D0647701

SETTING
NATIONAL
PRIORITIES
The 1973 Budget

Charles L. Schultze
Edward R. Fried
Alice M. Rivlin
Nancy H. Teeters

SETTING NATIONAL PRIORITIES
The 1973 Budget

715873

THE BROOKINGS INSTITUTION
Washington, D.C.

Copyright © 1972 by
THE BROOKINGS INSTITUTION
1775 Massachusetts Avenue, N.W., Washington, D.C. 20036

ISBN 0-8157-7758-2 (cloth)
ISBN 0-8157-7755-8 (paper)

Library of Congress Catalog Card Number 74-161599
9 8 7 6 5 4 3 2 1

Board of Trustees

Douglas Dillon
Chairman

John E. Lockwood
Vice Chairman

Robert Brookings Smith
Chairman, Executive Committee

Dillon Anderson
Vincent M. Barnett, Jr.
Louis W. Cabot
Robert D. Calkins
Edward W. Carter
George M. Elsey
John Fischer
Kermit Gordon
Gordon Gray
Huntington Harris
Luther G. Holbrook
William McC. Martin, Jr.
Robert S. McNamara
Arjay Miller
Herbert P. Patterson
J. Woodward Redmond
H. Chapman Rose
J. Harvie Wilkinson, Jr.
Donald B. Woodward

Honorary Trustees

Arthur Stanton Adams
William R. Biggs
Eugene R. Black
Leonard Carmichael
Colgate W. Darden, Jr.
Marion B. Folsom
Raymond B. Fosdick
Huntington Gilchrist
John Lee Pratt
Sydney Stein, Jr.

THE BROOKINGS INSTITUTION is an independent organization devoted to nonpartisan research, education, and publication in economics, government, foreign policy, and the social sciences generally. Its principal purposes are to aid in the development of sound public policies and to promote public understanding of issues of national importance.

The Institution was founded on December 8, 1927, to merge the activities of the Institute for Government Research, founded in 1916, the Institute of Economics, founded in 1922, and the Robert Brookings Graduate School of Economics and Government, founded in 1924.

The general administration of the Institution is the responsibility of a Board of Trustees charged with maintaining the independence of the staff and fostering the most favorable conditions for creative research and education. The immediate direction of the policies, program, and staff of the Institution is vested in the President, assisted by an advisory committee of the officers and staff.

In publishing a study, the Institution presents it as a competent treatment of a subject worthy of public consideration. The interpretations and conclusions in such publications are those of the author or authors and do not necessarily reflect the views of the other staff members, officers, or trustees of the Brookings Institution.

Foreword

ALTHOUGH THE MANDATE is couched in narrower language, the President is, in effect, required by law to present annually to the Congress his assessment of the nation's problems and his proposals for dealing with them. The federal budget, which is the main vehicle for communicating the details of the President's assessment and recommendations, is thus the chief instrument for forcing and recording executive branch decisions about national priorities—about the objectives the federal government should seek, the share of the nation's resources that should be devoted to each, and about who should bear the costs. The annual review necessitated by the preparation of the budget also gives the President and the Congress an opportunity to weigh the effectiveness of federal programs in achieving their purposes and to consider how they might be improved.

Because the federal budget is, unavoidably, a complex and abstruse financial plan, its significance as a comprehensive priority-setting document has in the past been obscured in a welter of technicalities. To deepen public understanding and stimulate informed discussion, the Brookings Institution in 1970 undertook to prepare an annual analysis that would highlight the priority-setting content of the budget and explain both the President's policy proposals and alternative strategies for dealing with national issues. The present volume is the third in this annual series. A substantial part of the book is concerned with the problems that dominate current discussion of national priorities and whose resolution will shape national policy this year and influence it for years to come.

Four chapters analyze the major problems of national defense. The authors identify the key decisions that shaped the 1973 defense budget and project their consequences for military forces and defense spending over the rest of the decade. The major elements of military forces and defense costs are examined separately; alternative policies are discussed, and several illustrative defense budgets are developed and analyzed.

In the chapters dealing with civilian programs, the authors emphasize the role of the federal government as an equalizer of resources among citizens and among state and local governments. Separate chapters examine federal income support programs, health insurance, child care services, the federal role in easing the severe fiscal problem of large cities, and federal assistance to local school districts. Another chapter deals with environmental problems and compares two alternative approaches to the control of pollution—regulation, and the use of economic incentives to improve the quality of air and water.

The authors then turn to some of the broader aspects of setting national priorities. The concluding chapters emphasize that the nature of the priority-setting problem has changed significantly in the past decade. Over those years, federal civilian programs have expanded sharply while federal tax rates were reduced. As a result, for the immediate future at least, economic growth can no longer be counted on to produce an automatic surplus of revenues available for launching new federal initiatives. In light of this development, the authors discuss alternative ways of increasing federal revenues and estimate the impact of each on the taxes paid by different income groups. In the final chapter, the authors discuss the problem of securing effective performance in the increasingly complex civilian programs of the federal government and suggest several approaches to this end. They also propose changes in budgetary procedures designed to focus the attention of the executive branch and the Congress on the longer-term consequences of their decisions.

Setting National Priorities: The 1973 Budget is not a compendium of "answers" to the vexing problems of national policy. Rather, the authors have sought to clarify the issues, to sort out the feasible alternatives, and to spell out their implications. In addition, they estimate budget revenues and expenditures over the next five years to suggest the framework within which decisions on priorities will have to be made.

In preparing many of the chapters, the authors relied on background papers written by other members of the Brookings staff and by outside experts. Those who provided background papers or other broad contributions to the analysis are named in the table of contents; contributors to specific parts of chapters are identified in footnotes. In all cases, however, the four authors bear full responsibility for the contents and conclusions of the chapters, and the listing of a contributor's name does not necessarily imply his or her agreement with the authors' treatment of the subject.

Research for the foreign policy and defense chapters was carried out under a continuing program of studies supported by a grant from the Ford Foundation. The project as a whole was supported by a grant from the Carnegie Corporation of New York.

Special mention should be made of Barry Blechman, who assisted in the preparation of Chapters 2 through 5 and coordinated the cost analyses. Chapter 2 also drew on contributions from Leslie H. Gelb, Arnold M. Kuzmack, Morton H. Halperin, and Henry D. Owen. Martin J. Bailey, a Rockefeller Visiting Professor at Brookings, and Colonel Delbert M. Fowler, USA, and Captain Chandler von Schrader, USN, both Federal Executive Fellows at Brookings, made helpful comments at each stage in the preparation of these four chapters. William W. Kaufmann, of the Massachusetts Institute of Technology, reviewed the manuscript and made useful suggestions.

Editorial assistance by the Brookings publication staff made it possible to publish this study four months after the President's budget was released on January 24, 1972. Ralph W. Tryon carried out the computer program used in making the economic and budgetary projections. Research assistance was provided by Mary S. von Euler, Gail R. Marker, Daniel J. Sullivan, and Nancy C. Wilson. To produce a volume of this size, with its many tables and numerical references, in a short period of time incurs serious risk of factual errors. This risk has been substantially reduced by Evelyn P. Fisher, who organized the checking of statistics.

The views expressed in this book are those of the authors and should not be attributed to the trustees, officers, or other staff members of the Brookings Institution, the Carnegie Corporation, or the Ford Foundation.

KERMIT GORDON
President

May 1972
Washington, D.C.

Contents

PART TWO: DOMESTIC PROBLEMS AND PROGRAMS

Tables

Chapter 9: Fiscal Problems of Cities

Chapter 10: Financing Elementary and Secondary Education

Chapter 14: Alternative Sources of Federal Revenue

Figures

Chapter 9: Fiscal Problems of Cities

Chapter 14: Alternative Sources of Federal Revenue

SETTING
NATIONAL
PRIORITIES
The 1973 Budget

1. Overview

ON JANUARY 24, 1972, President Nixon sent to the Congress his budget for the fiscal year ending June 30, 1973. This budget proposes that the federal government spend $246 billion in fiscal 1973 and estimates that it will raise revenues of $221 billion. The four volumes of budget documents contain 2,000 pages of detailed authorization and expenditure requests for more than a thousand federal programs administered by hundreds of federal agencies—nuclear weapons, cancer research, Indian reservations, preschool education, flood control, crime detection, aid to the blind and disabled. At first glance, writing a book about the federal budget might seem a little like writing about the Chicago telephone directory.

But the federal budget is far more than a collection of numbers proposing how much should be spent on the vast array of federal activities and how the money should be raised.

• The size of the budget and the way it is financed strongly influence national output, employment, and the rate of inflation.

• The budget is a means of determining how national resources should be allocated—the relative importance to be accorded public and private needs, defense and domestic spending, highways and health care.

• The choice of taxes to provide federal revenues determines how the burden of paying for government services is shared among various groups in the population.

• The budget is the most comprehensive single vehicle for examining practically every aspect of public policy. The defense budget, for example, involves far more than an answer to the question, "How important is national security?" It reflects a wide range of judgments

1

about the importance of various areas of the world to U.S. security, the survivability of our nuclear missiles in an attack, the ability of our conventional forces to deal with various contingencies, and the chances that U.S. arms programs will deter aggression or provoke additional arms spending by potential adversaries. Similarly, the budget for anti-poverty programs reflects far more than a decision as to how much should be spent for this objective. It reflects judgments about the feasibility and desirability of alternative methods of reducing poverty, such as cash benefits, job creation, education, training, or community action programs. Neither the administration nor the Congress reevaluates all of these judgments each year. But the budget does provide an important opportunity to examine how well the policies and programs of the government are working and to consider alternative approaches.

This book examines the fiscal 1973 budget in these four dimensions, in order to identify the choices open to the administration in preparing the budget and to explain some of the implications of choices made or not made. It does not propose an alternative budget, though it discusses a number of alternative spending levels and program strategies in many areas of the budget.

The Budget and the Economy

The principal way in which the budget affects the level of economic activity is through the gap between federal spending and federal revenue collections—the size of the deficit or surplus, and the changes in that deficit or surplus. When the budget is in surplus, the federal government withdraws more from the nation's income stream through taxes than it returns through spending. With a budget deficit, the reverse occurs; more is returned to the income stream than is taken from it. Compared to a balanced budget, therefore, budget deficits tend to stimulate economic activity, and surpluses to restrain it. At the same time, however, the state of economic activity itself influences the size of the budget deficit or surplus. For example, when unemployment is high and the economy is running at less than capacity, as is the case today, federal revenue collections fall below, and federal spending for unemployment compensation rises above, the levels they would reach under conditions of full employment. There is a two-way relationship: budget policies that change spending or revenues affect the level of economic activity, and the level of economic activity itself affects the size of the budget surplus or deficit that is actually realized.

To determine the stimulus or restraint that the budget is exerting on the economy, it is necessary to separate the effects on the budget of deliberate policy actions from those changes that result from variations in the level of economic activity. Perhaps the best way to isolate the effects of policy on the budget is to look at the full employment budget, a concept that the administration adopted in the 1972 budget and has continued to use since then. Under this concept, both revenues and expenditures are estimated at the level they would reach under conditions of full employment. Changes in the deficit or surplus in the full employment budget are therefore not influenced by variations in the economy, but are the result of government actions. An increase in the full employment deficit generally results from a shift in budget policy toward providing more economic stimulus; a move from a full employment deficit to surplus reflects a policy of restraint. On the other hand, if the full employment deficit in the budget is unchanged from one year to the next while the actual deficit increases, this will be the result not of a more stimulative budget policy but of a weakening economy. In fiscal 1972, for example, the actual budget deficit rose very sharply over the previous year. But only part of this increase in the deficit reflected deliberate action on the part of the government to stimulate the economy; the largest part of the deficit resulted from the reduced revenues accompanying increased unemployment and a decline in economic activity.

The 1972 Budget

In January 1971, when the President submitted his budget for fiscal year 1972, the unemployment rate stood at 6 percent, and the outlook for economic recovery in 1971 was uncertain. The administration took an optimistic view, however, forecasting an increase of 9 percent in the gross national product and a sharp reduction in the unemployment rate by the end of 1971. Consistent with this optimistic outlook, the administration projected a sharp rise in federal revenues. The fiscal 1972 budget submitted to the Congress called for a deficit of $11.6 billion. On a full employment basis, however, it was approximately in balance. The administration was apparently confident that economic recovery would proceed at a very rapid pace without the stimulus that a shift to a full employment budget deficit would provide.

A year later, in January 1972, a set of revised estimates was presented. The actual deficit projection was increased by $27.2 billion, from $11.6 billion to $38.8 billion. The principal factors contributing to this increase are shown in Table 1-1. The full employment budget was changed from an originally planned balance to a deficit of $8.1 billion. The increase in the latter deficit is the best measure of the additional stimulus provided by the revised 1972 budget.

The $27.2 billion increase in the actual deficit for 1972 stems from three sets of events, only the last of which is providing significant economic stimulus. *First,* the rise in economic activity turned out to be much less than was forecast in last year's budget, and unemployment stayed at 6 percent rather than falling. As a consequence, 1972 tax collections are lower and expenditures on unemployment compensation higher than originally forecast. *Second,* expenditures have risen above those indicated in the originally proposed budget. A large part of these expenditure changes have little or no economic impact—reductions in the planned sales of government owned mortgages and stockpile com-

Table 1-1. Factors Responsible for Increasing the Fiscal Year 1972 Budget Deficit above the Original Estimates

Billions of dollars

1972 deficit as estimated in the 1972 budget document		**11.6**
Shortfall of economic activity below budget forecast		14.6
Revenue loss	12.5	
Additional outlays for unemployment compensation	2.1	
Tax cuts and postponements		7.4
Revenue Act of 1971	4.4	
Other	3.0	
Expenditure increases[a]		5.2
Speedup in outlays[b]	2.0	
Reduced sales of mortgages, stockpile commodities, and so forth	2.5	
Other, net[c]	0.7	
1972 deficit as estimated in the 1973 budget document		**38.8**

Sources: Derived from *The Budget of the United States Government, Fiscal Year 1973,* and *The Budget of the United States Government, Fiscal Year 1972.*

a. Excludes increases in unemployment compensation, which are shown above in the first part of the table.

b. An approximate estimate. The 1973 budget document explicitly notes a $1 billion speedup in public assistance payments. (*The Budget of the United States Government, Fiscal Year 1973—Appendix,* p. 451.) Analysis of the defense budget and its relationship to the national income accounts data suggests that perhaps $1 billion of military spending was also speeded up.

c. This number is the net result of a large number of increases and decreases.

modities and a speedup in outlays achieved by shifting expenditures ahead several months. *Third,* the President proposed and the Congress enacted the Revenue Act of 1971, which cut taxes in fiscal 1972 by $4.4 billion. In addition a proposed increase in social security taxes was postponed for twelve months. These tax changes will reduce 1972 revenues by $7.4 billion and thereby provide a stimulus to the economy. The most recent data suggest that the actual budget deficit in 1972 will be smaller than the $38.8 billion estimated in the budget; revenues will be higher and expenditures possibly lower.

The 1973 Budget

The impact of the fiscal 1973 budget on national income and employment is more than usually difficult to predict. This year, the "unified budget," which is the accounting concept used to measure total revenues and expenditures in the budget document, presents a quite different picture than does the national income accounts (NIA) budget. The latter measure generally provides a better assessment of the economic impact of the budget.

In the unified budget, it is estimated that federal spending, after a $25 billion increase from fiscal 1971 to 1972, will rise by only $9.7 billion from 1972 to 1973. Spending is scheduled to increase sharply during the last quarter of fiscal 1972 and then to rise no further over the next twelve months. After the 1972 full employment deficit of $8.1 billion in the unified budget, a $700 million surplus is projected for 1973. The sharp deceleration of federal spending and the $9 billion swing from full employment deficit to surplus would portend a very marked shift from fiscal ease to fiscal restraint if these measures gave the real picture of the budget's economic impact.

The national income accounts budget tells a quite different story. Using this measure, budget expenditures rise by $25 billion from 1971 to 1972 and by $18 billion from 1972 to 1973—a deceleration, but one not nearly so sharp as in the unified budget. On the NIA basis, a full employment deficit of about $3 billion is expected in both fiscal 1972 and 1973.

A number of reasons explain why the two budget concepts tell such different stories. Two of the reasons are most important: In 1973 the federal government plans to sell a large volume of mortgages ($4.6 billion) from its portfolios, to dispose of commodities from its strategic stockpile ($0.7 billion), and to realize $3.1 billion from oil royalties and leases on the outer continental shelf. In calculating total expenditures in the unified budget, the proceeds from these transactions are treated as *negative* expenditures and are deducted from the outlays of the particular federal agencies involved. Because of the oil royalty proceeds, for example, the unified budget shows the entire Department of the Interior to have negative expenditures amounting to − $1.1 billion in 1973, compared to positive outlays of $1.1 billion in 1972. However, from the economic standpoint of hiring people, building dams, and maintaining parks, the Department of the Interior's activities will not decline by $2.2 billion from 1972 to 1973. They will actually expand. The national income accounts budget ignores most of these financial transactions and hence shows a larger increase in total budget outlays.

The government also plans to shift expenditures from the early months of fiscal 1973 back to the last month of fiscal 1972. In fiscal 1972 the states will receive thirteen months of payments for the federal share of public assistance and Medicaid, and only eleven months of payments in 1973. An examination of the patterns of military spending, relative to funds requested and contracts let, suggests that perhaps $2 billion of expenditures have been shifted, some from the early months of 1973 back to the last months of 1972 and some from late 1973 ahead to early 1974. These minor shifts in the timing of expenditures do reduce fiscal 1973 budget totals, but have little economic significance. The pattern of economic activity connected with the defense budget is not basically affected. The national income accounts budget makes an adjustment to correct for most, but not all, of these shifts in timing.

Table 1-2 shows the unified budget totals, adjusted to eliminate the major financial transactions and timing shifts discussed above, and compares these adjusted totals with the national income accounts budget. After adjustment, the unified budget shows expenditure increases of $26 billion from 1971 to 1972 and $18.5 billion from 1972 to 1973, matching the pattern of expenditure changes shown in the NIA budget. On a full employment basis, the NIA budget shifts from a surplus of $7.5 billion in fiscal 1971 to deficits of about $3 billion in both 1972 and 1973. Most of the deficit is concentrated in the second half of fiscal 1972 and the first half of fiscal 1973, that is, in calendar year 1972. Thereafter, according to the budget plan, the full employment deficit would become substantially smaller.

Table 1-2. Comparison of the Unified Budget, after Adjustment, with the National
Income Accounts Budget, Fiscal Years 1971, 1972, and 1973

Billions of dollars

				Change	
Budget item	1971	1972	1973	1971 to 1972	1972 to 1973
Unified budget					
Budget outlays as published	211.4	236.6	246.3	25.2	9.7
Plus major financial transactions resulting in negative expenditures	3.5	4.2	9.0	...	...
Plus timing shifts	−1.0	−1.0	3.0	...	...
Budget outlays, adjusted	213.9	239.8	258.3	25.9	18.5
National income accounts budget					
Budget outlays as published	212.4	237.8	255.9	25.4	18.1
Plus timing shift not adjusted in published NIA estimates	...	−1.0	1.0	...	...
Budget outlays, adjusted	212.4	236.8	256.9	24.4	20.1
Full employment surplus (+) or deficit (−)					
As published	+7.5	−4.3	−2.4	...	...
Adjusted for timing	+7.5	−3.3	−3.4	...	...

Sources: *The Budget of the United States Government, Fiscal Year 1973*; Charles A. Waite and Joseph C. Wakefield, "Federal Fiscal Programs," *Survey of Current Business*, Vol. 52 (February 1972), p. 16.

The Economic Forecast

The President's budget and his Economic Report forecast an increase in gross national product (GNP) of 9.4 percent between calendar 1971 and 1972, from $1,047 billion to $1,145 billion. The 9.4 percent gain is expected to reflect a price increase of about 3.2 percent and an increase in real output of about 6 percent.

If the 6 percent increase in real output is attained, some modest decline in the unemployment rate can be expected. Each year the labor force grows in numbers, and output per capita also increases as productivity rises. To absorb the added members of the labor force and to ensure that the growth in output per capita does not result in layoffs, total output must rise each year. In today's economy, output must expand by 4 to 4.5 percent a year simply to keep unemployment from rising. For every 1 percent growth in output, over and above this 4 to 4.5 percent requirement, the unemployment rate tends to be reduced by about one-third of 1 percent. If the administration's forecast proves correct, and if real output grows by 6 percent during 1972, the unemployment rate in the last quarter of the year might average about 5.25 percent compared to the 6 percent level at which it stood at the end of 1971. A continuation of this rate of economic advance beyond 1972 would reduce the unemployment rate to perhaps 4.5 percent sometime early in calendar 1974, and to 4 percent later in that year.

Is the administration's economic forecast likely to be realized? A year ago the official forecast was the subject of much controversy. The administration forecast an increase in GNP in 1971 that was some $15 billion to $20 billion higher than was estimated in forecasts being made by independent experts in business firms and universities. While these private forecasts differed among themselves, few if any of them predicted that economic activity would rise as rapidly as the administration expected. The private forecasts proved correct.

The economic outlook for 1972 as seen by the administration early in the year is much closer to the latest consensus of independent forecasters. The $98 billion gain in GNP between 1971 and 1972, reflecting a 6 percent increase in real output and a 3.2 percent rise in prices, is perhaps a shade more optimistic than the average of outside forecasts, but the difference is small. The official forecast was built on an expectation that every major category of expenditure for goods and services, with the exception of housing, would rise more strongly or decline less sharply in the coming year than it did in 1971. (Housing construction enjoyed a very rapid increase in 1971.) In no sector, however, does the forecast count on an explosive upsurge in demand; it assumes, moreover, that consumers will continue to save at higher than normal rates. The federal budget itself will help support the recovery in 1972. As was noted earlier, the NIA budget swings from a full employment surplus to a deficit, with the shift concentrated in calendar 1972. Thereafter, the budget calls for the full employment deficit to narrow. In the first months of 1972 no major developments could be observed that would indicate that the administration's forecast of moderate expansion in almost all sectors of the economy was either overly optimistic or excessively conservative.

The likelihood of achieving the expected slowdown in the rate of inflation, from a 4.6 percent price rise last year to a 3.2 percent rise in 1972, is particularly hard to judge. On the one hand, the continued existence of substantial unused capacity and the absence of excess demand in almost every sector of the economy, coupled with the restraining effects of wage and price controls, should work in the direction of moderating price increases. On the other hand, recent price developments in some sectors of the economy will make it quite difficult to achieve the hoped-for improvement. The Department of Agriculture in early February forecast a 4 percent rise in food prices, resulting in part from the delayed effects on meat prices of last year's corn blight. The prices of many services, where productivity gains are small, have been rising and may continue to do so at rates significantly greater than 3.2 percent. In these circumstances, if price increases are to average out at 3.2 percent, it will be necessary to hold price increases among nonfood commodities to well below that rate. If, for example, prices of food and services rise by 4 percent, retail prices of nonfood commodities can increase by only 2 percent. In recent years, retail prices of nonfood commodities have risen about 1 percent a year faster than manufacturers' prices. Should this trend continue, manufacturers' price increases can average no more than 1 percent if the overall price forecast is to be achieved. This may be a difficult target to reach, even if wage and price controls are fairly rigorous.

In sum, the budget is based on an economic forecast of a substantial, but clearly not improbable, rate of recovery. Prices seem likely to rise at a somewhat higher rate than is forecast, but the anticipated growth of real GNP could still be attained. Despite its apparent aura of restraint, the 1973 budget should provide a stimulus to economic activity this year roughly consistent with the goals of this year's economic forecast.

The Budget and National Priorities

Dramatic changes are hardly ever made in a single budget. Commitments to continue federal programs already on the books and obligations to meet the "built-in" cost increases in these programs eat up a substantial part of the available funds and prevent both the administration and the Congress from making major shifts in funds in any one year. While every new budget affords at least some room for the administration and the Congress to indicate their changing priorities, only a perspective that covers a number of years can illuminate the really large changes taking place in the scope and emphasis of federal activities.

Long-run Changes in Federal Expenditures

Over the years, the budget has reflected large changes both in the scope and in the nature of federal activity. For the first century and a half of the nation's history, the federal government played a minuscule role in the economy, except in wartime. Military expenditures fluctuated, but the civilian outlays of the federal government amounted to less than 1 percent of GNP until the 1930s.

During the depression of the 1930s, the federal role expanded rapidly, and civilian expenditures rose to about 5 percent of GNP. In the next thirty years, federal civilian outlays in relation to the size of the economy expanded only slightly. National security expenditures, on the other hand, increased dramatically, fluctuating around 10 percent of GNP in the 1950s and early 1960s.

Over the past ten years, total federal expenditures have increased more rapidly than GNP, rising from 18.4 to 20.5 percent of GNP between 1963 and 1973, as is shown in Table 1-3.[1] A small part of the increase in the ratio of expenditures to GNP was due to the fact that, on the average, the prices of what the federal government buys have risen a little faster than the overall price level. But most of the growth in the ratio represents an increase in the proportion of real income channeled through the federal government.

The rise in federal outlays was accompanied by a major change in the composition of federal expenditures. Combined outlays for defense, space, and international affairs programs were 53 percent of the budget in fiscal 1963, but only 34 percent in 1973, while the civilian programs' share increased from 47 to 66 percent and from 8.7 to 13.4 percent of GNP.

The largest increases in federal civilian expenditures came in two areas. Several longstanding programs that provide cash assistance to various groups of beneficiaries ("Older income maintenance programs" in Table 1-3) rose sharply, especially during the last three years of the decade. Social security, public assistance, and veterans' benefits account for the bulk of these outlays. The outstanding factor in budgetary growth in the past decade, however, is the introduction

1. To eliminate the effect of purely cyclical swings in the economy, expenditures have been adjusted to exclude unemployment compensation outlays resulting from unemployment in excess of 4 percent. Similarly, the potential GNP forthcoming at 4 percent unemployment levels is used in the denominator of the ratio.

Table 1-3. The Changing Composition of Federal Expenditures,[a] Fiscal Years 1963, 1970, and 1973

Category of expenditure	Billions of dollars			Percent of total		
	1963	1970	1973	1963	1970	1973
Defense, space, foreign affairs	58.9	87.7	88.0	53	44	34
Older income maintenance programs[b]	28.4	49.8	74.9	25	25	29
Major "Great Society" programs[c]	1.7	21.2	35.7	2	11	14
Commerce, transportation, natural resources[d]	7.6	11.6	16.5	7	6	6
President Nixon's new initiatives[e]	...	...	6.4	...	...	2
Interest (net)	7.7	14.4	15.5	7	7	6
Other programs	7.2	13.6	19.3	6	7	8
Total[f]	111.5	198.3	256.3	100	100	100
Expenditures as a percent of full employment gross national product						
Total	18.4	20.3	20.5	...	...	...
Total, less defense, space, foreign affairs	8.7	11.3	13.4	...	...	...

Sources: *The Budget of the United States Government*, for fiscal years 1973, 1972, and 1965.

a. Total expenditures and "older income maintenance programs" have been adjusted to exclude outlays on unemployment compensation resulting from unemployment in excess of 4 percent.

b. Social security and retirement programs, cash public assistance, veterans' benefits, and unemployment benefits.

c. Programs that were first inaugurated or substantially modified and expanded between 1963 and 1970. See text for discussion.

d. Excludes expenditures for regional economic development programs and environmental protection, which are included in "Great Society" programs.

e. Revenue sharing, family assistance plan, and emergency school assistance.

f. Figures are rounded and may not add to totals, and totals have been adjusted to eliminate the effect of major financial transactions that produce negative expenditures and timing shifts in the 1973 budget. See text for discussion. Individual expenditure categories have been similarly adjusted.

and rapid growth of a host of new (or sharply modified) programs, the "major Great Society programs" in Table 1-3. They have grown from a modest $1.7 billion in 1963 to a scheduled $35.7 billion in 1973. Of this total, some $20 billion is accounted for by programs that provide goods or services directly to people, principally the poor or the aged; housing subsidies to low- and moderate-income families; Medicare (for the aged) and Medicaid (for the poor); food stamps and school lunches; loans and scholarships for higher education. Instead of transferring cash to the beneficiary, as is the case with the older income maintenance programs, the new programs provide specific goods or services.

The remaining $16 billion of Great Society programs provide grants-in-aid to state and local governments and nonprofit institutions to accomplish a variety of complex objectives. These include grants for municipal waste treatment works to help clean up pollution; grants for establishing and operating community mental health centers; grants of various kinds to encourage better urban planning and rehabilitation of central cities; programs to increase the number of trained medical and paramedical personnel, and to develop improved methods of providing medical care; grants and loans to promote economic development in depressed areas; grants to communities and nonprofit groups and subsidies to industry to provide a wide range of manpower training services; and many other similarly complex programs.

Referring to these as "Great Society" programs is misleading in the sense that while a great many of them were introduced during the Johnson administration, they have been continued, and indeed their expansion has been accelerated, under the Nixon administration. There is widespread consensus, transcending party lines, that increasing equality of opportunity, improving the quality of public services, and rescuing the environment are, and should be, important concerns of the federal government. There is far less consensus, however, on how these objectives ought to be attained.

The Nixon administration has made some attempt to shape the domestic budget in accordance with an "income strategy" and a "new federalism." The income strategy implies less emphasis on direct provision of public services to people (for example, funds for model cities and community action programs have been increased only moderately) and more emphasis on programs to equalize access to private goods and services (for example, welfare reform, food stamps, student aid, and health insurance proposals). The "new federalism" implies strengthening state and local governments by giving them a share in federal revenues (general revenue sharing) and consolidating certain federally funded programs into block grants (special revenue sharing).

Expenditure Changes in the 1973 Budget

The President's fiscal 1973 budget is highly constrained by past decisions. Budget expenditures, after adjustment for the timing shifts and financial transactions explained above, are scheduled to rise by $18.5 billion from 1972 to 1973. Almost two-thirds of this increase is accounted for by items over which the President has little control, at least on a year-to-year basis. (See Table 1-4.) The largest single in-

Table 1-4. Changes in Budget Expenditures, Fiscal Years 1972 to 1973

Billions of dollars

Budget expenditure		Amount of change, 1972 to 1973
Total change, as published		9.7
Adjustment for financial transactions		4.8
Adjustments for timing		4.0
Total change, adjusted		18.5
"Built-in" changes		12.1
Pay and retirement	3.2	
Social security and Medicare	6.8	
Public assistance and Medicaid	0.5	
Veterans' benefits	0.6	
Interest, net	0.6	
Unemployment compensation	−0.6	
Other	1.0	
Military (except pay and retirement)		0.5
Major new proposals		3.7
Revenue sharing	3.4	
Family assistance plan	0.3	
Other discretionary changes		2.2
Manpower programs	0.7	
Civilian research and development	0.6	
Emergency school assistance	0.3	
Postal deficit	−0.5	
Other, net	1.1	

Source: *The Budget of the United States Government, Fiscal Year 1973.*

crease in this category, $6.8 billion, will go for social security and Medicare. About $3 billion of the increase is "uncontrollable," reflecting the growth in the number of beneficiaries and the rising costs of medical care; $2 billion results from the 5 percent benefit increase included in pending legislation to take account of increases in the cost of living; and the remaining $1.8 billion represents various improvements in social security and Medicare benefits contained in the same legislation. Pay increases for military and civilian personnel of the federal government, together with their growing retirement benefits, will add $3.2 billion to fiscal 1973 expenditures. (This does not include a $400 million request for additional pay incentives for the all-volunteer armed force.) Other expenditure increases of $2.7 billion are needed to meet commitments made in earlier years (for example, grants to local communities for constructing waste treatment works) or to pay benefits required by law (for example, educational benefits to GIs returning from Vietnam). All together, these "built-in" increases will require $12.1 billion in additional expenditures in 1973.

The central feature of the 1973 defense budget is the relatively large ($5.1 billion) increase in funds requested for military programs—an increase that occurs despite estimated budgetary savings of $3 billion from the reduced U.S. military role in Vietnam. Actual military spending, however, will not rise substantially in 1973, partly because it normally takes some time for an increase in available funds to be translated into additional spending and partly because special efforts were made to shift some expenditures back to the 1972 budget, as was explained above. The military programs and policies incorporated in the 1973 budget, however, will lead to significant increases in defense spending in 1974 and subsequent years. These are spelled out in Chapter 3.

After making provision for built-in expenditure increases and a small rise in military spending, $5.9 billion is applied to increases in other programs in the 1973 budget. Of this amount, $3.7 billion would go toward financing the added costs in 1973 of President Nixon's two major domestic initiatives—revenue sharing with states and localities, and welfare reform. Both of these were proposed last year and are still pending before the Congress. The bulk of this money is for revenue sharing. If passed by the Congress in this session, the administration's revenue sharing bills will give state and local governments $2.2 billion in fiscal 1972 and $5.6 billion in fiscal 1973. Even if welfare reform passes, only $350 million would be spent in fiscal year 1973, all for administrative expenses. Payments to beneficiaries under the program would not begin until July 1, 1973. Its first full-year cost would fall in fiscal 1974 and would amount to $5.5 billion. The administration's health insurance proposals, if passed by the Congress, would also appear in the fiscal 1974 budget.

The remaining $2.2 billion of net increases in spending are spread among a number of programs. Expenditures for manpower training will grow by $700 million, most of which will go toward expanding the newly enacted public service employment programs. Spending on civilian research and development programs will rise by $600 million, about one quarter of which will go to the National Institutes of Health.

Sharing the Cost of Government Services

While the expenditure side of the budget reflects relative priorities among government activities, the revenue side reflects decisions as to how the cost of government is to be shared among various groups in the population. Here again, past decisions weigh heavily, but tax changes in a single year can shift the burden significantly from one group to another.

In the past ten years, federal income tax rates have been reduced at frequent intervals and by large amounts. As a result of tax cuts in 1964, 1969, and 1971, federal personal and corporate taxes next year will be $35 billion lower than they would have been at 1963 tax rates. Excise taxes have also been reduced, by $10 billion. At the same time, payroll tax revenues, used to finance social security programs, have risen sharply because of increases both in payroll tax rates and in the proportion of wages subject to those taxes. Payroll tax collections in 1973 will be $18.5 billion greater than they would have been if 1963 rates and regulations had remained in force.

The shift from income to payroll taxes over the last decade has been substantial. Personal and corporate income taxes will account for only 60 percent of full employment revenues in 1973, compared with 66 percent in 1963. In the same period, payroll taxes will have risen from 18 percent to 28 percent of total revenue collections.

On balance, the tax changes enacted during the past ten years have reduced federal revenues substantially: full employment revenues in fiscal 1973 will be $27 billion lower than they would have been under the tax laws in effect ten years ago. Moreover, the recent reductions in tax rates and the expanded scope of the federal government's activities have produced a situation in which the annual built-in growth in federal expenditures now tends to absorb a very large part of the increase in federal revenues generated by an expanding full employment economy. Indeed, for the next several years the growth in federal expenditures under existing programs and those proposed in the 1973 budget may exceed the growth in full employment revenues under current tax laws. By 1977, revenue increases may have equaled the growth in expenditures, but they are not likely to produce a surplus for use in launching major new governmental programs to meet emerging national priorities. This situation is in sharp contrast to earlier periods in the nation's economic history, during which peacetime economic growth tended to produce larger gains in federal revenues than were absorbed by ongoing federal expenditure programs. As a consequence —in the near future at least—major new federal programs will have to be financed either from higher taxes or from sharp reductions in current activities.

Because of the shortage of federal revenues relative to long-term expenditure needs, a number of proposals have been made to seek new revenue sources. Several alternative means are available, but the proposal most frequently mentioned in recent months is to levy a federal "value added tax," which is roughly equivalent to a retail sales tax. The administration has such a proposal under serious review. Long-run problems of financing the federal government are discussed in Part 3.

Public Policy Issues: The "How" Questions

Making up a federal budget involves far more than deciding how much money should be devoted to various public purposes; it also involves the more important question of how these purposes are to be accomplished. Indeed, a reasoned decision as to how much should be spent cannot be made until the alternative policies available have been examined carefully and a judgment has been made about their effectiveness and cost. The bulk of this book is devoted to examining some of the basic policy issues whose resolution shaped the fiscal 1973 budget and whose impact will be felt in future years. These issues are summarized only briefly here and are treated at length in Parts 1 and 2.

Major Issues in Defense and Foreign Affairs

Military forces are by far the most costly of the nation's foreign policy resources. They serve foreign policy objectives by deterring conflict and, should deterrence fail, by defending the nation's security interests. Furthermore, the very existence of military forces influences the expectations of other countries, allies and adversaries alike, and thereby constitutes an important element in the conduct of foreign relations. These differing uses of military power imply differing requirements for the size, structure, and disposition of military forces. Additionally, several factors only remotely connected with foreign policy have a strong influence on the structure and cost of those forces. The relationship between foreign policy and other factors as determinants of the defense budget is discussed in Chapter 2.

Each year the defense budget reflects the administration's decisions as to the military posture most appropriate for the realization of security and foreign policy objectives. It is often forgotten that these decisions, presented and judged in the context of current economic and political circumstances, can represent commitments to long-term programs that will affect the structure of military forces and the size of the defense budget far into the future. A decision this year to authorize modest funds for developing a major weapon system can lead to a sizable investment for procurement over the next ten years and can affect operating costs over the next twenty years. In Chapter 3 the 1973 defense budget is examined not only in terms of its major current features, but also in regard to its long-term fiscal and force implications. Military expenditures for 1973 are projected to rise little from the previous year. However, the appropriations requested and the policies and programs outlined in the budget imply an increase in the defense budget of about $10 billion a year by 1977, quite apart from the impact on the military budget of future increases in wages and prices.

In the annual examination of the budget, attention is usually concentrated on the administration's plans for acquiring a limited number of major weapon systems. Decisions on these issues determine the pace at which military forces will be modernized. They involve such questions as:

• What should be the characteristics of new systems? Which ones should be procured, and how many are necessary?

• At what rate should new systems be introduced into the forces? Specifically, what are the political, military, and economic implications of accelerating or stretching out the process?

• How should the Defense Department acquire new weapon systems? How can innovations be encouraged without "gold-plating" and unmanageable cost overruns?

Controversy over military spending is focused primarily on weapon systems because they are readily identifiable by specific measures of output and by price. Advocates of increases or decreases in military spending usually define their positions in terms of moving ahead or cutting back on major weapon programs—and the administration defends its defense budget on much the same basis. As a result, another set of issues of equal or greater budgetary significance tends to be overlooked. Most of them concern force levels, readiness, and efficiency in the use of manpower and equipment, as well as the tradeoff among them. For example:

• What combination of force levels and readiness is preferable? Is it more effective, for example, to maintain sixteen ground force divisions partially manned or thirteen divisions fully manned?

• How should combat forces be supported—in what ratio of support to combat forces and in what ways?

• When should weapon systems be retired? In other words, at what point does the cost of maintaining and operating older aircraft and vessels clearly exceed their military or political value?

• How should military manpower be provided—through continued use of the draft or by volunteers alone? If the latter, what incentives would be best calculated to encourage the needed number of enlistments?

These issues tend to be neglected because existing congressional procedures for reviewing the defense budget are not designed to focus on them, because they are diffuse and hence difficult to assess systematically, and because strong incentives to make cost and effectiveness calculations are not built into the process of developing military budgets. Both sets of issues are examined in Chapters 4 and 5, first as they relate to particular military forces and then in terms of the defense budget as a whole.

Major Domestic Issues

Much of the discussion of domestic policy issues in this book deals, in one way or another, with the federal government's role as an equalizer of resources—among individuals or families and among state or local governments. Indeed, most of the domestic budget is devoted to these twin purposes—to providing income or specific services to people who are in need and to providing grants-in-aid to state and local governments, for either broad or specific purposes.

The size and scope of income support for individuals are not generally realized. As is pointed out in Chapter 6, income support programs (for veterans, civilian and military retirees, the aged, the blind, the disabled, survivors, the unemployed, and others with low incomes) amount to 39 percent of the fiscal 1973 budget, up from 28 percent in

1960. These programs have not developed in a coherent or consistent way. Some are designed to help special groups that are deemed particularly worthy of aid (veterans). Others are designed to provide replacement income for those who are unable to work (the aged, the blind, the disabled, the experienced unemployed, and mothers with dependent children). Until fairly recently, little attempt has been made to assist people who are needy but do not fall in these special categories. In the past decade, however, the difficulty of defining such arbitrary categories has become clear, and programs have been introduced that move toward providing essential items like food, medical care, and housing on the basis of income rather than category of person.

Decisions on basic issues concerning income support programs could greatly influence the size and allocation of the federal budget. A major question is the extent to which a distinction should be maintained between benefits for people unable to work and those who could work or are working but remain needy. Other questions involve the extent to which benefits should vary by state or region and the extent to which they should be related to the past status or contributions of individuals. Another basic issue is the emphasis to be placed on cash benefits rather than payments in kind, such as food stamps or medical insurance.

Chapters 7 and 8 deal with two types of in-kind benefits that raise particularly urgent issues for the next several budgets: health insurance and child care programs. The federal government already has two major health insurance programs (Medicare and Medicaid for the aged and the poor), but major concerns remain about the provision of health care. Inadequate access of the poor to care, the burden of catastrophic medical expenses on middle- and upper-income families, and the rapid escalation of the cost of medical care have focused national attention on alternative ways of designing and financing a broader national health insurance system.

The child care issue is at a different stage, since the federal government has so far financed only relatively small and experimental programs for preschool or out-of-school children. But pressure is now building for major federal financing of preschool education and day care for children of working mothers.

These programs raise some common issues. First, what is the justification for subsidizing these particular expenditures rather than giving people money to buy what they feel they need most? Second, should resources be concentrated on people with the lowest incomes, or should "need" be defined in other ways? This problem is evident in the area of health, where extraordinary expenses impose burdens even on those with high incomes. It is also apparent in child care, where present subsidy patterns appear to result in the provision of a more costly service to a minority of the very poor than is available to those with slightly higher incomes.

Third, how should conflicting objectives be balanced in designing these programs? For example, how should the conflict be resolved between helping those most in need (usually by relating benefits to income) and preserving incentives to work (which tend to be weakened if benefits decline as earnings rise)?

Finally, perhaps the biggest question concerns the extent to which the federal role should be restricted to mere financing or equalizing access of consumers as against regulating or subsidizing the producers of the service. Should the federal government directly subsidize suppliers of the service as a means of increasing output—for example, through subsidizing health maintenance organizations? Should quality standards be imposed? Should attempts be made to induce efficient delivery of the service or to hold down prices by direct regulation?

The discussion then shifts from individuals to the federal role in equalizing resources among governments. Chapter 9 focuses on the financial problems of large cities and what the federal government can do to alleviate them. Public expenditures per capita in big cities are generally higher than in the suburbs and are rising at least as rapidly. Revenues per capita, however, are growing much faster in the suburbs, where property values, sales, and income are all climbing more rapidly than in the city. The cities are caught in a fiscal squeeze, and many of the actions they might take to extricate themselves, such as raising taxes further or cutting services, are self-defeating because they would hasten the flight to the suburbs. Major help for the cities from the states or suburbs (through metropolitan government or tax sharing) seems politically unlikely, so the cities have turned to the federal government. The chapter points out that welfare reform will not help most city budgets appreciably and that revenue sharing may not improve the situation of the cities vis-à-vis the suburbs unless the formula is carefully designed to do so. The chapter also suggests that the federal government could contribute toward a solution by providing incentives for states and metropolitan areas as a whole to share some of the financial burdens of their cities.

Another fiscal problem, not peculiar to large cities, but faced by many local governments, is the financing of elementary and secondary education. The costs of education have been mounting rapidly while it has become increasingly difficult for local governments to raise additional revenue from the unpopular property tax. Finding a way to reduce reliance on the property tax as a source of funds for schools would help to solve the general problem of financing elementary and secondary education, but two even more intractable problems would remain. First, there are the great disparities among and within states in the expenditures devoted to a child's education, disparities that individuals are increasingly seeing as unfair and courts as unconstitutional. Second, even if expenditures per student were the same in all districts, the problem would remain of providing equal educational opportunity for racial minorities and the poor. Chapter 10 discusses these problems and alternative solutions to them that are open to the federal government.

The final set of major program issues addressed are those involving air and water pollution and other environmental problems. The nation, chiefly through the federal government, must set the standards of cleanliness it intends to seek in its air and water. Equally important and even more difficult to decide, however, is the question of how to go about securing clean air and clean water. Pollution is a complex phenomenon, and there are many technical means available for reducing pollution that vary widely in effectiveness and cost. The costs of cleanup are high and will be borne principally by consumers in the form of higher costs for the goods and services they buy. The discussion in Chapter 11 focuses on the choice between two alternative approaches to federal pollution control: (1) setting and enforcing through a regulatory agency specific limits on pollution for individual firms and municipalities, and (2) designing monetary penalties to discourage polluting activities.

The next three chapters review past and projected changes in the size and financing of the federal budget; the last chapter discusses the changing nature of federal civilian programs. As late as 1960, the civilian role of the federal government was limited to a fairly narrow range of activities. From the 1930s to the 1950s, much of the civilian budget

was devoted to income support programs that provided cash transfers to the elderly, the disabled, veterans, the experienced unemployed,
and some categories of the poor. Other major federal activities included certain kinds of physical investments (chiefly roads, dams, and
parks), subsidization of certain industries (such as agriculture and the
merchant marine), and, of course, the general housekeeping duties of
government. These were relatively uncomplicated activities, or so it
seems in retrospect. The major issues of public policy concerned
whether the federal government should undertake a particular activity
and *how much* should be spent on it, not *how* it should be carried out.
Once the decision was made and money provided, it was not an in-
superable task to make the program work. Moreover, results were
relatively easy to observe: veterans and old people received their
checks; farm prices were bolstered by subsidies and government purchases; contracts were let and roads built.

Then in the 1960s the federal government embarked on a new set of
programs aimed at more complex and more ambitious goals, and the
nation began to demand better performance in all federal programs,
old and new. The older income support programs were continued and
expanded, but new programs paying benefits in kind were added so as
to ensure more equal access to certain important goods and services,
such as food, medical care, housing, and higher education. Other programs sought to improve a vast array of public services, mostly
through grants to state and local governments for particular purposes,
or direct grants to certain private institutions, such as colleges and
hospitals. The objectives of these grant programs ranged from curtailing the pollution of air and water to assisting small colleges; from
early education for low-income children to literacy and job training
for adults; from improving community mental health centers to
stimulating urban planning.

By comparison with earlier federal objectives, the new ones were
complex and elusive. Achieving them involved not just federal action,
but changing the behavior of state and local officials, private firms,
schools and colleges, and many other institutions and individuals.
Even when a decision had been made to undertake a program, it was
often far from obvious how its objectives should be accomplished or
how success should be identified and measured.

Chapter 15 discusses some of the major problems and choices to be
faced in designing and carrying out programs of this kind. Since their

success depends on the decisions of many individuals, firms, and local governments, means must be sought to induce a large number of independent decision-makers to choose courses of action that are consistent with the aims of the programs. And so the chapter devotes attention to the problem of building *incentives* for effective action into federal programs.

In many cases very little is known about what works and what does not work in the areas of social and institutional behavior that are covered by the newer programs. The chapter discusses the uses of social experiments as a means of gaining knowledge. By deliberately trying alternative program designs on a small scale and carefully evaluating the results, the government can in some cases learn more about how to develop and manage more effective social programs.

2. What Shapes the Defense Budget?

DEFENSE CONTINUES to be by far the largest single government program, absorbing 30 percent of the national budget and directly employing 3.4 million people. By its size alone, the defense budget inevitably occupies a central position in the examination of national priorities. By its nature, defense spending invites controversy in that it can encompass both very high- and very low-priority expenditures. Not spending enough can threaten national security, and spending too much at best means a waste of resources that contributes nothing to national welfare and at worst a reduction in security instead of an increase. But what constitutes the nation's security requirements, and what are the level and the composition of defense expenditures needed to fulfill them?

Two general approaches to this problem can be distinguished. The first is exemplified by the President's Foreign Policy Report, the Defense Report of the secretary of defense, and the Budget Message itself. In these documents the proposed defense program reflects the administration's view of the minimum amounts that can safely be appropriated after systematic consideration of U.S. interests and commitments, the major threats to U.S. security, and the appropriate strategies for meeting them. Major issues and questions are raised in these presentations, but within a logical framework that emphasizes foreign policy objectives, treaty obligations, and force comparisons.

An alternative approach is based on the view that the problem of how much defense spending is enough simply does not lend itself to an orderly, unique solution such as would enable the policymaker to

24

proceed from a foreign policy assessment, to a defense strategy, to weapon system and force needs, and thence to a defense budget. Proponents of this view concede that considerable progress has been made over the past decade in building systematic relationships between military forces and national security interests. Nevertheless, they argue that analytic bases are still not available for comparing various kinds of defense forces and for determining how much should be spent on defense and for what forces. They contend that defense budgets are more the result of inertia and bureaucratic pressures (including interservice rivalries) than the logical consequence of foreign policy commitments or of questions concerning strategy and efficiency. Hence they believe that the best approach to the problem is to place a more or less arbitrary ceiling on defense expenditures (either as a fixed percentage of GNP or an absolute number of dollars, based largely on domestic considerations) without trying to relate the amounts to necessarily vague concepts of "national interest" or "foreign policy commitments."

The approach adopted here is to examine general relationships between foreign policy objectives and forces, as well as other determinants of defense spending, all of which are believed to be subject to systematic analysis. Actual budgets may not entirely reflect such analyses, but the goal should be to move further in that direction. The purpose of this chapter is to examine four general considerations shaping the defense budget—foreign policy, defense policy, manpower cost and efficiency factors, and domestic politics—and to outline the ways in which these factors can influence thinking on defense spending.

Foreign Policy Considerations

Defense requirements, at least in a general sense, flow directly from foreign policy assessments and decisions. The United States needs only relatively small conventional forces to defend its sovereign territory. Beyond that, conventional force requirements are based on the view that the United States has foreign policy interests, the defense of which requires the maintenance of additional military capabilities. These interests are expressed primarily through commitments to the defense of nations in Western Europe and Asia, but they are based on a more general belief that conflict elsewhere in the world can, in varying degree, adversely affect the security of the United States. The defense posture, therefore, depends in the first instance on an assessment of the intentions and capabilities of potential adversaries, the importance to the United States of the security of other countries, and the military contributions of allies. In short, what role does the United States intend to play in the world?

In this connection, some major features of the President's 1972 Foreign Policy Report merit special attention:

• With respect to the Soviet Union, a focus on adversary relations influences the tone and content of the message. The President sees U.S.–Soviet competition continuing in strategic arms development and in specific regions of confrontation, notably Europe and the Middle East. He hopes to persuade the Russians to move toward greater cooperation rather than rivalry with the United States. He implies that U.S.–Soviet relations could undergo major change either way and that the direction of change more than anything else will determine the character of the international environment.

• Great stress is placed on the evolution of U.S. relations with China, not in the expectation of resolving basic differences, but to replace animosity with a systematic exploration of possible areas of common interest. The results of the President's visit to China conform with this expectation. Moreover, whatever the specific results, the President's initiative brings the United States closer to a perception of China's capabilities and intentions that serves to support a more relaxed military stance in Southeast Asia.

• An ambivalent view emerges of U.S. relations with Western Europe and Japan. Both are close allies as well as strong economic competitors. As allies, they are reassured about the central position that they occupy in the definition of U.S. security interests and the constancy of U.S. military commitments to them; at the same time, they are pressed to contribute more to the common defense. As competitors, they are warned to improve conditions for U.S. trade and are urged to join the United States in seeking reform of the international economic system. There are many references to the need for change in the U.S. relationship with both Western Europe and Japan, but the substance of that change, in respect of either defense or economic policy or political organization, is not clearly defined.

• The discussion of U.S. security policy toward the Middle East and East Asia shows little change from last year's message. In the

Middle East the United States will seek a settlement and will try to deter or offset increased Soviet involvement. In Vietnam, the preferred solution is a negotiated peace, but the transfer of U.S. defensive responsibilities to the South Vietnamese will continue in any event. In the rest of East Asia, the United States will keep its various commitments to assist against local as well as Chinese aggression, but no attempt is made to distinguish the urgency or relative importance of each of these commitments. At the same time, the intention is reaffirmed to reduce the U.S. military presence in the area, which the increased defense efforts of our allies are to make possible, but the timing is left vague. Thus, ambiguities initially inherent in the Nixon doctrine remain unresolved. In part the ambiguities may be intentional, in order to enhance deterrence during a period of change and transition.

• U.S. policy toward Latin America, South Asia, and Africa, where threats to security are not seen to exist, is discussed without a sense of urgency. Development assistance, the main potential policy link between the United States and these regions, is endorsed, and programs to reform foreign aid are again advanced; but no major effort seems likely to be mounted to bring order out of the confusion that currently surrounds this area of U.S. policy. Evidence that the United States is moving toward a lower profile in dealing with countries in these regions is persuasive.

To what extent is the defense budget influenced by this view of the world, and to what extent would alternative foreign policy assessments call for changes in defense expenditures? A range of connections exists, notably in respect to three major issues: management of U.S.–Soviet relations, the view held of the U.S. role in Western Europe, and the assessment of requirements for stability in Asia.

U.S.–Soviet Relations

Over the past two years, the Nixon administration has expressed concern that the decline in total U.S. defense spending, even though it reflects mainly the winding down of the Vietnam war, might be taken by Soviet leaders to indicate that the United States would not maintain an effective military balance in the face of increases in the Soviet defense effort. This, it was feared, might cause Soviet leaders to conclude that the United States was not determined to defend its interests and allied leaders to lose confidence in the credibility of U.S.

guarantees. Thus, beginning with the fiscal 1972 budget, the administration has gone out of its way to emphasize its determination to match Soviet forces whenever it believed that the existing balance was threatened.

The increase in the total U.S. defense budget in itself might convey this political message to the USSR. But the general principle of force matching has been evident in a number of specific decisions. For example, the expanding role of the Soviet Navy has figured prominently as justification for accelerated U.S. naval construction; and the need to make sure that the USSR does not misread U.S. intentions has been an important underlying reason for not removing U.S. forces from Europe or otherwise disturbing the present military balance there.

In the strategic field, the Nixon administration has justified its decision to accelerate development of the undersea long-range missile system (ULMS) largely on the ground that the USSR is rapidly expanding the size of its strategic submarine force. While the administration has rejected the need to keep substantially ahead of the Soviet Union in all categories of strategic forces, it does see unfavorable foreign policy implications in a very great disparity in the total number of delivery vehicles.

Similar foreign policy considerations underlie the administration's use of the "bargaining chip" justification for force programs. For example, the administration has argued for several years that it must go forward with the antiballistic missile (ABM) program so that it can eventually trade off the program in return for a Soviet agreement to halt deployment of its large SS-9 intercontinental missile; and at times, the acceleration of the ULMS program seems to be justified as a bargaining chip the United States would give up in exchange for a halt in the Soviet submarine program.

In each case, the administration's force decisions are based on the belief that it is essential to negotiate with the Soviet Union from a position of strength and, when negotiations do not seem likely (as in the case of naval forces), to respond to Soviet programs with U.S. countermeasures. Thus, the initial result of a foreign policy that stresses replacing the era of confrontation with an era of negotiation is an increase in the defense budget.

Alternative approaches would be to seek superiority in strategic arms, which the administration has eschewed, or to exercise restraint in other defense programs and military deployments so as to minimize Soviet misunderstandings that would lead to an arms race, and to convey a signal of U.S. interest in détente and arms control. The former strategy would reflect the assumption that only superiority could ensure deterrence. The latter strategy would be based on a military assessment that existing military capabilities are sufficient both for deterrence and for successful negotiations, and that a course emphasizing arms limitation negotiations would not adversely affect the military and political posture of U.S. allies.

None of these strategies represents an all-or-nothing approach, nor would the adoption of any of them give a clear indication of the appropriate size of the defense budget. The "negotiate from strength" or "achieve superiority" approach need not mean that every new strategic system is a valuable bargaining chip; nor, conversely, does the opposite strategy mean that all weapon improvements should be forgone simply on grounds that restraint will bring détente. Nevertheless, the three strategies do imply differences in the size of defense budgets, however difficult it may be to translate each into specific budgetary magnitudes.

The U.S. Role in Western Europe

Requirements to assist in the defense of Western Europe are by far the most important determinant of the U.S. conventional force structure. More than half of the active U.S. conventional forces are specifically designed for this purpose; some are stationed in Europe and some in the United States. If the USSR should attack Western Europe, the United States is committed by treaty to intervene. But the posture it maintains to deter that contingency and to fulfill the commitment if it should occur can vary widely, ranging from heavy reliance on nuclear deterrence, either by strategic or by tactical nuclear forces, to heavy reliance on conventional forces—with very different foreign policy, as well as budgetary, consequences.

In regard to U.S. forces stationed in Europe, foreign policy considerations have consistently played a large role. During the Johnson administration, the reduction of forces agreed on in 1967 seems to have been limited more by Secretary of State Rusk's judgment as to political consequences than by Secretary of Defense McNamara's judgment as to possible adverse military implications. Similarly, President Nixon's decision not to withdraw U.S. forces from Europe, despite substantial domestic pressures to do so, stems in large measure from a foreign policy judgment that unilateral U.S. troop withdrawals would adversely affect a number of U.S. interests: the political stability and orientation of our European allies, particularly the Federal Republic of Germany; prospects for close U.S.–European partnership in other matters, notably economic policy; and Soviet policy toward the West, specifically in relation to the resumption of Soviet pressure on Berlin, recent agreements regarding that city notwithstanding. Maintenance of U.S. forces in Europe has also been justified in "bargaining chip" terms; the administration has argued that forces must be kept there to induce the Russians to negotiate a mutual and balanced force reduction in Europe.

With respect to the defense budget, however, the key issue is not the number of forces maintained in Europe but the size of the total forces maintained for European contingencies, whether they are stationed in Europe or in the United States. It costs no more incrementally to station forces in Europe than to station them in the United States. Bringing them back from Europe would not in itself save money. The units would have to be deactivated and the total force structure commensurately reduced, and this could be done as well by deactivating forces already in the United States as by returning and deactivating forces now stationed in Europe.

Thus the key foreign policy considerations affecting the budget are whether the United States should continue to attach as high a priority to the defense of Europe as have this and previous administrations, and how many U.S. forces are needed to meet this priority. It could be argued that the approaching balance with the USSR in strategic forces makes it essential to put more U.S. resources into assuring the existence of a balance in Europe in conventional forces. Such an argument assumes that having achieved rough parity with the United States in nuclear capabilities, the Russians may feel freer to employ their conventional forces on the European scene. Alternatively, military force planning for European contingencies could be based on a foreign policy assessment that emphasizes the following elements: a downgrading of the Soviet threat, based on détente, a revised estimate of Moscow's conventional capabilities, or a new view of the likelihood of Soviet intervention in Western Europe; a belief that Western Europe can contribute more to its own defense and would be more likely to do so if the United States reduced the size of its forces; and a revised assessment of the importance of Western Europe to the defense and welfare of the United States, such that Washington would ease out of its NATO commitments. Any of these reassessments would allow a cut in the size of U.S. peacetime forces and a smaller defense budget.

Force Requirements in Asia

A third group of issues arises from the changing political relationships in the Western Pacific and the implications for U.S. force planning of the emerging new power balance in the region. The U.S. withdrawal from Vietnam, the President's initiatives regarding China, the strains introduced into U.S.–Japanese relations by those initiatives and by recent economic differences, and the uncertain position of the USSR in this area introduce considerable ambiguity into U.S. military planning on at least three counts: To what extent should Japan be encouraged to play a greater military role in Asia rather than depend exclusively on U.S. commitments, and what risks, nuclear and otherwise, would this entail? In what contingencies, if any, should the United States be willing to commit forces, particularly ground troops, in Asia? And what role should be assigned to U.S. nuclear weapons, strategic and tactical, to deter conflict in Asia?

In 1971, under the rubric of moving from a two and one-half war to a one and one-half war strategy, the administration made substantial reductions in peacetime conventional forces, which for all practical purposes meant a reduction in forces based in Asia and of the type that would ordinarily fight in Asia. Beyond that, the administration's position has been hedged; while the withdrawal from Vietnam is near completion, U.S. deployments elsewhere in the Pacific are still significant, and the force structure as well as the budget continue to be based on the maintenance of substantial air and naval forces and some ground forces specifically for Asian contingencies. Alternatively, the United States could contemplate either a return to the two and one-half war strategy (reflecting the view that even with continuing Sino-Soviet enmity, major conflicts could break out in Europe and the Far East at the same time) or a decision implicit in some statements by the secretary of defense that the United States will not commit ground troops to a war in Asia. Moving toward these force planning strategies could result either in increases or reductions in conventional forces and in higher or lower defense budgets. Again, the ambiguities between policy statements and force deployments may be deliberate, for deterrence purposes.

Defense Policy Considerations

Even if there were no differences in specifying U.S. interests or interpreting U.S. commitments, adequate criteria for determining forces and budgets would still be lacking. An additional set of broad judgments that can be called "defense policy" are required. They include such factors as the strategies to be used in specific contingencies —rapid deployment and forward defense or slower deployment and a willingness to yield ground initially; the amount of warning time assumed to be available before an attack occurs; the projected capabilities of the potential enemy; the length and intensity of the war; the capabilities of U.S. allies; the extent to which peacetime forces are maintained in a fully active rather than a reserve status; and the concepts used in designing new weapon systems.

Foreign policy considerations affect decisions as to whether to enter into or keep commitments and whether to intervene militarily, whereas defense policy relates to weapons and force decisions as to how the United States can best avoid conflicts (deterrence), what risks it is prepared to run, and with what means it is ready to defend itself, should deterrence fail. Thus, defense policy provides those basic assumptions needed for the technical task of developing a detailed force posture consistent with foreign policy choices. Some of the major issues and their budgetary implications are noted briefly below.

Length of the War

Is it plausible to plan on a conventional war (with the Soviet Union or China directly involved) that would last for many months or years, or should it be assumed that such a war would not last for more than a few weeks before being either stopped or escalated to the point where nuclear weapons are used? Some analysts believe that a long conventional war in Europe is highly unlikely, but that prolonged conflict in Asia is entirely possible, as experience has shown. This question affects nearly every part of the general purpose force structure. For example, the size of stocks of ammunition and other consumables depends directly on the answer. It also affects the organization of forces. In the Army, a division of 16,000 men and its initial support increment of another 16,000 support troops can fight for about ninety days. To continue much longer would require an additional 16,000 support troops per division—the sustaining support increment—which can provide logistic support for an indefinite period. In the Navy, if it were assumed that a war would last only a few weeks, it would not be necessary to maintain antisubmarine warfare forces in either the present number or design, since the requirement to keep open sea lanes for the logistic support of prolonged combat would be greatly reduced. In the case of tactical air forces the assumption, for planning purposes, of a short war would downgrade or virtually eliminate the need for missions against supply lines deep in enemy territory, since the war would be too short for such interdiction to have much effect. This would argue for a smaller number of aircraft and for aircraft of simpler design and lower cost.

Recent U.S. force planning has been based on the assumption that wars may last for three months in Europe and for years in Asia, but this planning assumption has not been consistently applied. Planning for a relatively short war has determined the size of stocks of ammunition and other consumables. On the other hand, ground force divisions, tactical air forces, and antisubmarine warfare forces are designed, at least in part, on the assumption that a war in Europe will be relatively long.

Assumptions regarding the length of a war, whether expressed in days, months, or years, obviously cannot be arbitrarily applied, since the margin of safety will vary. For example, it is possible to work within a fairly narrow margin in stocks of consumables, since production could be increased rapidly following mobilization. But this is true to a lesser extent in the case of major weapons. A more subtle consideration is that if either side in a conventional war believes that it will be overwhelmed, it may quickly resort to nuclear weapons. Hence, substantial conventional capability for a rather long war may be a deterrent to a nuclear exchange. Nonetheless, military decisions must be based on a planning assumption as to the length of a war, and it makes a difference for both forces and budgets whether a relatively short or relatively protracted conflict is assumed.

Mobilization Lead-time

How much time, if any, should the United States assume it will have in which to mobilize its forces before the onset of hostilities? In the

Berlin crisis of 1961, there was a long period of mounting tension, and both sides were able to carry out at least some mobilization. But this might not be the case in a future crisis. The amount of lead-time both sides are assumed to have for mobilizing and deploying strongly affects such factors as the ratio of active forces to reserve forces (the latter being less costly to maintain), the level of peacetime deployment overseas, airlift and sealift requirements, and the general level of readiness. Recently the United States has assumed that neither the Soviet Union nor China could carry out a full-scale mobilization without its being detected almost immediately, but that it was necessary to hedge against lower levels of mobilization, which might be successfully concealed for a time. Alternative assumptions moving toward the "worst case" or toward the "best case" would also be conceivable, and each would have different budgetary implications.

Reliance on Allies

In the past, force planners have tended to discount allied forces and to assume in some contingencies that the United States would have to do all or most of the job. Discussions of the naval situation in the Mediterranean, for example, rarely mention the substantial naval forces operated by the other NATO countries in the area. The "total force planning approach" adopted by the Nixon administration is meant to give greater weight to allied forces to meet the contingencies for which U.S. forces are programmed. To this end, the administration has encouraged U.S. allies to improve their military capabilities, particularly in such areas as training, readiness, modernization, and logistic infrastructure.

In Europe this initiative has been directed toward strengthening NATO's total defense capability, not toward reducing the U.S. military contribution to the alliance. While European NATO countries are improving their forces, the United States is filling out units that are below strength in Europe and upgrading their readiness. The United States could have decided to reduce its forces as its NATO allies strengthened their forces. The judgments involved concern the questions: how much total defense is necessary for balance in Europe, and would European NATO countries do more if the United States did less?

In Asia, greater reliance on allied forces is associated with increased

U.S. security assistance and a possible reduction in U.S. forces. It is argued, for example, that it would be cheaper and entail less risk to subsidize South Koreans in uniform to deter another Korean war than to maintain Americans in uniform for the same purpose. If so, allied combat manpower could substitute for some U.S. combat manpower and make possible reductions in the U.S. defense budget that otherwise would not be possible.

Several issues are involved. Will the U.S. force reductions that are to result from increases in military assistance in fact be made? As in the case of troops in Europe, budgetary savings will depend not simply on bringing back troops that are now stationed in Asia, but on reducing the total force structure. Is this desirable? Is it in the interest of U.S. security for these countries to increase their own military spending, perhaps at the cost of economic development? Will high levels of military assistance strengthen the role of the military in the internal politics of these countries, and is this in the U.S. security interest? Finally, to what degree will this transfer of defensive responsibility from the United States to an ally involve political and military consequences that are destabilizing? Does substituting Asian forces for U.S. peacetime forces weaken the deterrent to conflict, even if aggregate capability is unchanged? If so, this defense policy initiative raises one of the central foreign policy issues discussed above: What forces should the United States maintain for Asian contingencies, and where should they be based?

Confidence Levels

Whatever conclusions are reached about these kinds of factors, there will still be a great deal of residual uncertainty about military potential. In a shooting war, leadership and morale can vary, and weapons systems can perform better or worse than anticipated. Estimated force requirements will always be greater if pessimistic assumptions are made, and they will be less if the assumptions are optimistic. Always to assume the worst may sometimes minimize risks, but this can be prohibitively expensive and may contribute to the arms race; always to assume the best may keep costs low, but may sometimes increase the risk of conflict by weakening deterrence. Thus, decisions must reflect a balance between the security confidence desired and the cost of defense expenditures needed to achieve it.

An example from the recent past illustrates the way in which questions regarding confidence can affect the relation between policy and force levels. One of the first acts of the Nixon administration was to request a reevaluation of U.S. military strategy, and in particular of the decision to maintain military forces sufficient to fight the initial phases of a major war in Europe and in Asia at the same time. The administration decided that these requirements were unnecessarily large and that it would maintain forces for a major war *either* in Asia *or* in Europe, but not in both at the same time. In effect, the administration came to a foreign policy judgment that a simultaneous outbreak of general war in Asia and in Europe was unlikely, and a fiscal judgment that the additional resources needed for a two and one-half war strategy could be better used for domestic programs. This defense policy decision, however, was not fully translated into force changes, in part because it raised questions of confidence levels that had previously been submerged. Most military planners had long argued that the United States could not be reasonably confident of actually meeting the requirements of a two and one-half war strategy with the forces being maintained under that strategy. They saw the decision to adopt a less ambitious strategy as narrowing, but not eliminating, the gap between requirements and forces, and they therefore pressed for maintaining existing conventional forces so that the United States could have greater confidence of being able to deal with a single major conflict in either Europe or Asia. Forces were in fact reduced, but not commensurately with the cutback in stated defense planning goals, if it is assumed that prior forces were adequate to achieve the stated goals.

Strategic planning offers the most explicit example of the effect of the confidence factor on force structure. The United States maintains three independent nuclear deterrents in the belief that redundancy is necessary as a cushion against technological surprises from potential adversaries or unexpected failures in its own systems. Some analysts argue, however, that a diad—two survivable systems—would be sufficient. Others maintain that the consequences of nuclear war are so catastrophic that a single nuclear system (a sea-based system is usually suggested because of its survivability) would be sufficient to deter Soviet leaders from launching a nuclear first strike.

Confidence, then, is central to the problem of defense insurance. How large a premium should the United States be willing to pay, as a society, to insure against low-probability contingencies, where the cost of being uninsured can be catastrophically high? Those who emphasize the remote character of the contingencies believe that present confidence levels are at least adequate, and they seek to reduce the premiums. Those who emphasize the huge cost of being wrong seek higher confidence levels, even at the expense of larger premiums.

Manpower Factors

Issues involving the pay and efficiency of defense manpower, though independent of foreign policy and only loosely related to defense policy, have been a major influence on the size of the defense budget.

In the case of manpower costs, two legislative decisions—the comparability pay standard for all government employees and the goal of an all-volunteer armed force—caused the fiscal 1973 defense budget to be $15 billion higher than it would have been at 1968 pay scales. About $7 billion of this increase in the defense payroll was due to the rise in the cost of living and $8 billion to an increase in real pay. In fact, pay legislation alone has increased the defense budget since 1968 by an amount almost equal to the budgetary savings realized from withdrawal from Vietnam.

The fact that manpower costs now compose more than half of the defense budget in itself highlights the importance of examining the efficiency with which manpower is used. In recent years there has been a marked trend toward a higher defense manpower overhead. The present ratio is roughly as follows: about 15 percent of military personnel have a combat job—that is, the primary mission of firing weapons at the enemy; the remaining 85 percent provide a variety of services to support these combat troops. Among the factors that explain this ratio are the large engineering and transport services deemed necessary in-combat organizations for mobility and combat effectiveness; the long logistics and personnel pipelines required to support the Vietnam war; improvements in the level of readiness; the larger manpower requirements for maintaining more advanced weapons systems; and the provision of services aimed at improving the standard of living for military personnel, partly to encourage enlistment. Thus, the ratio of combat to support manpower is not by itself a reliable measure of efficiency, but it should draw attention to alternative ways of meeting the same requirements at lower cost and to the possibilities for adjusting the requirements themselves. Examining defense costs in these terms dramatizes the fact that a sizable part of the defense budget is determined by policy issues that are related in large measure to efficiency rather than to foreign policy or strategy.

Domestic Considerations

Defense spending for the most part has not been subject to partisan politics, a notable exception having been the sharp debate over the existence of a "missile gap" in the presidential campaign of 1960. It is conceivable that in preparing the fiscal 1973 budget the administration, with such considerations in mind, wanted to forestall criticism from those who believe that the USSR is gaining a military advantage that the United States must try to overcome.

More mundane domestic considerations enter into the defense budget, principally because of its size in relation to the economy. For example, it is widely believed that there are too many military bases in the United States in light of the present level of forces, but closing them would cause a loss of jobs in the areas concerned and invite the strong opposition of congressmen whose constituencies were affected. The almost immediate effect of cutbacks in weapons procurement on the aerospace industry, which is heavily dependent on government contracts, inevitably is a restraining factor on defense decisions, both because of the effects on employment and because of concern over keeping specialized defense production facilities in operation. And in a soft economy, reductions in defense manpower—civilian or military—are politically sensitive and cause serious personal hardship, at least temporarily. Of the four general considerations affecting the defense budget, domestic factors are quantitatively the least important, but they illustrate the inherent pressure to maintain the status quo—irrespective of changes in the underlying justification—and the obstacles to making sizable year-to-year reductions in defense spending. On the other hand, the pressure of competing domestic requirements now exercises greater restraint on increases in defense spending than at any time since the end of the Second World War.

Conclusions

On the basis of this discussion, it is possible to draw a rough dividing line between the influence of foreign policy and that of other factors in determining the size of peacetime defense budgets.

There is no precise or automatic relationship between new conceptions of foreign policy objectives and obligations and the size of defense budgets. A redefinition of U.S. foreign policy interests is likely to change force requirements, but there are important qualifications. First, it takes time. While it may be widely believed that the world is moving either toward détente or toward greater hostility, such assessments would have to be well tested before a President would be willing to translate them into lower or higher forces and budgets; even then, a great deal of organizational inertia would have to be overcome. Second, budget levels would not be affected proportionately, since foreign policy most closely influences the number of major combat units—division forces, tactical air wings, and carrier task forces—and these account for only part of the defense budget.

Moreover, widely different defense budgets are possible with the same foreign policy. Other factors such as defense policy, manpower efficiency, and domestic concerns exert a major influence on the defense budget. In his Defense Report for fiscal 1973, Secretary of Defense Melvin R. Laird emphasizes the complexity of the issues and the need for "constructive discussion and constructive criticism" to help deal with them. This will require, he believes, not only consultation and cooperation with the Congress, but an enlightened public discussion. In the secretary's words: "Of equal importance—since national defense, in the last analysis, is the responsibility of all the American people—is the need for a public dialogue such as we have not had since the days of the genesis of the Marshall Plan."[1]

Chapters 3, 4, and 5 are intended to help meet this need. They outline some of the issues that lie ahead and the choices they may offer.

1. *Annual Defense Department Report, FY 1973*, Statement of Secretary of Defense Melvin R. Laird before the Senate Armed Services Committee on the FY 1973 Defense Budget and FY 1973–77 Program (Feb. 15, 1972), p. 17.

3. Changes and Trends in the Defense Budget

THE FEDERAL BUDGET for fiscal 1973 provides for a substantial increase in spending on national defense, the major impact of which will come in future years. The President proposes that the United States spend $76.5 billion for defense purposes—$700 million more than in fiscal 1972, and an amount representing 6.4 percent of the gross national product and 30 percent of the federal budget.[1]

In terms of outlays, the steady decline that began in 1969 in the *proportionate* claim that defense makes on the nation's resources will continue. In terms of authorizations to commit funds, the budget portends a perceptibly different trend. The President asks for $83.2 billion in total obligational authority for the Defense Department—up $5.1 billion from fiscal 1972. In the case of major procurement and research and development, it takes time for contracts to be let and purchases made. Once the contracts have been let, the contractor is usually paid in installments as the work is done. For this reason, when there is an increase in the defense program as measured by funds authorized, the accompanying increase in actual spending may not occur for some time, and it may be spread over several years. Much

---

1. The defense totals discussed in this section do not include approximately $1 billion for weapon development that is included in the Atomic Energy Commission's appropriation, which is an integral part of current national security costs. Nor does this chapter consider such appropriations as those for veterans' benefits or interest on the national debt, which are related to past expenditures on national security.

the same situation existed in the fiscal 1972 budget, when total obligational authority exceeded outlays by $2.3 billion. Taken together, the budgets for the two years provide authority for a substantial rise in defense outlays in the years immediately ahead.

This upward trend is more pronounced when account is taken of the implications for future spending of force and weapon decisions made in the 1973 budget, of future pay increases required under existing legislation, and of possible growth in the unit cost of technically advanced weapon systems now being developed or in early stages of procurement.

The reduction in the cost of the Vietnam war during 1973 adds an important perspective. The reduction in outlays is estimated to be $3.6 billion, and in total obligational authority $3 billion. When these are taken into account, the budget requests represent an increase in fiscal 1973 of $4.3 billion in outlays and $8.1 billion in total obligational authority for baseline, or peacetime, military forces. These financial comparisons are shown in Table 3-1.

In terms of force structure, the implications of the 1973 budget can be summarized as follows:

For *strategic forces*, modernization of all three offensive nuclear systems—sea-based missiles, land-based missiles, and bombers—but with a pronounced emphasis on expanding sea-based capabilities. A substantial investment is also being made in defense against bomber and missile attacks. As a whole, the program is reminiscent, and may soon reach the pace, of the early 1960s, when much of the present strategic posture of the United States was developed. In dollars of constant purchasing power, requested spending authority is roughly 10 percent below the 1961–64 average, but further increases are now clearly in prospect.

For *baseline general purpose forces*, the budget indicates a structure stabilizing at somewhat below the pre-Vietnam level in terms of divisions, carriers, air wings, and number of active military personnel, but with greater military firepower and effectiveness. Although smaller in size, the present baseline force costs about the same, in dollars of constant purchasing power, partly because of the effect of large catch-up and incentive pay increases and partly because the real cost of supporting force units has grown. In regard to programs for modernizing weapon systems, the proportion of funds going to the Navy has again risen, as was the case in the fiscal 1972 budget.

Table 3-1. Financial Summary of the Department of Defense Budget, Selected Fiscal Years, 1961–73

Billions of dollars

Description	1961	1964	1968	1972	1973
In current dollars					
Total outlays	**44.7**	**50.8**	**78.0**	**75.8**	**76.5**
Baseline force	44.7	50.8	58.0	68.7	73.0
Vietnam additions	...	...	20.0	7.1	3.5
Total outlays as percentage of gross national product	**8.3**	**8.3**	**9.4**	**7.0**	**6.4**
Total obligational authority	**46.1**	**50.7**	**75.7**	**78.1**	**83.2**
Baseline force	46.1	50.7	56.4	71.6	79.7
Vietnam additions	...	...	19.3	6.5	3.5
In 1973 dollars[a]					
Total outlays	**72.9**	**76.3**	**103.1**	**79.6**	**76.5**
Baseline force with conscription	72.9	76.3	77.1	70.2	69.9
Cost of moving toward all-volunteer armed force	...	...	...	2.0	3.1
Total baseline force	72.9	76.3	77.1	72.2	73.0
Vietnam additions	...	...	26.0	7.4	3.5
Total obligational authority	**75.2**	**76.3**	**99.0**	**82.0**	**83.2**
Baseline force with conscription	75.2	76.3	74.9	73.2	76.6
Cost of moving toward all-volunteer armed force	...	...	...	2.0	3.1
Total baseline force	75.2	76.3	74.9	75.2	79.7
Vietnam additions	...	...	24.1	6.8	3.5

Sources: U.S. Department of Defense, News Release 51-72, January 24, 1972; Department of Defense, "FY 1973 Budget Briefing" (January 22, 1972; processed); *Department of Defense Appropriations for 1972*, Hearings before a Subcommittee of the House Committee on Appropriations, 92 Cong. 1 sess. (1971), pp. 1164–65; Statements of Secretary of Defense to Senate Armed Services Committee, various years; Department of Defense annual reports, relevant years; U.S. Bureau of the Census, *Statistical Abstract of the United States, 1963*, p. 257. Vietnam costs for 1973 are authors' estimates.

a. Estimates of constant dollar costs of prior year authorizations differ from those used by the Department of Defense in two major respects: (1) the cost of the all-volunteer armed force is treated as a discretionary cost decision and not as an element of general inflation; (2) retired pay is calculated by multiplying the number of retirees in each stated year by the average cost of retiree benefits in fiscal year 1973, rather than by "straightlining" fiscal year 1973 costs for all previous years.

For *Vietnam*, the prospect is for further but diminishing savings arising from the decline of U.S. military activity and the withdrawal of U.S. forces, offset in small measure by increased military assistance to Southeast Asia. The war is no longer a significant budgetary factor; at most it may absorb 5 percent of the 1973 defense budget. Nor is it a source of significant savings in the future. The peace dividend has virtually been paid.

An estimated distribution of fiscal 1973 defense budget costs among these three categories, compared with similar data for past years, is shown in Table 3-2.

The secretary of defense has stated that the major force components contemplated in the 1973 budget represent the administration's thinking as to peacetime force needs over the next five years. These forces are shown in Table 3-3 and are compared with those maintained in selected prior years. Generally speaking, these data show: (1) in comparison with peak Vietnam war levels in 1968, a sharp across-the-board decline in general purpose forces; (2) in comparison with 1964, the last peacetime year, a moderate decline in the number of military personnel, divisions, air wings, and ships, and a steep cut in strategic defensive forces; and (3) in comparison with 1961, a marked change in the composition of both strategic and general purpose forces. These numerical force comparisons, it should be noted, do not

Table 3-2. Distribution of Department of Defense Budget, by Category, Selected Fiscal Years, 1962–73

Total obligational authority in billions of dollars

Category	1962	1964	1968	1970	1972	1973
In current dollars						
Strategic nuclear forces	12.6	13.9	13.6	14.7	16.9	18.6
Baseline general purpose forces	38.1	36.9	42.6	47.7	54.7	61.1
Vietnam additions	...	...	19.3	14.4	6.5	3.5
Total	50.7	50.8	75.7	76.8	78.1	83.2
In 1973 dollars[a]						
Strategic nuclear forces	20.8	21.6	18.4	17.5	17.4	18.6
Baseline general purpose forces	59.7	54.7	56.5	56.0	57.8	61.1
Vietnam additions	...	...	24.1	16.7	6.8	3.5
Total	80.5	76.3	99.0	90.2	82.0	83.2

Sources: Data in current dollars are derived from Department of Defense, News Release 72-71, January 29, 1971, News Release 51-72, January 24, 1972, and *Statement of Secretary of Defense Robert S. McNamara before a Joint Session of the Senate Armed Services Committee and the Senate Subcommittee on Department of Defense Appropriations on the Fiscal Year 1966–70 Defense Program and 1966 Defense Budget* (1965). Costs of strategic nuclear forces are the sum of the strategic forces program, half of the intelligence and communications program, one-tenth of the National Guard and Reserve program, 40 percent of the research and development program, and a varying percentage of three support programs, central supply and maintenance, training, medical and other general personnel activities, and administration, in proportion to the ratio of direct operating costs between strategic and all other forces. These estimates differ from those given in *Setting National Priorities: The 1972 Budget*, because of methodological refinements. The cost of baseline general purpose forces is the balance of the Defense Department's obligational authority less incremental Vietnam costs. The latter is given in *Department of Defense Appropriations for 1972*, Hearings before a Subcommittee of the House Committee on Appropriations (1971), pp. 1163–65, and Department of Defense, "FY 73 Budget Briefing" (January 22, 1972). Vietnam costs for 1973 are authors' estimates.

a. Estimates of constant dollar costs of prior year authorizations differ from those used by the Department of Defense in two major respects: (1) the cost of the all-volunteer armed force is treated as a discretionary cost decision and not as an element of general inflation; (2) retired pay is calculated by multiplying the number of retirees in each stated year by the average cost of retiree benefits in fiscal year 1973, rather than by "straightlining" fiscal year 1973 costs for all previous years.

Table 3-3. Structure of Department of Defense Military Forces, Various Fiscal Years, 1961–73[a]

					Estimated	
Description	1961	1964	1968	1970	1972	1973
Personnel (thousands)						
Active duty military	2,484	2,685	3,547	3,066	2,392	2,358
Reserve military	1,086	1,048	1,001	1,039	1,026	1,038
Civilian	1,042	1,035	1,287	1,161	1,041	1,036
Strategic forces						
Land-based missiles	28	654	1,054	1,054	1,054	1,054
Sea-based missiles	80	336	656	656	656	656
Strategic bombers[b]	1,654	1,277	648	517	512	511
Total offensive warheads[c]	3,900	4,900	4,200	4,000	5,700	6,900
Manned interceptor squadrons[d]	75	64	48	31	27	27
Surface-to-air missile batteries[e]	216	159	135	95	68	63
General purpose forces						
Ground forces						
Divisions (Army and Marine)	17	19⅓	23⅔	20⅓	16	16
Tactical air forces						
Air Force tactical wings[f]	32	36	48	44	36	35
Navy carrier attack wings	17	17	15	15	13	14
Marine air wings	3	3	3	3	3	3
Naval vessels						
Aircraft carriers[g]	24	24	23	19	17	16
Other vessels[h]	868	872	912	709	599	537
Average age, all vessels (years)	12.9	15.2	17.5	16.7	14.9	14.5
Airlift forces						
Strategic airlift squadrons	31	32	30	18	17	17
Strategic airlift capacity[i]	23.5	28.5	35.1	27.1	39.4	43.1

Sources: *The Budget of the United States Government*, various years; *The Budget of the United States Government—Appendix*, various years; Department of Defense, News Release 72-71, January 29, 1971, and News Release 51-72, January 24, 1972; *Fiscal Year 1972 Authorization for Military Procurement, Research and Development, Construction and Real Estate Acquisition for the Safeguard ABM and Reserve Strengths*, Hearings before the Senate Committee on Armed Services, 92 Cong. 1 sess (1971), Pt. 5; Department of Defense, "Fact Sheet" (May 1968; processed), p. 18; unpublished data from the Departments of the Air Force and the Navy. See also notes c and i below.

a. All figures are for the end of the fiscal year except for total offensive warheads for 1968 and 1970, which are for September 1 and December 31, respectively.

b. Includes, before 1968, medium-range bombers based overseas. These numbers represent active inventory.

c. The 1968 figure (for September 1) is from *The 1970 Defense Budget and Defense Program for Fiscal Years 1970–74, Statement of Secretary of Defense Clark M. Clifford* (January 15, 1969), p. 42. The 1970 figure (for December 31) is from *Fiscal Year 1972–76 Defense Program and the 1972 Defense Budget: Statement of Secretary of Defense Melvin R. Laird before the House Armed Services Committee* (March 9, 1971), p. 165. The 1972 figure is from *Annual Defense Department Report, FY 1973*, Statement of Secretary of Defense Melvin R. Laird before the Senate Armed Services Committee on the FY 1973 Defense Budget and FY 1973–1977 Program (February 15, 1972), p. 40. All other figures are authors' estimates based on reflect, for the most part, the steady increase in capabilities. In his statement on the fiscal year 1969 budget, Secretary of Defense Robert S. McNamara noted, as examples of this phenomenon, the substantial increase that had occurred between 1961 and 1968 in the firepower of ground force weapons, the payload capability of tactical aircraft, the mission effectiveness of Navy ships, and amphibious assault capacity.[2] Procurement programs since that time strongly suggest that those measures would show further increases. At the same time, however, the capabilities of potential adversaries have also increased.

Force structure aside, it is evident that three factors have dominated changes in the defense budget: the rising cost of manpower, the rising cost of weapon systems, and the diminishing cost of Vietnam. So long as the third factor, Vietnam war savings, was the most important, it made cuts possible in the defense budget. Now, rising manpower costs are the most important, and this exerts upward pressure on defense spending. In fiscal 1973, military and civilian pay, together with associated personnel costs, will take up 56 percent of the total defense budget. In 1964, when there were 300,000 more personnel in active service, this figure was 43 percent.

The fact that manpower costs will absorb the major portion of the additional resources the President proposes to commit to defense emphasizes this point further. Of the $8.1 billion increase requested for non-Vietnam military programs, nearly half is accounted for by price increases and by pay increases to make wages of government employees comparable to those in the private sector. The remainder, more than $4 billion, may be viewed as the discretionary increase in defense spending authority, expressed in dollars of constant purchasing

2. *Statement of Secretary of Defense Robert S. McNamara before the Senate Armed Services Committee on the Fiscal Year 1969–73 Defense Program and 1969 Defense Budget* (1968), pp. 87–94.

---

assumed force loadings. Cruise missile submarines, medium-range ballistic missiles, and tactical nuclear weapons are excluded from the calculations.

d. Active Air Force and Air National Guard units.

e. Includes Army and National Guard units, and Bomarc squadrons; note that some air defense batteries in the U.S. are not considered strategic forces (for example, eight Hawk batteries in Florida); they are included in these totals, however.

f. Includes fighter, reconnaissance, electronic warfare, and tactical airlift units.

g. Includes antisubmarine warfare carriers.

h. Excluding carriers and Polaris/Poseidon submarines.

i. Units in millions of pounds, maximum payload. Authors' estimates based on force levels and individual aircraft capabilities listed in John W. R. Taylor (ed.), *Jane's All The World's Aircraft* (McGraw-Hill), various issues; *Aviation Week and Space Technology*, Vol. 96 (March 13, 1972), p. 95; and unpublished data from the Department of the Air Force.

power. Military investment—consisting of procurement, research and development, and military construction—accounts for only $1.4 billion. The balance will be used largely for manpower programs, such as incentive pay increases, improved housing facilities, and better medical care to underwrite the all-volunteer armed force, and for increased costs of retired pay resulting from the growing number of military retirees.

The sharply rising costs of defense manpower highlight the need for a reassessment of several major aspects of the defense budget, in particular the balance between manpower and weapons in the combat forces, and the structure of support forces, which are disproportionately heavy consumers of manpower. It will be essential, in one way or another, to achieve greater efficiency in the use of manpower. The administration has indicated the hope that over the longer term defense spending can be kept at roughly current levels, with due allowance for inflation, or that at most no more than 7 percent of the gross national product will need to be allocated to the defense budget. As manpower costs continue to rise, achievement of this goal will increasingly require compensating adjustments—either in the number of people, or in weapons procurement, or in both. In his fiscal 1973 Defense Report, Secretary Laird makes the point succinctly: "It will not be easy to strike a balance between our equipment needs and our manpower needs."[3]

This and the next two chapters are designed to illuminate some of the difficult choices that lie ahead. The remainder of this chapter outlines the major features of the 1973 defense budget, including the decisions it reflects regarding strategic and general purpose forces, and projects their cost implications for the rest of this decade. Chapter 4 examines selected issues that bear on the consideration of alternative defense budgets, and Chapter 5 compares the 1973 budget with some illustrative alternatives, largely to indicate key decisions involved in arriving at defense spending levels.

Strategic Forces

Strategic nuclear forces account for about one-fifth of the 1973 defense budget. In the words of the President's 1972 Foreign Policy

3. *Annual Defense Department Report, FY 1973,* Statement of Secretary of Defense Melvin R. Laird before the Senate Armed Services Committee on the FY 1973 Defense Budget and FY 1973–1977 Program (February 15, 1972), p. 61.

Report, strategic forces, as the "most crucial" element of military power:

—Are the primary deterrent to nuclear attacks against the United States or its allies;
—Compel an aggressor contemplating less than all-out attacks to recognize the unacceptable risk of escalation; and
—Reduce the likelihood of intimidation or coercion of the U.S. or its allies.[4]

Strategic offensive forces consist of bombers, land-based missiles, and sea-based missiles. Each has an independent capability of absorbing an all-out Soviet attack while retaining enough force to inflict unacceptable damage in retaliation. This redundant deterrent is called the "triad." Strategic defensive forces include air and ballistic missile defense and early warning systems.

Factors Underlying Strategic Force Decisions

Strategic force planning is now based on the assumptions (1) that the USSR has reached a position of strategic parity with the United States and (2) that regaining strategic superiority would not be practical for the United States, for both technical and fiscal reasons, and would not contribute to U.S. security.[5]

On the other hand, while accepting the possibility of "minor quantitative imbalances," the President insisted in his 1972 Foreign Policy Report that the Soviet Union could not be permitted "to establish a significant numerical advantage in overall offensive and defensive forces."[6] At the same time, he emphasized that the United States must maintain an assured retaliatory capability despite any anticipated improvements—qualitative as well as quantitative—in Soviet strategic forces. While expressing a preference for mutual restraint and an agreement in the strategic arms limitation talks (SALT), the President said that "under no circumstances will I permit the further ero-

4. *U.S. Foreign Policy for the 1970's: The Emerging Structure of Peace*, A Report to the Congress by Richard Nixon, President of the United States (February 9, 1972), p. 156.
5. *Ibid.*, p. 157. It is also assumed that the Chinese will acquire a small intercontinental ballistic missile (ICBM) force before the end of the 1970s, but this does not appear to impose additional requirements for U.S. strategic force planning. Current offensive systems are sufficient to deter China as well as the USSR. Limitations on antiballistic missiles (ABMs) now in prospect in negotiations with the USSR would preclude building a thin nationwide defensive system specifically designed against a possible Chinese attack.
6. *Ibid.*, pp. 157–58.

sion of the strategic balance with the USSR."[7] Thus, two immediate major factors influenced the budget decisions on strategic forces: the Soviet strategic buildup and SALT.[8] These two factors are logically related in that progress in SALT, or the lack of it, could influence the assessment of the Soviet strategic threat. Each will be examined in turn.

The Soviet Strategic Force Buildup

An assessment of what Soviet strategic programs mean for U.S. force planning depends on three major elements: actual forces deployed, which are well known; the technical capability of these forces, which is considerably less well known; and Soviet objectives and plans, which are the most uncertain factors in the equation.

In recent years Soviet programs have been characterized by a steady expansion in intercontinental ballistic missiles (ICBMs) and submarine-launched ballistic missiles (SLBMs). The Defense Report states that during the past year there has been very little construction activity related to known Soviet missiles, but 100 new silos have been detected. These new silos could be for new systems, which would suggest a further expansion of land-based missiles, or simply for upgrading existing systems, which would suggest that the USSR is stabilizing the number of ICBMs at current levels. The Russians stopped testing multiple reentry vehicle (MRV) technology for their land-based systems in 1970, and there have been no indications that they have yet tested multiple independently targetable reentry vehicles (MIRVs). As for sea-based missiles, enough additional submarines are under construction to bring the Soviet submarine force into numerical parity with that of the United States by the end of calendar 1973.

Other elements in the Soviet strategic force—bombers, intermediate-range missiles, and air defense systems—have either remained constant in numbers or shown a slight decline since 1968.

Broadly speaking, strategic parity is believed to exist between the United States and the USSR. The USSR now has more ICBM launchers and operational defensive systems and is approaching parity in the number of strategic submarines; the United States is

7. *Ibid.*, p. 160.
8. A discussion of the major doctrinal issues that shape the U.S. strategic force posture appears in Charles L. Schultze and others, *Setting National Priorities: The 1972 Budget* (Brookings Institution, 1971), pp. 40–46.

ahead in number of bombers, in number of deliverable warheads (because of its continuing MIRV deployments), and in submarine technology.

Possible qualitative changes in future Soviet strategic forces are more crucial for U.S. strategic force planning than are simple numerical comparisons. This is reflected in a number of program decisions in the 1973 budget:

• The possibility of a breakthrough in Soviet antisubmarine warfare (ASW) technology that could threaten our present sea-based missiles is an important justification for the undersea long-range missile system (ULMS).

• The possibility that the USSR may develop an accurate MIRV technology and thereby threaten the survival of U.S. land-based systems is the primary justification for the Safeguard antiballistic missile (ABM) program and other substantial U.S. investments in protecting land-based missiles (for example, the site defense of Minuteman and Minuteman silo upgrade programs).

• The possibility that new Soviet interceptors and surface-to-air missiles could jeopardize the effectiveness of U.S. strategic bombers has led to U.S. investments in the development of a new strategic bomber, the B-1, in a new subsonic cruise armed decoy (SCAD), and in a new short-range attack missile for bombers (SRAM).

• The possibility that the Soviet Union may develop technology (particularly for firing missiles in depressed trajectories) and operating procedures for their sea-based missiles that would reduce warning time for our bombers has led to programs to disperse our B-52s and to enable them to react faster.

These technological uncertainties show the danger of associating numerical parity with strategic stability. Current evidence offers no indication that the Russians have yet achieved any of these technical advances, and the possibility that they will succeed in all areas over the next decade is remote. But they could succeed in some areas. Given the desire of the United States to maintain a stable strategic deterrent, the crucial problem is to decide which technological risks it is essential to hedge against, and which should receive low priority.

Uncertainty about Soviet intentions or even about medium-term projections of Soviet forces compounds the difficulty. The recent force buildup by the USSR could be viewed as disturbing, particularly if it continues. It is even more disturbing if appreciable weight is assigned to the possibility of rapid Soviet technological breakthroughs in most of the areas described above. It would then be possible to forecast a growing threat to all three areas of the U.S. strategic triad and a growing Soviet capability to apply political pressure on allies of the United States. The risk might be small, but the cost of doing nothing could be very great. Hence a tendency would exist to take countermeasures in all areas.

Alternatively, the Soviet buildup could be seen as motivated by the current Soviet view of requirements for achieving or maintaining parity with the United States, given the rapid increase in the number of U.S. warheads due to the MIRV programs, plus the need to deal with contingencies involving China. Compromises, logical or not, to resolve differences among Soviet leaders as to what should be done about strategic forces could also be a factor. This line of reasoning would suggest a willingness to delay countermeasures until Soviet intentions were more clearly defined. The businesslike Soviet attitude in SALT would support this position. From this point of view, the cost of a premature response to Soviet programs would be high, since it could cause the USSR to undertake new measures of its own in response to new U.S. programs. Continuing actions and reactions, stemming from uncertainty about each other's policies and stage of technological advance, would mean a step-up in the strategic arms race, in which case the United States as well as the USSR would be saddled with higher defense expenditures but would probably enjoy less security.

It may well be that proponents of both views exist within the Soviet hierarchy and that the choice between them is still a subject of controversy.

The Progress in SALT

A U.S.–Soviet strategic arms agreement would reduce uncertainty in both countries as to the other's policies. Limits on specific systems in themselves could achieve this result. In addition, the discussions greatly improve each country's understanding of how the other views the requirements for deterrence and stability. Much will depend, however, on the scope of the agreement.

A strong probability now exists that it will be possible in calendar 1972 to reach a first-round agreement consisting of a limit of 150–200 on the number of antiballistic missiles (ABMs) and a freeze on ICBMs.

It is also possible that the agreement will reflect some progress on restraining sea-based systems. And it probably will provide for a second round of negotiations looking toward a more comprehensive agreement.

It is noteworthy that neither country has suggested, at least not publicly, that air defense should be included in the negotiations. This is somewhat surprising in view of the agreement to discuss ABMs, the high cost of air defense systems, and their relative ineffectiveness. There may be a problem of definition here, since some of these weapons are used for tactical as well as strategic defense. Bureaucratic interests may also be a barrier, particularly in the USSR, which has made especially large investments in defensive systems.

Even a first-round agreement would have significant implications for U.S. force decisions. Limiting ABMs to no more than 200 missiles would mean that only two Safeguard sites could be maintained in the United States. Hence it would be unnecessary to build two additional sites or plan for a fifth site, which together would cost $2 billion over the next seven years and for which about $0.6 billion is requested in the 1973 budget. A freeze on the number of ICBMs would reduce but by no means eliminate concern over the survivability of the Minuteman. And this would suggest less need for other investment in the defense or upgrading of Minuteman sites, for which about $300 million is requested in the 1973 budget. On the other hand, a first-round agreement need not in itself affect expenditures on research and development, air defense, the Minuteman or Poseidon MIRV programs, or on expanding sea-based capability with ULMS. How a first-round agreement and arrangements for subsequent discussions affect these programs will depend on (1) the future development of Soviet programs and the interpretation placed on them, (2) the relationship believed to exist between spending for strategic forces and the likelihood of reaching further arms control settlements with the USSR, and (3) the strategic and psychological significance attached to numerical force comparisons. In any event, it is evident that failure to reach a first-round SALT agreement this year would exert a powerful force for even further expansion of strategic force programs.

Given the potential importance of continuing arms control discussions with the USSR for U.S. strategic force budgets (apart from their importance for other reasons), it is worth noting some major areas of difficulty that a second-round negotiation would seek to address.

The first difficulty concerns the definition of which strategic systems should be covered by a second-round agreement. The United States favors including all major strategic offensive systems—land-based and sea-based missiles, and bombers. Under this definition, Soviet intermediate-range ballistic missiles (IRBMs), which threaten Europe but not the United States, would be subject to limitation, but carriers and tactical aircraft, which can carry nuclear weapons, would not, on the ground that they are general purpose rather than strategic forces. In contrast, the USSR would have the negotiations cover any nuclear system that could threaten the homeland of the other country. This definition would include U.S. forward-based tactical aircraft and would exclude the Soviet IRBMs.

A second problem arises from the large disparity that exists in numbers, types, and qualitative characteristics of the long-range systems that each country maintains. In these circumstances, comprehensive limits on all offensive systems have proved difficult to negotiate. Whether a system-by-system approach will lead to a broad and durable agreement covering bombers, submarines, ICBMs, and air defense is still an open question. In the end, a comprehensive agreement may depend on a willingness on the part of each country to trade its advantages in one system for the elimination of its disadvantages in another.

Decisions in the 1973 Budget

The President has recommended a marked increase in spending for strategic forces, on the grounds that the Soviet buildup requires a broad-range U.S. response. While SALT continues to be a primary consideration in strategic plans, for the time being at least it is not preventing upward pressure on the budget. There are two main reasons for this paradoxical result. The first is that the President's decisions on force posture emphasize the effect of the strategic balance on U.S. political relations with allies as well as with potential adversaries. The second is the administration's apparent view that program requests for the improvement or expansion of offensive and defensive strategic systems are important bargaining chips in the negotiations with the USSR.

Total spending authority for strategic forces—including investment, operating, and indirect costs—is estimated to be $18.6 billion, up $1.2 billion over fiscal 1972. Improvements are requested for all three elements of the triad, but the increase in spending is concentrated on ULMS, the new sea-based missile system. Budget requests for air defense are also markedly higher. As is shown in Table 3-4, bombers and strategic defensive systems account for disproportionately large shares of the total strategic force budget. Furthermore, bombers and air defense in fiscal 1973 will together claim almost 60 percent of total strategic spending, but will make a less than equivalent contribution to deterrence—the primary objective of strategic forces.

These are the major decisions on strategic force programs reflected in the 1973 budget:

For sea-based systems, a dramatic increase from $105 million to $942 million in spending on ULMS. The purpose of the program is to build longer-range ballistic missiles and a highly survivable, quieter submarine of improved design that will be capable of launching them. In addition to underwriting further research and development, which is still at a relatively early stage, the budget includes more than $400 million for procurement and construction, which in itself indicates how rapidly the program is to be accelerated. The first ULMS sub-

Table 3-4. Allocation of the Strategic Forces Budget by Weapon System, Fiscal Year 1973

System	Cost (billions of dollars)	Percent of total
Offensive weapons, total	**11.8**	*63*
Land-based strategic missiles	2.4	*13*
Sea-based strategic missiles	3.6	*19*
Bombers	5.8	*31*
Defensive weapons, total	**6.8**	*37*
Ballistic missile defense	2.0	*11*
Air defense	4.8	*26*
Total offensive and defensive	**18.6**	*100*

Sources: Estimated from material in Department of Defense, "FY 1973 Budget: Major Weapon Systems" (January 24, 1972; processed) and material in the various authorization and appropriation hearings before the House and Senate on the Department of Defense budget for fiscal year 1972. Indirect costs are allocated among weapon systems in proportion to direct operating costs.

marine could enter the force in 1978, two to three years earlier than had previously been anticipated. At the same time, the Poseidon program to multiply the number of warheads on thirty-one of the forty-one existing missile submarines, for which $751 million is requested, continues on schedule. Secretary of Defense Laird has stated that the first ten ULMS submarines "could be replacements for our 10 oldest Polaris-type submarines"[9] (which are not being refitted with Poseidon missiles). Beyond that, ULMS submarines probably would be additions to the fleet, since the retrofitted Polaris submarines would not normally be phased out of service until the late 1980s at the earliest. In any event, ULMS would mean an increase in capability, since they are currently planned to carry twenty-four missiles each, compared to the sixteen missiles on each of the existing Polaris submarines.

For land-based missiles, continuation of the more than $2-billion-a-year program to modernize the Minuteman missile force and improve its pre-launch survivability and command and control system. The budget projects a slightly reduced investment to replace the single warhead Minuteman missiles with advanced versions that carry three independently targetable warheads (MIRVs). Substantially increased funds are requested for the Safeguard ABM program to protect these missiles, including funds for constructing the third and fourth Safeguard ABM sites and for planning a fifth site. A first-round SALT agreement presumably would mean withdrawal of the request for money to build these additional sites.

For bombers, a moderate increase in funding of the B-1, all for research and development. As now structured, the program envisages a production decision in fiscal 1975, with the possible introduction of the new bomber into the force in fiscal 1979. The total cost of the program would continue to rise throughout most of the decade, with procurement reaching $2 billion a year in the late 1970s.

The present strategic bomber force is to be left unchanged through the late 1970s; no further reductions are scheduled in the number of B-52s, and no funds are requested for additional FB-111s. Roughly $350 million is requested for a new missile and a new armed decoy, which will be used on the B-52s now and on the B-1s later.

For air defense, a sharp increase in spending for the new airborne

9. *U.S. News and World Report*, Vol. 72 (March 27, 1972), p. 44.

warning and control system (AWACS) and continued phasing out of older elements of bomber defense. For example, four squadrons of interceptors are being shifted from active service to the National Guard, and the last five squadrons of Bomarc missiles will be deactivated. While the evidence is still inconclusive, acceleration of the AWACS program and increased expenditures for engineering development of a new surface-to-air missile suggest that the administration intends to begin a major air defense modernization program.

Investments in the major new systems now being procured or for which heavy development expenditures are being made could total approximately $70 billion, of which $16 billion has been funded in previous budgets. These investments, along with estimated operating costs of each system, are shown in Table 3-5. They are overstated to the extent that a SALT agreement would preclude construction of twelve Safeguard sites, which the administration had originally planned, and restrict the program to the two sites already built. Or they could be understated in that they make insufficient allowance for cost escalation, which could be a particularly significant factor in these advanced technology programs.

With respect to broader force posture trends, the fiscal 1973 budget and developments in SALT may point toward less reliance on ICBMs as an independent and equal component of the U.S. strategic posture. There is no indication of funding requests for a follow-on missile to Minuteman III, and the expected freeze on ABMs in a SALT agreement would suggest acceptance of the potential vulnerability of land-based missile systems. Secretary Laird has noted that, in considering alternatives for a new strategic initiative, he decided on the ULMS program not only because of numerical imbalances, but because "the at sea portion of our sea-based strategic forces has the best long term prospect for high pre-launch survivability."[10] He specifically noted the risk that Soviet programs and Soviet technological advance "might offset the qualitative improvements we are planning for our land-based strategic forces." Therefore, large and continuing budget increases for the procurement of a new sea-based missile system and for the development of the follow-on bomber could ultimately lead to reliance on a bomber/submarine nuclear deterrent in place of the triad.

10. *Defense Department Report, FY 1973*, p. 69.

Table 3-5. Estimated Modernization and Direct Operating Costs of Major Strategic Programs

Billions of 1973 dollars

Program	Modernization cost[a]				Ten-year operating cost[b]	Total modernization and ten-year operating cost
	Through 1972	1973	Beyond 1973	Total		
Land-based missiles						
Minuteman (MIRV and other modernization)	3.8	0.9	3.8	8.5	2.0	10.5
Safeguard and site defense of Minuteman (SDM)[c]	5.2	1.6	11.0	17.8	4.0	21.8
Subtotal	9.0	2.5	14.8	26.3	6.0	32.3
Sea-based missiles						
Poseidon	4.8	0.8	0.7	6.3	2.5	8.8
Undersea long-range missile system[d]	0.3	0.9	13.8	15.0	2.3	17.3
Subtotal	5.1	1.7	14.5	21.3	4.8	26.1
Bombers						
B-1[e]	0.7	0.4	10.0	11.1	8.0	19.1
Air-to-surface missiles[f]	1.0	0.4	2.7	4.1	...	4.1
Subtotal	1.7	0.8	12.7	15.2	8.0	23.2
Air defense						
Various programs[g]	0.7	0.7	5.1	6.5	3.2	9.7
Total	16.5	5.7	47.1	69.3	22.0	91.3

Sources: Same as Table 3-4.

a. Includes research and development, procurement, ship construction, and military construction costs. Past investment includes that associated with the system as presently constituted; for example, Sentinel antiballistic missile system costs are not included.

b. Cost for the first ten years following initial operating capability. No allowance is made for indirect costs associable with these systems.

c. Cost for Safeguard program at twelve sites, four of which are augmented by the SDM program.

d. Assumes a force of 20 submarines, 24 missiles each.

e. Assumes 210 aircraft (unit equipment).

f. Short-range attack missiles and subsonic cruise armed decoys.

g. Specifically, 42 airborne warning and control systems, 350 improved manned interceptors, 84 surface-to-air missile firing units, and 3 over-the-horizon radar sites.

Strategic Force Financial Projections

Taken together, the strategic force decisions in the 1973 budget indicate that with no change in current policy, a steady and sizable rise in strategic force spending is likely over the next four or five years. Continuation of present programs at the currently indicated pace would mean an estimated further increase of more than one-fifth in the strategic force budget by 1977, in dollars of constant purchasing power. After that the strategic force budget would begin to decline. Put somewhat differently, the force programs now in prospect would usher in a strategic buildup comparable to, and more costly than, the programs of the early 1960s. Projected strategic force budgets based on these programs are shown on a year-to-year basis for the period 1972–79 in Table 3-6.

These projections make no allowance for program changes that could result from a first-round SALT agreement—a halt in the Safeguard program and possibly reductions in other programs to protect Minuteman missiles. Savings from these program changes, although large, would be only one-third as large as the projected budget increases resulting from the ULMS, B-1, and air defense programs, without allowing for cost escalation. The upward trend of strategic budgets therefore would still be pronounced, even after a first-round SALT agreement.

Nor does it necessarily follow that a second-round SALT agreement would reverse this trend. A comprehensive agreement could do this. But if a second-round SALT agreement were restricted to placing *quantitative* limits on offensive systems, it would not preclude increased expenditures for *qualitative* improvements of these systems and for strategic defense. The likelihood, however, is that a second-round agreement would measurably slow the pace of these programs.

Table 3-6. Projected Costs of Strategic Forces, by Category, Fiscal Years 1972–79

Total obligational authority in billions of 1973 dollars

Category	1972	1973	1974	1975	1976	1977	1978	1979
Major system acquisition[a]	4.2	5.5	6.0	6.6	7.3	7.3	6.7	5.5
Direct operating costs[b]	5.6	5.5	5.5	5.8	6.2	6.2	6.1	6.1
Indirect costs[e]	7.6	7.6	7.3	8.0	8.6	9.0	9.4	9.6
Total[d]	17.4	18.6	18.8	20.4	22.1	22.5	22.2	21.2

Sources: Derived by authors from data in the documents cited in Tables 3-1 through 3-4, above. See text for discussion.

a. Includes research and development, procurement, and military construction costs directly associated with major systems.

b. Includes military personnel and operations and maintenance expenses charged to strategic forces. Also includes estimate of procurement for strategic forces not associated with major systems, and portion of reserve forces appropriations traceable to strategic air defense.

c. Includes residual operations and maintenance, military personnel, research and development, and military construction costs and a proportionate share of defense agency and civil defense costs.

d. Does not include Vietnam war costs.

Baseline General Purpose Forces

The United States maintains general purpose forces to deter conventional and tactical nuclear attacks in a range of contingencies, primarily in Europe and Asia, and, if deterrence should fail, to protect the United States and its interests and commitments overseas. The budget requests for baseline or peacetime general purpose forces in all are estimated to absorb almost two-thirds of defense spending.

Factors Underlying the General Purpose Force Budget

Two general factors exerted a major influence on the fiscal 1973 general purpose force budget. The first concerns the administration's broad policy judgments regarding military strategy, which for convenience may be examined within the framework of the Nixon doctrine. The enunciation of this doctrine in 1970 and 1971 was accompanied by reductions in the baseline general purpose force. Evolution of the Nixon doctrine could further affect the size and composition of forces. The second factor concerns military manpower policies, which have a strong and immediate impact on how much the baseline force will cost.

Evolution of the Nixon Doctrine

This year's defense strategy statements show no marked changes, such as were reflected in the 1972 budget, in the way the administration relates force planning to possible contingencies in the areas where U.S. interests are, or could become, engaged. Nonetheless, the Nixon doctrine continues to hold a useful measure of ambiguity. Its main features may be currently restated as follows:

• In the words of the President's 1972 Foreign Policy Report, "approaching strategic parity with the Soviet Union and the developing Chinese nuclear capability" have, if anything, increased the importance of general purpose forces. Among other reasons, these forces must be strong so that they may be employed "to stabilize a local situation involving great power interests."[11]

11. *U.S. Foreign Policy for the 1970's*, p. 163.

• General purpose forces must be capable of meeting a major threat in Europe or in Asia, but not simultaneously in both. This expression of the shift from a two and one-half war to a one and one-half war strategy, while reaffirmed, is given less emphasis this year than in 1971. Indeed, the need is noted for "counterposing allied forces capable of maintaining a successful defense in either theater until reinforced."[12]

• A possible contingency in Europe continues to take priority in planning and is the factor that largely determines general purpose force requirements. U.S. forces must be kept in Europe and their readiness improved. Allied forces are to be taken into account more explicitly in determining requirements for the size and composition of U.S. forces.

• In Asia the U.S. nuclear shield is to protect our allies "from attack or coercion by a nuclear power."[13] But in addition to providing economic and military assistance, it "will continue to be essential to maintain strong forward American deployments" in Asia.

• Theater nuclear weapons continue to have a role in deterring conventional wars in both Europe and Asia.

• Stress is again placed on improving the readiness of guard and reserve forces.

These current statements of the Nixon doctrine suggest at least a temporary stabilization of the baseline force. In Asia, where force planning changes have been most in evidence, reliance is placed primarily on a combination of nuclear superiority and diplomacy to deter any threat from China, and primarily on U.S. ground, naval, tactical air, and security assistance to deter "subtheater" threats in Korea and elsewhere, with the direct role of U.S. ground forces reduced in importance, although not eliminated from contingency planning. Over the longer term, "allied military capabilities, especially in ground forces, are expected to improve substantially, making possible some further adjustments in U.S. deployments,"[14] and presumably in the force structure.

The distribution of U.S. general purpose forces in accordance with contingencies is estimated in Table 3-7, principally on the basis of the portions of the Nixon doctrine mentioned above. Ground combat

12. *Ibid.*
13. *Ibid.*, p. 165.
14. *Ibid.*

Table 3-7. Possible Distribution of Proposed Fiscal Year 1973 General Purpose Forces, by Geographic Contingency

| Type of force | For European contingencies | | For Asian contingencies | | For worldwide contingencies and strategic reserve | Total |
	Based in Europe	Based in continental U.S.	Based in the Pacific[a]	Based in continental U.S.	Based in continental U.S.[b]	
Active Army divisions	4⅓	⅔	2	...	6[c]	13
Marine division air wings[d]	...	1	1	1	...	3
National Guard and Reserve divisions	...	8	...	...	1	9
Navy carrier task forces[e]	1	4	1	6	4	16
Air Force fighter/ attack squadrons	21	4	16	...	31	72
Air National Guard and Reserve fighter/ attack squadrons	...	39	...	...	...	39

Sources: Based on Department of Defense, "Military Manpower Requirements Report for FY-1973" (February 1972; processed); International Institute for Strategic Studies, *The Military Balance, 1971–1972* (IISS, 1971); *Defense Department Report, FY 1973.*
a. Including Hawaii.
b. Small detachments are located elsewhere, primarily in the Western Hemisphere.
c. Three of the strategic reserve divisions are armored/mechanized units, specifically trained and equipped to fight in Europe. If these are added to the five Army and one Marine division listed for European contingencies, the total matches that cited in *Setting National Priorities: The 1972 Budget*, Table 3-5.
d. A small fraction of the Marine division forces are deployed forward on amphibious ships.
e. Assumes one carrier with home port in Greece and one in Japan or elsewhere in the Western Pacific. Agreements to permit these arrangements have not yet been completed. The total includes two ships previously designated as antisubmarine warfare (ASW) carriers. Because of this change, entries differ from those in Table 3-5 of *Setting National Priorities: The 1972 Budget*. The carriers designated for strategic reserve include the two that are normally in overhaul. There are 15 fighter/attack and 4 ASW air wings associated with these task forces, 4 of which are in reserve.

divisions oriented to European contingencies presumably include the three armored or mechanized divisions shown as available for world-wide employment. Similarly, divisions oriented to Asian contingencies could include, in addition to those now deployed in the Pacific, two infantry divisions that are shown as available for worldwide use but trained and equipped principally for use in the Asian theater. Forces planned for use in one theater can of course be used in the other theater in the event of conflict. But where forces are stationed and how they are equipped and trained, as well as political factors, will necessarily affect the feasibility and speed of such intertheater transfers.

Manpower Policies

Increases in manpower costs have become the most important single determinant of changes in recent defense budgets. The fiscal 1973 budget is no exception; the pay and other personnel actions for which it provides will mean an annual increase of $4.5 billion in costs associated with defense manpower. This continues a trend that began in 1968. Initially made for reasons of equity, and subsequently to underwrite the all-volunteer armed force, a series of legislative decisions have drastically revised military pay. A system in which heavy reliance on conscription resulted in the underpayment of personnel is being replaced by a recruitment system based on market forces. The element of the "free good" in military manpower—in other words, the element of cost hidden by conscription—has already been virtually eliminated.

Manpower costs as a result have changed dramatically. For example, between fiscal 1968 and 1973, when total military and civilian manpower was *reduced* by almost 1.5 million, payroll and other personnel costs *went up* by $10 billion. Since 1968, average military pay has about doubled, and the average pay of civilian employees of the Department of Defense is up by one-half. Military basic pay between fiscal 1968 and fiscal 1973 increased at twice the rate of the previous decade.

Four factors contributed to this result:

• Comparability pay legislation was enacted to bring federal salaries up to levels prevailing in the private sector. This was achieved by "catch-up" pay increases in fiscal 1969 and fiscal 1970 and subsequent annual increases equivalent to those in the private sector.

• The Military Selective Service Act of 1971 provided incentive increases in military pay and allowances to move toward the goal of an all-volunteer armed force. Pay increases under this legislation went predominantly to enlisted men—those just entering the service and others in the lowest grades. Military pay in these categories, which had been disproportionately low, was increased by roughly 60 percent. Pay in other military categories was increased only moderately.

• A higher grade structure now characterizes both military and civilian personnel. The sharp cut in total personnel that occurred after 1968 was a major factor in this change, since the reductions tended to affect persons with the fewest years of service. Conse-

quently, the present military and civilian grade structure is disproportionately heavy in higher-paid personnel; once manpower levels
are stabilized, however, the trend toward a higher grade structure
probably will end and conceivably could be reversed.

• The number of military retirees has increased (reflecting the
surge in military strength during the Second World War and the
Korean war), and retirement pay has increased, reflecting adjustments
for inflation and the higher pay levels of retirees leaving the service in
recent years.

The relative importance of each of the first three of these factors is
estimated as follows (in percent):

Components of pay increase, fiscal 1968–73

Source of increase	In active military pay[15]	In Defense Department civilian pay
Comparability with private sector		
To achieve comparability (catch-up)	8	6
To maintain comparability	54	40
Volunteer service—incentive pay	24	...
Higher grade structure	18	6
Total percentage increase	104	52

While much of this quantum jump in the cost of military manpower
is already accounted for in the 1973 budget, additional increases are
in prospect. Military and civilian pay under existing legislation will
continue to rise in line with wages in the private sector. This will bring
a continued increase in military manpower costs, even if no further
inflation should occur in the economy. Retired pay has grown since
1964 principally because the number of military retirees has more
than doubled; thus the share of the defense budget allotted to their
benefits has gone up from 2.4 percent in fiscal 1964 to 5.9 percent in
fiscal 1973. Since the number of retirees is certain to continue to rise
through the end of this decade, the cost trend in this program is
clearly upward.

Manpower policies therefore are crucial to understanding both
what has happened to the defense budget and what will happen in the

15. Not including allowances, such as those for quarters and subsistence, which remained relatively constant during this period. Because of these exclusions, military and
civilian rates of increase are not strictly comparable.

intermediate-term future. Pay increases have made it necessary to spend more for a smaller defense force, but their implications for the future are even more important. Increases in the cost of manpower call for (1) placing higher priority on achieving efficiency in the use of manpower, (2) recalculating the tradeoff between manpower and weapons systems, and (3) assigning greater weight to manpower costs in the design of both weapon systems and forces.

Decisions in the 1973 Budget

In the administration's view, the transition from wartime to peace-time forces is now virtually complete. The budget requests provide for important qualitative changes in conventional forces—notably in naval construction and in the readiness of guard and reserve forces—but the baseline structure is left unchanged. As Secretary Laird puts it, "fiscal year 1973 can be expected to be a year of leveling off" as disruptions in defense operations stemming from the transition become less pronounced. He specifically notes that "further reductions in both military and civilian personnel will occur," but "the rate of reduction will progressively slow down as we move toward our programmed base line force."[16]

The baseline general purpose force is estimated to cost $54 billion in fiscal 1973, or two-thirds of the total defense budget. The main features of this part of the defense budget are discussed here in terms of ground combat forces, naval general purpose forces (excluding tactical air squadrons), and tactical air forces. Cost data on a fourth category, airlift and sealift forces, will be shown but not discussed separately, since the funds involved are relatively small and significant change is not in prospect.

Ground Combat Forces

This primary element of our flexible response strategy accounts for 40 percent of the total cost of general purpose forces. Baseline ground forces consist of thirteen active Army divisions, three active Marine divisions, a range of combat support and general support forces, and reserve components making up nine divisions. Roughly half the total active manpower is in division forces, including combat support units. (At planned strength, a division force consists of almost 50,000

16. *Defense Department Report, FY 1973*, p. 156.

men, but in fiscal 1973 each Army division force will average only 30,000.) The balance of active ground force manpower is engaged in special missions (such as the Berlin Brigade), communications and intelligence, training, logistics, base operations, and headquarters and administration.

In the main, the 1973 budget requests for ground forces suggest no change in force planning contingencies, a modest increase in procurement, and continuing investments to improve the readiness of reserve forces.

Baseline manpower strength seems to be close to what the administration currently believes to be the peacetime minimum. Total active ground force manpower will be reduced by only 20,000 during fiscal 1973, suggesting that the bulk of the ground forces remaining in Vietnam on July 1, 1972, are considered to be part of the baseline force.

The change in expenditures on major ground force weapons systems is small. By 1975, however, as the new surface-to-air missile (SAM-D) moves into full-scale procurement, this part of the budget could increase by $1 billion. There is no evidence of significant change in the procurement of standard items, which is estimated to amount to about $2 billion a year. A question here is whether the high level of procurement for the Vietnam war will reduce normal replacement needs over the next few years. Ground combat forces presumably have come out of the war with relatively new equipment, but some of it is designed for Asian, rather than European, contingencies.

The administration projects a decline in the ratio of general support to combat forces as manpower is reduced, but the details of the program are not available. Rough data discussed in Chapter 4 suggest that this ratio will decline in fiscal 1973 but will still be high in comparison to 1968, the peak wartime year, or to pre-Vietnam standards.

A summary of the longer-term financial implications of the ground combat force budget is shown in Table 3-8. Baseline costs, in dollars of constant purchasing power, are projected to increase moderately during most of the period 1973–79, with savings from further small reductions in manpower being more than offset by increased costs for procurement of the SAM-D missile and increased investments in guard and reserve forces.

Navy General Purpose Forces

These forces include aircraft carriers, escort ships, attack submarines, amphibious assault vessels, a variety of support ships, land-

Table 3-8. Projected Costs of Ground Combat Forces, by Category, Fiscal Years 1972–79
Total obligational authority in billions of 1973 dollars

Category	1972	1973	1974	1975	1976	1977	1978	1979
Major system acquisition[a]	0.1	0.2	0.4	1.4	1.3	1.3	0.9	0.1
Direct operating costs[b]	9.1	9.8	9.7	9.7	9.7	9.7	9.7	9.7
Indirect costs[c]	10.8	11.8	11.6	11.6	11.7	11.8	11.8	11.8
Total[d]	20.0	21.8	21.7	22.7	22.7	22.8	22.4	21.6

Sources: Same as Table 3-6.

a. Includes research and development, procurement, and military construction costs associated with acquisition of surface-to-air missile (SAM-D) firing units earmarked for the general purpose force. This is the only ground combat procurement program of major proportions.

b. Includes military personnel and operations and maintenance costs charged to active forces. Also includes estimate of share of Army and Marine Corps procurement, and reserve forces accounts.

c. Includes residual operations and maintenance, military personnel, research and development, and military construction costs and a proportionate share of defense agency costs.

d. Does not include Vietnam war costs.

based antisubmarine warfare (ASW) and reconnaissance aircraft, and extensive shore facilities.

Naval general purpose forces are designed for two principal missions: to launch air strikes and carry out amphibious operations, and to keep open sea lanes in time of war by protecting ships against enemy attack. Over the past few years, principally in response to developments in the Soviet Navy and its widening presence outside Soviet waters, U.S. force planning has reflected greater emphasis on the second mission. This new stress on "sea control" in turn has caused increases in recent naval general purpose force budgets and changes in their composition.

The 1973 budget request for naval general purpose forces (excluding the cost of naval tactical aircraft) is estimated to be approximately $16 billion, a significant expansion for the second successive year. The budget again emphasizes naval modernization; funds requested for shipbuilding and conversion are twice the annual average for the years 1966–70.

Much of this spending increase is for ASW systems, reflecting the planning concept that, in a war, Soviet submarines would be the major threat to U.S. and allied shipping, particularly to sea lanes between the United States and Europe. Programs to expand ASW capabilities include new attack submarines, a new class of destroyer, new land- and sea-based ASW aircraft, the patrol frigate, the Mark 48 torpedo, and an entirely new sea control ship (SCS).

At the same time, the budget provides funds to buy long lead-time items for the fourth nuclear powered carrier (one is in operation, and two are now under construction) and to operate the sixteen carriers now in service. The latter include fourteen platforms previously designated "attack" carriers and two platforms previously designated "ASW" carriers. This reflects a recent decision to use carriers for multiple missions, varying the mixture of aircraft according to the requirements of the situation. This change will enable the Navy to maintain sea-based ASW aircraft without proportionately sacrificing attack carrier capability.

Even so, the number of carriers is likely to decrease to twelve by 1980 or soon thereafter. This would be the maximum number that could then be in service, since the seven carriers from the Second World War that are now in service will have been retired and only three new carriers, including the one for which funds are requested in fiscal 1973, will have been added. Furthermore, to maintain a force of twelve carriers through the 1980s and beyond, it would be necessary to begin construction of a new carrier every other year through the end of this decade—about the maximum rate sustainable by existing shipyards.

At some point in the mid-1970s the number of new ships entering active service will exceed the number being retired, thus ending the decline in the number of ships in the active fleet that has been taking place since 1968. Although the number of carriers is likely to continue to decline for the rest of the decade, the number of escort ships and attack submarines will begin to increase by about 1977. The main issues are whether this acceleration of the ASW program is required to meet the Soviet naval threat and whether it is an effective response in light of a realistic assessment of the survivability of the carriers.

To consider only the number of ships would be misleading. Newer vessels have tended to be larger than their predecessors, reflecting efforts to put multiple capabilities on single platforms. For example, the new Knox class destroyer escort (DE-1052) and the Spruance class destroyer (DD-963) are more than twice as large as their Second World War equivalents. Aside from questions of design efficiency, this illustrates a fundamental tradeoff in structuring naval forces: combining several capabilities in one vessel achieves economies, but it also increases the loss of combat capability when a ship is sunk, and reduces flexibility.

The Navy's awareness of these dangers is illustrated by its initiation of several programs to build relatively small, low-cost ships for operations against Soviet surface vessels and against Soviet submarine forces. Examples are the patrol frigate (a new, small ASW escort ship), the sea control ship (which will carry ASW helicopters and vertical takeoff fighter/attack aircraft), and the small hydrofoil patrol craft carrying surface-to-surface missiles. Most of these programs are still in the development stage; in budgetary terms the cost of the program as a whole is not likely to reach major proportions for several years.

Thus far the Navy has not had to make hard choices in shifting its priorities as to missions; it has been able to increase its emphasis on sea control and to initiate its other new programs without great sacrifice to its strike forces—specifically the carrier task forces. It has been able to do so and still avoid dramatic increases in its budget in part because the recent investment in new ASW programs was offset by savings in operating costs as ships from the Second World War were retired. Choices in the future may be more difficult since new ships will increasingly replace old ships on a one-for-one basis, thus eliminating savings in operating costs.

Nevertheless, the current force posture does not indicate significant increases through the 1970s in the Navy's general purpose force budget, principally because current financing levels already are high enough to underwrite the Navy's force structure initiatives. As is summarized in Table 3-9, this budget is projected to remain fairly steady in dollars of constant purchasing power. In making this projection it is

Table 3-9. Projected Costs of Navy General Purpose Forces, by Category, Fiscal Years 1972–79

Total obligational authority in billions of 1973 dollars

Category	1972	1973	1974	1975	1976	1977	1978	1979
Major system acquisition[a]	3.5	3.9	4.4	4.2	4.8	4.2	4.2	4.0
Direct operating costs[b]	6.1	5.9	6.1	5.9	5.8	5.9	6.0	6.1
Indirect costs[c]	5.7	6.0	6.0	5.9	5.8	6.1	6.1	6.2
Total[d]	15.3	15.8	16.5	16.0	16.4	16.2	16.3	16.3

Sources: Same as Table 3-6.

a. Includes research and development, procurement, and military construction costs directly associated with the acquisition of major systems.

b. Includes military personnel and operations and maintenance costs, procurement other than for major systems, and a share of reserve accounts.

c. Includes residual operations and maintenance, military personnel, research and development, and military construction costs and a proportionate share of defense agency costs.

d. Does not include Vietnam war costs. Also excludes naval tactical air costs, which are reflected in Table 3-11.

assumed that new carriers will be started every other year beginning in fiscal 1973, but no allowance is made for cost escalation, which has seriously troubled naval ship construction in recent years.

Tactical Air Forces

These forces are designed to serve a variety of combat, transport, and intelligence missions ranging from defense of both land and naval forces, to operations in close support of ground forces, to attacks on lines of communications and other targets far behind enemy lines. The annual cost of supporting the current baseline level of tactical air forces is estimated to be nearly $14 billion,[17] or one-fourth of the total baseline general purpose force budget. Much of the attention given to this part of the budget has focused on the rapidly rising cost of acquiring new weapon systems, and understandably so, if only because these costs more than others are subject to year-to-year discretionary decisions. Since the end of the Second World War a new generation of aircraft has come into service approximately every ten years, each costing six to eight times as much per airplane as the generation it has superseded. Nevertheless, it is important to recognize that almost two-thirds of the cost of tactical air forces consists of operating expenditures—for personnel, maintenance of equipment and facilities, and consumables. In turn, this part of the budget is also sensitive to the complexity of the new weapons that are introduced.

Budget requests for fiscal 1973, although $200 million higher than in the fiscal 1972 budget, are relatively restrained in view of the fact that six major new weapon systems are in various advanced stages of development or procurement. The budget will leave operating force levels virtually unchanged.[18] It features a slight decline from fiscal 1972 in procurement funds, which will probably result in a small reduction in the total aircraft inventory a year or two hence, as older systems wear out at a somewhat faster rate than replacements enter the ser-

17. Excluding the cost of aircraft carriers, from which the Navy's tactical air forces operate.

18. Strength tables show an increase over fiscal 1972 from twenty-one to twenty-two Air Force airwings and from thirteen to fourteen carrier airwings. This seems to be a temporary increase resulting from delays by both the Air Force and the Navy in carrying out previously announced plans to phase out older aircraft from the active service and transfer them to reserve units. Thus the Air Force and the Navy will each operate several more squadrons in fiscal 1973—a total increase of sixty aircraft—but present aircraft procurement programs would not permit maintaining these increased force levels in the future.

vice. Projected costs of the major new systems for which funds are requested in the 1973 budget are given in Table 3-10.

As these data show, the present budget is not yet half way through a procurement phase that is dominated by two very expensive aircraft—the Navy F-14 and the Air Force F-15. Controversy surrounds each, but both programs are currently scheduled to be completed within the next five years. Attention will then begin to focus on their eventual replacements, that is, on the design of the next generation of tactical aircraft. Thus a third major budgetary issue becomes significant: To what extent will a cost-motivated change in thinking result in a move away from big, expensive, multipurpose combat aircraft and toward specialized, single-mission types? Such a move is now reflected in development funds for the A-X close support fighter and in funds for early research on a lightweight fighter.

Table 3-10. Investment in Major Tactical Air Programs, by Primary Mission and Type of Craft
Total obligational authority in billions of 1973 dollars

	Investment			
Primary mission and type of aircraft	*1968–72*	*1973*	*Beyond 1973*	*Total*
Multipurpose				
F-14 aircraft (Navy), with emphasis on fleet defense[a]	2.7	0.7	1.8	5.2[a]
F-15 aircraft (Air Force), with emphasis on air superiority	1.0	0.9	5.4	7.3
Air superiority and air defense				
Phoenix missile (Navy)	0.5	0.1	0.7	1.3
Sparrow III-F missile (Navy)	0.1	0.1	0.9	1.1
Close air support				
A-X aircraft[b] (Air Force)	0.1	0.1	1.4	1.6
Cheyenne helicopter[b] (Army)	0.5	0.1	1.9	2.5
Total	4.9	2.0	12.1	19.0

Sources: *Department of Defense Appropriations for Fiscal Year 1972*, Hearings before a Subcommittee of the Senate Committee on Appropriations, 92 Cong. 1 sess. (1971), Pt. 3, pp. 1132, 1249, 1259, and Pt. 4, pp. 26, 730–32; *Fiscal Year 1972 Authorization for Military Procurement, Research and Development, Construction . . .* , Senate Hearings, Pt. 5, p. 3799; Department of Defense, News Release, January 24, 1972; "Close Air Support Report by Members of Congress for Peace Through Law," *Congressional Record*, daily ed., September 16, 1971, pp. S14392–402; *Armed Forces Journal*, Vol. 109 (October 1971), pp. 22, 24.
a. Provides for a total of 301 aircraft, "A" models. Grumman, prime contractor for the F-14, recently requested an additional $545 million to complete the 301 aircraft program. If approved, this request would raise total program acquisition costs to $5.7 billion.
b. No procurement funds have yet been authorized.

In the case of the F-14, the budget request reflects the Navy's earlier announcement that it was cutting the total program from 710 to 301 aircraft. In line with this reduction, the request to purchase only 48 planes in fiscal 1973 represents a slowdown in the rate at which the F-14 is brought into service. Furthermore, the F-14 was plagued by cost increases early in its development, and its problems could get worse; the 1973 budget request makes no allowance for the substantial price increase that the contractor insists is essential to continued production. On the other hand, if the design of the system, which includes the Phoenix missile as well as the aircraft itself, should eventually prove successful, the decision could be made to revert to the original program or to an even larger number—1,100 or more—if all F-4s on the carriers are replaced by F-14s on a one-for-one basis and if the Marine Corps also acquires F-14s. The procurement cost of this program over the next six years could then increase by at least $8 billion.

With the present cutback in F-14s, the largest single element in tactical air procurement is the F-15, the new Air Force plane designed primarily to achieve air superiority against the most advanced Soviet-designed fighters deep over their own territory. Procurement begins in fiscal 1973, when the first 30 will be purchased out of a total program of about 730 aircraft. Six air wings are to be in operation by 1980. Originally the cost of developing the F-15 engine was to be shared with the Navy, which intended to use a more powerful version in an advanced model of its F-14. Now that the F-14 program has been slowed, a greater share of the engine development cost will fall on the F-15. Partly for this reason, the F-15 is likely to show an increase in unit cost of at least 10 percent, or $1 million, within the next year.

Three other budget requests merit attention, even though they do not as yet involve large expenditures:

• Continued development funds ($48 million) for the A-X close support plane. The Air Force is believed to be planning to buy approximately 700 of these aircraft, which will probably cost $2.1 million each (including about $0.3 million for R&D). To the extent that these planes replace F-4s, they will generate considerable savings in operating costs. The Army and Marine Corps each has its own candidate for a close support system. The Army's is the technically troubled Cheyenne helicopter, which would cost more than twice as much as the A-X, mainly because of its more complex fire control system. The Marines are already buying 114 British-built Harriers at a unit cost of $4.5 million. The Harrier offers a vertical takeoff and landing capability in exchange for severe range and payload constraints.

• Development funds ($40 million) for a short-range air superiority plane, the lightweight fighter (LWF). Because of limitations on its range and payload, the LWF design lacks adaptability for use deep over enemy territory (a feature of the F-15), but it should be at least as maneuverable as the F-15 in air-to-air combat over friendly or contested territory. Since the unit cost of the LWF may be perhaps one-fourth that of the F-15, successful development of this fighter could raise the question whether it should substitute for some part of the F-15 program.

• Seed money ($10 million) for a new transport, the advanced medium short-takeoff-and-landing transport (AMST). It is described as a "tactical" aircraft, which suggests a capability to operate from marginal airfields near the battle area, but it will be large enough to fly long-range airlift missions as well. Thus it could become a multipurpose transport plane, involving an estimated acquisition cost on the order of $2.5 billion. In the strictly tactical role, the all-jet AMST might prove less capable than the turboprop C-130 it is intended to replace.

These budgetary decisions, in sum, imply moderately higher spending for tactical air forces through 1974 and a gradually declining budget thereafter as the F-14 and F-15 programs are completed. The financial projections for fiscal years 1972–79, as summarized in Table 3-11, encompass all programs now in development or procurement but do not allow for new initiatives beyond those relating to current programs, such as reconnaissance versions of the F-14 and F-15. A tapering off of spending is projected beyond fiscal 1974, though this could prove largely illusory for any combination of the following reasons: (1) a possible expansion of the F-14 program; (2) beginning about 1976 to 1978, the spending of sizable research and development funds for the next generation of multipurpose combat aircraft; and (3) a steep increase in cost, which has been endemic to these systems. An assumption favoring lower costs in the second half of the decade is that five A-X airwings will replace an equivalent number of F-4s, thus offsetting in part the increased costs of operating the F-14s and F-15s.

Table 3-11. Projected Costs of Tactical Air Forces, by Category, Fiscal Years 1972–79
Total obligational authority in billions of 1973 dollars

Category	1972	1973	1974	1975	1976	1977	1978	1979
Major system acquisition[a]	3.8	3.5	4.2	3.7	3.1	2.5	2.2	1.7
Direct operating costs[b]	6.1	6.5	7.1	7.0	6.8	6.7	6.8	6.9
Indirect costs[c]	3.8	3.9	4.3	4.4	4.5	4.5	4.6	4.6
Total[d]	13.7	13.9	15.6	15.1	14.4	13.7	13.6	13.2

Sources: Same as Table 3-6.
a. Includes research and development, procurement, and military construction costs directly associated with the acquisition of major systems.
b. Includes military personnel and operations and maintenance costs, procurement other than for major systems, and a share of reserve accounts.
c. Includes residual operations and maintenance, military personnel, research and development, and military construction costs, and a proportionate share of defense agency costs.
d. Does not include Vietnam war costs.

Instead, the A-X wings may be added to the F-4 force level; should this occur, both procurement and operating costs would be substantially higher toward the end of the 1970s than the projection indicates.

Reserve Forces

Each of the above force categories has reserve components. Improving the readiness of guard and reserve forces continues to be a major administration initiative. Budget requests for this program, more than half of which is for ground forces, will increase by one-sixth, or $600 million, in fiscal 1973. Two-thirds of the increase will be in expenditures for pay and training. In addition, the administration has proposed specific pay incentives beyond those provided in the budget to encourage enlistments in guard and reserve forces. Equipment in the hands of reserve units is also rapidly being modernized. For Army reserve components alone, more than $1 billion in equipment is scheduled to be issued in fiscal 1973, some of which will be transferred from the active forces. In addition, a sizable number of aircraft and naval vessels will be transferred to the reserves. The goal is to have all reserve components substantially equipped for early deployment by fiscal 1976. A key issue thus arises: Is this program for improved readiness of reserve components to be designed solely to supplement existing active forces, or eventually to substitute in some measure for active support or combat forces? There are no indications of the administration's intentions in this regard.

Vietnam War Costs

The cost of the Vietnam war is no longer a major factor in the defense budget. It has already fallen from a peak of $19.8 billion in fiscal 1969 (equivalent to approximately $25 billion in 1973 dollars) to $6.5 billion in fiscal 1972. These figures are official Defense Department estimates (in total obligational authority) of incremental costs; that is, of costs of the war over and above what would have been spent in peacetime.

We estimate the corresponding figure for fiscal 1973 to be $3.5 billion, of which $2.4 billion is for military assistance to Southeast Asia and $1.1 billion is the incremental cost of U.S. forces. This estimate arbitrarily assumes a residual U.S. force of 30,000 in Vietnam until the end of the year and a gradually declining level of air operations. Should U.S. participation end entirely during fiscal 1973, incremental costs could be reduced by perhaps an additional $500 million as the force of 50,000 that was there at the beginning of the year is phased out. The difference in the cost of these two assumed situations is small, principally because most costs of the war now consist of military assistance to South Vietnam, Cambodia, and Thailand. A review of how war costs declined between fiscal 1968 and 1972 in relation to troop levels, and estimated costs for 1973 are given in Table 3-12.

Vietnam war costs have three main components:

Cost of residual forces. It is assumed that a residual force of 30,000 in Vietnam would be part of the baseline force; that is, it would not be deactivated if it were withdrawn. Hence, incremental costs for these forces consist of combat pay, change-of-station costs, higher consumption of matériel, and similar factors, as well as logistical and administrative support for these forces located in the United States. We estimate these incremental costs to be $300 million.

Cost of air operations. Incremental costs in this category would consist of higher rates of ordnance consumption and weapon attrition, combat pay for forces in the area, including those in Thailand and on carriers stationed off Vietnam, and increased expenditures on personnel transfers and the support base in the United States. We estimate these costs to total $800 million, or about one-third their level in fiscal 1972.

**Table 3-12. Troop Levels and Incremental Costs of the Vietnam War,
Fiscal Years 1968–74**

Fiscal year	Number of troops[a]	Incremental cost, total obligational authority in billions of dollars
1968	534,700	19.4
1969	538,700	19.8
1970	414,900	14.4
1971	239,200	9.6
1972	50,000	6.5
1973	30,000[b]	3.5
1973	0[b]	3.0
1974	0[c]	1.0[c]

Sources: Troop levels, 1968–71: Department of Defense, Public Affairs for Vietnam office; 1972, President Nixon's troop withdrawal announcement of April 26, 1972. Costs: 1968–70, *Department of Defense Appropriations for 1972,* Hearings, p. 1163; 1971–72, Department of Defense, "FY 1973 Budget Briefing," p. 10; other data, authors' estimates.
a. Troop levels as of June 30.
b. Alternative assumptions.
c. Assumptions: no U.S. participation; residual assistance, military and/or economic, of $1 billion a year.

Military assistance. The defense budget includes $2.1 billion for service-funded military assistance to South Vietnam, Korea, and Laos. Military assistance for Cambodia and Thailand, which is appropriated under the military assistance program, is estimated at $300 million. Thus, total military aid comes to $2.4 billion. This figure does not include economic supporting assistance to South Vietnam, Cambodia, and Laos, which might be approximately $700 million in fiscal 1973, but which is appropriated as economic aid and not usually included in defense expenditures.

It is evident from these figures that additional savings from the war beyond fiscal 1973 depend largely on the level and duration of military assistance programs, where most of the remaining war costs are now concentrated. These data also indicate the margin that still exists for underwriting a shift from military to development assistance if the war ends. President Nixon's offer in the once-secret phase of the Paris negotiations to provide $7.5 billion in development assistance over a five-year period to all countries in Indochina presumably assumed such a shift.

With costs at this relatively low level and with data now available from the Department of Defense, it is worth reexamining two additional questions: (1) what happened to savings from Vietnam with-

Table 3-13. Vietnam and Non-Vietnam Defense Costs, and Changes,
Fiscal Years 1968–73
Total obligational authority in billions of 1973 dollars

Description	1968	1969	1970	1971	1972	1973	Net change, 1968–73
Amount							
Vietnam	24.1	24.2	16.7	11.0	6.8	3.5	−20.6
Non-Vietnam	74.9	75.5	73.5	72.9	75.2	79.7	+4.8
Total	99.0	99.7	90.2	83.9	82.0	83.2	−15.8
Change from previous year							
Vietnam	. . .	+0.1	−7.5	−5.7	−4.2	−3.3	−20.6
Non-Vietnam	. . .	+0.6	−2.0	−0.6	+2.3	+4.5	+4.8
Total	. . .	+0.7	−9.5	−6.3	−1.9	+1.2	−15.8

Sources: Current dollar Vietnam expenditures and total costs, 1968–70, *Department of Defense Appropriations for 1972*, Hearings, p. 1163; Vietnam expenditures, 1971–72, Department of Defense, "FY 1973 Budget Briefing," p. 10; Vietnam expenditures, 1973, authors' estimate; total costs, 1971–73, *Defense Department Report, FY 1973*, p. 189. Estimates of constant dollar costs of prior year authorizations differ from those used by the Department of Defense in two major respects: (a) the cost of the all-volunteer armed force is treated as a discretionary cost decision and not as an element of general inflation; (b) retired pay is calculated by multiplying the number of retirees in each stated year by the average cost of retiree benefits in fiscal year 1973, rather than by "straightlining" fiscal year 1973 costs for all previous years.

drawals, and (2) has deferred modernization of the baseline force been one of the costs of the war?

First, where did the peace dividend go? After adjusting for the effect of price and pay increases,[19] most of the dividend was available for other government programs or for private consumption through tax cuts. As is indicated in Table 3-13, of the estimated savings of almost $21 billion since 1968, less than $5 billion went to meet the increased costs of non-Vietnam forces, and nearly $16 billion was available for other programs. Two quite different periods can be distinguished: 1969–71, when the declining costs of non-Vietnam forces made it possible to pass on Vietnam savings, and more, to the nondefense sector; and 1972–73, when increased costs for non-Vietnam forces, including the cost of the all-volunteer armed force, absorbed most of the savings from Vietnam.

Second, have requirements for financing the war caused funds to be diverted from replacing obsolete equipment or undertaking essential modernization for baseline general purpose forces? Modernization

19. But excluding the effect of pay increases to underwrite the all-volunteer armed force, which is treated as a discretionary cost increase rather than one attributable to general inflation.

requirements pose an array of questions, some of which are examined in Chapter 4 as they apply to each of the major force categories. So far as the effect of the Vietnam war on this issue is concerned, the budgetary data show a mixed picture. Using 1964 as a base, military procurement for the period 1964–73, in billions of fiscal 1973 dollars, can be broken down as follows (in total obligational authority):

Procurement use	1964	1965–72 average	1973
Total procurement	20.3	23.9	19.3
Less procurement for:			
Strategic forces	5.3	3.2	4.1
Vietnam	...	6.1	1.6
Presumed procurement for baseline general purpose forces	15.0	14.6	13.6

These data suggest that procurement authority for baseline general purpose forces during most of the Vietnam war period averaged about 3 percent less a year than it was in 1964. War requirements imposed even greater constraints than these figures suggest on selected military production facilities, notably naval shipbuilding. On the other hand, the end of U.S. participation in the war will leave more modern equipment in the U.S. inventory than there was in 1964, and this has been charged to Vietnam war costs rather than to baseline procurement. Moreover, 1964 is not necessarily a representative base year, since it was part of a period in which a buildup occurred in both general purpose and strategic forces. The trend in strategic force procurement, it should be noted, was influenced by unique factors independent of Vietnam; procurement declined after the introduction of new systems in the early 1960s and is beginning to increase again as a consequence of the current phase of strategic force modernization.

It is also worth noting that while total military research and development authorizations declined during the war, the two key categories applicable to bringing new weapon systems into the force showed a contrary trend. Funding for new system development (engineering development and operational development) has remained, in real terms, above the fiscal 1964 level throughout the war years.

There is no reason to assume that these aggregate indications are a reliable guide for assessing modernization requirements, one way or the other. They suggest, however, that issues regarding modernization should be examined in terms of specific force needs and judged independently of Vietnam war costs.

Financial Implications of the 1973 Defense Posture

This section summarizes and restates the future cost consequences of defense policy decisions reflected in the 1973 budget. Assuming no change in the decisions on force structure, weapon system acquisitions, and manpower policies, it uses the preceding analyses to project the defense budget in the fiscal years 1973–79.

Two formulations are shown. The first, in Table 3-14, summarizes the data presented separately for the major force categories. Bringing them together distinguishes those parts of the force structure primarily responsible for projected changes in expenditures. The second formulation, shown in Table 3-15, outlines projected defense budgets in the appropriations categories acted on by the Congress.

A note of warning is necessary. These projections should not be viewed as predictions of future defense budgets. They lack such precision, not only because of the limitations inherent in the estimating procedures, but because actual budgets will depend on defense policy decisions, which change from year to year. They seek rather to mea-

Table 3-14. Projected Department of Defense Budget, by Mission Category, Fiscal Years 1973-79

Total obligational authority in billions of 1973 dollars

Mission category[a]	1973	1974	1975	1976	1977	1978	1979
Strategic forces	18.6	18.8	20.4	22.1	22.5	22.2	21.2
Tactical air forces	13.9	15.6	15.1	14.4	13.7	13.6	13.2
Navy general purpose forces	15.8	16.5	16.0	16.4	16.2	16.3	16.3
Ground combat forces	21.8	21.7	22.7	22.7	22.8	22.4	21.6
Airlift and sealift forces	2.6	2.3	2.3	2.3	2.3	2.3	2.3
Military assistance program and family housing	2.1	2.0	2.0	2.0	2.0	2.0	2.0
Baseline subtotal[b]	74.8	76.8	78.5	79.9	79.5	78.7	76.6
Vietnam	3.5	1.0	1.0	1.0	1.0	1.0	1.0
Subtotal	78.3	77.8	79.5	80.9	80.5	79.7	77.6
Retired pay	4.9	5.3	5.6	5.8	6.1	6.3	6.6
Total	83.2	83.1	85.1	86.7	86.6	86.0	84.2

Sources: Forces are from Tables 3-6, 3-8, 3-9, and 3-11, above. Military assistance, retired pay, and total for 1973 are from *Defense Department Report, FY 1973*, p. 189. Other data are derived by authors.
a. Indirect costs are allocated to mission categories in proportion to direct operating costs.
b. Components may not add to totals because of rounding.

Table 3-15. Projected Department of Defense Budget, by Appropriations Category, Fiscal Years 1973-79
Total obligational authority in billions of 1973 dollars

Appropriations category	1973	1974	1975	1976	1977	1978	1979
Military personnel	24.7	23.4	23.5	23.5	23.5	23.7	24.0
Operations and maintenance	21.2	21.2	21.3	21.3	21.3	21.6	21.8
Procurement	19.3	19.8	21.1	22.4	21.9	20.8	18.4
Research and development	8.5	8.5	8.5	8.5	8.5	8.5	8.5
Military construction	2.1	2.0	2.2	2.3	2.3	2.2	1.9
Military assistance program	1.3	1.9	1.9	1.9	1.9	1.9	1.9
Other[a]	1.1	1.1	1.1	1.1	1.1	1.1	1.1
Subtotal[b]	78.3	77.8	79.5	80.9	80.5	79.7	77.6
Retired pay	4.9	5.3	5.6	5.8	6.1	6.3	6.6
Total	**83.2**	**83.1**	**85.1**	**86.7**	**86.6**	**86.0**	**84.2**
Vietnam costs included in above categories	3.5	1.0	1.0	1.0	1.0	1.0	1.0

Sources: Authors' estimates, except data for 1973, other than Vietnam costs, which are taken from *Defense Department Report, FY 1973*, p. 189.
a. Includes family housing, civil defense, and special foreign currency.
b. Components may not add to totals because of rounding.

sure the future budgetary implications of current defense policies. Even so, they may be incomplete in that they take into account some, but not all, of the elements of change inherent in the defense posture.

The nature of these projections, detailed by force categories in the preceding sections, can be made more explicit by specifying the dynamic and static elements they contain. The former include the future cost consequences of fiscal 1973 decisions on the acquisition of major weapon systems, projected system by system; essentially minor force changes resulting from the retirement of obsolescent weapon systems; the end of U.S. participation in the Vietnam war; and predictable increases in the number of military retirees. However, the projections assume the following as constant: the number of major combat units; readiness (as reflected in training, maintenance, and deployments); procurement costs other than those related to major systems; efficiency levels; research and development expenditures; and manpower policies. As for major weapon systems, it is assumed that none will be canceled or added and that their costs will not grow as a result of cost overruns or inflation in the economy. Very small changes are projected in manpower; by implication, military personnel are projected to fall by 30,000 in fiscal 1974 and then to increase by around 5,000 a year through the end of the decade. The reduction in fiscal

1974 is traceable to the end of U.S. combat participation in Vietnam, while the subsequent rise would be required by the introduction of advanced weapon systems. Civilian personnel follow roughly the same trend.

With these caveats in mind, the major long-term financial implications of the 1973 defense budget, expressed in fiscal 1973 dollars, can be summarized briefly:

• The cost trend is clearly upward. By fiscal 1977 the current defense posture will cost $86.6 billion in funds authorized, an increase of $3.4 billion. Since it is assumed that $2.5 billion will be saved from the end of the Vietnam war, the total increase in funds for the baseline force will be almost $6 billion.

• Strategic forces will account for more than two-thirds of this increase, much of which represents higher rates of procurement. The costs of other major force components will change more moderately, both upward and downward.

• Retired pay will increase by $1.2 billion by fiscal 1977, absorbing fully 7 percent of the defense budget, and the trend will be upward.

• Defense will account for 6.0 percent of projected GNP, a slightly lower proportion than in 1973. Under the assumptions listed above, it could not be counted on to yield significantly to domestic needs in competing for shares in the increase of national output.

An examination of the elements of change not explicitly taken into account—those suggesting overstatement and understatement—indicates that this projected cost increase is likely to be on the low side.

The major factor suggesting overstatement is the absence of an allowance for the cost consequences of a SALT agreement. At a minimum, a first-round agreement would make it possible to curtail the Safeguard program at two sites and save on the order of $1 billion a year over the rest of the decade. A second-round agreement could, but would not necessarily, make possible substantial additional savings.

The major factors suggesting that the projected increase in defense spending is understated are new initiatives on weapon systems, cost escalation, and increased manpower costs.

In regard to new weapon systems, the pronounced "bow wave" effect evident in the forecast of major system acquisition costs is typical of long-term projections. New initiatives will probably be launched over the next five years that will increase research and development expenditures and, to a lesser degree, procurement. Examples include the beginning of research and development on tactical aircraft systems for the 1980s, of which remotely piloted vehicles are an example; research on surface effect ships (naval vessels riding on a cushion of air); and work on various aspects of an "automated battlefield," such as the use of automatic sensors and remotely controlled firepower. Work on such systems could cost an additional $1 billion a year by 1977.

Quantitatively, cost escalation is a far more important consideration. Costs typically increase because of technical uncertainties, errors associated with estimating procedures, and service-directed changes in performance or delivery requirements. The greater the degree of technological advance incorporated in a new system, the greater the possibility of cost escalation. In 1971 a General Accounting Office (GAO) survey[20] of fifty-two major weapon systems then being developed or procured showed that their projected cost had risen an average of 30 percent at the time of the survey over the cost estimates made when the preliminary design and engineering studies were completed. Presumably, additional cost growth will occur before these acquisition programs are completed. Comparable findings were made in a recent RAND study[21] of a number of aircraft, missile, and sensor systems developed in the 1960s. This survey differed from the GAO study in that it covered only weapon programs in which development had been completed. It showed an average growth in unit cost of 40 percent (excluding the effects of inflation) between the time the decision to develop each system was made and the time it went into operation. Since the major acquisition programs for the 1970s include several systems that incorporate major technological advances and are now in early stages of development, a similar cost growth could well be experienced. If so, cost growth associated with projected acquisitions in the fiscal 1973–79 period will be on the order of $25 billion to $35 billion. These added costs would show up in the budget between fiscal years 1974 and 1983, peaking at $3 billion to $5 billion a year during the fiscal 1977–79 period. Programs could, of course, be stretched out or reduced as a means of partially offsetting these increases.

Possible increases in manpower costs could be equally, if not more, significant. Existing legislation provides for government pay increases over the future comparable to those in the private sector. Even in the

20. Comptroller General of the United States, *Acquisition of Major Weapon Systems, Department of Defense*, Report to the Congress (March 18, 1971).
21. Robert Perry and others, *System Acquisition Strategies*, R-733-PR/ARPA (Santa Monica: RAND, June 1971).

absence of inflation, wages and salaries in the private economy will rise by roughly the amount of the annual gain in productivity—about 3 percent a year. As a consequence, the defense budget will have to provide for increases in military and civilian pay of that amount. By fiscal 1977 this will require an increase of $4 billion in the Department of Defense payroll. Moreover, it is still an open question whether current military pay scales will suffice to underwrite an all-volunteer armed force of approximately 2.3 million military personnel. If the answer turns out to be no, and the force level is not changed, another incentive pay raise will be required, but evidence is not yet available to indicate whether this will be necessary and, if so, how large an increase will be needed.

If these additional factors are taken into account, the current defense posture could mean a defense budget of as much as $95 billion in fiscal 1977, rather than the $87 billion shown in the projections. It is emphasized that these estimates are in constant or 1973 dollars. Put differently, assuming no offsetting force reductions, the combination of a rapid pace of modernization and high manpower costs could mean a real increase of 6 to 15 percent in the defense budget by fiscal 1977. At the high end of this range, defense expenditures would be rising more rapidly than total output, so the share of defense in GNP would increase to 7 percent.

These projections are made in terms of funds authorized. They show that under the various assumptions spelled out above, funds could rise from $83 billion in 1973 to somewhere between $87 billion and $95 billion by 1977, an increase ranging between $4 billion and $12 billion. Since proposed defense outlays in 1973 are only $76.5 billion as against $83.2 billion in requested authorizations, the increase in actual defense spending between 1973 and 1977 could be $6 billion greater. This would mean that as expenditures rise gradually toward the level of authorizations, the increase in actual defense spending could range from $10 billion to $18 billion by 1977. Using the midpoint of this range and allowing for the effects of continuing inflation (as assumed in Chapter 13), defense expenditures in current dollars could be approximately $100 billion in 1977.

4. Special Defense Issues

THIS CHAPTER EXAMINES EIGHT ISSUES bearing on the U.S. defense budget. The first section, by way of introduction, briefly discusses the Soviet defense budget, Soviet military planning assumptions, and their possible implications for U.S. force planning. The next four sections outline alternative illustrative budgets for each of the major U.S. force categories and relate each alternative to the foreign and defense policy decisions on which it is based. The final three sections discuss defense support, manpower policies, and weapon acquisition policies; here the alternatives rest principally on cost and efficiency factors.

In examining alternative force levels, a deliberate effort has been made to outline a relatively wide range of options; and this has been done, moreover, without fully taking into account the effect of a low or high option in one force category on requirements in other force categories. The purpose of this approach is to highlight key decisions underlying each component of the force structure and thereby to provide a basis for the subsequent examination, in Chapter 5, of major national security options. In the alternatives laid out in Chapter 5, relationships among specific force components are explicitly taken into account.

The Soviet Defense Budget*

Since the Soviet Union is the most powerful potential adversary of the United States, that country's defense program figures prominently in the formulation of the U.S. defense posture. Moreover, a propor-

* Based in part on a background paper prepared by Herbert Block.

tion of U.S. combat forces have as their primary mission to deter or to meet contingencies involving possible Soviet military initiatives. Hence specific Soviet force programs, as well as Soviet research and development activity, are frequently seen as calling for countermeasures by the United States. Furthermore, changes in the level of total Soviet spending sometimes suggest a U.S. response to avoid adverse political reactions. Conversely, the USSR is influenced by what the United States does. The ways in which the United States and the Soviet Union influence each other differ, however, since the two superpowers have different security objectives and foreign policy interests and are under different constraints from domestic political and organizational interests. This section deals primarily with how Soviet military programs influence the United States, but the other side of the equation should be kept in mind.

Trends in Total Soviet Defense Spending

First a note of warning should be given. Estimates of what the Soviet Union spends in real terms on defense vary widely for a host of reasons, notably because the estimates require highly uncertain interpretations of published Soviet data (given the extraordinary secretiveness surrounding the Soviet defense economy) and because it is difficult to compare what a defense ruble and a defense dollar can buy. Soviet defense expenditures are spread among a number of budget categories. The principal allocation is that for the Ministry of Defense. Published as only a single amount, it specifies neither the overall sum nor the composition of Soviet military spending. The USSR uses it to portray its international posture and sometimes to convey a political message. A second defense allocation is included in "science," partly under the budget category "social and cultural measures." Additional military expenditures lie hidden in various other budget categories.

These caveats notwithstanding, U.S. experts agree that the Soviet military budget has increased sharply since 1960. The data presented in Table 4-1 show the nominal "defense" authorization and the "science" authorization, which is partly defense, compared with an estimate of the actual defense budget that is near the center of the range of estimates by U.S. experts. The data on actual defense budgets indicate restrained military spending in much of the 1950s; a sharp increase in the early 1960s; a period of restraint toward the end of the Khrushchev regime and during the reappraisal that followed the take-

Table 4-1. Soviet Defense Expenditures, Selected Years, 1950–72

| Year | *Official Soviet figures (billions of current rubles)* | | | *Estimate of actual defense spending (billions of rubles at 1955 factor costs)* |
	Total budget	Ministry of Defense allocation	Science allocation[a]	
1950	41.3	8.3	0.9	8.7
1952	46.0	10.9	n.a.	11.6
1955	54.0	10.7	1.2	11.6
1958	64.3	9.4	1.8	11.4
1960	73.1	9.3	3.3	11.8
1961	76.3	11.6	3.8	14.7
1962	82.2	12.7	4.3	16.1
1963	87.0	13.9	4.7	17.7
1964	92.2	13.3	5.2	17.3
1965	101.6	12.8	5.9	17.3
1966	105.6	13.4	6.5	18.4
1967	115.6	14.5	7.2	20.0
1968	128.6	16.7	7.9	22.8
1969	138.5	17.7	9.3	24.4
1970	154.6	17.9[a]	12.0[b]	25.1[c]
1971	165.1	17.9[a]	13.2[b]	25.9[c]
1972	173.5[a]	17.9[a]	14.4[b]	26.7[c]

Sources: Official figures were compiled from Soviet statistical handbooks and budget data; estimates of actual spending were developed by Stanley H. Cohn (State University of New York, Binghamton, 1972). Cohn's estimates seek to account for changes in prices by using official price changes in analogous civilian industries.

The official figures and the estimate of actual spending are not comparable since the former are in current rubles and the latter is expressed in terms of constant 1955 prices. Official data are shown to indicate how trends in this index, over time, compare with trends in the estimate of actual spending.

n.a. Not available.

a. The science allocations for 1958–72, the Ministry of Defense allocations for 1970–72, and the 1972 total budget figure represent planned, rather than actual expenditures.

b. Since 1970, the science allocation has included investments associated with research facilities. This explains a portion of the large increase in that year.

c. Preliminary estimates.

over by Brezhnev and Kosygin in late 1964; and a renewed armament drive in 1966, which began to moderate in 1970.

Measuring the burden of defense on the Soviet economy also involves heroic assumptions, but here again a consensus exists regarding general trends. Paralleling developments in the United States, a brief period of demobilization and conversion after the Second World War was interrupted by growing international tension and rearmament; in the early 1950s defense spending probably absorbed about 15 percent of the Soviet gross national product (GNP). Khrushchev, who had his own version of "massive retaliation" and a strong interest in shifting priorities to the civilian economy as part of his program to overtake the United States, managed to reduce this share to about 9 percent during the latter part of the 1950s. In the 1960s military spending probably averaged 10 percent of GNP, with moderate variations during the period—higher at the beginning of the decade, lower in the middle, and higher again in the period 1965–69. Recently the rates seem to have dropped to about 9 percent, and possibly less.

A comparison of these Soviet military spending estimates with the U.S. defense budget requires still another judgment: What would Soviet military budgets amount to in U.S. dollars if the cost of Soviet weapons and manpower were calculated at U.S. prices? A determination of this "military purchasing-power parity" exchange rate must take into consideration the fact that the Soviet defense sector is much more efficient than its civilian counterpart and that Soviet military manpower costs much less than U.S. military manpower. For these and similar reasons, Western experts differ as to what ruble–dollar exchange rate is appropriate for comparing military spending between the United States and the USSR.

In fact, very few estimates of the dollar value of Soviet military spending are publicly available, and most of these fall within a relatively narrow range. Data in Secretary Melvin R. Laird's 1972 Defense Report suggest that Soviet military spending is about equal in value to U.S. military spending, and even somewhat higher if Vietnam costs are excluded.

Without placing too much reliance on these data, it seems reasonable to conclude that (1) Soviet military spending has increased markedly in recent years; (2) at the current level it results in a military establishment that, in a loose sense at least, is nearly comparable to its U.S. counterpart; and (3) maintaining this rough comparability places an appreciably heavier burden on the Soviet than on the U.S. economy. Aggregate comparisons, however, can be dangerously misleading. What has the USSR bought for its defense rubles, and on what force planning assumptions have its decisions been based?

Strategic Forces

The rapid buildup of Soviet strategic forces since 1967 indicates that a significant portion of the post-1965 increase in military spending went to strategic programs. The beginning of this buildup coincided roughly with the coming to power of Brezhnev and Kosygin. The nature of the program has been discussed in Chapter 3; the concern here is with Soviet motivation and planning goals.

It is possible to interpret the strategic buildup as a straightforward attempt to gain parity with the United States and specifically to do so before reaching arms limitation agreements that would freeze the relative capabilities of the two superpowers. On this reasoning, the USSR has sought to make up, through the number of its launchers and the size of its warheads, for U.S. technological superiority and for the rapidly growing U.S. lead in the number of warheads resulting from its multiple independently targetable reentry vehicle (MIRV) programs. There have indeed been signs that Soviet strategy has shifted toward a concept of deterrence similar to U.S. doctrine. This could explain the continued expansion of the Soviet submarine-based missile force. Moreover, Soviet statements and behavior at the strategic arms limitation talks (SALT), notably in proposing limits on antiballistic missiles (ABMs), show a growing awareness of the importance of stability and the value of mutual restraint in weapon acquisition. Since 1969, public statements by Soviet leaders have expressed interest in mutual deterrence and concern over the destabilizing nature of ABMs—both cases representing a reversal of earlier Soviet positions.

On the other hand, some Soviet deployments are not consistent with announced doctrine. The size and character of the SS-9 intercontinental ballistic missile are matters of particular concern. Secretary Laird has alluded to the possibility that the Soviet Union may be striving for a first-strike capability. This fear has been based on the large payload of the SS-9s, on their appearance in substantial numbers, and on the possibility that the USSR will eventually achieve a breakthrough in delivery technology. In addition, given past Soviet attitudes toward the political use of strategic power, the administration has expressed concern that Moscow is seeking superiority in the number of launch vehicles for political advantage.

Or again, one can read the evidence as reflecting mainly the bureaucratic and military-political momentum of ongoing programs in the face of ambivalent or differing views among Soviet leaders.

While the issue remains unresolved, recent indications of a halt in the SS-9 program, and the current Defense Department appraisal that it will be a long time before the Soviet Union develops a MIRV technology, point in the direction of less worrisome interpretations. Attainment of a first-round SALT agreement and provision for follow-on negotiations would be additional, though not necessarily conclusive, evidence that Soviet programs are designed principally to achieve parity. In any event, even modest arms limits should reduce concern over future Soviet strategic threats.

Naval Forces

Contrary to popular impressions, there has not been a major recent expansion in the size of the Soviet Navy, although its quality has improved. Since 1958, a turning point in the evolution of Soviet naval power, manpower in the Soviet Navy has been cut by more than one-third, naval aviation by two-thirds, and the attack submarine fleet has been considerably reduced. (See Table 4-2.) The surface force is the same size but considerably newer; sixty vessels are less than five years old.

Trends in the near future will vary. The Soviet submarine force will be further reduced in number, reflecting the increasing obsolescence of the *W* class submarines, which now compose a large share of the conventional submarine force. The number of surface combat vessels is likely to grow only moderately, if at all, as modern units replace those built shortly after the Second World War. In brief, the Soviet Navy has followed a course similar to that of the U.S. Navy, accepting lower force levels in return for modernization. It is not clear that the Soviet Navy has increased its share of the total Soviet defense budget; if it has, the increase cannot have been very large.

Nonetheless, the Soviet Navy is now a far more capable force than it was earlier. Perhaps 25 percent of the fleet has been constructed in the past decade, and as a whole it incorporates technologically advanced propulsion, detection, communication, and weapon systems. Particularly striking has been the widespread deployment of cruise missiles on a variety of platforms; more than any other single event, the sinking of the Israeli destroyer *Eilat* by such a weapon seems to have contributed to recognition of the potential threat wielded by Soviet naval forces. Deployment of cruise missile–equipped surface naval ships to areas of traditional Western naval dominance, such as the Mediterranean, has detracted from the political impact of U.S. and other Western naval forces on station there. More important, the fact that some sixty Soviet submarines and several hundred aircraft are equipped with these weapons adds to the problem of the survivability of U.S. aircraft carriers in confined areas, such as the Mediterranean, where the possibility of concealment is limited, where Soviet sub-

Table 4-2. Changes in Size and Characteristics of the Soviet Navy, 1958–71

Characteristics	1958	1971
Major surface combatants[a]		
Number of units	255	255
Total tonnage[b]	815	679
Number of surface-to-air missiles[c]	...	114
Number of surface-to-surface missiles[c]	...	144
Number of torpedo tubes	1,762	1,554
Number of antisubmarine rockets[d]	1,984	7,668
Total mine capacity, maximum number	19,310	11,000
Coastal, attack, and cruise missile submarines[e]		
Number of nuclear units	3[f]	56
Number of diesel units	474	290[g]
Total tonnage[b]	400	610
Number of surface-to-surface or subsurface-to-surface missiles[c]	...	380
Number of torpedo tubes	2,496	2,190
Minor surface combatants[h]		
Number of units	121	270
Total tonnage[b]	39	75
Amphibious warfare vehicles		
Number of units	120	200
Naval aircraft		
Number of units	3,000	1,000
Total Navy		
Number of personnel (thousands)	750	450–500

Sources: Based on data appearing in Raymond V. B. Blackman (ed.), *Jane's Fighting Ships* (McGraw-Hill), 1958–59 and 1971–72 editions; International Institute for Strategic Studies, *The Military Balance, 1971–1972* (IISS, 1971), and 1959 edition of *The Military Balance;* Siegfried Breyer, *Guide to the Soviet Navy,* translated by M. W. Henley (Annapolis: United States Naval Institute, 1970).

a. Surface combatant vessels—helicopter carriers, cruisers, destroyers, and escorts—greater than 750 tons standard displacement.

b. Maximum listed standard (surface for submarines) displacement in thousands of tons.

c. Number of launcher rails.

d. Number of launcher barrels; if ship may be configured with rockets or depth charges, the former was assumed.

e. Excludes strategic missile–carrying submarines.

f. The three nuclear units listed for 1958 reflect a supposition made at the time.

g. Recent statements by U.S. officials indicate that 50–100 of these have been retired.

h. Coastal escorts, fast escorts, patrol vessels, and submarine chasers displacing at least 200 tons.

marine forces can be concentrated, and where the carriers are within range of land-based Soviet planes.

The increased willingness of the USSR to deploy naval forces in regions distant from the Soviet homeland has also contributed to pessimistic Western assessments of the naval balance. The first official visit of a Soviet naval vessel to a noncommunist nation was as recent as 1955. Until 1956, maneuvers were held strictly inside the Black, Baltic, and Barents Seas, extending only gradually through the North

Sea and into the North Atlantic over the following twelve years. Surface warships first appeared in the Pacific in 1963 and in the Caribbean in 1969. Soviet warships were not kept continuously in the Mediterranean until 1964, and their numbers did not become significant until mid-1967. The deployment of Soviet warships in the Indian Ocean began in 1968 and off the west coast of Africa in 1970.

The widening presence of the Soviet Navy should not obscure the fact that it is primarily a defensive force, designed to blunt nuclear attacks on the Soviet homeland that are launched by carrier-based aircraft and strategic submarines. In other respects, the Soviet Navy continues to have serious deficiencies. First, its amphibious warfare forces are small, and it has no sea-based, fixed-wing aircraft. These factors severely limit the Soviet Navy's ability to intervene in conflicts that are distant from the Soviet homeland. Second, the lack of sea-based airpower limits the USSR's ability to maintain surface ships in a hostile environment at any great distance from its own shores. Third, the Soviet Navy cannot support distant and prolonged deployments in wartime. Fourth, Soviet submarines are not as quiet as U.S. submarines and are more susceptible to detection. Nevertheless, a force with these deficiencies can be effective in varying degrees: (1) to make it potentially costly and thus to deter the United States from intervening with sea-based aircraft or amphibious forces in crisis situations; (2) to attack shipping between the United States and its allies during war; (3) to use naval forces for political coercion, as in the Soviet recourse to "gunboat diplomacy" against Ghana in 1969; and (4) to weigh in regional balance-of-power calculations, as in the Middle East.

General Purpose Forces for Land Combat

A striking paradox in U.S.–Soviet force comparisons is the fact that the USSR has now virtually completed its move toward a two and one-half war military planning strategy as the United States has moved away from it. In other words, Soviet planners want to be able to fight major wars in Europe and Asia simultaneously, if need be. A sizable part of the increase in the Soviet military budget during the 1960s, and particularly during the second half of the decade, probably was used to finance the buildup of Soviet forces on the border with China. According to the International Institute for Strategic Studies and other published sources, these forces now consist of thirty-three divisions in the Soviet Far East and Mongolia plus twenty-eight divisions in the Caucasus and West Turkestan, most of which are now stationed at, or could be quickly redeployed to, the Sinkiang border region. These division forces, plus associated combat units (tactical aviation, air defense, offensive missile troops) as well as support units, construction troops, and border patrol forces, may now be approaching 1 million men, an increase of some 500,000 since 1965. This has been a costly buildup because it was accomplished chiefly by increasing the total size of the Soviet Army rather than by reducing Soviet forces in Eastern Europe,[1] and because the long logistic line to the Soviet Far East is very expensive to maintain.

While the USSR did not reduce its forces in Eastern Europe, the buildup in the Far East did require some reductions in the size and combat readiness of forces held in reserve in Western Russia for European contingencies. Weapon modernization programs in Europe may also have been affected.

How long will the Soviet Union continue to build up its forces in the East? Will it soon, or eventually, have to sacrifice military capabilities in Eastern Europe in order to do so? At the moment this does not seem to be a serious issue, since the present forces in the Soviet Far East are sufficient to support the Soviet political posture toward China and to deal with any military contingencies short of a full-scale invasion of China. In effect, the price of the buildup in these land combat capabilities has already been paid; the cost was substantial but apparently bearable and not unduly disruptive to the Soviet military position elsewhere. Over the longer term, however, the growing Chinese nuclear capability may require the USSR to think in terms of a flexible response strategy in the Soviet Far East as it already does in Europe—and to undertake a larger force buildup in Asia to this end. In that event, the USSR may be under fiscal as well as military pressure to reexamine alternatives.

Two other possible sources of the increase in Soviet defense spending should be mentioned. First, the Soviet Air Force (SAF) has undergone extensive modernization since the mid-sixties. Included among the new aircraft now being developed or phased into the force are a new high performance fighter (Foxbat), a prototype of a new stra-

---

1. In fact, Soviet forces in Eastern Europe were increased from twenty-six to thirty-one divisions during and after the invasion of Czechoslovakia. See International Institute for Strategic Studies, *The Military Balance, 1971–1972* (London: IISS, 1971), p. 6.

tegic bomber (Backfire), and experimental versions of vertical or short takeoff and landing (V/STOL) aircraft. Particularly impressive has been the growth in the Soviet Air Transport Command and in the logistic support and mobility of the Soviet Air Force itself. Soviet airlift capabilities have been demonstrated on several occasions in recent years—the massive armaments airlift into the Middle East in 1967, the invasion of Czechoslovakia in 1968, and several less extensive but difficult operations in the Middle East (Yemen, 1967–68; Sudan, 1969–71; and Egypt, 1971).[2]

The other potential source of spending increases is logistics, long one of the weakest points in the Soviet military. Soviet logistics have been reorganized in the past ten years, with the result that the credibility of their conventional military power has improved. There seems to have been a major effort to increase the mobility, flexibility, and sustaining power of Soviet ground and air combat forces. These costly steps support the thesis that the USSR in recent years has been planning in terms of more protracted conflicts rather than rapid escalation to nuclear levels.

Prospects and Implications

On the assumption that there will be no appreciable change in the international situation, what can be said about the Soviet defense posture in the years ahead?

The present Soviet defense burden is heavy, but not unduly so for a great power that is intent on being recognized as such, on maintaining control in Eastern Europe, on keeping pressure on China, and on projecting its power in the Middle East—all the while suffering from an invasion trauma. While Soviet leaders may prefer to reduce the burden of defense, they are unlikely to do so. In part, Soviet defense spending is a reaction to their assessment of U.S. and Chinese policies. Despite the "era of negotiations," Soviet leaders are probably disposed by history and dogma to regard the longer outlook as highly uncertain and are not prepared to discount future dangers heavily. Moreover, Soviet military spending is also shaped by political considerations and other factors that are independent of what other powers may or may not do. In these circumstances, defense outlays will con-

2. See the assessment by John Erickson, *Soviet Military Power* (London: Royal United Services Institute for Defence Studies, 1971).

tinue to move upward, probably by less than, or at most by as much as, the rate of increase in the Soviet GNP—say, by 3 to 5 percent a year. This would suggest that Soviet military spending might increase at about the same, or a slightly higher, rate than that projected in Chapter 3 for U.S. defense outlays, given the current U.S. defense posture.

Domestic factors alone would probably push the Soviet defense budget upward. Manpower costs are rising as the standard of living improves. These costs are also being pushed higher because the term of conscription has been shortened and because the increased technological sophistication of Soviet weapons requires more highly skilled military personnel. As in the United States, the armed forces in the USSR are trying to make military careers more appealing; only recently, two senior noncommissioned officer ranks dating back to czarist days were revived. Furthermore, Soviet leaders would hesitate to provoke the military; generals do not control the Soviet regime, but the civilian leaders must be acutely aware that competing factions could use military displeasure to their own advantage. In any event, the defense burden is not likely to be a source of overt popular discontent, particularly since it would permit a continued increase of about 3 percent annually in per capita consumption—less than in the 1960s, but still a respectable rate of improvement.

A more likely source of restraint on Soviet defense spending is a lackluster performance by the civilian economy. This is possible, if not probable, given the great difficulty of achieving satisfactory, sustained increases in the productivity of labor in the civilian sector. Soviet leaders might be tempted to draw on the concentration of engineering, scientific, and management resources in the defense sector, which is by far the most innovative force in the economy and potentially a stimulus to civilian economic growth. Similarly, the armed forces are the choicest reservoir of skilled and semiskilled manpower for civilian employment in case a manpower squeeze should develop. Khrushchev moved in this direction in the mid-1950s, and it paid off. Nevertheless, the prospect of a similar initiative in the 1970s is at best highly uncertain, in view of the factors indicated above.

The prospect, then, is for increases in Soviet defense outlays and hence for some pressure on the United States to match them. While concern is warranted, and Soviet programs having adverse consequences for the U.S.–Soviet military balance could require U.S. countermeasures, automatic responses are not warranted. In the first place, the magnitude and meaning of Soviet defense spending are difficult to judge with any assurance. Furthermore, a significant part of any increase in Soviet military spending would be directed against China and could not be readily deployed against the United States or its allies. Another part would result from rising manpower costs and thus would not represent an increase in military capabilities. That leaves some part that is geared to Soviet policies toward the United States— both as a means of exerting pressure and as a response to U.S. military actions.

All of this suggests that the United States should predicate its responses to Soviet military spending on an analysis of the specific military uses of Soviet spending and their consequences for U.S. interests. To do otherwise would, at best, mean a diversion of U.S. resources from more important security and domestic needs. At worst, it could stimulate further increases in Soviet expenditures and jeopardize moves toward tacitly or explicitly agreed U.S.–Soviet arms limitations.

Strategic Force Alternatives*

Four related questions underlie decisions on the size and composition of strategic forces. (1) How many independent offensive systems are necessary? (2) At what force levels should these systems be maintained? (3) How rapidly should they be modernized to assure their effectiveness? (4) How much emphasis should be placed on defensive systems? Answers to these questions depend on the amount and character of redundancy that is judged necessary to provide a high level of confidence in the U.S. strategic deterrent.

This fundamental issue concerns the need to maintain the triad— a concept that evolved gradually during the 1960s as land- and sea-based missile forces were added to the strategic bomber force. Because of differences in basing and in modes of penetrating Soviet defenses, the capability of each component to survive a Soviet preemptive strike and to respond against targets in the USSR is relatively independent of the others. With respect to the future of the triad, Secretary Laird in 1972 in his Defense Report stated the administration's view as follows:

Turning to specifics in our planning, although each element of our strategic offensive forces at the present time possesses a substantial capability in its own right, we plan to maintain a combination of land- and sea-based missiles and manned bombers during the program period. This will enable us

* Based on an analysis by Barry Blechman and Alton H. Quanbeck.

to take advantage of the unique capabilities inherent in these different systems, to provide a hedge against enemy technological breakthroughs or unforeseen operational failures, either of which might adversely affect our deterrent, and to complicate Soviet and PRC [Peoples Republic of China] offensive and defensive strategic planning.[3]

Strategic defensive systems play a secondary role in U.S. strategic deterrence, although, as was pointed out in Chapter 3, it is a relatively expensive one. The administration has specifically ruled out the option of seeking a nationwide defense of urban-industrial complexes because it would be costly, technically difficult, and destabilizing to relations with the USSR. Hence strategic defensive forces are limited to protecting fixed land-based systems and the national command authority (mainly through ABMs and related programs) and to defending against light or accidental attacks by missiles and bombers.

A third group of systems, consisting of warning and surveillance programs and command and control systems, provides support for both offensive and defensive strategic forces. They are essential to the survivability and responsiveness of the strategic forces, but because they are so diverse, because in some cases they are highly classified, and because judgments concerning requirements for them are largely qualitative, no attempt will be made to analyze them here.

In this section, U.S. strategic forces are examined in terms of specific strategic weapon system issues, with the analysis focusing on the budgetary significance of alternative decisions on each. A number of strategic questions, however, do not involve appreciable differences in funding, one way or the other. Examples are whether to improve missile accuracy, or to deploy additional penetration aids on missiles and bombers, or to upgrade the reliability of command and control systems. While these issues for the most part are not considered in this section, it should be recognized that they could have an important impact on security, principally because of their stabilizing or destabilizing consequences for the U.S.–Soviet strategic relationship.

What about U.S. Land-based Missiles?

Land-based intercontinental ballistic missiles (ICBMs) pose a particularly difficult set of questions because they are the part of the triad in which there is least confidence. Most experts believe that the Min-

3. *Annual Defense Department Report, FY 1973.* Statement of Secretary of Defense Melvin R. Laird before the Senate Armed Services Committee on the FY 1973 Defense Budget and FY 1973–1977 Program (February 15, 1972), p. 66.

uteman force at some point in the future would be vulnerable to a
Soviet first strike *if* the USSR chose to allocate a large part of its
ICBM capability to that task and *if* it made improvements in missile
accuracy and achieved a MIRV technology. For example, John S.
Foster, Jr., recently testified:

Analysis of the latest projections concerning Soviet missile growth rates
and accuracy improvements indicate considerable variation in the time
period in which our Minuteman forces would be seriously threatened. In
cases where small Soviet growth is assumed, Minuteman forces do not appear threatened until the early 1980's or beyond. For middle range assumptions, Minuteman could have less survivors in 1980 or before. If the most
severe of the postulated SS-9 and SS-11 type missile forces were directed
at Minuteman, the Minuteman force (assuming that the silos are unde-
fended, but are upgraded in hardness) could be drawn down as early as the
mid-70's. Prudence requires that we take the more pessimistic projections
seriously.[4]

In the face of such uncertainties, steps were taken over the past few
years to improve the survivability of these missiles. The Safeguard
program is the most costly and most ambitious; others are programs
to strengthen silos and to pursue research and development on special
radars and missiles, now known as the site defense of Minuteman
(SDM) program. These programs continue to be funded in the 1973
budget.

Nevertheless, ICBMs remain potentially vulnerable, and this would
be true even with a full twelve-site Safeguard system and completion
of the other programs now under way or being developed to improve
their survivability. A SALT agreement that precluded additional
Safeguard sites and possibly prohibited some of the other missile
defense programs, however, would raise the fundamental question
whether efforts should be continued to maintain a survivable land-
based offensive system. Several alternative positions are possible.

Consideration has been given in the past to developing an entirely
new technology—for example, a mobile land-based system or super-
hardened silos. None of the proposals has proved practicable. Furthermore, they would merely postpone the vulnerability problem
rather than offer the possibility of solving it.

Moving in the opposite direction, programs to protect these missiles
could be discontinued, the missile force components eventually

4. "Statement by the Director of Defense Research and Engineering, Dr. John S.
Foster, Jr., On the Safeguard—Site Defense of Minuteman, before the Armed Services
Committee, U.S. Senate," 92 Cong. 1 sess. (1972), p. 8.

phased out as they became vulnerable, and no follow-on programs initiated. The Minuteman III MIRV program would be completed (550 missiles), but additional Safeguard and other missile improvement programs would be ended. These reductions in missile defense could result in a saving of $1.4 billion a year during the period 1973–79.

Leaving aside the ultimate role of ICBMs, given these survivability questions, it would be possible to consider phasing out the less effective components of the land-based missile system now, specifically the 54 Titan missiles and the 450 Minuteman II missiles. If this were done within the next year or so, either unilaterally or as part of a SALT agreement, there would be a saving of $600 million a year in direct and indirect operating costs.

If it were deemed politically important to maintain a rough balance with the USSR in the total number of missile systems, phasing out the less effective missiles could be accomplished bilaterally by negotiating reciprocal reductions through SALT. If this did not prove possible, the United States could nevertheless reduce the number of land-based missiles or phase them out entirely and transfer this capability to the more survivable sea-based systems. In this event, savings would be more problematical.

Sea-based Missile Forces

The sea-based missile force is the cornerstone of the U.S. strategic deterrent. Mobility and concealment of submarine platforms currently provide assurance of the invulnerability of the system and therefore of maintaining a secure retaliatory capability. Now and for the indefinite future, submarines appear likely to offer better prospects for survivability than do either land-based missiles or bombers.

Confidence as to the survivability of sea-based systems rests on the following kinds of considerations. There are no indications that the USSR has developed, or is close to developing, an antisubmarine warfare (ASW) capability that could endanger the present Polaris force. Severe technological and geographic obstacles stand in the way. The detection and precise locating of quiet, slow-moving submarines is difficult at long distances. The effectiveness of acoustic means (sonar) is limited by the characteristics of the water and ocean bottom, and nonacoustic means apparently do not have the capability to search

the vast expanses of the oceans. Furthermore, the Russians are handicapped by their lack of land bases that are contiguous to the Polaris
patrol areas. Finally, if the USSR should substantially improve its
ASW capabilities, the United States could take any of a large number
of available countermeasures, such as changes in tactics and patrol
areas and the use of deception devices.

Moreover, the destructive potential of the U.S. sea-based force
alone is very large. When conversion of thirty-one Polaris submarines
to permit them to carry Poseidon missiles is completed in 1976, the
United States will have more than 5,000 warheads deployed on sea-
based missiles. (Each Poseidon missile can carry ten to fourteen small-
yield MIRV warheads, and there are sixteen missiles on each submarine.) Allowing for submarines in overhaul or otherwise not on
station and for less than complete missile reliability, at least one-half
of these warheads—or about 2,500 of them—could be delivered on
targets in the USSR in reaction to a Soviet first strike. This capability
alone, it could be argued, would be sufficient for deterrence (all the
more so if Soviet ABMs remain at low levels), with the redundancy
supplied by bombers and land-based ICBMs providing a hedge
against unexpected developments or miscalculations.

Nevertheless, a follow-on to the Polaris/Poseidon force will eventually be required if for no other reason than the high cost of maintaining and operating older submarines. The undersea long-range
missile system (ULMS) is meant to fill this role. The central issues are
when it will be necessary to bring a follow-on system into operation
and in what numbers.

In the 1973 budget, the administration proposes to accelerate the
ULMS program with the objective of bringing the new system into
operation by 1978 rather than by 1981, as had previously been contemplated. Several reasons have been advanced to justify this proposed speedup:

• The need to replace the ten oldest Polaris submarines.

• Improving crew morale by allowing strategic submarines to operate from bases in the United States.

• Using ULMS as a hedge against improvements in Soviet ASW,
primarily through the enlargement of the operating range of U.S.
submarines made possible by a longer-range missile.

• Matching the USSR in numbers of missile launchers for political
reasons.

• Using ULMS as a bargaining chip to encourage the Russians to agree to limits on submarine-based systems in the SALT negotiations.

• Transferring the capability of U.S. land-based Minuteman missiles to sea.

The first two reasons do not seem urgent enough to justify accelerating the ULMS program. The ten oldest Polaris submarines will not become obsolete before 1980 (they are only nine to twelve years old now), and the present Polaris Atlantic fleet could be based in the United States with only a small sacrifice of on-station time. A hedge against possible improvements in Soviet ASW capabilities, the third reason noted above, could be provided by a longer-range missile alone, which under the earlier ULMS program would be available before the end of the seventies.

Thus, the main arguments for accelerating the ULMS program are (1) to induce the Russians to accept limitations on strategic submarines in SALT, (2) to avoid possible international or domestic consequences of the appearance of Soviet gains in the strategic balance, and (3) to substitute for Minuteman, assuming that these missiles will become vulnerable in the late 1970s.

The costs of the accelerated program and of the more orderly schedule recommended in the 1972 budget, assuming in both cases that twenty submarines will be built, can be compared as follows:

Total obligational authority
(millions of fiscal year 1973 dollars)

Fiscal year	Accelerated program: initial operating capability about 1978	Previous program: initial operating capability about 1981
1973	945	400
1974	2,000	700
1975	2,500	900
1976	2,700	1,000
1977	2,700	1,500
1978	2,800	2,000
1979	2,700	2,500

On the average, the accelerated program would increase costs by approximately $1 billion a year during the rest of this decade. However, this is not an accurate reflection of the comparative costs of the two programs. If force levels were the same, the principal effect of the slower schedule would be to defer costs into the 1980s. Accelerating the program, on the other hand, would increase the likelihood of real cost growth because of inefficiencies associated with concurrent development and production and with the necessity of proceeding on the basis of poorly defined contracts. It also would raise the danger that the design of the system would be fixed before the nature of the threat was well understood. Finally, if an accelerated schedule were tantamount to a decision to increase force levels, that factor alone would be the most important element in comparing the costs of the two schedules.

Size and Composition of the Bomber Force

Manned bombers were the mainstay of the U.S. strategic force from the end of the Second World War until ballistic missiles became available in large numbers in the mid-1960s. The number of bombers declined from more than 1,600 planes in the late 1950s to about 500 in 1972; the force now consists of B-52s and a small FB-111 component.

The newer B-52s (255 G–H models built between 1958 and 1962) are the core of the bomber force and are being equipped with new short-range attack missiles (SRAM) and subsonic cruise armed decoys (SCAD) to aid their penetration ability. To improve their survivability against possible concentrated missile attacks launched from Soviet submarines, the Air Force is improving warning systems, dispersing the bases from which the B-52s are flown, and reducing the time it takes them to react.

About 40 percent of the bomber force is kept in a state of readiness to launch on warning of an impending attack. This alert force could be expected to survive any preemptive attack. Its destructive potential is large. In the case of the late-model B-52s, each of the approximately 100 planes on alert at any given time, when newly equipped, will be capable of carrying twenty nuclear tipped air-to-surface missiles as well as high-yield gravity bombs. This adds up to a total payload equivalent to 600 megatons. Assuming that only one-third of these weapons were delivered, this part of the alert bomber force alone would have the capability to destroy more than 20 percent of the Soviet population and 70 percent of Soviet industry.[5]

5. *Statement of Secretary of Defense Robert S. McNamara before the Senate Armed Services Committee on the Fiscal Year 1969–73 Defense Program and 1969 Defense Budget* (1968), p. 57.

The remainder of the operational strategic bomber strike force consists of 142 older B-52s (D and F models built between 1955 and 1957) and 66 FB-111s (a variant of the F-111). The former are considered too old to be worth reequipping with the new air-to-surface missiles; hence their primary weapons are gravity bombs, which must be dropped over the target. The FB-111s, although they are new planes, have a severely limited range and payload; they were introduced into the force in fiscal 1971, replacing the B-58.

Tankers, the third component of the bomber force, are essential because each B-52 would have to be refueled en route to its destination. There are 615 KC-135 tankers now in operation, a number that has remained unchanged over the past four years despite reductions that have occurred in the interim in the number of operational strategic bombers. Tankers, it should be noted, are also used to refuel aircraft on nonstrategic missions, such as the redeployment of tactical squadrons or tactical air operations in Southeast Asia.

The cost of operating the strategic bombers and tankers is substantial. Direct and indirect operating costs are estimated to be approximately \$5 billion a year, or almost 80 percent of the estimated total annual cost of the strategic bomber program.

In light of these considerations, two central features of the administration's strategic bomber program should be considered. First, the program calls for the development of the B-1—a follow-on manned bomber—at about the pace anticipated in the fiscal 1972 program. The amount requested for development in the 1973 budget is \$445 million. If the procurement decision is made, the first planes could be operational by the end of this decade. Second, the program seems to envisage continuation of the present bomber force levels until B-1 replacements are available. At least no deactivation of older model planes is indicated in the 1973 budget, in contrast to the deactivation of three squadrons of older model B-52s provided for in the 1972 budget.

As for the first item, if the United States is to maintain a strategic bomber force indefinitely as an independent element in the strategic deterrent, it will be necessary to introduce a follow-on bomber sometime in the mid-1980s, when it will no longer be economical to maintain the B-52s. What should be the characteristics of a new bomber? The B-1 is now the sole candidate. As now conceived, it incorporates marginal improvements over the B-52 G–H models in speed, low altitude capability, radar cross-section, payload, and pre-launch survivability (the last factor being measured in terms of engine start time, airframe vulnerability to nuclear blast, and flyout speed after takeoff). The range of the B-1 is inferior to that of the newer B-52s. Concern exists that the improvements do not greatly increase its capability to penetrate advanced Soviet air defenses.

Concern about the B-1 also centers on its high procurement cost. Estimates range from $30 million a plane to as high as $60 million. Direct and indirect operating costs for each B-1 and its supporting tanker force will be approximately the same as for the B-52s, about $10 million a year.

A decision on whether to procure the B-1 is scheduled to be made in 1975. If these concerns prove to be justified, the program presumably will be ended, leaving no feasible alternatives available. What options exist?

One approach would be to assume that the time problem is not urgent and that there would be merit in waiting to see what the requirements might be in the mid-1970s, particularly in light of the results of SALT negotiations in the interim.

Another alternative would be to start now on the parallel development of a manned bomber prototype designed to carry standoff cruise missiles, either continuing the B-1 program at its present pace or slowing it down. Since a standoff bomber would not need to reach the Soviet mainland and penetrate its air defenses, it could be large and subsonic like a Boeing 747 or a Lockheed C-5 aircraft, while incorporating improvements in ground alert and rapid takeoff capability like the B-1. Its payload would consist of cruise missiles carrying nuclear warheads, such as the Air Force SCAD, which would penetrate at a very low altitude and present a very small radar target. Not being required to reach the Soviet Union or descend to low altitudes, a standoff bomber would be able to carry more fuel than the B-1 and not require tankers for refueling.

Research and development costs for a standoff bomber would be relatively low since it would be based on aircraft and missile systems now operational or under design; and because it could carry many more air-to-surface missiles than the B-1, not as many aircraft would be required. Two kinds of cost comparisons between a standoff strategic bomber and the B-1 are worth noting. If it were developed in place of the B-1 and procurement started in fiscal 1976, costs over the remainder of the decade would average $700 million a year for the standoff bomber, compared with $1.1 billion a year projected for the present B-1 program.

A very approximate total cost comparison of the two systems would work out as follows: Assuming that 120 standoff bombers are comparable in capability to 240 B-1s (the presently contemplated number), the total ten-year system acquisition and operating costs of the B-1 program are estimated to be $19 billion, and for a comparable standoff bomber system approximately $12 billion.

Maintaining the less effective components of the strategic bomber force also would raise significant budgetary issues. The older model B-52s and the FB-111s, as was noted earlier, add little to the penetration capabilities of the strategic bomber force but cost a great deal to operate. If, over the next year or so, these planes and an equivalent number of tankers were taken out of operation and put into active storage, possible savings in operating costs would be an estimated $1.2 billion a year. In weighing this alternative, consideration would have to be given to its possible impact on, or use as a bargaining chip in, the SALT negotiations.

Air Defenses for the Future

Should U.S. air defenses be improved, or should they be reduced to a surveillance role? They now include a total of twenty-seven squadrons of fighter/interceptors, the Bomarc and Nike Hercules surface-to-air missiles, and associated radars and command and control networks. In his 1972 Defense Report, Secretary Laird specified as objectives for these forces:

—Deterring air attacks by defending strategic retaliatory forces, and key military and urban/industrial targets.
—Defending the National Command Authority.
—Limiting damage from deliberate or unauthorized small air attacks.
—Restricting the unauthorized overflight of U.S. airspace.[6]

He also pointed out, however, that these objectives are well beyond the capabilities of the present force. In fact, his appraisal of the pres-

6. *Defense Department Report, FY 1973*, p. 66.

ent system indicates that part of it is obsolete now and that virtually the entire system will become so by the end of this decade.

Faced with this situation, the administration is phasing out some surface-to-air missiles (all Bomarc squadrons) and transferring some Air Force interceptor planes to the National Guard. At the same time a large-scale research and development effort has been initiated to achieve a modernized air defense force capable of meeting the ambitious objectives outlined above. These efforts are concentrated on developing new warning systems—for example, the airborne warning and control system (AWACS) and over-the-horizon radars. If the program were to be carried through to procurement, it would eventually require a substantial investment in new warning systems, interceptors, and missiles.

An alternative approach would be to cut back heavily on objectives and instead to view air defense as being useful principally for surveillance and for protection against unauthorized entry of isolated aircraft, from whatever source. This approach would be analogous to the one taken with respect to a nationwide ABM system when the administration rejected large-scale defense of cities as being impractical and destabilizing to U.S.–Soviet strategic relations. The present Soviet bomber force is small; even if it were greatly strengthened, it still would not threaten the U.S. strategic retallatory capability. Hence, arguments for bomber defenses must rest on the objective of limiting damage to cities and industry in the event of nuclear war. This justification is open to question simply on the grounds that there is little point in trying to protect the population against Soviet bomber attacks when it has already been determined that it would be self-defeating to try to protect the nation against the substantially greater destructive potential of the Soviet missile force.

Comparative costs for the two approaches to air defense for fiscal years 1973–79 are shown below (total obligational authority in billions of fiscal year 1973 dollars):

Alternative	1973	1974	1975	1976	1977	1978	1979
Modernized force	3.2	3.2	4.6	5.2	5.2	5.0	4.8
Surveillance force	3.0	2.2	2.0	2.0	2.0	2.0	2.0

The projected cost of a modernized air defense force is based on the development and deployment of AWACs, over-the-horizon radar, an advanced surface-to-air missile (SAM-D), and an improved manned interceptor aircraft. The lower cost option would limit the air defense role to surveillance and would require only warning systems and a much smaller number of existing interceptor aircraft.

Area Missile Defenses

The area defense portion of Safeguard as currently conceived is designed to provide protection from accidental launches from any source and at most to limit damage from a Chinese nuclear attack. A first-round SALT agreement of the sort outlined above would make it impossible to seek attainment of this objective with current technology.

In the absence of a SALT agreement, the administration presumably would want to complete the Safeguard program, on the grounds that it is technically feasible and politically, as well as strategically, essential. Its plans call for a twelve-site Safeguard system, an unspecified number of the sites being augmented by radar and interceptor modules (site defense of Minuteman, or SDM).

The first Safeguard site will not become operational before fiscal 1975, and at present rates the twelfth site would be completed in fiscal 1986. The additional cost of building the full Safeguard program, beyond the cost of two sites that are now well along, is estimated to be $1.4 billion a year over the period 1973-79. This estimate includes the cost of additional improvement programs (for example, SDM).

An alternative would be to terminate the program at the two sites that are already under construction, even in the absence of a SALT agreement. The argument would be that U.S. strategic offensive forces would deter the Chinese from attempting either nuclear attack or nuclear blackmail, just as they have deterred the Soviet Union. Additionally it could be argued that moving ahead to complete the twelve-site program, particularly in the dangerous atmosphere created by a breakdown of the SALT negotiations, would lead to uncertainty on the part of the USSR concerning U.S. strategic objectives and would cause the Russians to undertake counterprograms.

Whatever position is taken on the size of the Safeguard program, there is general agreement that an active research and development program in ABM technology should be continued. It would make defensive options more readily available and would improve understand-

ing of the techniques by which offensive ballistic missiles can penetrate ABM defenses. Research and development costs on ABMs to
maintain this technology would amount to approximately $400 mil-
lion a year.

Seven Illustrative Budgets

Discussions of strategic force alternatives tend to focus on acquisition issues (Should new systems be procured and, if so, at what pace?)
or on strategic doctrine (Is it necessary to maintain a triad, or would a
diad or a single system be enough?). These questions are certainly important, but, as the discussion above indicates, the question of maintaining less effective forces—both offensive and defensive—has potentially at least equal budgetary significance. Positions taken on this last
set of issues depend on the relative importance placed on cost and
effectiveness considerations as opposed to essentially nonquantitative
judgments on the consequences of changes in force levels.

Seven alternative strategic force levels, together with their cost implications in constant 1973 dollars, are outlined below. In general they
are based on differing views regarding strategic doctrine, the appropriate rate of weapon system modernization, and necessary force
levels. They are summarized in Table 4-3.

*Alternative 1 is a projection of the administration's program based on
the assumption that a first-round SALT agreement will be reached in
1972.* The program can be characterized as designed to maintain the
triad, with extensive modernization. Its main features are (1) accelerated development of ULMS, (2) continued development of the B-1,
(3) continuation of the MIRV programs for Poseidon and Minuteman
missiles, and (4) expanded research and development to modernize
air defenses. The strategic bomber force would be maintained at present levels, with existing bombers phased out only after being replaced
by the B-1. As a result of a SALT agreement, however, it is assumed
that the Safeguard program would be limited to two sites.

It is estimated that the average annual cost of this program, including indirect costs, would be $18.8 billion over the period 1973–79.

*Alternative 2, a higher option, is based on the assumption that the
SALT talks break down or that no SALT agreement is reached in calendar 1972.* This alternative consequently projects the present program,
including provision for a twelve-site Safeguard system. In addition,

Table 4-3. Average Annual Cost of Strategic Force Alternative Programs, Fiscal Years 1973–79

Total obligational authority in billions of fiscal year 1973 dollars

	Program components					
Alternative	*Land-based missiles*	*Sea-based missiles*	*Bomb-ers*	*Air de-fenses*	*Mis-sile de-fenses*	*Total cost*[a]
1. The present posture, assuming a limited SALT agreement[b]	2.0	4.4	6.5	4.4	1.5	18.8
2. An accelerated program, assuming no SALT agreement[c]	2.5	4.4	7.0	4.4	2.9	21.2
3. A diversified program, assuming no SALT agreement[d]	1.8	3.6	6.7	4.4	2.9	19.4
4. A diad, with accelerated development programs for sea-based missiles and bombers, and limited air defenses[e]	1.1	4.4	7.0	2.2	0.5	15.2
5. A triad, with less effective forces eliminated[f]	1.4	4.4	5.3	2.2	1.5	14.8
6. A triad, with slow modernization[g]	1.8	3.4	5.0	2.2	1.5	13.9
7. Transition to a completely sea-based force[h]	1.1	4.4	2.7	2.2	0.5	10.9

Source: Authors' estimates.

a. This total does not include the proportionate share of the defense agency costs attributable to strategic forces or the cost of civil defense. Under alternative 1, these costs amount to $600 million a year.

b. MIRV Minuteman III; complete Poseidon, accelerated ULMS schedule; moderate B-1 schedule; heavy air defense modernization; two-site Safeguard.

c. MIRV Minuteman II and III; complete Poseidon, accelerated ULMS schedule; accelerated B-1 schedule; heavy air defense modernization; twelve-site Safeguard plus SDM.

d. MIRV Minuteman III; complete Poseidon, moderate ULMS development, development of submarine-launched cruise missile; slow B-1 development, development of standoff bomber; heavy air defense modernization; twelve-site Safeguard plus SDM.

e. Phase out Minuteman and Titan; complete Poseidon, accelerated ULMS development schedule; accelerated B-1 development schedule; air defense for surveillance only; phase out Safeguard and terminate SDM.

f. MIRV Minuteman III, phase out Minuteman II and Titan; complete Poseidon, accelerated ULMS development schedule; phase out older B-52s and FB-111s, moderate B-1 development schedule; air defense for surveillance only; two-site Safeguard.

g. MIRV Minuteman III at slower rate; complete Poseidon, moderate ULMS development schedule; slow B-1 development; air defense for surveillance only; two-site Safeguard.

h. Phase out Minuteman and Titan; complete Poseidon, accelerated ULMS development schedule; phase out bombers; air defense for surveillance only; phase out Safeguard and terminate SDM.

because of the atmosphere generated by failure to reach a SALT agreement, the B-1 program would be accelerated, and all Minuteman missiles would be equipped with MIRVs.

The average annual cost of this alternative is estimated to be $21.2 billion—$2.4 billion more than the present program *with* a SALT agreement.

Alternative 3 seeks further diversification of strategic systems as a means of increasing strategic capability. It also assumes a breakdown in SALT, but would require a much smaller increase in expenditures than alternative 2. The rationale for this alternative is that greater diversification would reduce the importance of any one system and therefore would increase the level of confidence in U.S. strategic deterrence. The objective, however, would be to seek greater diversification by slowing the rate of modernization and thereby limit the increase in cost of any reactions to an impasse in U.S.–Soviet strategic negotiations.

Possibilities for diversification include programs to develop a large subsonic bomber carrying standoff missiles, surface ships carrying ICBMs, and submarine-launched cruise missiles. To offset the cost of these new programs the ULMS and B-1 programs would be slowed down. As in alternative 2, planning would proceed on the basis of a twelve-site Safeguard system, given the assumption that no agreement had been reached in SALT.

This alternative would pose the danger of creating uncertainty in the USSR as to the strategic policies of the United States and would therefore create a danger of Soviet countermeasures. Furthermore, the introduction of new systems would complicate the problem of eventually reaching a SALT agreement.

The average annual cost of this alternative is estimated to be $19.4 billion, $600 million a year more than alternative 1.

Alternative 4, a lower option, would rely primarily on modernized sea-based missiles and bomber forces, phasing out land-based ICBMs as they became vulnerable. Emphasis on air defense would be reduced. In this alternative, concern over the vulnerability of land-based ICBMs is strong enough to cause abandonment of programs to protect them. Planning is based on the assumption that the Minuteman force would be phased out by 1979. ULMS would proceed at an accelerated pace, and an increase in submarine force levels would be explicitly assumed. The B-1 bomber program would be accelerated, on the grounds that the bomber force, as well as the submarine force, would have to be modernized rapidly to make up for phasing out one element of the triad. On the other hand, programs to defend land-based missiles would be terminated, and air defense would be reduced to a surveillance role.

The average annual cost of this alternative would be an estimated $15.2 billion, $3.6 billion less than alternative 1.

Alternative 5, also a lower option, maintains the triad with heavy modernization, but eliminates less effective forces and reduces the role of defensive systems. In this alternative the emphasis would be on efficiency; older model B-52s, the FB-111s, and their associated tankers would be phased out in a year or so because of their marginal contribution to the strategic bomber capability, as would the Minuteman II and Titan missiles. Air defenses would be reduced to a surveillance role, and the Safeguard program would be terminated when the two sites now under construction were completed. The ULMS and B-1 modernization programs would continue at the rate projected in the 1973 budget.

In this alternative, force levels and costs would be reduced more than in proportion to capabilities. Moving in this direction would mean applying a heavy discount to force matching and bargaining chip considerations. It might have the advantage of contributing to stability in the U.S.–Soviet strategic relationship, depending on how it was interpreted by the USSR.

The average annual cost of this alternative is estimated to be $14.8 billion, or $4 billion less than alternative 1.

Alternative 6, a still lower option, maintains the triad with only essential modernization and reduces emphasis on defensive systems. This alternative would reflect confidence that present forces are adequate for deterrence and somewhat reduced concern over growth in Soviet forces generally and over the need to match changes in specific Soviet forces. Development of ULMS and the B-1 would be slowed and their introduction into the force delayed, though the Minuteman III and Poseidon MIRV programs would be completed on schedule. Safeguard deployment would be limited to two sites and air defense reduced to the surveillance role.

The average annual cost of this program is estimated at $13.9 billion, or $4.9 billion less than alternative 1. It would cost almost as much as alternative 5, indicating that the difference between the cost of an accelerated and a slow pace of modernizing offensive systems is about equal to the savings that could be realized from immediately phasing out less effective forces.

Alternative 7, the lowest option, would move gradually to reliance on a sea-based system alone. This option would rest on the justification that a large and modernized sea-based force would be sufficiently effective to provide a high level of confidence in strategic deterrence for the indefinite future. It might be based on the further argument that moving in this direction would make the greatest contribution toward reaching further agreements in SALT and stabilizing the U.S.–Soviet strategic relationship.

The ULMS program would be accelerated as proposed in the 1973 budget, and planning would call for increased submarine force levels in the 1980s. Bomber and land-based missile forces would be phased out by the end of the decade, when ULMS would come into operation. A research and development program on ABM technology would continue, and air defenses would be limited to surveillance.

The average annual cost of this program is estimated to be $10.9 billion, or $7.9 billion less than alternative 1.

Ground Combat Force Alternatives*

The choice among alternative ground combat forces hinges principally on manpower issues: How much manpower will be required? Into what kinds of force units should this manpower be organized? What is the best mixture to maintain between active and reserve components? Should manpower be mobilized through conscription or by an all-volunteer system? And how should ground combat manpower be supported?

These issues are applicable to all military forces, but more so to ground combat forces than to others simply because alternative ground force plans involve chiefly changes in manpower. By the same token, procurement and modernization issues are quantitatively far less significant for ground forces than for other forces. Excluding strategic systems, procurement composes only one-tenth of the Army budget in fiscal 1973, compared with about one-fourth for the Air Force and about one-third for the Navy. Moreover, Army procurement is mostly for equipment having a relatively low unit cost and for consumables; ammunition alone accounts for approximately 40 percent of the total. Only two major acquisition programs are for conventional ground combat forces: a follow-on surface-to-air missile (SAM-D) and ground force candidates for close support aircraft (the Army's Cheyenne and the Marine Corps' Harrier).

In this section, ground force manpower requirements other than for support functions[7] will be discussed in relation to foreign policy con-

---

* Based on an analysis by Martin Binkin and Delbert M. Fowler.

7. Support requirements in relation to combat units are discussed in a later section of this chapter as a factor applicable to all force categories.

siderations, readiness factors, and the constraints imposed by an all-volunteer armed force. Views on these issues in turn provide a basis for outlining ground combat force alternatives.

Foreign Policy

Three broad foreign policy considerations bear heavily on the level and structure of ground combat forces.

First is the relation between strategic objectives and conventional force capabilities. The U.S. posture of strategic "sufficiency," which in effect amounts to acceptance by the United States of approaching nuclear parity with the USSR, is based on recognition by both countries of the unacceptable cost of nuclear warfare. In this sense, strategic parity may be said to emphasize the decoupling of nuclear and conventional force capabilities in regard to the deterrence of conflict. If so, it might increase the risk of conventional war and require a hard reappraisal of what conventional forces are needed for deterrence. In his 1971 Foreign Policy Report, the President stressed this point:

To serve as a realistic deterrent, our general purpose forces, together with those of our allies, must be such as to convince potential enemies that they have nothing to gain by launching conventional attacks. . . .

We and our allies together must be capable of posing unacceptable risks to potential enemies. We must not be in a position of being able to employ only strategic weapons to meet challenges to our interests.[8]

Second, it can be argued that the size of ground combat forces has a unique foreign policy significance, even apart from any consequences flowing from the strategic balance. The number of U.S. ground combat units, where they are deployed, and year-to-year changes in those deployments may be interpreted as signals of U.S. intentions regarding the role it intends to play in world affairs. On this reasoning, reductions in U.S. ground combat forces, or perhaps even an unwillingness to match force buildups by adversaries, could have seriously adverse political and military consequences. For example, it could reinforce the view, already widely held in the world, that the United States will not be able, let alone willing, to protect its allies and to deter conflict. If so, the argument goes, this could encourage adven-

---

8. *U.S. Foreign Policy for the 1970's: Building for Peace*, A Report to the Congress by Richard Nixon, President of the United States (February 25, 1971), p. 179.

turism on the part of potential adversaries of the United States and cause disarray among U.S. allies, especially in an era of nuclear parity when conventional force is the only usable power.

On the other hand, it can be argued that changes in the size, structure, or location of U.S. ground combat forces could stem from a careful reassessment of U.S. interests, of what allies could contribute, and of what potential adversaries would be willing and prepared to do—without raising the dangerous specter described above. For example, U.S. military planning could be based on the view that the United States will not become involved in a ground war in Asia unless an ally is attacked by China. Secretary Laird came close to saying just that in 1971 in his Defense Report:

With regard to U.S. force capabilities in Asia, we do not plan for the long term to maintain separate large U.S. ground combat forces specifically oriented just to this theater. . . . If a large land war involving the United States should occur in Asia, we would, of course, be prepared to mobilize, and would initially use our non-NATO-committed forces as well as portions of those forces based in the U.S. and earmarked for NATO. . . .[9]

One inference that might be drawn from this is that U.S. allies in Asia would be able to deal with "subtheater" or non-Chinese threats with their own military forces, supplemented as necessary by U.S. military assistance or by U.S. air and naval support. Further, the move toward less hostility between the United States and China could be taken to portend less risk of future direct conflict with China; U.S. interests in Southeast Asia might then be reassessed, leading to the conclusion that other contingencies in that area would not warrant U.S. involvement in large-scale ground conflict. In consequence, reductions might be warranted in U.S. ground combat forces based in the Pacific, or based in the continental United States but equipped and oriented toward Asian contingencies.

This point of view could be carried a step further by applying it to the forces the United States maintains for European contingencies as well. The argument here would rest on the proposition that the movement toward East-West détente is well enough established to permit a somewhat less cautious approach to military planning. On this rea-

9. *Fiscal Year 1972–1976 Defense Program and the 1972 Defense Budget*, Statement of Secretary of Defense Melvin R. Laird before the House Armed Services Committee (March 9, 1971), p. 77.

soning, the United States might unilaterally reduce its forces oriented toward European contingencies in order to encourage its European NATO allies to do more themselves to make up for any security deficiencies that emerge. It is argued that reductions in forces, whether for Asia or for Europe, could be carried out in ways that would not provoke precipitate actions either by allies or by potential adversaries. The main point is that the United States, on the basis of a revised foreign policy assessment, would operate on the assumption that it had wider leeway in planning force levels.

Readiness

How quickly will ground forces have to be built up and committed overseas in a crisis or in a conflict? The answer, which depends on factors ranging from the assumed amount of warning time to the assumed international and domestic consequences of mobilization measures, influences decisions on the fundamental structure of ground combat forces.

One such decision concerns the reliance to be placed on reserve forces. In general, the reserve components cost about one-fifth as much to maintain as their active force counterparts. Pay for reserve forces, which are part time, averages one-sixth of that for active forces, but procurement, operations, and maintenance costs are more nearly comparable. While costs are much less, reserve forces obviously would not be as ready for combat as active forces; they would have to be mobilized first and would take longer to prepare for the contingency at hand. Steps could be taken, as they are in the administration's current program, to increase the training of reserve forces and modernize their equipment, but the reserves would still be less usable than active forces at the onset of conflict.

Another variable affecting readiness is the degree to which active forces are maintained at full strength. For example, during the period of large-scale U.S. military activity in Vietnam, divisions in Asia were maintained at full strength, but divisions in Europe and in the United States were maintained at levels ranging as low as 80 percent of full staffing. The same practice was followed in peacetime during the second half of the 1950s, when three of the fourteen active army divisions were in fact training organizations rather than readily deployable combat units. This approach would be adopted in the expectation of saving money at some sacrifice in readiness, which would be kept to acceptable proportions by preparations to have divisions filled out with reservists during a period of crisis.

Conscription versus the All-Volunteer Armed Force

The administration's decision to move rapidly toward an all-volunteer armed force introduces an important fiscal constraint into the consideration of ground force alternatives.[10] The full cost of an all-volunteer force cannot yet be determined, since experience with the system is just beginning to provide information, and the outcome in any event will depend in part on general economic conditions in the United States and on intangible factors, such as prevailing attitudes toward military service. Nevertheless, it is evident that a serious constraint will exist. An increase in ground combat forces without compensatory manpower reductions elsewhere will almost certainly require further incentive pay increases and, consequently, a more than proportionate increase in manpower costs. Furthermore, should recruitment levels with an all-volunteer armed force prove unsatisfactory, additional pay incentives would be required to maintain even present force levels. In itself, this would create pressure to reduce those levels, assuming that the present ratio of manpower to weapons is to be maintained within a reasonably constant total budget.

In theory, conscription could be continued if the all-volunteer armed force proved too costly. The administration is committed, however, to abolishing the draft. The analysis that follows assumes the commitment will be carried out and shows the costs of moving in that direction.

Present Size and Distribution of Ground Force Manpower

Before considering alternative ground force levels, it is useful to note prevailing views as to the adequacy of present forces for European contingencies, since they place the greatest demands on ground forces and therefore are the most significant in determining their level. The military balance in Europe is much better understood now than it was even as recently as ten years ago. For example, total Soviet

10. Issues concerning the all-volunteer armed force are examined later in this chapter.

divisions are no longer compared on a one-for-one basis with forward deployed NATO divisions, since it is recognized that they are vastly different in size, equipment, and capability; furthermore, greater weight is now assigned to the Soviet need to maintain forces in the Far East as a factor limiting the forces that the Russians would mobilize for an invasion of Europe. The question is still moot whether NATO forces could hold off a well coordinated, determined surprise attack by the Warsaw Pact countries. Many military experts flatly deny that they could. However, the doubt rides as much on such questions as the location of different parts of the forces, the mixture of forces available, and the readiness of forces, as it does on the numerical superiority of the Warsaw Pact countries.

In the critical Central European area, immediately available Warsaw Pact troops outnumber NATO's troops by 1.6 to 1; after thirty days of mobilization and reinforcement, the Warsaw Pact could increase its troop superiority to slightly more than 2 to 1. Generally speaking, however, the longer the mobilization continued, the more NATO could overcome its initial inferiority in ground force strength. The Warsaw Pact would have an advantage in tanks, whereas NATO would be stronger in antitank weapons and would have a qualitatively superior tactical air force.

These technical comparisons do not provide a persuasive answer, one way or the other, as to the stability of the present military balance in Europe. Political and other factors carry great weight. Even in military terms, opinion ranges from the optimistic view that a nonnuclear balance could be maintained with a substantially smaller Western effort, to despair of being able to redress imbalances. Holders of the extreme views are in the minority. Leaving political considerations aside, most military experts believe, and the statistics themselves suggest, that total NATO forces—if they are kept ready and are given adequate warning—may be close to the strength that is needed to continue to deter a conventional attack.[11] Furthermore, the U.S. component of these forces at strength levels near those maintained in the 1960s and programmed for the 1970s is believed to be a plausible backup to the NATO commitment.

Apart from questions about the adequacy of forces in relation to requirements, it is useful to understand how U.S. military and civilian

11. John Newhouse with others, *U.S. Troops in Europe: Issues, Costs, and Choices* (Brookings Institution, 1971), especially pp. 50–65.

manpower is employed in the sixteen active divisions and nine reserve divisions that now compose the ground forces. In Table 4-4, manpower use is shown separately for active ground combat forces, for active support forces, and for the reserve components.

For planning purposes, each Army division is assumed to require 48,000 men to conduct sustained wartime operations. About 16,000

Table 4-4. Manpower Composition of Active and Reserve Ground Combat Forces, End of Fiscal Year 1973

	Army			Marine Corps		
		Manpower *(thousands)*			Manpower *(thousands)*	
Description	*Number*	*Military*	*Civilian*	*Number*	*Military*	*Civilian*
Active forces, total	. . .	841	440	. . .	198	20
Ground combat forces, total	. . .	435	35	. . .	79[a]	. . .
Divisions	13	190	. . .	3	54	. . .
Combat support increments	14	200	. . .	3[b]	25	. . .
Special mission forces[c]	. . .	45	. . .	. . .	. . .	. . .
Other combat forces, total[d]	. . .	7	13	. . .	28	. . .
Support forces, total	. . .	399	392	. . .	91	20
Communications, intelligence, research and development, free world support	. . .	52	37	. . .	2	. . .
Base operations, training, command, and logistics	. . .	347	355	. . .	89	20
Reserve forces, total[e]	. . .	714	. . .	. . .	46	. . .
Ground combat forces, total	. . .	566	. . .	. . .	36	. . .
Divisions	8	120	. . .	1	18[a]	. . .
Combat support increments	28	446	. . .	1	18	. . .
Other combat forces, total	. . .	9	. . .	. . .	10	. . .
Support forces, total	. . .	139	. . .	. . .	. . .	. . .

Sources: Derived from U.S. Department of Defense, "Military Manpower Requirements Report for FY-1973" (February 1972; processed); and *The Budget of the United States Government—Appendix, Fiscal Year 1973.*

a. Includes helicopter squadron personnel from Marine air wings.

b. The Marine Corps does not use the same support increment planning concept as the Army. By implication, however, the Marine Corps has about 25,000 personnel performing duties similar to those performed by Army combat support increments. Also, the Navy provides some support to the Marine Corps.

c. Includes missile forces and special brigades in Panama, Alaska, and Berlin.

d. Other combat forces, for the Army, consists of strategic forces, and for the Marine Corps, primarily of Marine tactical air wings.

e. In paid status.

of these are assigned to the combat division; the remaining 32,000 are assigned to nondivisional units of battalion size or smaller that support the combat forces. For analytical convenience, these units are grouped into support increments of a size applicable to a division. Support in this sense includes artillery battalions, cavalry regiments, and helicopter combat units, as well as engineering, communications, and maintenance units. About half of the support manpower (about 16,000) is in units considered necessary for division operations in the initial stages of combat (initial support increments). The remainder are assumed to be needed only to sustain combat operations (sustaining support increments) and thus do not have to be deployed until after sixty days of combat.

The reduction in active Army manpower from the Vietnam peak has fallen somewhat disproportionately on support increments, as evidenced by the fact that the ratio of combat support units to active army combat divisions has declined from 1.4 in fiscal 1971 to 1.1 in fiscal 1973. This implies that greater reliance would be placed on reserve components for sustaining combat support functions should a conflict arise. No compensating increase has occurred in reserve manpower.

In the case of the Marine Corps, the basic division is somewhat larger than the Army division but has a smaller combat support element outside the division structure. Despite experience to the contrary in Korea and again in Vietnam, the theory is that Marine divisions would be immediately committed to high intensity combat and then be relieved by Army units if the conflict were protracted; hence, they do not have to be as fully staffed for sustained operations. The three active Marine divisions are designed and equipped primarily to provide a seaborne capability for armed intervention. In this capacity they presumably would be required more for contingencies in Asia, Africa, the Middle East, and the Western Hemisphere than in Europe. A Marine division has not been used in the European area since the First World War, but one is now earmarked for European contingencies.

Six Illustrative Budgets

In the following discussion, six alternative ground combat force structures are outlined, each emphasizing different foreign policy and readiness requirements. Cost projections assume that conscription will end in 1973 and that any significant increase in military manpower would require additional pay incentives. Where it is appropriate, a specific allowance is included for this factor. It should be emphasized, however, that there is a wide margin of uncertainty in allowing for this factor, which is of crucial importance in estimating the costs of alternative ground force structures. There is no persuasive evidence that the pay incentives provided in the 1973 budget to achieve an all-volunteer force at the present manpower level will in fact be adequate. At higher manpower levels, the margin of uncertainty widens greatly, all the more so when qualitative as well as quantitative requirements are introduced.

The rationale for each posture and the organizational structure it calls for are described below. Cost and force level data for the period 1973–79 are summarized in Table 4-5.

Alternative 1 is a projection of the administration's present program. It puts priority on maintaining strong U.S. ground forces for NATO, deployed both in Europe and in the United States, and in using this posture to press the European NATO countries to strengthen their contribution to NATO's conventional force deterrent. The position on Asia is hedged; substantial ground forces continue to be maintained for Asian contingencies, including two divisions deployed in the Western Pacific and Korea, but intervention in a major ground action in Asia would require the use of a large part of the ground forces maintained for European contingencies.

Under this program, sixteen active division forces (thirteen Army and three Marine) would be maintained through the 1970s. Each division force would average 30,000 men, divided about equally between the combat division itself and combat support units. Planning calls for the reserves to supply the additional combat support units that would be needed in the case of sustained conflict. Therefore, this program calls for substantial investment to modernize their equipment and to improve their readiness.

The cost of the administration's program (in constant 1973 dollars), allowing for indirect costs and for some modest future reductions in military manpower as outlined in Chapter 3, would average $22.2 billion a year over the period 1973–79.

Alternative 2, a higher option, would emphasize the need to improve the readiness of active ground combat forces for deterrence, in view of

Table 4-5. Active and Reserve Ground Combat Force Alternative Structures and Budgets, Fiscal Years 1973–79

Description	Alternative					
	1	*2*	*3*	*4*	*5*	*6*
	Present program	*Increase in readiness*	*Increase in force structure*	*Mixed active and reserve divisions*	*No ground war in Asia*	*No ground war in Asia; reduced reserve forces*
Active forces						
Army						
Combat divisions	13	13	16	13[a]	11	11
Combat support increments	14	26	17	14	12	12
Manpower (thousands)[b]	835[c]	1,035	950	800	740	740
Marine Corps						
Combat divisions	3	3	3	3	2	2
Manpower (thousands)	198	198	198	198	158	158
Reserve forces						
Army						
Combat divisions	8	8	8	8[a]	10	8
Combat support increments	28	16	31	28	30	26
Manpower (paid status)						
(thousands)	714	544	759	714[a]	774	684
Marine Corps						
Divisions	1	1	1	1	2	1
Manpower (paid status)						
(thousands)	46	46	46	46	71	46
Average annual cost, 1973–79 (total obligational authority in billions of fiscal year 1973 dollars)	22.2	25.4	24.8	21.7	20.6	19.9

Source: Derived by authors.

a. In alternative 4, the thirteen active Army divisions comprise seven divisions with three active brigades each and six divisions of two active brigades each. The third brigade in these six divisions is a reserve brigade associated with the active division for training and administration. Under this alternative, the number of reserve divisions remains at eight, since it is assumed that the reserve brigades assigned to active divisions were nondivisional units. Reserve manpower would be unchanged.

b. Manpower totals include support manpower other than combat support. In the present program (alternative 1), non-combat support amounts to 399,000. (See Table 4-4.) In alternatives calling for an increase in divisional manpower, a minimal allowance is made, primarily for training requirements. In alternatives calling for a reduction in divisional manpower, this support manpower is proportionately reduced.

c. Fiscal year 1973 Army end-strength is programmed to be 841,000. When further Vietnam withdrawals and the effects of technological improvements are considered, the average Army baseline strength is estimated to be 835,000.

approaching U.S.–Soviet strategic parity. Priority would be placed on removing doubt as to the ability of the United States to fight a protracted war in Europe, and in particular to achieve a strong ground force position there during the first three months of conflict. During this critical period, the availability of reserve forces might be restricted by a possible delay in the decision to mobilize and by the time required to bring them up to a satisfactory level of readiness.

Under this alternative, the present thirteen active division forces would be provided with a full complement of support for sustained operations. The manning of all units, however, would remain at the normal peacetime standard of 90 percent. Thus, each division force would average approximately 43,000 men.

An increase in active military manpower of approximately 200,000, including an austere allowance for training and support needs, would be required. This raises the question of how large a pay incentive would be needed to attract the necessary number of volunteers. The estimates cover a wide range because of uncertainty stemming from lack of experience with a volunteer service and because the answer depends partly on the approach taken. If heavy reliance were placed on enlistment bonuses paid only to new Army recruits, the additional cost might be as little as $750 million a year, but the rate of reenlistment might be too low. At the other extreme, heavy reliance on across-the-board pay increases for all military personnel would drive the cost to more than $4 billion a year. For present purposes $1.5 billion a year is allowed for this factor on the assumption that incentive pay, while not restricted to bonuses, would be concentrated on pay raises for the lowest grades.

In addition, this alternative would mean higher operating and maintenance costs for the active forces but significant offsetting savings from a reduction in reserve forces.

The average annual cost of this alternative is estimated to be $25.4 billion, or $3.2 billion more than the present program.

Alternative 3, also a higher option, would increase ground combat strength by emphasizing structure rather than readiness. A move in this direction would be intended to provide more flexibility to intervene in strength in Asia as well as in Europe. It would represent a return to the ground force structure of the 1960s, whether or not it was described as a force appropriate to a two and one-half war strategy.

Under this alternative, three additional Army divisions would be activated. They would be manned at the current level of 30,000 each, and reserve components would continue to be relied on for sustaining support forces. The additional manpower requirement, including a minimum allowance for nondivisional personnel, would then be 115,000 in active strength and approximately 45,000 reservists to provide sustaining support for the three new divisions. Maintaining these higher force levels would cost about $800 million a year for incentive pay increases. In addition, three division sets of equipment and sustaining procurement would be needed.

The average annual cost of this alternative is estimated to be $24.8

billion a year, somewhat lower than alternative 2, but $2.6 billion a year more than the present program.

Alternative 4, a lower option, would rely more heavily on reserve components in manning the present number of ground force divisions. Under this alternative, one active brigade in each of six Army divisions based in the United States would be deactivated and replaced with a reserve brigade. (Each division is composed of three brigades.) The Army divisions deployed outside the continental United States and the three active Marine divisions would continue to have three active brigades each.[12]

Maintaining sixteen ground force divisions would reduce possible adverse political effects stemming from the reduction in active strength. Readiness of the six reorganized divisions would be dimin ished. At the same time, the readiness of the six reserve brigades would be improved, since they would train alongside their active counterparts, use modern equipment, and benefit from experienced commanders.

This alternative would reduce active military strength by about 35,000—less than the equivalent of two divisions because supporting increments would not be proportionately reduced. The average annual cost of this alternative is estimated to be $21.7 billion, or $500 million a year below the present program.

Alternative 5, a lower-cost option, would be based on the planning assumption that the United States would not become involved in a localized ground conflict in Asia. This option would represent a fairly literal interpretation of the one and one-half war strategy; in practice, it would indicate either that the United States placed heavy reliance on nuclear deterrence of a major war in Asia or that it clearly disassociated itself from defense commitments in that region. If the United States should be required to intervene against a Chinese attack, or even against a North Korean action against South Korea, planning would call for the large-scale use of forces oriented to European contingencies. Maintaining priority for Europe probably would require the withdrawal of ground forces now deployed in Asia.

Under this alternative, two Army divisions and one Marine division would be deactivated. As a hedge against mobilization requirements for a major conflict either in Europe or in Asia, these divisions would

12. This reorganization would leave the eight National Guard divisions intact if the brigades assigned to active divisions were taken from nondivisional reserve forces. Reserve manpower also would be unchanged.

be added to reserve forces. The reduction of 135,000 in active military manpower (including reductions in general support) for this alternative probably would assure attainment of an all-volunteer armed force without pay incentives beyond those provided in the 1973 budget. On the other hand, increasing the number of reserve divisions would aggravate the problem of recruiting reserves and would necessitate pay incentives for this purpose.

The estimated average annual cost of alternative 5 is $20.6 billion, or $1.6 billion less than the present program.

Alternative 6, a still lower option, would be the same as alternative 5, except that it would leave the number of reserve divisions unchanged. Total strength would be reduced by three active division forces and by two reserve support increments. The reasoning in this case would be that the likelihood of conflict had declined enough to make unnecessary the margin of safety that additional reserve strength might provide.

The average annual cost of alternative 6 is estimated to be $19.9 billion, or $2.3 billion less than the present program.

Navy General Purpose Force Alternatives*

Naval procurement budgets and future force levels are closely linked. Decisions taken over the next few years on key shipbuilding programs will largely determine force levels in the 1980s. Therefore, in considering current procurement requests it is essential to decide first on future force level objectives. Three questions are particularly important: (1) How many aircraft carriers should the United States maintain? (2) How many escort ships should defend these carriers and carry out other defensive missions? And (3) what other forces should be maintained to protect sea lanes in time of crisis or conflict? The carrier question is overriding, since it affects all the others. In this section these three issues are examined in turn and are used as a basis for outlining alternative naval force levels and budgets.

How Many Carriers?

While the United States now operates seventeen carriers, a decline to twelve by the end of the 1970s is probably unavoidable. Several fac-

* Based on an analysis by Arnold M. Kuzmack.

tors combine to account for this: the block obsolescence problem that characterizes the present carrier fleet; the long time that is needed for building a carrier; limits on shipbuilding capacity; and fiscal pressures, since a new carrier now costs approximately $1 billion. In these circumstances, three broad carrier force level alternatives can be distinguished:

• *To postpone the reduction to twelve carriers as long as possible*, operating the Second World War carriers now in the fleet until they become overage. This policy would be based on the view that more carriers are needed, even though the force will have to go down to twelve by about 1980.

• *To reduce the present carrier force to twelve*, retiring four Second World War carriers now before they become overage. This policy would be based on the view that some reduction in the number of carriers is feasible now because carriers will become increasingly vulnerable in a war involving the USSR, and because in any event it would be advantageous to put greater reliance on land-based tactical air forces because of cost considerations.[13]

• *To reduce the current carrier force to nine*, on the assumption that this force would be adequate from now through the 1980s. This policy would assume that carriers would not be usable against land targets in a war with the USSR and that nine carriers would be sufficient for other missions in a war in which the USSR was involved, for other types of wars, and for peacetime political and crisis needs.

These alternative force levels imply significantly different long-term carrier construction programs, which can be calculated on the basis of the following assumptions: (1) that the carrier has a useful life of thirty years, the usual Navy planning assumption for major ships (or, put differently, that the carrier can be operated for more than thirty years only at increasingly higher maintenance and operating costs); and (2) that it takes six years to build a carrier from the time it is authorized. These assumptions would mean that the seven Second World War carriers now in service will have been retired by 1980. They also highlight the block obsolescence problem stemming from the fact that seven carriers (Forrestal class) were commissioned between 1955 and 1961. In order to maintain a twelve-carrier force that

13. Considerations affecting the vulnerability of the aircraft carrier and their effect on carrier force requirements are discussed in Charles L. Schultze and others, *Setting National Priorities: The 1972 Budget* (Brookings Institution, 1971), pp. 71–81.

includes no ships older than thirty years, seven new carriers would have to be authorized between 1979 and 1985, or an average of more than one a year. Without attempting a temporary acceleration in construction at very high cost, the United States could deal with this bulge in the replacement schedule by any, or a combination, of the following approaches: begin replacements earlier; keep some carriers in operation for more than thirty years; or reduce the number of carriers—say, to nine—which was noted above as the lowest force requirement for the 1980s.

The carrier construction schedule implications of these three alternative approaches are shown in Table 4-6. They indicate the following conclusions. To maintain a twelve-carrier force in the 1980s and beyond, it will be necessary to authorize the next carrier in fiscal 1974, as the administration proposes, and to authorize a new carrier every other year for a virtually indefinite period. Or construction could be slowed to about one new carrier every two and one-half years by main-

Table 4-6. Illustrative Aircraft Carrier Construction Schedules, 1973–2005

Force level: twelve carriers; authorize construction every 2 years		Force level: twelve carriers; authorize construction every 2½ years		Force level: nine carriers; authorize construction every 2½ years	
Authoriza-tion year for each new carrier	*Age of the carrier It would replace (years)*	*Authoriza-tion year for each new carrier*	*Age of the carrier it would replace (years)*	*Authoriza-tion year for each new carrier*	*Age of the carrier it would replace (years)*
1974	30	1974	30	...	...
1976	27	1977	28	...	...
1978	28	1979	29	...	...
1980	29	1982	31	1979	28
1982	29	1984	31	1982	29
1984	29	1987	32	1984	29
1986	31	1989	34	1987	32
1988	33	1992	37	1989	34
1990	31	1994	35	1992	33
1992	30	1997	35	1994	32
1997	30	1999	32	1997	30
1999	30	2002	33	1999	30

Average retirement age (years)

29.8	32.3	30.8

Year of initiation of new cycle

2004	2004	2005

Source: Derived by authors.

taining a twelve-carrier force and replacing them at an average age of slightly more than thirty-two years instead of thirty. (However, two would have to be operated until age thirty-five and one until age thirty-seven.) This approach would mean lower procurement costs and higher operating costs, but it would also suggest the need to authorize construction of the next carrier in fiscal 1974 as part of an orderly replacement program. Or, finally, if it were decided to move to a nine-carrier force, the construction of a new carrier could be postponed until near the end of the decade, but it would be necessary to build one new carrier every two and one-half years during the 1980s. Obviously, other combinations of construction schedules, average carrier life spans, and force levels are possible.

How Many Escort Ships?

Escort ships are designed to protect naval task forces and merchant ship convoys from attack by enemy submarines, aircraft, or other surface ships. All of the ships involved are equipped with antisubmarine warfare (ASW) detection systems and weapons to provide an antisubmarine screen around the escorted force. Some escort ships are also equipped with guided surface-to-air missiles (SAMs) to defend against enemy aircraft or to shoot down enemy missiles launched by surface ships, aircraft, or submarines. In addition, the Navy is designing a new surface-to-surface missile, called Harpoon, which will be installed on escort ships and increase their capabilities to combat enemy surface ships.

The Navy now operates 226 escort ships of all types. About 80 of them date from the Second World War and will be retired over the course of this decade. Two major procurement programs are intended to replace many of these ships. First is the purchase of 30 new destroyers (DD-963), each costing about $90 million; 16 were previously authorized, and $612 million is requested in the fiscal 1973 budget to build 7 more. Second is the contemplated purchase of 50 new destroyer escorts designated the patrol frigate (PF), costing $45 million to $50 million each. In the 1973 budget, $193 million is requested to complete the design and to build the first patrol frigate. Because the ships dating from the Second World War will have to be phased out more rapidly than the new ones are introduced, the total number of escort ships will decline until 1976–77 and then begin to rise. By the early 1980s, when the two new programs are completed, the Navy will have 230 to 240 escort ships, or slightly more than it has now.

A determination of escort ship requirements depends on four functions: (1) to protect carriers, (2) to protect the ships needed to support and replenish carrier task forces, (3) to protect amphibious forces in an assault operation, and (4) to perform "other missions," notably to protect convoys of merchant ships carrying supplies to military forces deployed overseas during the early phases of a war, and "surveillance," which may include coordinated antisubmarine operations with ASW aircraft.

The number of ships needed to perform these functions depends principally on the number of carriers in the force (since carrier protection is the largest single requirement), on whether it is assumed that the carriers will be engaged in action against Soviet naval forces or limited to actions where they would face less sophisticated threats, and on whether it may be assumed for force planning purposes that additional ships do not have to be specifically maintained to perform "other missions." In addition, the characteristics of the ships need to be considered, since the escort function includes protecting against submarine, air, and surface attacks. Requirements also would vary depending on whether the task force is all nuclear-powered or whether it includes conventionally powered elements.

Alternative escort ship requirements based on these factors are shown in Table 4-7. While these force levels are illustrative in character and the presentation is highly simplified, the calculations themselves are based on the specific characteristics of the ships that are, or will be, in service, and on requirements for carrying out specific functions. They suggest the following conclusions:

• By the early 1980s, present programs will provide a level of escort ship protection that is roughly 50 percent higher than the levels that would result from applying the planning factors of the late 1960s to a twelve-carrier force. The need to protect U.S. carriers against Soviet land-based air and submarine attacks are the dominating factor in these requirements. Indeed, if the objective of improving the survivability of the carrier in all circumstances were carried to its logical conclusion, increased expenditures would be needed in many areas, including research and development in antisubmarine warfare and perhaps for escort ship programs as well.

• Applying the lower planning factors used in the late 1960s would

Table 4-7. Escort Ship Requirements under Alternative Assumptions Regarding Size of Carrier Force and Enemy Capabilities

Number of ships

Size of carrier force and purpose of ships	Enemy threat		
	High[a]	Medium[b]	Low[c]
Twelve-carrier force			
To protect carriers	88	68	48
To protect carrier support ships	55	33	27
To protect amphibious forces	56	56	40
For other missions (surveillance, military convoys, and so forth)	30	...	...
Total	229	157	115
Nine-carrier force			
To protect carriers	64[d]	50	36
To protect carrier support ships	50[d]	30	25
To protect amphibious forces	56	56	40
For other missions (surveillance, military convoys, and so forth)	30[d]	...	...
Total	200	136	101

Source: Authors' estimates. These figures are based on detailed calculations that take into account the mix of different types of escort ships needed: those equipped with surface-to-air missiles for air defense; those having the necessary speed to keep up with carriers; and those that are nuclear propelled and suitable for use in all nuclear powered task forces. For a discussion of methodology, see Arnold M. Kuzmack, *Naval Force Levels and Modernization: An Analysis of Shipbuilding Requirements* (Brookings Institution, 1971), App. B.

a. High threat assumes aircraft carriers could be involved in most actions against Soviet forces and that other missions require additional escort ships.

b. Medium threat assumes planning factors roughly equal to those used during the 1960s. No allowance is made for other missions on the ground that this function can be carried out by escort ships not otherwise engaged, by the U.S. reserve fleet, and by allied ships maintained by other NATO countries.

c. Low threat assumes aircraft carriers would not be used in most actions involving Soviet forces.

d. Based on the mechanical application of the assumed planning factors, even though the carrier forces would be out of balance with the assumed threat.

mean that the United States already had enough modern escort ships in service or authorized to meet requirements for a twelve-carrier task force in the 1980s. These planning factors assume that such functions as protecting military convoys could be carried out by ships allocated to protect amphibious assaults (since amphibious groups would not be continuously employed), by ships in the U.S. reserve, and by the approximately 200 destroyer-type ships maintained by U.S. allies in NATO. Since no additional escort ships beyond those already funded through fiscal 1972 would be needed at least until the end of the 1970s, it would be possible to cancel the DD-963 program beginning with the 1973 budget request, as well as the patrol frigate program.

• A nine-carrier force in the 1980s, whose rationale (discussed in the preceding section) assumes that carriers would not be used where Soviet forces could concentrate against them, would lead to an escort ship force less than one-half the size of the force currently programmed. In fact, even without any further construction, the existing force of escort ships would be greatly in excess of requirements.

Other Force Requirements to Protect Sea Lanes

As Soviet naval forces have been modernized and have ranged out more widely, the United States has placed growing emphasis on "sea control," or the ability to retain use of the seas despite attempted interdiction by enemy forces. Aside from escort ships, carrying out this mission would require other U.S. naval forces (leaving aside the question of how much reliance should be placed on allied forces to perform this mission). Two of those forces are considered here: land- and. sea-based ASW aircraft, and the Navy's newly proposed "sea control ship."

Land- and Sea-based ASW Aircraft

Approximately $900 million is requested in the 1973 budget for acquisition of these systems, of which three-fourths is for sea-based and one-fourth for land-based aircraft. This program is likely to continue at roughly this level for several years.

Although few dispute the need for land-based ASW aircraft, there is considerable controversy over force requirements for their sea-based counterparts. The idea of sea-basing ASW aircraft was developed as a result of the severe range limitations on land-based ASW planes during the Second World War and the consequently large areas in the mid-Atlantic that were not protected by aircraft. Such arguments are of less importance now, since the mission radius of the P-3C, our present land-based ASW aircraft, is on the order of 1,500 nautical miles. This range permits coverage of the entire Mediterranean from a single base in Greece or Italy, of the entire Norwegian Sea from one base in either Great Britain, Iceland, or Norway, and of the North Atlantic convoy lanes from U.S., Canadian, and British bases. Trans-Pacific convoy lanes can be covered from bases on U.S. territory (Hawaii, Midway, Wake, Guam) and one or two bases near the other ends of the lanes—Japan, Korea, the Philippines, or Thailand. Thus dependence on foreign bases, which might be unreliable, would be at a minimum. Furthermore, present land-based ASW aircraft reflect the technology of the late 1950s: newer airframes are now available that could be adapted to ASW use and permit mission radii on the order of 2,500 or 3,000 nautical miles.

Given these considerations, it is argued that the major justification for modernizing the sea-based ASW aircraft force is to protect U.S. naval and merchant shipping in areas where land bases may not be available—mainly the Indian Ocean, the South Atlantic, and the South Pacific, where the United States has few commitments and its security interests are of low priority. The cost of maintaining this capability is substantial, since it involves, in addition to the aircraft, the need to build and operate carrier decks and their escort and supporting vessels. Hence, alternatives to the present program can be considered that would call for reducing the procurement of sea-based ASW aircraft (S-3A) and for placing more emphasis on land-based ASW aircraft, at some sacrifice in flexibility but at a reduced cost.

The Sea Control Ship

Only $10 million is requested in the fiscal 1973 budget for the sea control ship, but the SCS could develop into a major procurement program. This vessel, eight of which might be purchased initially, would be a relatively austere ship capable of carrying aircraft and costing only $90 million. The actual composition of the aircraft group it carries would be tailored to the particular mission of each vessel. A typical deck load would consist of ASW helicopters and vertical or short takeoff and landing (V/STOL) fighters, up to a total of seventeen. The ship would not be able to operate conventional fixed-wing aircraft, as it would not be equipped with catapults or arresting gear. Additionally, the SCS would be limited to speeds of about twenty knots in order to keep costs down.

Proponents of the SCS program stress the vessel's multimission potentiality. First, it would be used to protect merchant shipping from air, surface, and submarine threats. V/STOL fighters would be used to defend against the first two, and helicopters against the third. Second, it is argued that the SCS could play a unique peacetime, or crisis-control, role in situations that require a U.S. naval presence—for example, to carry out an armed evacuation of American citizens abroad —but in which the dispatch of a full-sized aircraft carrier might seem provocative.

On the other hand, it can be argued that the SCS would be a redundant and unnecessary element in the already substantial shipbuilding program. This view rests on the following contentions. First, the SCS would have little capability to defend against air and surface threats to U.S. or allied merchant shipping mounted by the Soviet Union. This requirement is likely to be an all-or-nothing proposition: either the threat will not exist, or it will be so substantial as to require aircraft carriers or land-based air defense. Second, the ship's ASW capabilities would, in effect, consist of keeping three helicopters continuously in the air, plus holding a few additional helicopters in reserve for reaction purposes. The cost of acquiring this capability would be $210 million ($90 million for the ship and $120 million for thirty ASW helicopters, the number necessary to keep seventeen on board). The question is whether this function could be carried out about as well and at less cost by putting small helicopters on escort ships and building more of the ships, if needed. Third, it is argued that the peacetime and crisis-control mission could be carried out by ships now in service or under construction, particularly by air-capable amphibious assault ships (such as the LHA or LPH) or by two or three destroyers carrying the Harpoon missile.

Four Illustrative Budgets

On the basis of the discussion above, four illustrative force level alternatives and their cost implications for fiscal 1973–79, in constant 1973 dollars, can be outlined. They are shown in detail in Table 4-8 and are summarized here.

The first is a projection of the administration's program. The reduction to twelve carriers would be postponed as long as possible, and a new nuclear-powered carrier would be authorized every other year beginning in fiscal 1974. The number of escort ships would provide a high level of protection compared to previous standards. All obsolete sea-based ASW aircraft would be replaced, and procurement of land-based ASW aircraft would continue at the present rate of twenty-four a year, with transition to a follow-on aircraft in fiscal 1978. The first sea control ship would be authorized in fiscal 1974, and two a year in subsequent years. Procurement of nuclear-powered attack submarines would continue at the rate of six a year, as is proposed in the 1973 budget; beginning in fiscal 1975, they would be equipped with cruise

Table 4-8. Naval General Purpose Force Alternative Structures and Budgets, Fiscal Years 1973–79

	Alternative							
	1		*2*		*3*		*4*	
	Present program		*Greater sea control*		*Less stringent planning factors*		*Smaller carrier force*	
Type of ship or craft and budget item	*1973*	*1979*	*1973*	*1979*	*1973*	*1979*	*1973*	*1979*
Number of units at end of fiscal year								
Aircraft carriers	16	14	16	14	12	12	12	9
Sea control ships	...	5	...	7	...	5	...	3
Escort ships	207	200	227	204	157	165	157	141
Nuclear attack submarines	60	83	60	84	60	83	60	74
Antisubmarine warfare (ASW) sea-based air groups	4	4	5	5	4	4	...	...
ASW land-based air squadrons	24	24	24	32	24	24	24	30
Number of units procured, 1973–79								
Aircraft carriers	3		3		1		...	
Sea control ships	11		18		11		5	
Nuclear frigates (DLGN)	...		7		...		...	
Destroyers (DD-963)	16		16		...		...	
Destroyer escorts (PF)	59		82		...		...	
Nuclear attack submarines	42		48		42		...	
Sea-based ASW aircraft (S-3A)	162		192		162		...	
Land-based ASW aircraft (P-3C)	120		144		120		96	
Land-based follow-on ASW aircraft (VPX)	64		106		64		88	
Average annual cost, 1973–79 (total obligational authority in billions of fiscal year 1973 dollars)	16.2		17.8		14.2		12.1	

Source: Derived by authors.

missiles. The cost of this program, including indirect costs but excluding the cost of naval tactical aircraft, would average $16.2 billion a year over the period 1973–79.

The second, and higher, alternative would be based on a perceived need to provide greater defensive capabilities so as to be credible against the Soviet Navy, particularly against the submarine threat to shipping. Major changes from the administration's present program would be provision of larger escort ship forces, both by postponing retirement of older ships and increasing procurement programs; a moderate increase in procurement of the sea control ship and submarines; procurement of one nuclear-powered guided-missile frigate a year; and, logically, an increase in research and development expenditures on ASW, which for these purposes is arbitrarily set at a total of $300 million a year. The total cost of this program would average $17.8 billion a year, or $1.6 billion more than the estimated annual cost of the current posture.

The third, and lower, alternative would provide for moving to a twelve-carrier force now and for reductions in the level of escort protection. It would be based on two assumptions: (1) that the arguments in favor of a twelve-carrier force in 1980 are equally valid today, and (2) that a somewhat more relaxed view of the Soviet naval threat or a less ambitious response to it is warranted. This option would make possible a saving in carrier operating costs between now and 1980. Also, the fourth nuclear-powered carrier would be authorized in fiscal 1974, but authorizations of any additional carriers would be postponed for the balance of the 1970s—at the cost of keeping some carriers in operation for more than thirty years during the second half of the 1980s. This would be consistent with a lower emphasis on carrier-based tactical aircraft. It also would reflect uncertainty as to the nature of naval requirements in 1990 and hence an unwillingness to make large expenditures in the near future to satisfy uncertain requirements in the far distant future.

Under this alternative, escort requirements for carrier protection and other purposes would be based on planning factors developed in the late 1960s, rather than on the much higher figures reflected in the present program. This would mean lower force levels now and no escort ship procurement during the period of the projection. In other re, spects, a strong ASW program would be maintained: procurement of ASW aircraft and attack submarines would be virtually unchanged from alternative 1. The cost of this program would average $14.2 billion a year, or $2.0 billion a year less than alternative 1. It would also call for reductions in naval tactical air programs, which are discussed in the next section.

The fourth and still lower alternative would provide for moving toward a nine-carrier force over the next two years and for corresponding reductions in escort and support ships and in ASW procurement. This alternative would be based on the proposition that aircraft carriers are too vulnerable to be relied on in any situation in which the

Soviet Union could concentrate its land-based aircraft and submarines against them. Authorization of the fourth nuclear carrier could be postponed until the end of the 1970s. The drastic reduction in ASW requirements stemming from the assumptions underlying this alternative would justify the following measures: no additional procurement of escort ships or attack submarines for the remainder of the decade; canceling procurement of new sea-based ASW aircraft (S-3A), compensated partially by an increased purchase of land-based ASW aircraft; and reducing the proposed sea control ship program. The annual cost of this alternative would average $12.1 billion a year, or more than $4 billion a year less than alternative 1. It would also call for terminating F-14 procurement, as is pointed out below.

Tactical Air Alternatives*

There has been a steady trend since the end of the Second World War to substitute firepower and mobility for combat manpower on the battlefield. Tactical airpower presents an outstanding example of this trend, yet nowhere is the question of economic justification for new weapons more pressing, or more elusive, than for these forces. New aircraft not only cost several times as much as current aircraft to procure, but cost more to operate and maintain; consequently their extra costs extend throughout their service life and affect budgets up to ten years ahead. If the geometric cost growth of the past twenty-five years continues, the next generation of aircraft—that is, the systems that will begin coming into use in the mid-1980s to replace today's F-14s and F-15s—are likely to cost $40 million to $50 million each. Hence, controversy over the number and type of force levels and weapon systems is likely to intensify.

In considering alternative force levels, three related sets of issues should be kept in mind. First, what missions are to be carried out? Second, are they to be performed by specialized or multipurpose aircraft? Third, how do decisions on specific aircraft relate to missions, force levels, and costs?

Missions and Design Philosophy

Traditionally, air power doctrine distinguishes two broad operational areas, strategic and tactical. Where strategic missions are flown

* Based on an analysis by William D. White.

against an enemy's heartland, tactical missions are, as a rule, closely confined to the battlefield, though in the case of deep interdiction, which is aimed at stemming the flow of supplies near its sources of origin, this distinction often blurs.

Tactical air missions can be classified as follows:

• *Air superiority,* viewed by the Air Force as the first-priority mission, aims at achieving freedom of operation over a defined area, usually by destroying or driving off the enemy's air forces. It can also entail attacking specialized ground targets, such as airfields and air defense installations. Air superiority permits the other tactical air missions greater freedom of operation.

• *Close air support* bolsters the firepower of ground forces on the battlefield. It delivers munitions directly against an enemy's forward combat forces, usually when they are in proximity to friendly ground units. In this role, close air support is a highly mobile though expensive addition to, or substitute for, artillery.

• *Interdiction* aims to reduce the initiatives open to the enemy by disrupting his supplies and communications, and by inhibiting the movement of his combat forces. Interdiction might be described as "battlefield," "forward," or "deep," depending on which part of the enemy's lines of communication are attacked.

• *Air defense* strives to prevent enemy close air support or interdiction missions against one's own forces, wherever air supremacy over the battlefield is not otherwise assured. If a competent ground control and early warning radar network exists, aircraft for this mission need not have great range and payload capabilities nor elaborate avionics systems. This is the mission for which most Soviet tactical aircraft, especially the MIG series, are best suited.

• *Reconnaissance and electronic warfare* are specialized aircraft missions. Reconnaissance collects visual, photographic, and electronic intelligence data useful for such purposes as selecting targets and deploying ground forces. Electronic warfare missions use electronic countermeasures to reduce the effectiveness of the enemy's air defenses.

• *Tactical airlift* provides short-range, high-speed mobility for friendly ground forces. Where land lines are insecure, it may also be the best way to support forward deployments. Helicopters, as well as fixed-wing aircraft that can operate from marginal landing fields, are used in this role.

From the standpoint of aircraft design, this diversity of missions calls for a variety of performance characteristics. The relevant questions are, first, what is the aircraft intended to do—fight other aircraft, attack ground targets, gather intelligence, or transport troops, equipment, and supplies? Second, where and under what conditions must the aircraft operate—over the battlefield, in a contested or permissive air environment, or deep over enemy territory? Finally, what fraction of full effectiveness should tactical air forces have in bad weather? The cost of all-weather avionic equipment can be very high, and the equipment itself has a profound influence on the design of the aircraft.

Two contending schools of thought exist as to how to deal most efficiently with this diversity in mission requirements. The "commonality" school argues for fewer types of aircraft, reasoning that large savings, primarily in development costs but also in production, operations, and maintenance, can be realized by designing one airplane capable of carrying out a variety of missions with only minor modifications. The most celebrated example of this approach is the much-criticized F-111, though the less controversial F-4 Phantom II fighter/bomber has effectively served the Air Force, the Navy, and the Marine Corps in many roles since the early 1960s. There are two basic disadvantages to this approach. Although the multipurpose aircraft can do several jobs, it is generally less efficient in any one of them than is an aircraft designed specifically for that purpose. A second problem is that the plane usually ends up being designed to meet the specifications of the most demanding mission—in the case of tactical aircraft, the deep interdiction mission with an all-weather capability. In Southeast Asia, these expensive qualities proved not only unneeded but actually a hindrance in performing missions such as close air support.

The alternative is to design and build specialized aircraft to perform one particular mission. Proponents of this approach argue that it is more efficient for two reasons: unit costs are lower because many of the expensive, but not always needed, features built into multipurpose aircraft are omitted; and special-purpose aircraft, being designed for one mission, perform it better. The disadvantages are the loss of the economies that are potentially available from standardization and, more important, the loss of flexibility that multipurpose aircraft can provide, unless this flexibility is purchased through larger forces. Over the years, the United States has gradually increased its reliance on multipurpose aircraft for combat missions. Whether this trend should be reversed in the face of mounting unit costs is now a major issue.

Design philosophy and costs inevitably are linked to the controversy over the relative importance to be assigned to various tactical air missions. For example, how worthwhile are deep penetration missions for air supremacy and interdiction in view of their high cost and the questionable effectiveness of these missions in the past? Second, how feasible would it be to use carriers in a conventional war with the Soviet Union? The answer to the latter question is crucial for decisions on the type and number of aircraft needed for carrier defense and, more generally, on the appropriate mixture of land-based and sea-based aircraft in the force. Another issue concerns the amount of close air support a combat division requires in various contingencies. Finally, to what extent can tactical airpower employed in a close support role substitute for ground weapons and forces?

The escalating costs of multipurpose aircraft, which tend to outrun the cost rise for most specialized aircraft, are likely to make the economies of specialization look better for the future. As this happens, today's doctrine, specifically its mission priorities, will be increasingly challenged: can explicit planning judgments be made that result in the deemphasis or elimination of missions that are expensive to carry out and yield the most uncertain returns? For purposes of outlining alternatives, the two most important judgments concern the emphasis to be placed on maintaining a deep interdiction capability and the requirements believed to be necessary for carrier defense. Positions taken on these two questions exert an overriding effect on weapon system decisions, force levels, and budgets.

Specific Aircraft Issues

Against this background, it is useful to examine the current debate over major aircraft procurement decisions and to identify the underlying issues.

The Navy's F-14

The purpose of this system is to replace the F-4 in defending carriers. Its potentialities lie in its swing wing, which will permit it to remain aloft for longer periods in anticipation of an air attack, and in the long range and altitude agility of the Phoenix missile, which the F-14 is designed to carry. If the F-14 and the Phoenix missile measure up to design criteria, the system will be a substantial improvement over the F-4 in the role of carrier air defense.

Whether the improvement is worth the cost or, more fundamentally, whether aircraft carriers are defensible even with the F-14 against attack by a concentration of Soviet submarines, missile-carrying surface vessels, and land-based aircraft is an open question. Differing answers to this question lead to a dramatic variation in the possible range of budgetary costs. If it is believed that the carrier could be defended in all circumstances with F-14s and if the F-14 were also procured for the Marine air wings, the eventual purchase could rise to 1,000 or more planes instead of the 301 now contemplated. The increase in cost over the present program could be on the order of $8 billion. At the other extreme, if it is assumed for planning purposes that the carrier would not be used against land targets in a war involving the Soviet Union, there would be no need for F-14s, since the F-4 is satisfactory for carrier defense in all other contingencies. In this event, the F-14 program could be terminated, with a saving in procurement costs of approximately $3 billion.

In any event, another factor has to be considered. There continues to be an appreciable technical risk that the F-14 system, particularly the highly complex Phoenix missile, will not perform fully up to its specifications.

The Air Force's F-15

Also intended as a successor to the F-4, this time in its capacity as the Air Force's first line fighter, the F-15 is designed primarily as a long-range air superiority aircraft capable of penetrating far into hostile air space to defeat an enemy's most advanced fighters. Like the F-14, it will be a large airplane—around 40,000 pounds—that can readily be configured to attack ground targets on all types of interdiction missions as well.

Because the F-15 design is similar in some respects to that of the Navy's F-14, it has periodically been suggested that the Defense Department economize by dropping one program or the other and letting both services use the survivor, as they now use the F-4 and were supposed to have used the F-111. Savings from such a move now, however, would probably be relatively small, since most of the research and development money in both programs has been spent.

The key budgetary issue in this case relates to mission requirements, not to possible savings from common use. Whether the F-15 is needed depends on where it is necessary to achieve air superiority and by what means—aerial combat or with emphasis on attacking air bases. For deep interdiction missions, air superiority is necessary far into hostile territory, and this is what the F-15 is designed to achieve. If deep penetration missions were deemphasized or eliminated, and if the United States were willing to settle for less than air supremacy, which can be achieved only by air base attacks, the F-15 program presumably would be canceled in favor of a new lightweight fighter. Such an aircraft could do a better job of fighting enemy aircraft over the battlefield and probably could be built in quantity at a cost well below that of the F-4—that is, at about one-fourth the cost of the F-15. The Air Force is just starting a program to develop a lightweight fighter. These planes could be substituted for an equivalent number of F-15s to save money, or within the same budget the Air Force could buy and operate nearly four lightweight fighters at the same cost as a single F-15. Various combinations obviously would be possible. At the outside, replacing the F-15 program with a lightweight fighter program on a one-for-one basis would save approximately $3.5 billion in acquisition costs and several hundred million dollars annually in operating costs. In that event, deep penetration tactical missions could be carried out on a relatively small scale by the F-111 and by whatever F-4s were retained in the force structure, although the feasibility of doing so without an F-15 escort against improved enemy interceptors in the years ahead might be questionable.

Close Air Support Aircraft

The third key issue concerns the place close air support should occupy in the hierarchy of mission priorities and which weapon system, or combination of systems, is needed for that purpose. The Air Force, the Army, and the Marines have all put forth candidates for the role. Also in the competition are the already operational A-7 light attack aircraft and several improved helicopters developed independently by private industry. Among these contenders, only the Army's technically troubled Cheyenne helicopter gunship has to date drawn heavy congressional criticism. Largely because of its complex avionics, the Cheyenne is also the most expensive proposed system, costing more than $5 million each. The Marine Corps' program to procure 114

British-built Harriers has not been subject to serious controversy, perhaps because the total cost (though not the unit cost of $4.7 million) is relatively small. The Air Force A-X is received with considerable enthusiasm by cost-conscious critics as a relatively inexpensive (about $2.1 million) replacement for part of the multipurpose aircraft inventory.

Both the Army and the Marine Corps cite special needs as the primary justification for their respective systems. The Army wants an all-weather tank killer for NATO defense (the Cheyenne armed with wire-guided missiles); the Marines want an aircraft (the V/STOL Harrier) that can come ashore just behind the land forces in an amphibious operation, flying close support first from aboard ship, then from the beachhead, and finally from forward positions as the ground forces move inland. The Air Force, which is strictly a supplier, not a consumer of close air support, believes the A-X could adequately meet requirements across the board with greater accuracy and at less than half the unit costs of any of its rivals. With its simplicity of design and redundant flight systems, the A-X is expected to be much less vulnerable to ground fire than the complex Cheyenne and will have a very great range and payload advantage over the Harrier. As critics see it, the A-X's main disadvantage is its lack of an all-weather avionic system—a factor that is largely responsible for its lower price. An all-weather A-XB at nearly double the cost could become a reality sometime after 1975.

As matters now stand, the Air Force plans to buy about 700 A-Xs through fiscal 1979, enough to equip five or six wings, probably concurrently phasing out several wings of F-4s to the Air National Guard. The Marines will have three Harrier squadrons in operation by fiscal 1976. The Army's Cheyenne has thus far failed to achieve a firm procurement schedule. Should the Cheyenne program be terminated, the Army has at least two less expensive alternative helicopter gunship designs ready to put forward in its place.

Two key budgetary issues relate to close air support systems. First, will the A-X become the standard for all services, and if so, how many A-X aircraft should be designed to have an all-weather capability? The difference between the low- and high-cost options on this issue probably would be on the order of $1 billion in acquisition costs over the remainder of the 1970s. Second, should A-X squadrons be added to present force levels, as might be inferred from the Nixon doctrine's emphasis on air support for threatened allies, or should they replace an equivalent number of F-4 squadrons? Adding them to the force and retaining five wings of F-4s would mean at least $0.5 billion in acquisition and operating costs over the period 1973–79.

Four Illustrative Budgets

Alternative decisions on the major issues discussed above could be combined in many different ways. For simple comparative purposes, they may be grouped into four alternative force levels and budgets, each corresponding to a sharply defined posture. The four illustrative postures are (1) a projection of the administration's program on the basis of previously announced plans and the decisions in the fiscal 1973 budget; (2) a higher budget, such as might accompany an increased role for tactical air power under the Nixon doctrine, based on more extensive modernization and higher force levels; (3) a lower budget, based on nearly the same force levels as in alternative 1 but with a slower pace of modernization and somewhat greater reliance on less expensive specialized aircraft; and (4) a still lower alternative that greatly deemphasizes deep penetration missions, thereby permitting reduced force levels made up of specialized rather than multipurpose aircraft. The four alternatives are summarized below in terms of rationale, key procurement decisions, and force levels. Table 4-9 lists 1973–79 force levels and cost data, in constant 1973 dollars.

Alternative 1 is a projection of the administration's present posture. As was pointed out in Chapter 3, the current posture is dominated by the prospective introduction of the F-14 and the F-15 into the force. In projecting this program through the rest of the 1970s, it is assumed that the F-14 program will drop to the minimum rate needed to maintain a production capability after 301 aircraft are acquired; that, as presently contemplated, about 730 F-15s will be procured; and that the 15 A-X squadrons expected to be in operation by 1979 will replace an equal number of F-4 squadrons. It is assumed that the lightweight fighter, like previous short-range fighter designs, will not be procured in quantity. A gradual conversion of tactical airlift forces to all-jet aircraft is also assumed. The number of aircraft assigned to operational units is projected to decline slightly between 1973 and 1975 and remain about level thereafter. Capabilities should continue to increase throughout the period as a consequence of the newer types being

Table 4-9. Tactical Air Force Alternative Structures and Budgets, Fiscal Years 1973–79

	Alternative							
	1		*2*		*3*		*4*	
	Present program		*Faster modernization and increased force levels*		*Slower modernization*		*Reduced emphasis on the deep interdiction mission*	
Type of aircraft and budget item	*1973*	*1979*	*1973*	*1979*	*1973*	*1979*	*1973*	*1979*
Number of squadrons at end of fiscal year								
F-14	1	12	1	37	1	6	1	...
F-15	...	15	...	15	...	...	...	...
A-X	...	15	...	24a	...	15	...	15
Lightweight fighter (LWF)	...	...	...	...	...	6	...	15
F-4b	76	47	76	27	76	48	69	23
Other fighter and attack	80	68	80	79	70	62	70	59
All other tactical	113	109	113	117	113	109	107	85
Total	270	266	270	299	260	246	247	197
Number of aircraft procured, 1973–79								
F-14		270c		940		60		...
F-15		730		730		...		...
A-X		700		1,060		700		700
LWF		...		...		300		650
F-4		100		140		360		...
Other fighter and attackd		710		930		600		560
All other tactical		740e		1,200e,f		480		310
Total		3,250		5,000		2,500		2,220
1973–79 average annual cost (total obligational authority in billions of fiscal year 1973 dollars)		14.3		18.0		11.9		10.5

Source: Derived by authors.

a. Includes three wings of all-weather version (A-XB).

b. Air force squadron total adjusted to 24 unit equipment equivalents.

c. Assumes continued procurement funding for 15 aircraft per year beyond present program in order to sustain production capability.

d. All options include 300 F-5Es for military assistance to U.S. allies.

e. Includes reconnaissance versions of F-14 and F-15, and advanced medium short takeoff and landing transport (AMST) to begin replacing C-130s.

f. Includes light vertical or short takeoff and landing aircraft to replace C-7s and C-123s, plus aircraft to form additional operations squadrons.

introduced. The average estimated cost of this alternative, including indirect costs, is $14.3 billion a year over the period 1973–79.[14]

Alternative 2, a higher option, postulates more extensive modernization and gradually increasing force levels for both the Air Force and the Navy in fiscal 1975 and beyond. In general this option would maintain the historical pace at which new weapons have been introduced, despite escalating costs, on the grounds that cost and effectiveness factors are too elusive to be used with confidence and that tactical air modernization is the most appropriate expression of U.S. conventional force deterrence. In terms of mission priorities, this option

14. This does not include costs associated with aircraft carriers, which are included in Navy general purpose forces.

would rest on the argument that increased U.S. tactical airpower, both over the battlefield and on deep penetration missions, is necessary as a substitute for U.S. ground forces under the Nixon doctrine and to counter possible Soviet aircraft modernization programs.

The following changes from the present program would be made: (1) Procurement of the F-14 would revert to the initial Navy program for 710 aircraft, enough to equip 14 carrier air wings, plus an additional 300 for the Marine Corps; (2) the A-X program would be expanded to include an additional 360 "B" models with an all-weather capability, and all A-X squadrons would be introduced as additions to force levels, not as replacements for existing F-4 squadrons; (3) the program to buy a new jet transport to replace the C-130 would be accelerated, and another program would be initiated to develop and procure a smaller V/STOL tactical transport; and (4) the Navy would add backup air wings, plus an extra squadron for each of its Nimitz class carriers.

Under this program, costs would rise rapidly, averaging $18 billion over the period, or almost $4 billion a year more than the projected cost under present plans.

Alternative 3, a lower option, would maintain nearly the same force levels as the present program but cut back heavily on the pace of modernization. It would be argued in support of this option that weapon technology is no longer providing improvements in capability at a fast enough pace to justify the cost of buying new systems every ten years, as has been the practice since the Second World War. On this reasoning, introducing new systems should await technological breakthroughs or at least an accumulation of innovations; meanwhile, improvements should be added insofar as possible as modifications to existing designs. In terms of mission priorities, this alternative would be based on the view that carriers would have a diminished role in a conventional war with the USSR and that some deemphasis of the deep interdiction role is warranted.

Procurement of the Navy's F-14 would be ended after fiscal 1973, with provision for an orderly phase-out of the program and enough aircraft initially to equip three carrier air wings. Further development of the Air Force F-15 would be halted; none would be procured. In place of the F-14 and F-15, an improved version of the F-4 would be procured gradually by both services to replace operational attrition of the earlier models and thus to maintain a deep penetration capability. This option assumes that development of the lightweight fighter would continue, but that only a small number (two wings) would be procured in the second half of the 1970s to provide limited battlefield air cover.

Procurement of the Phoenix missile, developed primarily for the F-14, would also be halted. Research and development for a similar missile would continue at a reduced level and would concentrate on the problem of adapting the system to the improved F-4.

Alternative 3 would leave the present A-X program unchanged, but would drop Cheyenne development immediately on grounds of cost, vulnerability, and the contention that an all-weather close air support capability would not be essential.

Airlift modernization would be shifted from the large four-engine jet now envisioned toward the development of a smaller tactical V/STOL transport. The argument would be that the C-130 does not need a replacement, but that a need exists for a smaller transport to fill the gap between the helicopters and the C-130.

Force levels would remain constant except for a reduction of two naval air wings corresponding to an accelerated move toward a twelve-carrier Navy, as called for in alternative 3 under Navy general purpose forces.

The cost of this program would average $11.9 billion a year, or $2.4 billion less than the current posture.

Alternative 4, a still lower option, would virtually eliminate the deep penetration requirements associated with interdiction and total air supremacy missions. Instead, greater reliance would be placed on less expensive special-purpose aircraft, and force levels would be reduced. It would be consistent with maintaining a force of nine carriers, operated on the assumption they would not be used against land targets in a war involving the Soviet Union.

The F-14 and F-15 programs would both be terminated, including cancellation of F-14 procurement in fiscal 1973. Rather than procuring an improved F-4, as in alternative 3, the Air Force would begin reducing its F-4 strength immediately, eliminating four wings altogether and replacing the remaining ten with five wings each of A-Xs and lightweight fighters as they became available. (Development of the latter would be accelerated.) Tactical air capability over the battlefield would almost certainly be increased rather than diminished by this shift in force composition, though U.S. forces could not expect to have absolute air supremacy. The planned three wings of A-7s and four wings of F-111s would be retained, the latter primarily for deep penetration with tactical nuclear weapons.

Some capability to attack well beyond the battlefield would be retained in the form of Navy A-6s and F-4s. Option 4 also assumes a gradual reduction in the number of Navy carrier air wings to nine and a reduction in Marine Corps tactical air strength to two wings. The former would be consistent with reduced carrier strength; the latter would be justified on the ground that two Marine air wings would be adequate to support the scale of amphibious operations possible with present sealift capabilities.

The cost of this program would average $10.5 billion a year, or almost $4 billion less than the current posture, as outlined in alternative 1.

Support Level Alternatives*

In examining alternatives for the major combat force categories, it has been assumed that the ratio of support to combat forces remained constant. Obviously, this would not necessarily be the case. Choices exist on such questions as how many military units to place on one military base, how much training to give, how often to overhaul equipment, how frequently to rotate personnel, or how large a headquarters staff to have. Decisions on how forces should be supported have a decided impact on the size of the defense budget, and, since they involve manpower almost exclusively, their impact will grow as manpower costs rise. Unfortunately, the criteria of sufficiency for support forces lack precision, perhaps more so than for other forces.

Analysis of the desirable ratio of support to combat forces is plagued by a problem of definition. For present purposes, combat capability is measured by an Army combat soldier, an Air Force flying hour, and a Navy ship steaming hour. Strictly speaking, these are not measures of military output, but they are the major elements of the demand for support. The cost of supporting this combat capability has direct and indirect components.

Direct support consists of activities performed within a major combat command. Thus, it includes personnel in combat units (for exam-

* Based on an analysis by Martin Binkin.

Table 4-10. Support Costs per Unit, Army Combat Soldier, Air Force Flying Hour, and Navy Steaming Hour, Selected Fiscal Years, 1964–73

Total obligational authority in thousands of fiscal year 1973 dollars

Unit	1964	1968	1970	1972	1973
Army combat soldier					
Direct support	6.5	7.9	7.3	7.5	7.1
Indirect support	11.7	15.9	15.3	17.5	16.8
Air Force flying hour					
Direct support	1.4	1.4	1.4	1.4	1.4
Indirect support	1.3	1.4	1.5	1.7	1.7
Navy ship steaming hour					
Direct support	2.2	2.2	2.6	2.6	2.3
Indirect support	2.3	2.3	3.3	3.4	3.2

Sources: *The Budget of the United States Government—Appendix*, various years; and, for activity measures, *Department of Defense Appropriations*, Hearings before the Senate and House Committees on Appropriations, various years. Support costs include operation and maintenance costs and military personnel costs. Direct support costs are assumed to be in the same proportion to total direct operating costs as direct support military manpower is to total direct military manpower.

ple, clerks and drivers) and complete support units assigned to a combat organization (for example, an engineering battalion in an Army division force).[15] *Indirect support* includes centralized or service-wide activities that are not identifiable with a single defense mission (for example, logistics, training, personnel, headquarters, communications, and intelligence).

On the basis of these definitions, trends in total support have been estimated for selected fiscal years over the period 1964–73. The results, calculated in dollars of constant purchasing power, are shown in Table 4-10. The contrast between trends in direct and in indirect support is striking. Over the years 1964–73, direct support costs per unit of combat capability remained constant for the Air Force, varied little for the Navy, and changed moderately for the Army. Even in the case of the Army, where direct support costs are now approximately 10 percent higher than in 1964, the trend seems to be sharply downward. On the other hand, indirect support costs per unit of combat capability are 30 to 45 percent higher for all three services than they were in 1964 and substantially higher than in 1968.

Caution should be used in drawing inferences from these data. First, no significance should be attached to the wide differences in the ratio of support to military output among the three services. Neither the

15. The initial and sustaining support increments discussed under ground forces fall in the category of direct support.

measurements of activity used nor the data lend themselves to such a comparison. Second, comparison of support costs between any two years must take into consideration the change in sophistication and effectiveness of weapons during the period. For example, while the data in Table 4-10 show that it will cost $16,800 to provide indirect support for one Army combat soldier in fiscal 1973, compared to $11,700 in 1964, it could be argued that the soldier today is better trained, better equipped, and has more firepower than his 1964 counterpart, and that his increased effectiveness is in part the consequence of better support. This argument would have less force in comparisons with 1968. It is more difficult to point to significant improvements in capability since fiscal 1968 that would justify the continued increase in support levels; in fact, support levels in fiscal 1968, at the peak of the Vietnam war, probably were abnormally high because of the long logistic and personnel pipeline the war required.

What decisions would be involved in considering alternative support levels?[16] While there is a wide range of issues, budget costs would depend heavily on a relatively small number of decisions. These concern the movement and training of military personnel and the maintenance of equipment. For example, shorter tours of duty would mean higher costs for training, transportation, and personnel movement. During the war in Vietnam, the cost of these activities was necessarily very high because tours of duty there were restricted to one year. And it remains high even though the war has diminished; military personnel in fiscal 1972 moved, on an average, every ten months. A change of only one month in the average tour length would involve costs or savings of $200 million a year.

Training is another important variable. All military personnel are given basic training, and a large fraction are given additional specialized training. Relatively small changes in the length of training courses, or in the size and number of formal training courses in relation to on-the-job training, would mean substantial differences in the number of personnel needed for the training establishment. For example, a change of 10 percent in the length of specialized training courses would involve costs or savings of $100 million a year.

That support costs sometimes depend on other than military con-

16. A comprehensive examination of the issues and choices appears in a staff paper by Martin Binkin, *Support Costs in the Defense Budget: The Submerged One-Third* (Brookings Institution, 1972).

siderations is evident in regard to military bases. The costs of operating these bases in fiscal 1973 will account for nearly 10 percent of the defense budget. Since 1968 the number of bases has not declined in proportion to the reduction in military forces and manpower, presumably because of domestic political constraints. Deputy Secretary of Defense David Packard estimated that $1 billion would be saved if excess military bases could be closed.[17]

The budgetary significance of this range of issues, specifically those applying to indirect support costs, can be stated as follows. If fiscal 1973 baseline combat forces were supported at the fiscal 1968 level, support costs would be reduced by $3 billion; if they were supported at the fiscal 1964 level, support costs would be reduced by $6 billion. No precision is claimed for these figures as indicators of support requirements. However, two implications seem warranted: (1) The reduction in military personnel since 1968 has been applied more than proportionately to combat forces and less than proportionately to the support base—the naval shore establishment and the Army and Air Force training and logistical systems; and (2) analysis of support force requirements and specific decisions concerning them merit at least as much attention as those concerning the major combat force categories.

Manpower Policy Issues*

This section discusses the cost of, and prospects for, an all-volunteer force, the method of computing military pay increases, and proposals to reform the military retired-pay system. The first issue—the all-volunteer armed force—could be centrally important to future budgets and force plans. The other two subjects are examples of the kinds of questions that must be considered now that manpower costs absorb so much of the defense budget.

The All-Volunteer Armed Force

President Nixon has set as a goal an all-volunteer armed force by June 1973. The fiscal 1973 budget provides $3.1 billion for this pro-

---

* Based on an analysis by Martin Binkin.
17. *Washington Post*, Dec. 14, 1971.

gram, of which $2.5 billion represents the cost of pay raises legislated by the Congress in 1971, $200 million is for administrative items such as barracks improvement and recruitment expenditures, and $400 million is earmarked for pay incentives that will be offered during the fiscal year.

The Congress pushed this program at a faster pace, and in somewhat different directions, than the administration intended. In its 1972 budget the administration had proposed a two-phase program: it planned to spend $1.5 billion in fiscal 1972 and to base its request for 1973, as to both the size and the composition of incentives, on the results achieved in the first year. In acting on the program, the Congress took the view that the full pay increases would have to be offered in fiscal 1972 if there were to be a reasonable chance of achieving the goal within two years. Hence, it almost doubled the size of the first year program to $2.7 billion[18] and thus virtually precluded the experimental approach the administration had proposed.

In comparison with the 1970 estimates of the President's Commission on an All-Volunteer Armed Force (known as the Gates Commission), the 1972 program as passed by the Congress is nearly the same in total cost but different in composition. The Gates Commission would have concentrated almost all of the incentive pay increases on the lower grades. It specifically concluded that compensation for the higher military grades was already comparable to civilian pay scales and that personnel in these grades did not need additional pay incentives to encourage them to remain in the service. The program as enacted substantially increased pay in the lower grades, but at the same time provided some increases for all other grades.

Given the present program, what are the prospects for achieving the goal? As matters stand now, the draft will end in June 1973. In his 1972 Defense Report, Secretary Laird took an essentially noncommittal position in assessing these prospects. He noted an encouraging increase in the rate of enlistment even before the pay incentives came into effect but emphasized that results were still far short of what would be needed to attain an all-volunteer force. To date, experience is lacking on which to base a conclusive judgment.

Two different requirements may be said to exist—a short-run, or transitional requirement, and a long-run, or sustaining requirement.

18. The actual cost in fiscal 1972 is estimated at $1.9 billion, since the pay raise will be in effect for only part of the year.

In the transitional period—the next two years—requirements will be higher because of the need to replace the large number of draftees and draft-motivated enlistees now in the service. Most of them will leave when their terms of service expire. After that, retention rates presumably will rise, and the annual need for new enlistments will decline. The Defense Department estimates that it will be necessary to enlist 515,000 volunteers in fiscal 1973 to sustain the present active force. No official estimates are available for longer-term requirements. The data presented by the Gates Commission indicate that once an all-volunteer force is attained, sustaining requirements could be on the order of 350,000 enlistments a year.

How many volunteers can be expected in fiscal 1973? Available evidence based on actual experience in 1971, adjusted for the existence of the draft, suggests that 265,000 would volunteer for the armed services even without allowance for the effect of pay incentives. According to the Gates Commission, the effect of these pay increases can be estimated by applying an "elasticity factor" of 1.25; that is, a 10 percent increase in pay should increase enlistments by 12.5 percent. Wide differences of opinion exist as to what elasticity factor should be used, and, given the lack of direct experimentation, this is understandable. Estimates made by others are both higher and lower than the average figure of 1.25 used by the Gates Commission. Applying the Gates Commission elasticity estimate to the increase in the compensation of recruits since November 1971 would indicate that approximately 115,000 additional volunteers will be enlisted, which would mean total enlistments of 380,000 in fiscal 1973.

This estimated rate of enlistment would be ample for the longer-term or sustaining requirement, but would fall short by approximately 135,000 of meeting the transitional requirement in fiscal 1973 and, by a smaller amount, of meeting requirements in fiscal 1974. The short-term problem could be managed by one or more of the following measures:

• Request funds for an additional pay incentive—for example, special enlistment bonuses for the next two years. This might cost $3 billion if bonuses were paid to all new enlistees over the two-year period.

• Relax intelligence and physical standards. A large number of potential volunteers are now turned away because they do not meet present requirements.

• Increase quotas for women. Women volunteers are often turned away not because they fail to meet standards, but because of limits on the number of positions for which they are now considered to qualify.

• Allow military manpower levels to go down temporarily, perhaps with undermanning concentrated in support units.

• Substitute civilian for military personnel. The Gates Commission estimated that this could extend to 106,000 military positions with no loss in effectiveness. It should be noted that possibilities for "civilianization" are considerably greater for the Air Force (76,000 of the 106,000), which has a heavy concentration of U.S.-based support personnel, than for the other services.

• Extend the draft for one year, perhaps with a reduced ceiling on the number to be drafted.

Apart from the prospective shortfall in enlistments during the transitional period, the all-volunteer force will also create problems for maintaining the reserve components at desired levels. The number of volunteers for reserve and guard units has fallen sharply since the threat of the draft has been reduced. These units are understrength now. While reserve personnel benefited from incentive pay increases at the same rate as active personnel, early indications are that these incentives will not be sufficient to attract enough enlistments. The 1973 budget therefore requests $80 million for enlistment bonuses for reserves. Should a shortfall nevertheless occur, the measures suggested above for the active military forces could be used also for the reserve components.

These considerations highlight the need to develop alternative approaches to the problems of attaining an all-volunteer armed force in calendar 1972—before the expiration of the draft law exerts pressure for precipitate action. An example of precipitate action would be to base the ultimate decision on an all-volunteer armed force—whether to achieve it or abandon it—principally on the transitional rather than on the longer-term enlistment requirements. Both requirements must be faced, but they call for different measures. If this distinction is not kept in mind, the question may be decided on the wrong grounds, and resources may be wasted as well.

Computing Military Pay Increases

Applying the comparability pay legislation to military personnel involves a special problem in that part of military compensation consists of pay, and part of various allowances, some of which are furnished in kind. For example, an average of 73 percent of military compensation[19] is in basic pay, 14 percent in quarters allowances, 8 percent in subsistence allowances, and 5 percent in tax advantages. In the military pay act of 1967, the Congress directed that (1) when federal civilian pay was increased, comparable increases for military compensation were to apply to allowances as well as to basic pay; and (2) the total increase was to be reflected in basic pay alone. Thus a given percentage increase in federal civilian pay has been accompanied by a higher rate of increase in basic military pay. In January 1972, for example, when federal civilian pay was increased by 5.5 percent, basic military pay was increased by 7.2 percent, the difference being the increase in basic pay estimated to be necessary to provide a 5.5 percent increase in allowances.

This formula has resulted in several anomalies:

• Military personnel who receive quarters and subsistence in kind are now in addition being compensated for the effects of inflation. In 1972, for example, 58 percent of military personnel were furnished quarters in lieu of allowances.

• Those military personnel not receiving quarters had their monetary allowances increased in fiscal 1972 as part of the package of incentives to achieve an all-volunteer service. In this sense, this group has been compensated twice for the same purpose.

• Additionally, retired pay costs are higher than they would otherwise be because they are calculated solely on basic military pay rather than on total military compensation.

Initially, this formula probably was designed to benefit those in the lower enlisted grades, though it applies automatically to the higher grades as well. Almost all of those in the lower grades receive quarters and subsistence in kind. In 1967, at the time of the military pay act, their compensation was inordinately low. Since then, however, the comparability and incentive pay increases combined have presumably corrected this inequity. Maintaining the formula now tends to increase compensation for some military personnel above the amount required to keep military pay comparable to pay in the civilian sector;

19. Military compensation defined in this way is called "regular military compensation." It does not include special bonuses such as combat and flight pay, or fringe benefits such as exchange, commissary, and medical privileges, and a noncontributory retirement system.

eventually it may overshoot the pay level required for an all-volunteer force. For example, if those receiving quarters in kind had not at the same time received cost-of-living adjustments for this factor, the total cost of the military pay increase in fiscal 1972 would have been approximately $100 million lower. Furthermore, by 1977 the cost of retired pay would be about $100 million a year less than is now projected. It follows that continuing the present formula will have a cumulative future impact on both pay components.

A more fundamental question is worth noting. The military pay structure is already so complex that military personnel understandably have difficulty in valuing accurately the various elements that make up military compensation. In 1967 a special Department of Defense study group (the Hubbell Committee) recommended an overhaul of the military pay system that would replace military basic pay and allowances with a salary system. This recommendation was subsequently endorsed by the Gates Commission. Making the method of military compensation similar to practice in the civilian sector would avoid misunderstandings and at the same time improve the accuracy of comparisons between military and civilian pay. Both are the more important because of the growing cost of defense manpower and the goal of achieving an all-volunteer armed force.

Proposals to Reform the Military Retired Pay System

In Chapter 3, the cost of military retirement benefits was projected to increase, in constant dollars, from $4.9 billion in fiscal 1973 to $6.6 billion in fiscal 1979. This rising trend is likely to continue through the 1980s, causing retired pay to absorb an increasing share of the defense budget. Partly because of this trend, the President established an interagency committee to study the system and to develop legislative proposals. The fiscal 1973 budget provides $300 million to cover the first-year cost of changes in the system, but no indications are given as to the intended use of these funds.

To show the nature of the issues that could be involved in changing the system, some of the major proposals of the interagency committee are summarized below:

• To increase benefits for those remaining in the service more than twenty-five years and to reduce benefits for those staying less than twenty-five years. This change would have the effect of reducing personnel turnover in the active service as well as the total cost of retired pay.

• To base retired pay on the average of the highest three consecutive years, as in the federal civil service, rather than on pay at the time of retirement.

• To reduce social security benefits for military retirees. At present, military retirees, by contributing to social security, are eligible for benefits under that program in addition to benefits under the military retirement system.

• To align military retirees' survivorship benefits with those applicable to federal civil service retirees.

• To make comparable changes in retired benefits for reserve personnel.

The committee also addressed itself to the thorny problem of whether military retired pay increases, which are now pegged to changes in the cost-of-living index as is the case for federal civilian retirees, should be recomputed each time there is a real increase in active duty pay. Recomputation was the rule before 1958, and there is considerable pressure from military retirees to resume this practice. The committee recognized the equity arguments for doing so but concluded that a return to continuing recomputation was unwarranted. As a compromise, it recommended a one-time recomputation for persons now retired, which would be made under specified conditions as to age and length of service.

Some of the proposals would increase retirement costs, and others would reduce them. The committee estimated that its proposals, taken together, would result in the following costs (−) or savings (+) in future years (in millions of current dollars):

Year	Annual cost or saving
1973	−250
1975	−386
1980	−228
1990	+1,900

Each proposal must of course be examined on its merits. The point is that these kinds of changes would almost inevitably increase costs in the short run, so as to avoid penalizing those already in the system, but would result in very large savings over the long term. Indeed, the committee estimated that the cumulative effect of its proposals would be a net saving of $35 billion by the year 2000. While no significance need be attached to the specific figure, it indicates the stakes involved. If present trends continue, military retired pay will impose a growing burden on the defense budget that is largely independent of current defense requirements.

Weapon Acquisition Policies*

Concern over U.S. weapon system acquisition policies exists inside and outside the government. In reporting out the fiscal 1972 defense appropriations bill, the Senate Committee on Armed Services said:

> If defense budgets are to remain more or less constant, as now seems likely, and consume an ever smaller part of the nation's resources, then the present development and procurement policies are no longer open to us. They only point the way to burdensome increases in defense spending, inadequate forces for defense, or to both of those unacceptable alternatives.[20]

In presenting the fiscal 1973 defense budget, Secretary of Defense Laird shared the congressional concern:

> All of our new national security strategy planning , , , will be undermined if we are not able to continue the progress that has been started in improving our weapons acquisition process. . . .
> But I must say again that we are not out of the woods.[21]

Outside the government, criticism of Defense Department weapon programs has been widespread and harsh for several years. Charges leveled at the "military-industrial complex" have gained credibility because of serious trouble in weapon acquisition programs. Dissatisfaction centers principally on the cost and performance of new systems and on the lack of choices in weapon development.

Costs and Performance

The problem of costs has two aspects. First is the consistent record of sizable growth in the cost of a weapon system during the period of

* Based on an analysis by Lester Fettig.

20. *Authorizing Appropriations for Fiscal Year 1972 for Military Procurement, Research and Development, for the Construction of Facilities for the Safeguard Anti-Ballistic Missile System, Reserve Component Strength, and for Other Purposes*, S. Rpt. 92-359, 92 Cong. 1 sess. (1971), p. 19.

21. *Defense Department Report, FY 1973*, pp. 15, 16.

development and production. This aspect of the problem was described in Chapter 3. The second is the marked increase in the unit cost of a weapon system from one generation to the next. Between 1950 and 1968 the real cost of the average bomber and military transport plane increased three times and of the average fighter nearly eight times. This cost experience resulted principally from the higher performance demanded of each system and the increasing complexity of the system needed to achieve it. These factors can be expected to drive up costs no matter how well the programs are managed. Sooner or later, moreover, increasing unit costs will mean that fewer and fewer weapons can be ordered—a tradeoff that cannot continue indefinitely. At some point, less sophisticated equipment will be preferable simply because it can be provided in much greater numbers.

In theory, program managers can restrain cost growth by accepting reductions in system performance or slippage in acquisition schedules. A 1971 RAND study of a representative sample of weapon programs in the 1960s indicated that average production schedules slipped 15 percent, or about one year in seven, but that system performance came out on the average as predicted.[22]

Thus, performance requirements that drive up unit costs tend to be met at the expense of moderate schedule slippages and more serious excesses of cost over original estimates.

Lack of Options

Perhaps the most frustrating aspect of current acquisition policies has been the lack of room for choice among weapon systems being developed. The number of systems under development has dropped off dramatically since the Second World War. For example, the number of military aircraft (bombers, fighters, attack) reaching the point of demonstration flight has shown a continuous decline from thirty-eight in the five-year period 1945–49 to a total of only three in 1965–69. (See Table 4-11.)

It is significant that as the number of systems under development declined, the proportion entering service rose sharply. In the most recent period, 1965–69, all three aircraft under development went into service—including the F-111, which was regarded by critics as a fiasco.

22. Robert Perry and others, *System Acquisition Strategies*, R-733-PR/ARPA (Santa Monica: RAND, June 1971), pp. 7, 8.

Table 4-11. United States and USSR Military Aircraft Development Projects, Five-year Periods, 1945–69

	United States			Soviet Union		
		Entered service			*Entered service*	
	Total			*Total*		
	number of	*Number*	*Percentage*	*number of*	*Number*	*Percentage*
Period	*projects*	*of aircraft*	*of total*	*projects*	*of aircraft*	*of total*
1945–49	38	20	53	45	14	31
1950–54	26	24	92	21	8	38
1955–59	13	11	85	18	9	50
1960–64	7	5	71	9	7	78
1965–69	3	3	100	11	5	45
Total	87	63	72	104	43	41

Source: Robert Perry and others, *System Acquisition Strategies*, R-733-PR/ARPA (Santa Monica: RAND, June 1971), p. 36.

In contrast, while the output of new aircraft in the USSR has also declined, the Russians have conducted more demonstrations and have exercised the choice of which aircraft *not* to produce much more often than has the United States.

Improvements in the weapons of potential adversaries compel the United States to keep pace, but many congressional critics feel crowded into a corner. The Congress complains that "in each area there is only a single weapon system available to modernize the forces—and this system is often a very costly one. This means that Congress is faced with the decision of approving the procurement of that system or denying modern weapons to our armed forces."[23]

Reforms under the Present Administration

In his three years as deputy secretary of defense, David Packard led a campaign for reform of weapon acquisitions. His policies, which were designed to reduce total costs and at the same time provide more choices, emphasized the following:

• Greater realism in program estimates, with independent checks on the estimates at key decision times.

• Deliberate balancing of cost and schedule against performance goals during development.

23. *Authorizing Appropriations for Fiscal Year 1972 for Military Procurement . . , and for Other Purposes* (1971), p. 19.

• More reliance on hard data from prototypes and testing and less concurrence between development and production—that is, "Fly before you buy."

• Decentralization and delegation of authority—giving the military services greater responsibility for programs while confining civilian leaders to setting policy, approving claimed weapon needs, and monitoring the execution of policy.

Deputy Secretary Packard introduced many new procedures to implement these policies, including changes in contracting procedures, greater authority for the military program managers, and an adjustment of the phases through which the development process proceeds. The status and influence of the operational testing agencies of the military services have been increased, giving them an early say in the development process. The new post of deputy director for test and evaluation was created in the Office of the Director of Defense Research and Engineering to coordinate and establish policy for all test and evaluation matters. Finally, new prototype programs were initiated independently of the formalized procedures and practices of the major weapon system acquisition cycle.

The Key Issue: Has Reform Gone Far Enough?

Over the past twenty-five years, a number of groups inside and outside the government have made proposals for improving the development and procurement of new weapon systems. The most recent were the wide-ranging recommendations of the Blue Ribbon Defense Panel in 1970. A fundamental problem that has been consistently exposed is the need to redefine the relative responsibilities of the military services and the civilian leaders in the Defense Department. The military services have what amounts to a conflict-of-interest problem. They identify military requirements, specify the system needed to fulfill them, and then serve as judge and jury over each weapon project.

The reforms of the current administration have alleviated some aspects of this problem but not others. Independent and more thorough supervision of the development processes, with a testing program designed to give the right warning signals when a development program is in trouble, is surely a step in the right direction. In the past, the developing agency in each service had full control of testing and evaluating the weapon until the time of the procurement decision. At that point, so much money and prestige were invested in a project that the testing and evaluating agencies came under extreme pressure to find the system operationally acceptable. Even then, they had no authority to question whether the new weapon was a sufficient improvement over the old one to justify its higher cost. The strengthened test and evaluation procedures should prevent a repetition of some of the disastrous failures of the past, notably with respect to cost overruns.

The conflicts of interest remain, however, and decisions will still involve power struggles among the interested services and the civilian offices in which rational appraisal will suffer. This prospect is reinforced by the strong emphasis on decentralized authority under the current administration, which in effect will strengthen the role of the military services in defining requirements and the weapon systems to meet them. Consequently, whether new procedures will reverse the trend toward fewer options and higher unit costs is open to question. Although it will be several years before the effectiveness of these reforms can be judged, the prospects and the issues on which they depend may be summarized as follows:

First, the new prototype effort could potentially increase options and restrain unit costs. Approximately fifteen new prototype programs have been initiated by the services. The lightweight fighter (about 20,000 pounds) discussed earlier in this chapter is a good example of both the possibilities and the problems. It merits careful consideration as an attractive low-cost alternative to fulfill some of the requirements for which high-cost aircraft (about 40,000 pounds) are now being designed or procured. However, as Deputy Defense Secretary Packard recently commented:

It is very hard to get a service to even try alternate approaches for fear they may jeopardize their pet project. If you doubt this, see what luck you have in getting the Air Force to support a prototype fighter over 25,000 lbs. or the Navy to support a prototype fighter at all.[24]

Second, the range of choice that prototypes offer over the future will depend on the latitude permitted by the services in defining requirements. Two contrasting examples illustrate the point. A Navy request to contractors for a V/STOL fighter/attack aircraft appeared

24. Speech delivered before the National Security Industrial Association, St. Louis, February 23, 1972, as reported in *Aviation Week and Space Technology*, Vol. 96 (March 6, 1972), p. 7.

on a single page of *Commerce Business Daily*. Absent were specifications on weight, range, payload, or even the technological approach. An Army request for competitive prototypes of a new helicopter covered more than 800 pages, detailing the engines, performance specifications, and a host of special design constraints, including the type of landing gear. The first approach will encourage a wide range of options to meet the need, but it will require investments in the near term to explore them. The second approach virtually precludes options, but aims to limit the cost and delay in obtaining a system to meet the need as that need has been defined.

Third, a large share of procurement funds is going to major acquisition programs in which the need for hardware testing and evaluation before the procurement commitment runs into conflict with the military determination that there is an urgent need to bring the system into operation. ULMS is an example: the military judgment on timing dictates that development and procurement take place concurrently.

In sum, the prospects for improvement remain uncertain, principally because change may not have gone far enough. Examples of more far-reaching changes that were not adopted are the Blue Ribbon Defense Panel's recommendations that theater commanders be given a major voice in defining requirements for new weapons and in procuring them, and that a new set of civilian offices replace the Office of the Director of Defense Research and Engineering so as to develop an arm's-length relationship between the advocates of a new system and those responsible for evaluating it. Drastic reforms of this nature would have much greater potential for improving the acquisition process, but would carry with them the uncertainties associated with a fairly large-scale dislocation of any operating bureaucracy.

In assessing the scope of needed change, it is important to recognize that improving the process of weapon acquisition is more than a matter of eliminating cost overruns. It concerns all the issues discussed in this chapter—those affecting the size, composition, and missions of the military forces. Weapon development is among the most important of these issues because it is where so much of the trouble begins.

5. Major National Security Options

IN PRESENTING THE 1973 BUDGET, the administration also outlined its proposed defense posture for a time of peace. The end of U.S. military involvement in Vietnam will bring marginal additional savings but will have virtually no impact on future force levels. Defense spending in real terms has been brought down from peak Vietnam war levels to amounts close to those spent on military forces before the Vietnam war. This in itself reverses a significant trend. When military spending stabilized after the Second World War and again following the Korean war, it did so at higher than prewar levels.

Nonetheless, as the preceding two chapters have indicated, programs now under way will increase defense spending in the years ahead, and a wide range of choice exists as to force levels, force structure, modernization rates, and manpower use. The range of uncertainty within which reasonable people can and do disagree as to what is needed to satisfy the same defense objectives is probably on the order of $20 billion, or 25 percent of the defense budget. Moreover, the same budget and force structure can be interpreted as a risky means for achieving an ambitious worldwide strategy or as a relatively safe means for carrying out a restricted and more selective strategy.

In this chapter the present defense program is compared with a lower and a higher cost option. Both are illustrative in character. Each reflects the fiscal consequences of one set of choices among the many posibilities presented in the preceding two chapters. Other combinations are, of course, possible. Neither option stems from an arbitrary judgment as to how high or how low the defense budget should

159

be. In the final sections of this chapter, the three alternatives are ex-.
amined in terms of their impact on the domestic economy and their
implications for public and congressional review of the defense budget.

Defense Budget Options

If alternative defense budgets are to be usefully compared and assessed, they must be based on the same international setting. For
present purposes, it is assumed that there will be no sudden or drastic
shift in the present pattern of international relations over the rest of
this decade. This assumption obviously does not preclude differing
assessments of the risks this international setting implies and the military forces it requires; as has been noted, such differences are often a
major factor underlying controversy over the size of the defense
budget.

In addition, the following specific assumptions apply to the cost
projection of the current defense posture and of the higher and lower
options discussed below: (1) U.S. military involvement in Vietnam
will end in fiscal 1973; assistance to Southeast Asia (military or economic) of $1 billion a year will continue for the rest of the decade.
(2) Research and development expenditures over the period 1974–79
will be $8.5 billion a year, the amount requested in the 1973 budget,
and about 10 percent higher in real terms than the average for the
past three years. (3) A first-round SALT agreement that specifically
limits ABMs and imposes some restraints on offensive missiles will
be reached in calendar 1972. No allowance is made for the effects of a
possible second-round SALT agreement. (4) The draft will end in
June 1973, and the pay incentives already requested will suffice to
attract the necessary number of volunteers for the current defense
posture.

Given these assumptions, the defense posture reflected in the 1973
budget is projected to have the following major force planning features over the 1970s:

• Maintenance of a redundant, diversified, strategic deterrent characterized by modernization of sea-based and land-based missiles,
bombers, and air defense. Marked emphasis is placed on expanding
sea-based capabilities. With a first-round SALT agreement, sizable
reductions would be made in programs to defend land-based missiles.
The number of missiles and bombers is maintained at current levels

over the remainder of the decade, with a steady increase in the number of warheads as a consequence of MIRV programs.

• Sufficient ground forces—thirteen Army and three Marine divisions—to maintain a strong conventional capability to deter a war in Europe and to provide a residual capacity for dealing with contingencies arising from localized conflicts in Asia.

• A gradual reduction in the number of aircraft carriers, leading to a baseline force of twelve in the early 1980s, accompanied by an accelerated shipbuilding program and aircraft and missile development programs for carrier protection and sea control.

• An essentially constant number of tactical Air Force squadrons, steadily modernized by the introduction of new high-performance aircraft for air-to-air combat and specialized aircraft for close support missions.

• Military manpower stabilized at 2.3 million, or almost 15 percent below pre-Vietnam levels.

The illustrative higher option would be based on the judgment that U.S.–Soviet strategic parity increases the risk of conventional military confrontations and on greater concern over the modernization of Soviet general purpose forces. Both factors would point to the need for selective offsetting improvements in U.S. general purpose forces, but no change would be required in strategic forces beyond those that can be projected from current administration proposals. The major force differences between this option and the present defense posture would be:

• An increase in Army division forces from thirteen to sixteen, manned at current levels of 30,000 each, with only essential increases in general support. (Average cost increase: $2.6 billion a year.)

• An expansion of naval antisubmarine warfare (ASW) programs —principally submarines, ASW aircraft, and research and development on ASW—to protect carriers and shipping against the Soviet Navy. (Average cost increase: $1 billion a year.)

• An enlargement of the F-14 program (up to the 710 aircraft originally planned rather than the 301 now programmed) to improve carrier defense, and the addition of A-X squadrons to present force levels, partly to support the increase in U.S. combat divisions, partly to augment capabilities for air support to allies in Asian contingencies. (Average cost increase: $1.7 billion a year.)

• An increase in military manpower to 2.5 million, which would also increase the cost of achieving an all-volunteer force. (This cost increase is apportioned among the programs above.)

The illustrative lower option would be based partly on a different interpretation of the international setting and of Soviet capabilities, but principally on cost and efficiency factors. It would aim at rapidly phasing out the less effective components in military forces and selectively slowing down weapon modernization. In general, the political importance attached to numerical force comparisons would be downgraded. The major force differences between this option and the current defense posture would be:

• The elimination of older model B-52s and Minuteman II and Titan missiles. The air defense system would be restricted to a surveillance role, which would mean deactivating part of the existing force, ending the airborne warning and control system (AWACS) program, and not procuring new interceptors and surface-to-air missiles for the defense of the United States. Current programs for the modernization of strategic offensive systems, however, would remain unchanged. (Average reduction in cost: $4 billion a year.)

• Maintenance of the present number of ground force divisions with a modest reduction in active strength. One active brigade in each of six Army divisions based in the United States would be deactivated and replaced by a reserve brigade that would be assigned to, and train with, the division. The reduction in readiness of these six divisions would be partially offset by an improvement in readiness of the reserve units. This change would test the possibility of relying more heavily in the future on reserve components in force planning. (Average reduction in cost: $500 million a year.)

• An immediate move to the twelve-carrier Navy projected for the 1980s. This would mean retiring the four oldest carriers in 1973 rather than gradually over the decade, authorizing one rather than three new carriers over the remainder of the decade, and greatly reducing the escort ship program. (Average reduction in cost: $2 billion a year.)

• A marked reduction in tactical air force modernization programs, principally by halting further development of the F-15 and ending the F-14 program at the end of fiscal 1973. However, plans for introducing new specialized aircraft—the A-X and the lightweight fighter—would go forward. Tactical air force levels would remain constant, except for limited reductions in naval tactical air forces corresponding to the accelerated move toward a twelve-carrier Navy. (Average reduction in cost: $2.4 billion a year.)

• A reduction in the ratio of support to combat forces to the level prevailing in 1968. Most of this reduction would result from base closures and changes in personnel assignment and training policies. (Taking into account the lower force levels under this option, the average reduction in cost would be $2.7 billion a year, of which $500 million would be allocated to strategic forces and $2.2 billion to general purpose forces.)

• A reduction in military manpower to 2.0 million, which would probably assure achievement of the all-volunteer force with currently planned pay incentives.

The three defense budget projections are summarized in Table 5-1 as they apply to strategic forces, general purpose forces, and other programs. Shown separately are allowances for increased procurement costs arising from cost growth and weapon system initiatives over the period, and for increases in real pay called for by comparability pay legislation. These allowances have been adjusted for differences among the three options in the pace of weapon procurement and

Table 5-1. Projection of Average Annual Cost of Optional Department of Defense Budgets, by Type of Force and Cost Allowance Factors, Fiscal Years 1973–79

Billions of fiscal year 1973 dollars

Type of force and cost factor	Option 1: Present program	Option 2: Selective increases in general purpose forces	Option 3: Elimination of less effective forces and a selective slowdown in modernization
Strategic forces	19.4	19.4	14.9
Baseline general purpose forces	55.0	60.3	47.9
Other[a]	9.2	9.2	9.2
Subtotal	83.6	88.9	72.0
Allowance for growth in real cost of new weapon systems and of initiatives[b]	2.0	2.2	1.5
Allowance for real pay increases[c]	3.0	3.7	2.6
Total	88.6	94.8	76.1

Source: Authors' estimates based on the projections in Chapters 3 and 4.

a. Includes retired pay, family housing, military assistance, and fiscal year 1973 incremental costs of the war in Vietnam.

b. The allowance for the growth in the real cost of new weapon systems is roughly half the amount that could be projected from the RAND and General Accounting Office studies cited in Chapter 3, p. 80. An allowance for new initiatives of $500 million a year under the current defense posture compensates in part for the "bow wave" effect in long-term projections. Allowances for both factors have been adjusted upward in option 2 and downward in option 3 in accordance with the assumed rate of modernization and major weapon systems procurement.

c. Assumes real pay increases of 3 percent a year corresponding to the average increase in productivity in the private sector. The allowance is higher for option 2, both because of increases in manpower and because of further incentive pay increases to meet the higher enlistment requirements for this option. It is lower in option 3 because of a reduction in manpower levels.

modernization and in manpower levels. The projected average annual cost of the current defense posture, in 1973 dollars, is almost $89 billion, compared with $95 billion for the higher option and $76 billion for the lower option.[1]

The full effect of moving in the direction of a higher or a lower option would not be felt immediately. In the first place, the projections are based on authorizations, and changes in expenditures lag behind changes in authorizations. Second, in moving toward a lower option, it would be necessary to incur one-time costs for terminating acquisition programs or reducing manpower levels. Presentation of the options in terms of average annual costs makes it possible to take these time lags into account.

Differences among the three options stem not from differing views of the contingencies to be met, but from differing interpretations of the military capabilities needed to meet them. Consequently they represent a range of alternatives that is by no means extreme, even though a potential difference of $130 billion is involved over the seven-year period. The significance of this range can be highlighted by comparing the average annual cost of the alternative projections with fiscal 1973 defense outlays, both in absolute terms and as a proportion of national output.

• Under the high option, average defense expenditures would be $18 billion more than defense outlays in fiscal 1973. Comparison with outlays magnifies this amount because of the large difference between outlays and authorizations in the fiscal 1973 defense budget, as noted in Chapter 3. Over a longer period, outlays could be expected to catch up with authorizations. The lower option illustrates the measures that would have to be taken to keep defense outlays approximately constant in real terms at the fiscal 1973 level.

• As a proportion of national output, the high budget option would average 6.5 percent of GNP, or about the 1973 level. This means that defense expenditures in real terms would increase by slightly more than 4 percent a year, the full employment rate of increase projected for GNP. The lower option would mean a decline in the defense burden to about 5 percent of GNP.

1. The current dollar costs of these three defense budget options in fiscal 1977, the final year of the budget projection given in Chapter 13, would be $100 billion for the present defense posture, $107 billion for the high option, and $86 billion for the low option.

A wider range of defense budget options could readily be developed on the basis of the alternatives for the major force categories outlined in Chapter 4. They would depend, however, either on a significant change in U.S.–Soviet relations or on a deliberate modification of selected military missions. Thus the high option might be increased by $5 billion a year as the result of a sudden breakdown in U.S.–Soviet arms control negotiations and the heightened international tension that would follow. Conversely, the low budget option might be reduced by $5 billion as the result of the following force planning decisions: to eliminate ground forces oriented toward use in local conflicts in Asia; to limit the role of carriers in contingencies involving the Soviet Union; and to cut back heavily on tactical air force requirements for deep penetration missions. If at the same time the United States moved toward relying solely on a sea-based strategic deterrent, the defense budget would be reduced by $4 billion more a year.

Beyond this range, changes in defense budgets would depend on fundamental shifts either in the way the United States defines its interests in the world, or in the way it chooses to protect them. Far more than a modification of military missions would be involved. For example, the United States might drastically restructure its military forces after reassessing the importance of its close connections with Western Europe and Japan, or after deciding that it could maintain those connections and protect its interests by relying principally on nuclear deterrence. Shifts of this magnitude, in either foreign policy or military strategy, occur only over an extended period of time. They have not been taken into account in developing the foregoing alternatives either for the major force categories or for the defense budget as a whole.

Impact on the Domestic Economy*

A question that consistently arises in the consideration of defense spending is the impact of alternative defense budgets on domestic output and employment. Should increases or decreases in defense spending that are determined on security grounds be postponed either to avoid adding to inflationary pressures when the economy is expanding, or adding to unemployment when the economy is slack?

* Based on an analysis by Martin J. Bailey.

Defense spending uses resources in the form of manpower, capital, and materials. Those resources could be used to produce other goods and services, public or private; hence they constitute the real cost of the defense budget. When defense spending changes, deliberate fiscal and monetary policy actions must be taken to create offsetting changes in other spending. The resources released by a cutback in the defense budget will be used to produce other goods and services only if national economic policy provides an increase in the demand for them. Otherwise, cuts in defense spending can lead to overall reductions in employment and output. Conversely, during periods of full employment, increases in defense spending not accompanied by actions to reduce other demands for goods and services will lead to inflation.

Changes in defense spending have played a role either in starting or helping to stop three of the five recessions since the Second World War. In addition, the drop in real GNP from 1944 to 1947 was associated with the abrupt decline in military production at the close of the Second World War. The fact that a recession did not materialize in 1967 was in part the result of the buildup in military outlays for Vietnam. The most recent example of the impact of defense spending on the state of the economy is now in progress.

During most of the past several years, as the administration scaled down the Vietnam war and defense-generated employment was falling, national economic policy was directed toward temporarily slowing the growth in economic activity in order to reduce inflation. As a consequence, monetary and fiscal policies until recently were not addressed toward providing offsetting changes in nondefense spending, and the cuts in defense employment were not adequately matched by increases in employment elsewhere. The decline in defense spending did not cause the recent recession but it clearly played a role, principally because the anti-inflationary program severely limited the possibilities for offsetting the employment effects of defense cuts.

Types of Employment Effects

Future changes in the level of defense spending, rather than the present absolute amount, will affect domestic economic prospects. Before examining the possibilities, it is useful to distinguish the ways in which defense spending can affect employment.

First is the *direct* effect, consisting of Department of Defense civilian and military employment and the distribution of military procurement appropriations to prime contractors for the production of aircraft, weapons, and other equipment and supplies. Spending for the latter purposes has a *derived* employment effect arising from the subsequent redistribution of part of the prime contract funds among subcontractors at many levels and among firms that provide supplies and raw materials to both prime contractors and subcontractors.

Beyond these employment consequences, defense spending has secondary effects on the economy. When workers directly or indirectly employed by the Defense Department lose jobs as a result of a reduction in defense spending, they cut back on personal spending until they find new employment. Similarly, firms losing defense contracts or subcontracts reduce their inventories and purchases because of poorer expectations for the future. As a result, additional unemployment may be generated beyond that stemming from the direct and derived impact of the reduction in the defense budget. Conversely, an increase in defense spending can have secondary expansionary effects on the economy. For present purposes, no attempt is made to estimate these secondary effects, both because they are less predictable and because they merge imperceptibly into a range of other factors that have an independent influence on the general level of private employment.

The impact of alternative defense budgets on total national employment depends on whether monetary and fiscal actions are taken to provide compensatory changes in spending on other goods and services. If such actions are taken, total employment need not be affected, except perhaps during a transition period. Nevertheless, even if total employment is held constant by appropriate monetary and fiscal actions, there will be employment consequences for particular industries and regions. Employment changes associated with compensatory nondefense spending usually will not be distributed by industry or location in the same pattern as the defense spending it replaces.

Moreover, the impact of alternative defense budgets on specific industries and regions will vary according to the composition of a given change in defense spending. Defense budget changes concentrated on personnel tend to be fairly evenly distributed over the country; those concentrated on procurement fall disproportionately on regions with large defense industries. For example, about 16 percent of defense-generated private employment is concentrated in California, and about 12 percent in New York State.

Table 5-2. Comparison of the Employment Effects of Optional Department of Defense Budgets and Offsetting Government Actions, by Industry, Fiscal Year 1973

Thousands of jobs

Industry	Estimated employment generated by 1973 defense budget	Employment change generated by:			Employment change generated by:		
		Higher defense budget option	Offsetting tax increase and monetary restraint[a]	Offsetting reductions in other government expenditures[b]	Lower defense budget option	Offsetting tax cut and monetary ease[a]	Offsetting increases in other government expenditures[b]
Agriculture	45	+1	−14	−64	−3	+30	+135
Mining	25	+4	−3	−5	−7	+6	+10
Construction	40	+5	−25	−64	−9	+54	+135
Manufacturing	1,315	+166	−109	−112	−337	+230	+238
Services	595	+60	−285	−191	−114	+600	+402
Department of Defense (military and civilian)	3,400	+200	0	0	−450	0	0
Total	5,420	+436	−436	−436	−920	+920	+920

Sources: Authors' estimates. The first column is adapted primarily from Richard P. Oliver, "Employment Effects of Reduced Defense Spending," *Monthly Labor Review*, Vol. 94 (December 1971), pp. 3–11. All other estimates are adapted from Bernard Udis (ed.), *Adjustments of the U.S. Economy to Reductions in Military Spending*, Prepared for the United States Arms Control and Disarmament Agency, ACDA/E-156 (December 1970).

a. Assumed to produce an across-the-board change in private spending, almost all in consumption.

b. Assumed to involve an across-the-board change in all nondefense government programs.

Employment Impact of Alternative Budgets

Defense-generated employment is currently estimated at about 5.4 million jobs, of which 3.4 million represent Defense Department civilian and military personnel, and 2 million represent direct and derived private employment. Total employment attributable to the defense budget is 6.1 percent of the labor force, or a slightly lower proportion than defense spending constitutes in the GNP. About two-thirds of the private employment generated by the defense budget is in manufacturing.

How would the role of defense in the domestic economy change as a result of moving toward either the higher or lower budgets outlined in the previous section? The high option, which would eventually increase defense spending by $6 billion a year, would imply an increase in defense-generated employment of well over 400,000 jobs, about 40 percent of these going to the Defense Department and about 60 percent to private civilian employment. The low option, which would eventually result in a reduction of $12 billion a year in defense expenditures, would reduce defense-generated employment by more than 900,000 jobs, slightly more than half of which would be in private employment and slightly less than half in Defense Department employment.

With compensatory government actions, these changes in defense spending would mainly create problems of adjusting to a different pattern of demand rather than cause either a rise or a fall in total employment. The nature of these adjustment problems can be illustrated by outlining two kinds of government action designed to offset the aggregate employment effect of changes in defense budgets. One program would consist wholly of tax changes and monetary measures to change private spending, the other of changes in civilian government expenditures. Each program would have aggregate fiscal and employment effects equal to but offsetting those resulting from a move to either the higher or the lower defense budget option. The distribution of employment effects under these alternatives is shown in Table 5-2.

By assumption, these government actions would create just enough employment to make up for the jobs lost by a reduction in defense spending or reduce employment by just enough to offset the stimulus resulting from an increase in defense spending. Changes in defense spending, however, tend to affect employment in manufacturing more heavily, while offsetting government actions tend to have greater impact on employment in the service industries and in construction. Thus a change in defense spending creates adjustment problems even though it is offset by government action. Workers losing defense-generated jobs in manufacturing would have to move elsewhere in the manufacturing sector or to other locations to stay in the same field of employment, or shift to service industries and construction. In the case of adjusting to increases in defense spending, shifts would be required in the reverse direction.

Policy Implications

These employment effects of changes in defense spending naturally concern the executive branch and the Congress and limit their freedom to decide defense questions solely on security grounds. For example, both the present and past administrations have encountered strong domestic political opposition when they have tried to close military bases they considered excess to needs. Similarly, curtailing military procurement arouses concern over the employment consequences in certain areas and over the survival of the aerospace industry.

These are serious concerns, but they should be placed in a broader perspective. Offsetting government actions can greatly reduce the aggregate employment effects caused by changes in defense spending, and adjustment assistance programs pinpointed to depressed areas and industries can ease the impact of dislocations. Retraining programs and liberal financial and other assistance could reduce the hardships associated with looking for new jobs and perhaps having to move to other areas to find them. Even large investments in these programs would more than pay for themselves if they enabled the government to avoid wasteful spending decisions or to initiate more efficient policies.

It should be recognized that possible dislocations from changes in defense spending, though potentially sizable in any one year, may be outweighed by employment dislocations caused by other kinds of economic change such as shifts in consumer taste, new antipollution requirements, interregional shifts of industries, and changes in the level and composition of imports. Hence, adjustment assistance policies should be addressed to a wider problem than the dislocations resulting from defense changes alone. In general, adjustments are comparatively easy to make when the economy is prosperous and people in search of jobs can readily find them. They occur more slowly and painfully when the economy sags, as in the recent recession.

A tendency to permit employment effects to determine defense spending would raise issues that are central to the problem of how the nation should allocate resources. It would suggest, in effect, that government programs should be frozen at current levels or allowed only to increase. Resources could not be shifted from programs that had become obsolete, inefficient, or otherwise unnecessary, to other public or private uses. There is, in short, no readily available substitute for assessing the force structure and the defense budget against an array of security, foreign policy, and efficiency considerations. Employment effects should be dealt with through economic adjustment policies; they should not become an obstacle to wise defense planning.

Reviewing the Defense Budget

Most public and congressional discussion of the baseline defense budget is concentrated on a surprisingly few issues, and even for these, important interrelationships are often overlooked. Examples in recent years are (1) the debates over whether to build the Safeguard system, or a new manned strategic bomber, or a new nuclear carrier; (2) the attention paid to cost overruns or mismanagement in the case of the C-5A transport, the F-111, and the F-14; and (3) the recurring controversy over maintaining large U.S. forces in Europe. These are indeed important questions. Individually or collectively, however, they affect only a small part of the defense budget. Moreover, issues of this kind are raised almost fortuitously instead of being the result of a systematic examination of the defense program. Too much attention is paid to a few individual defense issues that are generally unrelated, and too little to the objectives of the defense program and how they are being carried out.

Consideration of the national security options outlined in this chapter, or of the choices as to major force categories illustrated in Chapter 4, would require a very different approach to reviewing and approving defense spending. Major emphasis would be placed on the following factors:

• *Force levels.* How many major force components are needed, in what combination, and to serve what political and military purposes?

Questions of force size and structure also involve the pace at which new weapon systems should be introduced and, equally, the pace at which older, less effective systems should be phased out.

● *Support levels.* How should combat forces be supported? In part this is a question of efficiency. It also involves readiness—how quickly must U.S. combat forces respond to contingencies, and how long will they need to be sustained? Readiness requirements cannot be assumed to remain constant, for they change from time to time as changes in the international situation become reasonably well defined. Moreover, unless it is assumed that there are no constraints on total defense spending, the relationship between readiness and force levels must be regularly assessed, since the tradeoff inherent in this relationship is a fundamental factor in determining the defense posture. In general, the assessment of support levels requires examination of numerous diverse elements in the defense program that are small individually but together account for one-third of military spending. No other set of issues highlights so well the importance of the undramatic in reviewing the defense budget.

● *Short-term versus long-term implications.* What time horizon should govern defense budget decisions? The defense posture is made up of weapon systems that require a long lead time to develop and procure, of forces whose training entails costly investments, and of forward deployments that are the product of political alignments developed over the years. Concentrating on current year outlays sharply limits the scope of the review and the opportunity to consider fundamental changes. Furthermore, changes that can result in savings over the longer term frequently involve initial one-time costs. A reluctance to accept such costs can mean forgoing opportunities to improve the defense program.

These factors are fundamental to the process of formulating the defense budget in the executive branch. Why, then, is there not a parallel examination outside the executive branch? In large measure, the answer lies in current congressional procedures, which determine not only the form and content of congressional scrutiny of defense appropriations, but also the character of the public debate.

The legislative process is in two stages, authorizations and appropriations, each of which is the responsibility of separate committees. Authorizations cover only selected aspects of the defense program, principally procurement of major weapon systems, research and development, and military manpower levels. Appropriations cover the entire defense budget, but in categories that are largely independent of those used by the executive branch for force planning purposes. Both the authorization and appropriation procedures tend to concentrate on the exceptional items of change in the current budget; neither focuses on the issues noted above—force levels, effectiveness, support, readiness, and the necessary tradeoffs among them. Furthermore, they are almost exclusively concerned with spending requests for the current fiscal year; the long-range consequences of spending decisions receive less attention.

This approach is the more surprising in that the congressional review process is initiated by the secretary of defense's report on the five-year defense program, which states the purposes of the program and outlines the force decisions needed to achieve them. Since 1971, moreover, the Defense Department has provided the Congress with an annual report on military manpower requirements for the coming fiscal year, based on major missions. And the presentation of both reports is preceded by the President's foreign policy report, which places defense requirements in the broader setting of the administration's assessment of the international situation and its statement of U.S. foreign policy objectives. These reports unfortunately are the only formal link between force planning in the executive branch and the congressional review of the defense budget. After the Congress receives them, the legislative process follows its separate path.

How could the Congress organize its review and approval of defense spending in terms of the purposes of U.S. military forces, as does the executive branch in formulating the defense program? Basing congressional authorization and appropriations on the five-year defense program would be one way to begin. This would require that congressional deliberation be structured according to force levels, manpower levels, and procurement schedules for each mission function rather than on the basis of the budget categories now in use. The Congress would continue to review and approve defense spending annually, but would do so with explicit awareness of the longer-term implications for costs and for force capabilities. Each year the executive branch would propose amendments to the five-year program that reflected the most recent information, possible changes in planning strategy, and estimates of requirements for the new final year of the planning period. The Congress, through its Armed Services Committees, would review the administration's recommendations and explicitly authorize a new five-year program. Subsequently, through its appropriation process, the Congress could decide on funding for the first year of the new program, with its five-year implications specifically in mind.

Such a fundamental change would require a transition period for developing the necessary information and new procedures. From the outset, the Congress could authorize funds for the five-year defense program. Initially, however, it could continue within this five-year framework to authorize and appropriate funds according to existing budget categories such as procurement, military personnel, and military construction. The new budgetary information classified by missions—that is, by major force categories and support—would provide important new data that for the time being would be supplementary in character. Eventually, the Congress could begin authorizing and appropriating funds on the basis of the new categories, should that be justified by experience gained in the interim.

Even with the same planning information and following the same general approach, the Congress presumably would apply somewhat different criteria than does the executive branch to its evaluation of the defense program. But these differences would not detract from the basic advantage of reviewing the defense program in a long-term framework: the opportunity it provides to consider changes in planning contingencies and improvements in efficiency.

Moving in this direction would not in itself result in abrupt changes in the defense budget or in the way the government manages the defense program. To the contrary, the objective would be orderly change brought about by focusing public and congressional reviews of defense spending on the most important questions.

6. Income Support

FEDERAL PROGRAMS that provide individuals and families with income support in the form of cash or goods and services are now the largest component of the federal budget. Expenditures for these programs have risen rapidly as more people have become eligible for existing income maintenance programs and as new programs have been inaugurated. In 1950, federal income support payments were $13 billion and accounted for 29 percent of federal expenditures, or nearly 5 percent of gross national product (GNP). By 1973, these payments will exceed $102 billion, account for 39 percent of federal expenditures (60 percent of civilian outlays), and amount to nearly 9 percent of GNP, as is shown in Table 6-1. The number of people receiving some form of income support will have risen from just under 17 million in 1950 to between 55 million and 60 million in 1973.

The various federal income support programs have been introduced piecemeal over many years, each with its own eligibility requirements, benefit levels, and, in some cases, its own sources of financing. These programs can be classified in several ways:

1. Most income support programs were originally designed to meet the needs of persons who are retired or who for other reasons cannot work—the blind, the disabled, and female heads of families with dependent children. Having a low income is not sufficient in itself to make a family eligible for payments, except in a few of the newer programs such as food stamps and housing subsidies. The working poor receive few benefits.

2. In some programs, entitlement to benefits is considered by recipients to be more or less a "right," earned by having paid prior contributions (social security, civil service retirement) or by past service

175

Table 6-1. Federal Expenditures for Income Support Programs, Selected Fiscal Years, 1950–73

Program	1950	1960	1970	1973 Estimate
	Billions of dollars			
Retirement and related, total	**3.8**	**16.7**	**49.2**	**72.6**
Veterans' compensation and pensions	2.2	3.4	5.2	6.4
Military retirement and medical benefits	0.2	0.7	3.0	5.1
Civil service retirement	0.3	0.9	2.6	3.9
Railroad retirement	0.3	0.9	1.6	2.1
Old age, survivors, and disability insurance	0.8	10.8	29.7	44.7
Medicare	...	...	7.1	10.4
Unemployment compensation	**2.0**	**2.6**	**3.1**	**5.9**
Public assistance and related, total	**1.0**	**2.3**	**8.3**	**16.1**
Aged, disabled, and blind	0.8	1.4	1.9	2.8
Families with dependent children	0.2	0.7	2.2	4.7
Medicaid	...	...	2.7	3.8
Food stamps	a	a	0.6	2.3
Other nutrition	a	0.1	0.4	0.7
Housing subsidies	a	0.1	0.5	1.8
Other, total	**3.2**	**3.7**	**5.1**	**7.1**
Student aid	1.6	0.4	1.3	3.4
Farm price supports	1.6	3.3	3.8	3.7
Total benefits	**10.0**	**25.5**	**65.7**	**101.7**
Cash benefits	10.0	25.1	54.4	82.7
Benefits in kind	a	0.4	11.3	19.0
	Percentage of federal expenditures[b]			
Total benefits	**23.2**	**27.7**	**33.8**	**39.4**
Cash benefits	23.2	27.2	28.0	32.0
Benefits in kind	a	0.4	5.8	7.4
	Percentage of gross national product			
Total benefits	**3.8**	**5.1**	**6.9**	**8.6**
Cash benefits	3.8	5.1	5.7	7.0
Benefits in kind	a	a	1.2	1.6

Sources: *The Budget of the United States Government*, for fiscal years 1952, 1962, 1972, and 1973, and *Special Analyses of the United States Government*, for fiscal years 1972 and 1973.
a. Less than $50 million or 0.1 percent.
b. Components and budget totals adjusted for shifts in timing and financial transactions as explained in Chapter 1. Details may not add to totals because of rounding.

(military retirement, veterans' compensation and pensions). In other cases, chiefly welfare and related programs, benefits are not based on past contributions or past service; hence the receipt of welfare benefits carries a social stigma in the eyes of many people.

3. Most of these programs pay benefits in the form of cash. But several of the more recently established ones provide "in-kind" benefits in the form of goods and services—food, medical care, housing, and higher education.

4. The benefits received under many of the programs are uniform throughout the nation. But for public assistance, Medicaid, and unemployment compensation, benefits and eligibility requirements are determined by each state and vary from state to state.

The varied nature of these programs suggests the basic questions that need to be asked. Presumably, the major purpose of income support programs is to provide a decent living standard to those who would not otherwise be able to achieve it. Is it necessary to have so many diverse programs to accomplish this objective? Is the present emphasis on categorical status instead of need appropriate as a condition of eligibility? To what extent should benefits be tied to prior contributions, and how should those contributions be levied? What is the rationale for providing benefits in kind, instead of paying cash and letting beneficiaries decide how to spend it? Finally, how should benefits be set—how much variation from state to state or community to community is appropriate, and how should benefits be changed over time to reflect inflation and general increases in living standards?

After a brief review of the major income support programs, this chapter addresses the questions posed above.

Summary of the Programs

Before the 1930s there were only three federal income support programs, each addressed to a special group in the population: veterans' compensation and pensions dating back to the Revolutionary War, the military retirement program begun during the Civil War, and federal civil service retirement started in 1920. It was not until the thirties that a broad system of social insurance programs was inaugurated as one of the major New Deal reforms: the social security system to provide income to workers in retirement or to their survivors in case of death; the unemployment compensation program to provide a temporary source of income to experienced workers who had lost their jobs; and a public assistance program through which the federal government helped the states provide welfare payments to those who could not work—the aged poor who had not earned sufficient social security benefits, the disabled, the blind, and families with dependent children, chiefly headed by women. While the coverage and benefits under these programs were increased during the forties and fifties and the social security system was extended to disabled workers, the next major expansion of income support payments came in the sixties, when several new programs were launched to provide benefits in kind —Medicare, Medicaid, housing subsidies, food stamps, and student aid for higher education.

Retirement and Disability Programs

The retirement and disability programs—veterans' compensation and pensions, federal civilian and military retirement, railroad retirement, and the social security system (including Medicare)—pay benefits on the basis of prior employment in the armed forces or in the civilian sector. Together they will pay almost $73 billion in 1973 and account for about 70 percent of total federal income support payments.

Veterans' compensation and pensions, by far the oldest of the income support programs, are available only to persons who served in the armed forces during a war or other specified contingency. Compensation is paid for service-connected disabilities and is supposed to make up for the reduction in earning power that such handicaps create. Veterans' pensions are awarded to aged veterans or their dependent survivors primarily on the basis of need, although disability (not necessarily service connected) is taken into account. In fiscal 1970, 4.7 million persons were receiving veterans' compensation or pensions at a cost of $5.3 billion, an average annual benefit of $1,128 per recipient. In fiscal 1973, the number of beneficiaries is expected to reach nearly 5 million, and total expenditures $6.4 billion. The growing number of veterans' beneficiaries reflects two factors—increasing compensation payments arising from disabilities incurred in the Vietnam war, and increasing numbers of pensioners, reflecting the rising age of veterans of earlier wars, particularly the Second World War.

Military retired pay is the second oldest retirement program, dating back to 1861, when men with forty years' service were permitted to retire with full pay of the highest rank they had attained. Today, men and women of the armed forces are permitted to retire after twenty years' service, with 50 percent of their last basic pay, or they can continue for a total of thirty years' service, at which time their retired pay is equal to 75 percent of their final basic pay. Eligibility for military retired pay depends only on rank and length of service. Since a person can join the armed forces at age seventeen, it is possible to qualify for retired pay at thirty-seven. Because there are no income restrictions or minimum age requirements, many military retirees have full-time nongovernment jobs and also draw retired pay.

Retirement benefits for civilian employees of the federal government were legislated in 1920. Civil service retirement is based on the number of years of service and the average salary earned during the three years of highest salary. Benefits range from slightly more than 15 percent of previous salary for ten years' service to slightly more than 75 percent with forty years of service. However, federal employees must be at least fifty-five years old and have thirty years' service to receive full retirement benefits.

Both military and civil service retirement pay are automatically adjusted for increases in the cost of living. If the consumer price index has risen by more than 3 percent since the last automatic adjustment and remains 3 percent higher for three months, retirement benefits are increased by the amount of the cost-of-living increase, plus 1 percent. On the whole, benefits under federal employee retirement programs are somewhat more generous than those paid by the typical private employer.

Civil service retirement is financed in part by a levy on the employee's pay, in part by federal government contributions. The employee rate has risen from 2.5 percent originally to 7 percent at present. The government pays the full cost of the military retirement system. By fiscal 1973, 2.0 million people are expected to be receiving military and civilian retirement benefits at an annual cost of $8.7 billion. These benefits are simply an employment cost that the federal government bears as does any other employer. In that sense they are unlike the other income support programs, which were adopted to serve particular social objectives.

One other retirement program came under federal direction before the enactment of the social security laws in 1935. The *railroad retirement* system was enacted in 1934 to consolidate and to assure benefit payments from the private pension plans of the various railroads. The benefits, determined by length of service and pre-retirement earnings, are higher on the average than social security benefits, and are financed by a 19.9 percent tax paid jointly by the employer and employee. By 1973, nearly 1 million persons are expected to be receiving railroad retirement benefits at an annual cost of $2.1 billion.[1]

The largest of the employment-related programs is the *old age, survivors, disability, and hospital insurance program* (OASDHI). The original legislation levied a 2 percent tax on the first $3,000 of wages earned by workers in commerce and industry. Half the tax is paid by the employer and half by the employee. Since 1937 the tax rate has been raised eleven times and the wage ceiling increased six times. At present the first $9,000 of earnings are subject to a 10.4 percent combined employer-employee tax. The program provides retirement and survivor benefits and, since 1956, benefits for disabled workers. Medical benefits for persons over sixty-five were begun in 1966. Starting in 1950, the coverage of the system was gradually expanded, until by 1969, 90 percent of all wages were earned in occupations covered by social security. The growth in expenditures reflects four major factors: a growing number of aged persons; an increase in the proportion of the aged and disabled covered by social security; increases in average benefits to keep up with the cost of living; and increases in the real value of benefits, over and above cost-of-living increases. The total number of persons receiving benefits increased from 3 million in 1950 to 25 million in 1970 and is expected to exceed 28 million by 1973. As Table 6-2 shows, average benefits per person have risen sharply over the same period, growing substantially faster than the cost of living.

The growth in the real size of average benefits is the result of two factors. An individual's benefits are based on his average wages during the years since 1951, omitting from the calculation the five lowest years. Wages have been rising steadily in the American economy; consequently, each year those who retire are entitled, on the average, to higher benefits than are those who retired in prior years. In addition, the Congress has periodically raised the benefit levels for those who have already retired, by amounts more than sufficient to compensate

1. The railroad retirement system currently faces the problem that the number of retirees is continuing to grow, while the total number of railroad employees is declining. In 1950, there were 1.2 million railroad employees supporting fewer than 400,000 retired or disabled annuitants. By 1970, fewer than 566,000 active employees were supporting nearly 979,000 retirees.

Table 6-2. Average Annual Old Age and Survivors Insurance and Disability Insurance Benefits in Current and Fiscal Year 1973 Dollars, Selected Years, 1950–73

Type of benefit	1950	1960	1965	1970	1973 Estimate
		Current dollars			
Old age and survivors insurance	438	753	876	1,215	1,564
Disability insurance	...	838	835	1,091	1,479
		Fiscal year 1973 dollars			
Old age and survivors insurance	757	1,050	1,155	1,347	1,564
Disability insurance	...	1,169	1,101	1,210	1,479

Sources: *Social Security Bulletin*, Vol. 35 (March 1972), p. 40; *The Budget of the United States Government —Appendix, Fiscal Year 1973*, pp. 465–67.

for increases in the cost of living. Since 1965 there have been four across-the-board increases that have raised benefits by more than 50 percent. During the same period, prices rose by about 25 percent. As a result, real benefits have increased by more than 20 percent.

While benefits are related to prior wages, they are not proportional to those wages. The formula for calculating benefits is so constructed that the lower the prior wages, the higher the ratio of benefits to wages. Moreover, there is a ceiling beyond which additional wages are not counted, either for paying taxes or for calculating benefits. Table 6-3 shows how the ratio of benefits to wages is related to prior wage history. There are minimum benefits to which a person is entitled if

Table 6-3. Ratios of Old Age and Survivors Insurance Benefits to Selected Average Monthly Earnings, 1971 Benefit Schedules

Average monthly earnings of insured worker during working years[a] (dollars)	Implied average annual salary (dollars)	Single retired worker		Couple	
		Monthly benefit (dollars)	Ratio of benefit to prior earnings	Monthly benefit (dollars)	Ratio of benefit to prior earnings
250	3,000	145.60	0.58	218.40	0.87
417	5,000	198.80	0.48	298.20	0.72
583	7,000	251.80	0.43	377.70	0.65
750[b]	9,000	296.00	0.39	444.00	0.59

Source: "H.R. 1," Report 92-231, 92 Cong. 1 sess. (1971), pp. 7, 8.

a. Average monthly earnings, upon which the OASI benefit is based, is the average of monthly taxable earnings after 1950 after up to five years of lowest (or zero) earnings have been omitted: (total earnings after 1950 minus 5 years of lowest earnings) ÷ (total months after 1950 minus up to 60 months).

b. In 1971, no one could have had average monthly earnings of $750 because the ceiling on wages subject to social security tax was below the $9,000 covered annual salary implied by the $750 monthly wage during all prior years. The highest average monthly earnings possible with the ceilings on wages in effect to tax after 1950 was $472.

he has worked the necessary forty quarters, regardless of his prior wage history. Special minimum benefits are given to persons over age seventy-two who do not fit into any of the categories of eligible beneficiaries. Thus the concept of need as well as previous employment is recognized in the program. While social security is often thought of as an insurance program in which individuals and their employers "buy" retirement benefits through payroll tax contributions, the benefits are only loosely related to past contributions and contain large welfare elements.

In 1956, benefits for disabled workers were added to the social security program. By 1970, nearly 2.6 million people were receiving disability payments at an annual cost of $2.8 billion. To qualify, an employee must have worked twenty of the forty quarters immediately preceding his application for benefits. (Special provisions are made for younger workers.) Under present law a disabled worker must wait six months before he becomes eligible, though legislation currently under consideration would reduce this period to five months.

Disability under the social security programs is defined as "inability to engage in any substantial gainful activity by reason of any medically determinable physical or mental impairment which can be expected to result in death or has lasted or can be expected to last for a continuous period of not less than 12 months."[2] Although this definition is rigorous, the program has grown rapidly. Part of this growth reflects the expansion of coverage of the social insurance programs to more and more groups of workers; part reflects liberalization of the eligibility rules. When the program first began, disability benefits were available only to those who were more than fifty years of age. This requirement was modified in 1960, and the number of beneficiaries grew rapidly in the first half of the 1960s. The rate of growth has recently moderated, and the average annual rate of growth in the number of recipients in the near future is expected to be between 6 and 7 percent a year.

The equity of protecting retirement benefits from the effects of inflation has gained general recognition and congressional support. The military and federal civilian retirement programs already provide for automatic increases in benefits to compensate for increases in the cost of living. Under H.R. 1, the social security bill passed by the House last year and now pending in the Senate, OASDI beneficiaries would

2. *Compilation of the Social Security Laws*, H. Doc. 266, 90 Cong. 2 sess (1968), Vol. 1, p. 117.

also receive automatic cost-of-living increases financed by automatic increases in the wage ceiling.

H.R. 1 provides for a 5 percent across-the-board increase and a number of other liberalizations in social security benefits that would become effective July 1, 1972. In addition, automatic annual increases would occur whenever the consumer price index rises by 3 percent and no legislative increase in benefits has been enacted. The chairman of the House Ways and Means Committee has declared that he now favors a 20 percent benefit increase, and similar legislation has been introduced in the Senate. It is very likely, therefore, that the social security legislation that emerges from the Congress this year will provide for a much larger benefit increase than the 5 percent contained in H.R. 1.

In 1966 the social security cash retirement system was substantially expanded by the addition of *Medicare*, which provides government insurance for the medical care of the elderly. The program is in two parts: (1) Hospital insurance helps to cover the cost of inpatient hospital care and post-hospital care through nursing homes and home health services, and (2) supplementary medical insurance helps to pay the costs of physicians' services and other outpatient care. Hospital insurance is financed by a special payroll tax added to the regular social security payroll tax. Supplementary medical insurance is financed half through monthly premiums paid by the beneficiaries and half by the federal government from general revenues. Some 21 million persons are eligible for Medicare benefits, and 16 million are expected to receive benefits in fiscal 1973. (See Chapter 7 for a fuller description of the program.)

Unemployment Compensation Benefits

The unemployment compensation program was designed to replace part of the income lost due to periods of unemployment. The program was enacted in 1935 (as part of the basic social security legislation) with the imposition on employers of a 1 percent federal tax on the first $3,000 of wages. The tax rate has since been increased three times and is now 3.2 percent of the first $4,200 of wages. By agreeing to federally imposed conditions, including the payment of certain minimum unemployment benefits, the states receive most of this tax to finance their unemployment compensation programs, which—despite the federal minimum conditions—vary substantially from state to state. So long as its reserve fund for meeting future benefits exceeds a certain minimum, a state may reduce its tax rate on each employer according to the past unemployment experience of his work force. During periods of high unemployment the reserve funds of many states are depleted, and to build them up again they must often raise their tax rates back to 3.2 percent. Tax rates therefore vary from state to state, from employer to employer within the state, and from time to time.

Although the tax receipts are deposited with the Treasury, the program is administered at the state level. Coverage may be extended beyond the groups required by federal law at the option of the state. The size of the weekly benefit is established by state laws, usually as a certain percentage of previous earnings with a maximum amount. Both the proportion of workers eligible and the percentage of prior earnings paid during periods of unemployment vary from state to state. In fiscal 1970, when unemployment averaged 4 percent, 5.8 million persons received benefits at an annual cost of $3.0 billion. Both the number of beneficiaries and annual outlays rose as the 1970–71 recession developed. In fiscal 1972, with average unemployment expected to be close to 6 percent, the number of persons receiving benefits at some time during the year will rise to about 8 million at an annual cost of $5.8 billion.

Most persons with some work experience are now covered by unemployment compensation programs. In November 1971, the average weekly benefit for the country as a whole was $53.31, but there was wide dispersion about that average, ranging from $22.62 in West Virginia to $62.47 in Colorado.

Federal laws require the payment of twenty-six weeks of unemployment insurance benefits to eligible workers. Legislation passed in 1970 provided that an additional thirteen weeks of benefits are to be paid to all eligible workers if the unemployment rate among insured workers for the nation as a whole equals or exceeds 4.5 percent for three consecutive months.[3] This extension of benefits can also be triggered on a state-by-state basis if the state unemployment rate among insured workers is 4 percent or higher for thirteen consecutive weeks

3. The unemployment rate among insured workers is always lower than that among all workers. The total work force includes many who are not covered by insurance, often because they are just entering the work force. Unemployment rates are typically higher for them than for experienced workers.

and the unemployment rate is at least 20 percent above the rate in the preceding two years. During calendar 1971, twenty-two states activated extended benefits at some time during the year because of state unemployment rates. By the end of 1971, the number of states still paying extended benefits was declining. For a short period, from the beginning of January 1972 to the middle of March 1972, the national covered unemployment rate was high enough to activate the program for the whole country. Late in 1971, legislation was enacted that permitted a still further extension of unemployment benefits to fifty-two weeks for states with unusually high rates of unemployment—above 6.5 percent. The second extension is to expire on June 30, 1972.

An issue related to unemployment compensation is whether the extension of benefits beyond twenty-six weeks of unemployment should be conditional on the rate of unemployment, in the state or in the nation. On the one hand, it is argued that when the unemployment rate in a particular locality is very low and job opportunities plentiful, twenty-six weeks is more than ample time for a person who has been laid off to find another job, and that the availability of unemployment compensation over a longer period would reduce his incentive to find one. It is only when the overall unemployment rate is high and job opportunities scarce that people cannot be expected to find work, and in those circumstances they should be carried by unemployment benefits for an extended period.

The other side of the argument stresses the fact that even when unemployment rates are generally low, some individuals have skills that cannot be matched with job openings. Without extended unemployment compensation, they would be forced to take much less desirable jobs and perhaps suffer a permanent loss of income. Moreover, this argument continues, unemployment compensation benefits are sufficiently lower than a worker's prior wages that most workers would be unlikely to avoid suitable jobs for long periods of time, since the reduction in their living standards would be substantial. Hence, the extension of unemployment benefits to thirty-nine or even fifty-two weeks should not be switched on and off depending on the unemployment rate, but should be made available on a continuing basis.

Welfare and Related Programs

Before the social security system was established, income maintenance for needy persons was supplied—if at all—by their families, by private charities, by some state and local governments, and by a limited number of private pension plans. Federal grants to share in the costs of state welfare programs were part of the original social security legislation of the 1930s. They were viewed as interim programs to aid those unable to work, during the transition period, until everyone had earned protection under the social security programs against loss of income. Benefits were provided for the disabled, the blind, the aged not entitled to social security (or entitled to only very low benefits), and to families with dependent children. Because eligibility for benefits is subject to a means test, families with incomes above a certain level are not eligible.

The states were given the responsibility for determining the standards of eligibility and the level of benefits. Hence, the standards of eligibility vary from state to state, and the level of benefits varies not only from state to state but among the various welfare programs. How widely benefits in each of the cash public assistance programs vary from state to state is shown in Table 6-4, which lists the five highest- and five lowest-benefit states in each public assistance category. Only South Carolina consistently falls in the lowest group for each type of welfare payment, and no state consistently pays the highest amount for every type of benefit. Each state makes different judgments about the relative needs of each kind of beneficiary and sets the benefits accordingly.

The number of persons receiving public assistance because of age or blindness has declined in the past several decades, in part because of the increased coverage and benefits paid under the social security program. (See Table 6-5.) However, despite the introduction and liberalization of the disability insurance program, the number of persons receiving public assistance because of disability has continued to rise, growing at an average annual rate of nearly 12 percent. Moreover, the rate of growth has accelerated since 1968, to 14.5 percent in 1969 and 16.5 percent in 1970. But the total numbers involved are still small; less than one-half of 1 percent of the population receives public assistance benefits because of disability.

The "crisis" in welfare has not arisen from these programs for adults but from aid to families with dependent children (AFDC). Table 6-6 shows the number of recipients, average benefits, and total expenditures for selected calendar years from 1950 to 1970, and the increase projected in the fiscal 1973 budget.

Table 6-4. The Five States Paying the Lowest Benefits and the Five Paying the Highest Benefits in Each of Four Welfare Programs, September 1971

Dollars per month per recipient or family

State	Old age assistance	Aid to the blind	Aid to the disabled	Aid to families with dependent children
U.S. average	75.21	103.31	98.64	186.83
Lowest				
Mississippi	. . .	63.70	. . .	53.78
South Carolina	48.84	66.71	56.76	72.56
Louisiana	. . .	. . .	55.60	75.68
Tennessee	49.83	70.74	. . .	. . .
Texas	54.18	. . .	62.66	. . .
New Mexico	54.30	. . .	. . .	. . .
Georgia	54.46	70.38	. . .	. . .
Alabama	. . .	70.30	52.60	58.46
Indiana	. . .	. . .	56.72	. . .
Florida	. . .	. . .	. . .	92.12
Highest				
New Hampshire	165.74	161.85	144.28	. . .
Alaska	129.25	174.19	172.51	. . .
Hawaii	. . .	132.68	147.19	293.65
New York	. . .	. . .	. . .	280.94
Minnesota	. . .	. . .	. . .	268.35
New Jersey	. . .	. . .	. . .	265.05
Connecticut	107.88	. . .	. . .	263.54
Iowa	126.36	. . .	152.71	. . .
Delaware	. . .	. . .	143.10	. . .
Massachusetts	. . .	153.72	. . .	. . .
California	. . .	153.03	. . .	. . .
Wisconsin	120.15	. . .	. . .	. . .

Source: *Social Security Bulletin*, Vol. 35 (February 1972), p. 59.

The rate of increase in the number of persons receiving AFDC benefits accelerated rapidly after 1965, more than doubling in the next five years, as is shown in Table 6-6. The rapid growth in the number of recipients and dissatisfaction with the wide variation in eligibility standards and benefit payments has resulted in the welfare reform proposals now before the Congress. Under the current program, the number of beneficiaries is expected to continue rising through fiscal 1973, reaching 12.6 million people in 3.3 million families.

WELFARE REFORM. The public assistance program has come under increasing attack in recent years, both from those who point to its in-

Table 6-5. Number of Persons Receiving Public Assistance because of Age, Blindness, or Disability, and Total Money Payments, Selected Years, 1950–70

Year	Old-age assistance	Aid to the blind	Aid to the disabled	Total
	Number receiving payment in December (*thousands*)			
1950	2,786	98	69	2,953
1955	2,538	104	241	2,883
1960	2,305	107	369	2,781
1965	2,087	85	557	2,729
1970	2,082	81	935	3,098
	Cash benefit payments, calendar year (*millions of dollars*)			
1950	1,454	53	8	1,515
1955	1,488	68	135	1,691
1960	1,626	86	236	1,948
1965	1,594	77	417	2,088
1970	1,861	98	985	2,944

Sources: *Social Security Bulletin*, Vol. 34 (October 1971), p. 53, and Vol. 34 (May 1971), p. 50; *Social Security Bulletin, Annual Statistical Supplement, 1969*, p. 132.

Table 6-6. Number of Families and Children Receiving Public Assistance under Aid to Families with Dependent Children, and Average Monthly and Total Payments, Selected Years, 1950–73

Year (calendar, 1950–70; fiscal, 1971–73)	Number receiving payment in December (thousands)			Average monthly payment in December (dollars)		Total payments during the year (millions of dollars)
	Families	Children	Total recipients[a]	Per family	Per recipient	
1950	651	1,661	2,233	71.45	20.85	547
1955	602	1,661	2,192	85.50	23.50	612
1960	803	2,370	3,073	108.35	28.35	994
1965	1,054	3,316	4,396	136.95	32.85	1,644
1970	2,553	7,034	9,660	187.95	49.65	4,852
	Average monthly number receiving payment in fiscal year (*thousands*)					
1971	2,532	6,962	9,556	...	...	5,656
1972 estimate	n.a.	n.a.	11,073	...	...	6,713
1973 estimate	n.a.	n.a.	12,572	...	...	7,843

Sources: *Social Security Bulletin*, Vol. 34 (December 1971), pp. 54–55; *The Budget of the United States Government—Appendix, Fiscal Year 1973*, p. 452.
n.a. Not available.
a. Includes as recipients the children and one or both parents or one caretaker relative in families in which the requirements of such adults were considered in determining the amount of assistance.

adequacies in meeting the needs of the poor and from those who decry its rapid growth. As one of his major innovations in domestic policy, President Nixon proposed in August 1969 a thorough reform of the welfare system. The President's proposal, substantially modified, has passed the House of Representatives twice, most recently in June 1971 as H.R. 1. The Senate has held extensive hearings on the proposal but has not yet brought it to a vote.

While all the major components of the current public assistance program have serious shortcomings, most controversy has centered around aid to families with dependent children. Critics point out that the AFDC program is a failure because:

1. It is inequitable. Families are treated very differently depending on where they happen to live. Fifty-four jurisdictions set benefit levels and eligibility standards. In some states benefits are extremely low, providing bare subsistence; in others they are more nearly adequate.

2. It excludes large numbers of poor families. Federal law permits states to provide benefits to families headed by unemployed males, but not all states do so. There are no federal benefits for the families of men working full time at low wages—the "working poor." This exclusion creates perverse incentives. A father earning very low wages can improve the income of his family by leaving them and making them eligible for AFDC.

3. It discourages work. Until 1967, families on welfare had no incentive to go to work because their welfare benefits were reduced by $1 for every dollar they earned. Amendments to the public assistance law in 1967 allowed recipients to keep $30 a month and 33 cents of each dollar earned, but this is a modest work incentive. It is equivalent to a 67 percent tax rate on earnings. Since welfare recipients who go to work also have to pay the social security tax and may lose medical and other benefits, they may find that their income is reduced if they take a job.

4. It is undignified. The very nature of the program, with its complex eligibility requirements, rigid means tests, and distinctions between broken families and other families, is demeaning for the recipients and often leads to abuse of the poor by program officials.

While various approaches to welfare reform have been vigorously advocated,[4] it is now widely agreed that AFDC should be replaced by a system that

4. For a fuller discussion, see Charles L. Schultze and others, *Setting National Priorities: The 1972 Budget* (Brookings Institution, 1971), Chapter 8.

• guarantees every family a basic benefit determined by family size, to ensure that all families with children have enough income to buy the necessities of life; and that

• reduces the basic benefit by substantially less than $1 for each dollar earned, to ensure that families have an incentive to seek employment.

For example, the basic benefit might be set at $3,000 for a family of four and the benefit reduced by 50 cents for each dollar earned. Under such a system, a family with $2,000 in earnings would have their basic benefit reduced by half that amount, or $1,000. They would therefore receive $2,000 in benefits, which, added to their $2,000 in earnings, would give them a total income of $4,000. Smaller benefits would be received by families with earnings up to $6,000.

This kind of system has been called a negative income tax, by analogy with the regular or positive tax system. Positive taxpayers now have to share with the government a fraction of each additional dollar earned. That fraction is called the marginal tax rate. In the same fashion, recipients of negative tax payments would find their payments reduced as their earnings rose. They too would have to share a fraction of each dollar earned with the government. From their point of view, that fraction is a marginal tax rate.

A negative income tax is a simple idea, but shifting from the present crazyquilt of benefits under AFDC to a negative income tax would be an extraordinarily complex problem. At present, welfare benefit levels vary widely among the states, as do the wages of the working population. Suppose the country adopted a negative income tax with a basic benefit near the poverty line, or about $4,000 for a family of four—approximately the level of benefits now received by welfare recipients in the more generous states. This would be extremely expensive. The change would greatly increase the benefit payments to those groups already eligible for welfare, since most states have much lower benefit levels at present, and it would extend benefits to a very large group of newly eligible families—the working poor. If the basic benefit were $4,000 and the marginal tax rate were 50 percent, benefits would be extended to families earning as much as $8,000. Moreover, a national basic benefit as high as $4,000 might encourage substantial numbers of people to drop out of the labor force in areas—especially the Deep South—where wage levels are low. Some money could be saved by raising the marginal tax rate, but this would discourage working. On the other hand, if the basic benefit were set low—say, $2,000 for a family of four—persons already on welfare in the higher-income states would be worse off than they are now unless provisions were made to maintain their benefits at a higher level.

The administration's original proposal of 1969 necessarily represented a compromise in which movement toward the basic objective was conditioned by the problems listed above. Under the original proposal, all poor families with children would be eligible for a basic benefit; for a family of four with no income, the benefit would be $1,600, and it would be scaled up or down from that level depending on family size. The first $60 per month of earnings would entail no reduction of benefits, and for each dollar of earnings above that level benefits would be reduced by 50 cents. For the first time, the working poor would be eligible for benefit payments.

The cost of this basic program would be paid by the federal government. States that currently had benefits in excess of this federal minimum—and most states do—would be required to supplement the federal benefit in order to maintain total benefits at the old level. The federal government would pay 30 percent of the cost of these supplements.

When H.R. 1 emerged from the House in 1971, it was substantially different from the administration proposals. The basic cash payment of $1,600 for a family of four was raised to $2,400—but since food stamps would be eliminated, total benefits would not be raised for most families, and for some families they would be reduced. States now paying more than the federal benefit would not be required to provide supplementary benefits but could do so if they wished.

Work requirements for welfare recipients would be substantially increased and monetary incentives for work reduced. Recipients of public assistance would be divided into two groups, those with an adult available for employment and those without. All family members would be considered employable except the disabled, those under the age of sixteen (for students, twenty-two), mothers of children under the age of six (after 1974, under the age of three), those needed at home to care for incapacitated family members, and wives of family heads. Employable adults would be required to register for and accept training or work; failure to do so would reduce benefits by $800. For every dollar earned above $60 a month, welfare benefits would be cut by 67 cents. (The substance of these work requirements

was separately enacted into law in December 1971.) In 1971 about
1 million adults in AFDC families fell into the employable category
and 1.5 million in the unemployable, under the concepts in H.R. 1:

	Number (*in thousands*)
Characteristics of family head	
Disabled fathers	246
Unemployed fathers	193
Mothers with preschool children	1,258
Mothers with school-age children	839
Total	2,536
Available for employment (unemployed fathers and mothers with school-age children)	1,032

For welfare recipients, the combination of reduced welfare benefits
and the social security payroll tax would eliminate much of the monetary advantage of working, unless they succeeded in finding a relatively high-paying job. Table 6-7 shows how little the net income of a
welfare family of four would improve when a family member found a
job. The last column of the table, labeled "marginal tax rate," indicates the percentage of any additional earnings that would be taken
away by a reduction in welfare benefits or by taxes. In the range of
earnings between $720 and $4,200 a year, welfare recipients would keep

Table 6-7. Relationship under H.R. 1 between Earnings, Welfare Benefits, Taxes, After-
Tax Income, and Marginal Tax Rate for a Family of Four, at Selected Earning Levels
Dollars

Annual earnings	*Welfare benefits*	*Income before taxes*	*Social security taxes*[a]	*Individual income taxes*	*Income after taxes*	*Marginal tax rate*
0	2,400	2,400	0	0	2,400	0
720	2,400	3,120	39	0	3,081	5.4
1,200	2,080	3,280	65	0	3,215	72.0
1,800	1,680	3,480	97	0	3,383	72.0
2,400	1,280	3,680	130	0	3,550	72.0
3,000	880	3,880	162	0	3,718	72.0
3,600	480	4,080	194	0	3,886	72.0
4,200	0	4,200	227	0	3,973	85.4
5,400	0	5,400	292	155	4,953	18.3
6,000	0	6,000	324	245	5,431	20.4

Source: Calculated by authors from provisions of H.R. 1, cited in source to Table 6-3.
a. The employee payroll tax rate of 5.4 percent, established in H.R. 1 for 1973 and 1974, is assumed in
these calculations.

only 28 cents or less of each additional dollar earned. Since Medicaid and housing subsidies would also decline as income rose, the value of additional earnings for many welfare recipients would be even less than that shown in the table.

As now incorporated in H.R. 1, welfare reform would establish nationwide eligibility requirements, provide a basic minimum benefit, and include the working poor—at least if they were in a family with children. But it would continue to rely upon—indeed it would strengthen—the use of administrative controls as a means of enforcing work requirements, while providing little monetary incentive for recipients to seek work themselves.

IN-KIND BENEFITS. In addition to cash welfare benefits, other federal programs provide benefits to the needy in the form of specific goods or services, usually called "transfers in kind."

The *Medicaid* program pays for medical care for recipients of cash public assistance, and in some states for poor and near-poor families who do not qualify for public assistance. This program is described in Chapter 7. In almost all states, need alone is not enough to qualify an individual to receive benefits; one must also be an aged, blind, or disabled person or in a family eligible for aid to dependent children. Eligibility requirements and benefits vary substantially from state to state. In fiscal 1973 the Medicaid program will cost $7.2 billion, of which $3.8 billion will be paid by the federal government and the rest by states and localities. For the needy aged, the Medicaid program in many states pays the premiums, deductibles, and coinsurance required under the Medicare program.

Food subsidies are provided by five programs—food stamps, child nutrition, special milk, disposal of surplus commodities, and the emergency food program that is being absorbed into the food stamp program. The largest of these is the food stamp program, established in 1964. Participation by states and individual counties originally was optional. In 1971, however, the provision of food stamps became a mandatory part of state welfare programs. The new legislation established uniform standards of eligibility based on income and family size. A family of four with an income below $360 a year receives without charge food stamps worth $108 a month. At higher incomes a charge is made, reaching 25 percent of income at the $2,000-a-year level. With incomes of $2,000 to $4,000, the cost of stamps as a percentage of income remains fairly constant—not more than 27 percent.

An eligible family buys the stamps and uses them instead of cash to buy food. The purchasing power of the stamps is higher than their cost to eligible families, by an amount that is greatest for very low-income families.

The total number of participants in the food stamp program has risen rapidly in recent years—from 3.2 million in 1969 to 10.5 million in 1971. Unlike most other programs providing assistance to the poor, benefits are uniform throughout the country. Because eligibility is based on need alone, non-aged childless couples and the working poor may also participate.

The child nutrition and special milk programs consist of grants to states to subsidize the cost of milk and of school meals. In recent years, the program has been expanded to include breakfasts as well as lunches, and child care centers as well as schools. Legislation passed in 1970 provides additional assistance to schools with needy children. In addition, surplus food commodities obtained under the farm income stabilization program are donated to schools and other institutions, including community action programs, for distribution. Federal expenditures for food subsidies in fiscal 1973 are as follows (in millions of dollars):[5]

Recipient group	Expenditure
Aged	221
Disabled	97
AFDC and unemployed persons	3,002
Non-needy children	602
Total	3,922

Housing subsidies of various kinds are provided for poor and moderate-income families. The older low-rent public housing program consists of federal low-interest construction loans and annual subsidy contracts to local housing authorities, who build and operate public housing projects for the poor. Family income levels determine eligibility, and the federal subsidy makes it possible for local housing authorities to charge no more than 25 percent of tenants' income as rent. Income eligibility varies from community to community, depending on the level of rents for blue-collar housing in the community.

A newer set of housing programs subsidizes the cost of home owner-

5. *Special Analyses of the United States Government, Fiscal Year 1973*, pp. 191, 193, 197.

ship or rent in private dwellings for families at the moderate-income level. The federal government subsidizes interest payments for home owners and rents for tenants who meet the income eligibility requirements. The subsidies are calculated to bring the cost of home ownership down to 20 percent of income and the cost of rent (including utilities) down to 25 percent of income. As in the case of food stamps, eligibility for housing subsidies is based solely on income rather than on the "employability" categories established for cash public assistance. Most of the funds for housing subsidies are for *new* low-cost housing units, of which about 500,000 are being built each year under various public programs. The federal government plans to sponsor some 6 million such units by 1978, by which time the estimated cost of the subsidy will be $7.5 billion a year (compared to $1.8 billion in fiscal 1973). During the intervening years, however, the number of families who meet the income tests will continue to be larger than the number of new subsidized units becoming available. Hence subsidies have to be rationed, and waiting lists are common.[6]

Other Major Income Support Payments

The farm price support program raises the income of farmers. At the present time the program pays direct cash subsidies to farmers in return for which they agree to restrict the acreage planted in certain crops. This restriction raises prices and helps to increase farm income. There are no "needs" tests, and both large and small farmers are helped by this program. Since the benefits of the program are roughly proportional to the amount of farm products produced, large farmers receive the bulk of those benefits. One study estimated that in 1969 the largest 19 percent of farmers (in terms of their sales) received 63 percent of the benefits from the price support programs. The average income of those farmers from farming and nonfarming sources was $21,000. At the other end of the scale, the smallest 50 percent of farmers received only 9 percent of the benefits.[7]

Federal grants and loans to students for higher education are another major in-kind transfer program. Tuition payments and cash

6. For detailed discussions of federal housing programs, see Henry J. Aaron, *Shelter and Subsidies: Who Benefits from Federal Housing Policies?* (Brookings Institution, 1972), and Charles L. Schultze and others, *Setting National Priorities: The 1972 Budget* (Brookings Institution, 1971), Chapter 14.

7. Charles L. Schultze, *The Distribution of Farm Subsidies: Who Gets the Benefits?* (Brookings Institution, 1971), p. 29.

Table 6-8. Federal Expenditures for Income Support, by Major Program Characteristics, Fiscal Year 1973

Billions of dollars

| Program | Federal expenditures (estimate) | Criterion for eligibility and size of payment | | Program characteristics | | |
		Retirement or other employability status	Need	Based on prior contribution	Payment in cash or in kind	Nationwide benefit (NW) or varies by state (S)
Retirement and related, total	72.6	...	...	...	...	...
Veterans' compensation and pensions	6.4	Yes	Partially[a]	Yes[b]	Cash	NW
Military retirement and medical benefits	5.1	Yes	No	Yes[c]	Cash	NW
Civil service retirement	3.9	Yes	No	Yes	Cash	NW
Railroad retirement	2.1	Yes	No	Yes	Cash	NW
Old age, survivors, and disability insurance	44.7	Yes	Partially[d]	Yes	Cash	NW
Medicare	10.4	Yes	No	Yes	In kind	NW
Unemployment compensation, total	5.9	Yes	No	Yes	Cash	S
Public assistance and related, total	16.1	...	...	...	...	...
Aged, disabled, and blind	2.8	Yes	Yes	No	Cash	S
Families with dependent children	4.7	Yes	Yes	No	Cash	S
Medicaid	3.8	Yes	Yes	No	In kind	S
Food stamps	2.3	No	Yes	No	In kind	NW
Other nutrition	0.7	No	Yes[e]	No	In kind	NW
Housing subsidies	1.8	No	Yes	No	In kind	NW
Other, total	7.1	...	...	...	...	...
Student aid	3.4	No	Yes	No	In kind	NW
Farm price supports	3.7	No	No	No	Cash	NW
All programs, total	101.7	...	...	...	...	...

Sources: *The Budget of the United States Government, Fiscal Year 1973; The Budget of the United States Government—Appendix, Fiscal Year 1973; Special Analyses of the United States Government—Fiscal Year 1973.*

a. Pensions are inversely related to other income.
b. Participation in a war or other specified emergency is required in order to qualify for pensions.
c. Considered deferred pay.
d. Benefit formula gives larger benefit relative to wage history to lower income groups than to higher income groups.
e. Includes some programs, such as special milk program for schools, that are not based on need.

allowances were first made available to veterans after the Second World War to help them to obtain or complete their college education. Expenditures under this program declined sharply after the great surge of returning veterans had finished school in the late 1940s and early 1950s. Currently the program provides a basic stipend of $175 a month to cover the tuition and living expenses of veterans attending approved educational institutions. The number of persons using these benefits is expected to rise as veterans returning from Vietnam increase the numbers eligible. Total expenditures for this purpose are expected to grow from less than $1 billion in 1970 to nearly $2.2 billion in 1973.

Increasing amounts of money are now being made available for higher education to students other than veterans. They include educational opportunity grants for financially needy undergraduate students, work-study grants, loans, graduate fellowships, and subsidies to reduce interest costs on private loans to students.

Characteristics of Payments

Federal budget expenditures for income support now total $102 billion a year, absorb 60 percent of the civilian budget, and are growing rapidly. Table 6-8 summarizes the main components of the system —a patchwork of programs having widely varied characteristics and providing widely differing treatment to individuals and families in the same economic circumstances.

A recent study made for the Joint Economic Committee of the Congress contains dramatic illustrations of disparities in the current system.[8] In Detroit, for example, a nonworking mother of three children on welfare can receive cash, food, and medical benefits worth $4,894 a year—benefits equivalent to $5,373 before taxes. If the same family moved to Atlanta it would be eligible for $2,710 in benefits, but if the family head were a male it could receive only $474 a year (in food benefits). Moreover, if the mother of three children in Atlanta found a job and earned $3,200 a year, her total income support would drop to only $126. By working forty hours a week, fifty weeks a year, she would add only $616 to her family's income; net, her work would pay

8. James R. Storey, "Public Income Transfer Programs: The Incidence of Multiple Benefits and the Issues Raised by Their Receipt," A Study Prepared for the Use of the Subcommittee on Fiscal Policy of the Joint Economic Committee, *Studies in Public Welfare, Paper 1*, 92 Cong. 2 sess., April 10, 1972.

her only 31 cents an hour. An elderly couple in Detroit, entitled to minimum social security payments and with no other income, would receive cash, medical, and food benefits sufficient to bring their income up to $5,200, while the same couple in Atlanta would receive $3,320.

The wide variety and differing characteristics of the existing programs can be explained by the particular historical context in which they were introduced. But since both the programs and the circumstances have changed over the years, many of the differences have lost their original justification. The social security and unemployment compensation programs, as conceived in the 1930s, emphasized prior attachment to the labor force, in which people would work and earn rights to such benefits as retirement, survivors, disability, and unemployment insurance. The question of public assistance for persons with no prior attachment to the labor force was viewed as a temporary depression-induced problem, and benefits for persons in this group who were considered able to work, or who worked but still had very low incomes, were not provided at all. But the employment-related benefits, even after thirty years and much greater economic prosperity, still do not provide adequate income support for large segments of the population. More recently it has been deemed important to supplement cash benefits with transfers in kind, in an effort to ensure that food, medical care, and housing are provided to the poor or the elderly. In many cases, the philosophy and eligibility requirements of these in-kind programs are more need oriented, and less related to prior employment or categorical status, than are the older programs.

Alternative Strategies for Reform

How can the patchwork system of income support programs be improved? To what extent should programs be consolidated and differences in approach eliminated, and to what extent do those differences still make sense? Rather than try to suggest a specific set of solutions, the remainder of this chapter explores some of the alternative directions that a reform of the system might take and considers the advantages and disadvantages of each.

Universal versus Means-tested Support Payments

Most federal income support payments are subject in some degree to a means test—that is, the benefits are reduced as income increases.

Exceptions are benefits under federal civilian and military retirement programs, veterans' disability compensation, farm price supports, and Medicare. Under social security, the test of retirement—up to age seventy-two—is whether a person is earning significant amounts of wages or salary, and retirement benefits are reduced for outside earnings. Public assistance benefits, veterans' pensions, food stamps, Medicaid, and housing subsidies are all means tested.

In many other countries, a number of universal benefits are provided to broad categories of people, regardless of income. In the Western world, children's allowances are paid universally in Australia, Canada, Denmark, Iceland, Ireland, Israel, the Netherlands, New Zealand, Norway, Sweden, and West Germany. The only eligibility requirements are residency and children. In the United Kingdom the children's allowances start only after the birth of a second child. In a large number of other countries, especially in South America and Africa, employers are required to pay allowances for children of their employees and pensioners.

Universal medical care is provided by the government in seven countries. A much larger number require employers to provide medical insurance for employees in industry and commerce. There are a few universal retirement systems, principally in the Scandinavian countries, under which pensions are granted on the basis of age and residence, with no income test. Canada and Denmark have a two-tier system—a basic universal pension and a second pension that is income tested.

The main advantage of programs with universal benefits is that they avoid the social stigma that is attached to income-tested programs. If everyone receives the grant or benefit, there is no singling out of the poor and no need to reveal the financial status of the family to become eligible. They also avoid the problems associated with detecting "cheaters," since everyone is eligible.

The major disadvantage of universal systems is their very large cost when they are extended to categories of the population who need little or no income support. Providing social security benefits to those over seventy-two, with no reduction for earnings, costs very little extra because few persons over seventy-two have earnings. Doing the same for social security beneficiaries at age sixty-five, however, would become more expensive, compared to the present system, because more of them do have earnings. And providing universal children's allowances of sufficient size to be a real aid to poor families would be exceedingly expensive: for every dollar paid to poor and near-poor families, three to four dollars would be paid to families in the middle- and upper-income brackets. That is why benefits are very small in countries that do have children's allowances. In Canada, for example, the allowances range only from $6 to $10 a month, depending on the age of the child. In general, unless most of the particular population to be helped is unlikely to have outside earnings (for example, those over seventy-two), universal payment systems are a very inefficient means for helping those with low incomes, since the benefits are not concentrated where the need is greatest. Large numbers of families would receive allowances and at the same time have their taxes increased to pay for the allowances. Tax rates would have to be raised simply to channel money from the family to the government and back to the family again.

Contributory versus Noncontributory Programs

The social security (old age, survivors, disability, and hospital insurance—OASDHI) and unemployment compensation programs are called contributory insurance systems.[9] By paying a certain percent of his wages, a person establishes a right to future benefits payable on retirement, death, disability, or unemployment. As the earlier discussion pointed out, however, these systems are not like private insurance, in which benefits are closely related to what an individual (or his employer) has contributed to the system in the past. Retirement benefits under social security are higher relative to past wages for those whose wages have been low; they are higher for a retired worker and his wife than for a single person; and for all retirees taken together they are substantially higher than past contributions alone would warrant.

Despite their welfare-oriented benefit schedules, the contributory programs have much greater political and social acceptability than do the noncontributory public assistance programs. Beneficiaries consider them an earned right with no social stigma attached, and the public in general does not think of them as "welfare" programs. For this reason, one plausible strategy for consolidating and rationalizing

9. The federal civil service and railroad retirement programs are also called contributory.

income support would be to merge at least some of the welfare programs with the social security programs.

Current legislation is moving in this direction. As one step, H.R. 1 would transfer the administration of the adult categories of welfare (aid to the aged, blind, and disabled) to the Social Security Administration and would provide uniform minimum benefits in all parts of the nation. Benefits under these programs would still be means tested —that is, eligibility would depend on income levels. But this is also true of social security benefits themselves insofar as earnings from wages and salaries are concerned. The difference is that the receipt of other forms of income, such as dividends, interest, private pension payments, and the like, does not reduce social security benefits, although their receipt does reduce or eliminate public assistance payments. But it would not be too great an additional step to integrate the two systems: one part of social security benefits could be provided solely on the basis of past earnings (adjusted for changes in the cost of living, or other factors, if desired), with no reduction for outside income; the other part of the benefits could be related to income, with the benefits tapering off as the income level of the beneficiary rose.[10]

Similarly, it has been suggested that the administration of Medicaid for the aged, the disabled, and the blind be turned over to the Social Security Administration. A modest additional step could combine Medicaid for those categories of the needy with Medicare, under social security. The premiums, deductibles, and coinsurance under Medicare would be paid by the government, totally or in part, for the poor and near poor.

If these proposals were adopted, one major system would provide cash and medical service benefits for the elderly, the blind, and the disabled. The system would be basically contributory, but with special supplements for low-income recipients whose benefits, based on past contributions, still would leave them below the poverty line. This approach would have the advantage of providing a single system for all and, it is hoped, of removing or reducing the stigma now attached to public assistance. Some supporters of the existing social security system might object that the changes would introduce a means test into what is now largely a wage-related system. But, as has been pointed

10. For a fuller description of a two-tier system, see Joseph A. Pechman, Henry J. Aaron, and Michael K. Taussig, *Social Security: Perspectives for Reform* (Brookings Institution, 1968), Chapter 9.

out, an income test already exists for social security beneficiaries under age seventy-two insofar as wage and salary earnings are concerned. The change to an integrated system, with an income test for part of the benefits, might not seem such a large step after all.

The Categorical versus the Need Approach

Under almost all the current income support programs, individuals and families become eligible by being in certain categories—retired, aged, disabled, blind, experienced unemployed, female heads of families with dependent children, farmers, and veterans. While low income is a criterion of eligibility in the cash welfare programs and in Medicaid, few programs have benefits that are based *solely* on income levels. As an alternative to consolidating some of the welfare programs into the contributory social security system, what are the merits of eliminating the categorical approach and paying benefits solely on the basis of need, through a comprehensive negative income tax?

Replacing all the existing income support programs with a universally applicable negative income tax is clearly not a plausible alternative. Many of these programs, in whole or in part, deal with problems other than poverty. The social security system pays retirement income related in part to prior contributions and provides retirement benefits even to those who have other sources of income. Federal military and civilian employee retirement programs are not poverty related: they are intended solely to provide retirement benefits and quite properly are not reduced for outside income. The unemployment compensation program provides, for workers who have been laid off and are looking for a job, temporary income support in amounts quite appropriately related to their prior earnings.

The more relevant question is whether a single negative income tax program could be designed as a basic support for all individuals and families whose income from work, retirement benefits, unemployment compensation, or from any other source is too low to provide a minimum decent standard of living. Under such a system, a single set of minimum income guarantees would be provided for all families, appropriately adjusted for family size and other family characteristics, and a single formula would be used to reduce benefits as income increased (that is, a single marginal tax rate). Eligibility would not depend on categorical status—whether the recipient was aged, disabled, or the mother of dependent children—but simply on income. Prior work-related benefit payments available to the family under social security, unemployment insurance, or other programs would count as income and reduce the basic negative income tax benefits.

This approach has many advantages. It would base the poverty-related income support programs solely on need, eliminating the inequities and perverse incentives that inevitably occur when eligibility or benefit size is made dependent on categorical status. It would provide monetary incentives for work. But granted that the negative income tax is a desirable approach to the poverty-related programs, should there be one universal system, with a single set of minimum guarantees and a single marginal tax rate for all, or should there be separate systems for different groups of the poor?

Several factors enter into this determination. A high minimum guarantee and a high marginal tax rate would provide generous income support for the very poor, but work incentives would suffer since every dollar of earnings would result in a large reduction in benefits. Conversely, a low minimum guarantee and a low marginal tax rate would be conducive to work effort but would not provide a decent income for those who cannot work. For the aged and severely disabled, preserving work incentives is not so important; consequently, a high minimum and a high marginal tax rate would be appropriate. But for those groups who can work, a lower marginal tax rate and perhaps a lower minimum would be desirable. The problem, of course, is to decide who can (or should) work. For the aged and severely disabled the decision is fairly easy. But what about other potential recipients? Should families headed by mothers with preschool children be treated differently from families, otherwise similar, in which the children are in school, or from families in which both parents are present? Should childless couples or single persons be treated separately?

While some distinctions may seem logically desirable, tailoring the minimum guarantee and the marginal tax rate to different categories of people inevitably leads to the arbitrary distinctions and perverse incentives that characterize the present system—as when unemployed fathers find that their families are financially better off if they desert. Consequently, while it might be feasible to have two negative income tax systems—one for the aged and disabled and one for non-aged families—establishing still further categories would probably raise more difficulties than it would solve. Therefore a universal, or dual, negative income tax system inevitably would have to incorporate a compromise between the option that concentrates most of the benefits on the poor who cannot work (high minimum, high marginal tax rate) and the option that emphasizes work incentives and income supplements for the working poor (a lower minimum and a lower marginal tax rate).

A transitional problem in moving to a negative income tax system was discussed earlier in this chapter in connection with the administration's welfare reform proposals. At the present time, benefits under the existing categorical programs are diverse and vary from state to state within each program. Two courses of action are available to avoid reductions in benefits for many recipients if a new system were introduced: the new benefits could be set equal to the highest of the benefits available under the current programs; or the states could be required (with federal assistance) to make up any difference between the new benefits and the existing ones. Since the former alternative would be prohibitively expensive, the latter course seems the more feasible.

The Payroll Tax as a Means of Financing

The earmarked payroll tax was first used in financing the civil service retirement fund in 1920 and was later extended to the social security and unemployment compensation programs. Of the $83 billion spent in fiscal 1973 for cash income support payments, $64 billion, or 77 percent, will be financed from payroll taxes.

A person's cash benefits from the social security program are not directly related to what he has paid, though the recorded wages on which he paid taxes are used in a complex way to determine the size of his benefits. This has been an efficient method of providing beneficiaries with replacement incomes related to their previous standard of living. Benefits could also be related to past wages even if the system were financed from general revenues rather than from earmarked payroll taxes. But the linkage of payroll taxes and the wage records used to calculate benefits has enhanced the concept of a contributory system: taxpayers see themselves paying into a fund and getting back "what they put in."

The tax has been a highly productive source of revenue for the social security system. Over the years, the Congress has raised the tax along with the benefit levels and has met little political opposition —perhaps because the wage earner sees only half the tax deducted from his pay check (the other half being paid by his employer) and considers the deduction a "contribution" rather than a tax.

The political and computational conveniences associated with the payroll tax, however, should not obscure the fact that it is highly regressive. As was noted earlier, both employer and employee pay a 5.2 percent tax on wages, for a combined rate of 10.4 percent. The ceiling on wages subject to tax, currently set at $9,000, is scheduled in H.R. 1 to rise to $10,200 next year. The ceiling is primarily responsible for the regressive nature of the tax. The tax is a constant percentage of earnings up to the ceiling but then becomes a smaller and smaller fraction as earnings rise. The payroll tax has no personal exemptions, no deductions, and no low-income allowance. Moreover, it treats families of the same income level differently, since the amount of tax a family pays varies according to the number of wage earners. A family with total earnings of $18,000, earned equally by the husband and wife, pays twice as much in payroll taxes as does a family in the same income bracket with one earner. So long as the combined earnings do not exceed the ceiling, the tax is proportional to earnings. And, at any given level of family earnings below the ceiling, the single-earner family receives larger benefits than does the multi-earner family.[11] Not only is the tax regressive, but it taxes families with equal earnings unequally.

There are several reforms that could eliminate the regressive features of the tax, while still retaining it as a generally accepted means for financing the social security program.

One basic reform would be to remove the wage ceiling entirely, adjusting both the employee and employer tax rates downward to compensate for the expansion in the tax base. Such a reform would have the advantage of making the tax proportional to earned income. Making it a tax on all earnings would also remove the inequities between single- and multi-earner families in the same income bracket. Since raising the wage ceiling, under the current system of computing benefits, increases the benefits a worker will receive in the future, some

11. For example, if the $9,000 ceiling were in effect long enough for a single-earner family to receive maximum benefits under that wage history, the man and his wife would receive $5,584 annually in benefits. If the husband had earned $5,000 and the wife $4,000, the separate annual benefits would total $4,667. If the split were $7,000 and $2,000, the wife would receive a larger amount by taking her benefit as a wife based on her husband's earnings than she would by taking the benefit based on her own earnings—despite the fact that she has paid taxes on her earnings.

maximum benefit level would have to be established if the wage ceiling were removed.

A second reform would be to make it a family tax, with personal exemptions for employees and perhaps a low-income allowance for poor families. As one example, a $750 personal exemption for the worker and each of his dependents would exclude from the tax the first $3,000 of earned income for a family of four. Retaining the employer's tax on all wages and salaries, with no allowance for employees' personal exemptions, would ensure that taxes had been paid for everyone who subsequently became entitled to benefits.

This set of reforms would, in effect, convert the employers' portion of the tax into a flat-rate tax on wages and make the employees' tax approximately the same as an earmarked portion of the individual income tax.

Cash versus In-Kind Benefits

Until recent years, income support consisted largely of cash payments that the recipient could spend according to his preferences. While some benefits in kind have existed for a long time—particularly public housing—the growth of programs subsidizing "worthy" expenditures (for food, medical care, housing, and education) has been very rapid since 1960. Expenditures on in-kind payments rose from $400 million in that year to an estimated $19 billion in 1973.

Several rationales underlie the provision of benefits in kind rather than in cash:

1. Consumption of a minimum level of certain kinds of goods and services may be considered socially desirable; if poor people were given money only, it is assumed they would buy less than that minimum level. Food stamps reduce the price of food to zero for the very poor and by lesser amounts for poor families with some income, as a means of inducing them to buy more food. Part of the rationale for Medicare and Medicaid is to encourage people to seek medical care when they need it. Since benefits in kind often seem more acceptable politically than cash benefits, they make it possible to provide the poor with greater assistance than would otherwise be feasible.

2. Often some essential expenditures have to be made in large, discrete sums rather than continuously over time. Poor families, pressed to meet the ordinary expenses of living out of their low incomes, cannot be counted on to save in advance for such expenditures; moreover,

they often find it impossible to borrow. Providing additional cash benefits equal to average yearly medical expenses would still leave families unable to meet unusually large medical bills and often unable to cover even the usual run of medical bills, since they would have spent the cash benefits for other purposes. The high cost, over a relatively short time, of acquiring a higher education is one reason—though not the only one—for the government's provision of grants and loans to students.

3. Still another rationale for payments in kind rests on the judgment that one person's consumption of certain goods or services benefits the rest of society. Higher education is thought to result not only in added earning power for the individual, but also in benefits to society as a whole, in the form of a better and more informed citizenry. Similar arguments are made in favor of subsidizing day care and child development programs. Some proponents of housing subsidies argue that decent housing for the poor leads to better neighborhoods and less crime.

4. Sometimes an income support program is used as a means to improve the supply of the good in question. Through the housing subsidy programs, it is argued, the federal government can locate low-cost housing outside of central city slums and, because of the size of its program, can stimulate the development of new technology in the building of low-cost housing. Medicare and Medicaid, particularly if they were expanded into a national health insurance program, could be used to influence the way health care is delivered and thereby improve the efficiency and distribution of health care services.

5. Finally, the provision of benefits in kind can be used to ration the payments. Subsidies to low-income students for higher education are paid only to those who have the desire and the ability to enter college. Those who do not, receive no subsidy. If the cash equivalent of the subsidy were paid to all poor families as part of the cash welfare program, the amounts involved would be much larger. Housing subsidies are currently received by only a small fraction of the families whose low income makes them eligible. As new housing is built under the subsidy program, the number of units available for occupancy with a subsidy increases each year, but it will be many years before enough units are available to provide one for each eligible family.

The desirability of paying benefits in kind rather than in cash depends on the importance one attaches to the particular rationale for making in-kind payments and the degree to which the particular program meets the objectives sought. Of all the in-kind programs, food stamps probably have the weakest justification. Food purchases, unlike medical care, do not involve huge lump-sum expenditures. They are less likely than higher education to provide social benefits to anyone other than the recipient. And, unlike housing subsidies or medical insurance, the food stamp program does not seek to improve the efficiency or effectiveness of the supplying industry. Basically it is an attempt to substitute the judgment of the government for the judgment of the family as to how its income should be spent. The program does have the advantage that income is the sole test of eligibility—unemployed fathers of families and the working poor may receive stamps. But the "advantage" lies in the eligibility rules, not in the provision of food itself. Reform of the cash welfare system to make income the chief criterion of eligibility would remove this advantage.

The other in-kind payments have more substantive justification. This is not to say that each of them always effectively accomplishes its purposes. There has been much criticism, for example, of poor quality housing furnished under the housing subsidy program, with large profits accruing to speculators. But such criticisms do not necessarily argue for converting a program to cash benefits; rather, they call attention to the need for reforming the program itself.

How Should Benefits Be Set?

Three kinds of questions arise in determining how the benefits under various income support programs should be set.

First, to what extent should benefits vary from one part of the country to another, to take into account differences in prices or in real standards of living? Benefits under the federal government's retirement, survivors, and disability programs are uniform throughout the nation for persons with similar wage histories, largely because these are viewed as insurance programs whose benefits are related to past contributions. The public assistance programs, as noted earlier, pay benefits that vary widely from state to state. Since those variations are not primarily related to the cost of living, the real purchasing power of benefits varies substantially among the states. In general, poorer states pay lower public assistance benefits, but there is no close relationship between a state's per capita income and the welfare benefits it pays.

Because the cost of living differs from place to place, a uniform federal standard for public assistance benefits would result in higher real purchasing power for some recipients than for others; what would be a meager income in New York City would be fairly generous in rural Mississippi. Conceptually, two approaches to adjusting benefits in different parts of the country could be used to avoid these anomalies. Under one approach, benefits would vary from place to place, depending only on differences in the cost of living. Benefits would have the same real purchasing power in each location. Since real standards of living differ throughout the country, however, this approach would give to public assistance recipients in, say, the rural South, benefits that were much higher relative to the earnings of a typical blue collar worker in that area than would be the case in northern industrial centers. The alternative approach would provide benefits that everywhere bore a constant relationship to the earnings of a typical moderate-income working family. A practical way to do this would be to vary benefits according to differences in the wages paid to semiskilled and unskilled workers in the various locations.

The first approach—adjusting benefits only for cost-of-living differences—faces two difficulties. There are no good measures of differences in the cost of living on a state-by-state or county-by-county basis. The existing data are collected principally for a limited number of metropolitan areas. Recent surveys show a 20 percent difference in the cost of a low-income family budget between the most expensive and the least expensive metropolitan areas in the continental United States. But this difference may not accurately reflect differences in prices; it may to some extent reflect variations in the quality of goods and services typically bought in areas with different living standards. Even if much larger resources were devoted to the collection of price data and the survey were extended to more cities and to rural areas, it would be difficult to construct valid price indexes measuring area differences in the cost of living. Moreover, should such data be collected and benefits be adjusted for cost-of-living differences, one still might question the fairness of providing beneficiaries in one part of the nation with much higher living standards relative to their working neighbors than in other parts.

Wage data are more readily available than price data for a large number of areas. To vary public assistance benefits in accordance with differences in area wages would be more feasible and probably more equitable as well.

A reason other than equity argues for taking account of wage variations in setting national benefit standards for public assistance. As was noted above, setting a single uniform benefit under public assistance would be very expensive, since the benefit level would have to be set at or close to that of the highest states to avoid a sharp reduction in benefits for recipients in those states. In general, the states with high benefits are also the ones with high wage and income levels. Setting a national average standard for benefits, with variations about the average dependent on wage levels in different areas, would reduce but not solve the problem. The patchwork of state variations in welfare benefits could be reformed by establishing a wage-related federal standard and requiring states whose benefits are now above the federally determined level to make up the difference to benefit recipients; the federal standard would be gradually increased over a period of years until the remaining gaps were closed. The use of differences in wage levels to adjust benefits is by no means a perfect solution, but it might be the only practical way to achieve a completely national system of benefits.

A second problem is what to do about increases in the cost of living over time. Both the military and civil service retirement programs are automatically adjusted for increases in the consumer price index. Pending legislation includes provisions for automatically increasing social security (OASDI) benefits as prices increase. But rising prices obviously erode the purchasing power of welfare benefits too, and these are not automatically adjusted. The advantage of providing for automatic adjustment in benefits is that it assures the beneficiaries that their real purchasing power will be maintained. The main disadvantage is that the automatic adjustments could become another factor spreading inflationary pressures during periods of overheated demand and rapidly rising prices. This disadvantage is probably of more theoretical than practical significance. The Congress has always been fairly prompt in legislating social security benefit increases as the cost of living has risen. And those who receive public assistance payments, being generally the poorest of the nation's population, should not be singled out to bear the burden of restraining inflation. Adjustments in tax policies or in other expenditures are a fairer means of reducing inflationary pressure.

A third problem is the extent to which benefits should be increased to keep up with real increases in the nation's standard of living. Per capita levels of real income in the United States have been rising at about 3 percent a year, doubling every twenty-five years, in line with increases in productivity. Rising productivity brings rising real wages. Since a worker's social security benefits are tied to the wages he received, the rise in real wages keeps increasing the benefits to which he will be entitled on retirement. But once he has retired, even if his benefits are adjusted in line with cost-of-living changes, their real value does not rise (in the absence of specific legislation increasing benefits), while living standards continue to increase for those around him.

Concepts of poverty and a decent living standard are clearly relative. What people consider a poverty-level income is much higher now than it was a generation ago and incomparably higher in the United States than in the less developed countries. If benefits for retirees, public assistance recipients, and others receiving income support are not raised periodically along with increases in per capita incomes generally, living standards of families who depend on these benefits for most of their income will fall further and further behind those of the rest of the population.

In the long run, benefit levels should be raised in line with advancing living standards. But this does not necessarily imply that the benefits should be increased automatically under some prescheduled formula. Making such adjustments would give both the executive branch and the Congress an opportunity to review periodically the entire schedule and relationship of benefits among different programs.

A Combination of Alternatives

The discussion of the various alternatives considered above suggests some general directions for reform and consolidation of federal income support programs that may be both desirable and attainable:

1. *Consolidation of the adult categories of public assistance (aid to the aged, disabled, and blind) with the old age, survivors, and disability insurance programs.* The consolidation would eventually result in a two-tier system, as explained above; part of the benefits would be based on past contributions and made available without regard to income, and a second part would be inversely related to income. Similarly, Medicaid for the adult welfare categories could be integrated with Medicare by having the federal government pay all or part of the Medicare deductibles and coinsurance for the poor. Cash and medical benefits that were income related would be financed from general revenues rather than from payroll taxes, since they are welfare oriented and should not be financed by the wage earner's contributions. The civilian and military retirement programs of the federal

government could also be integrated with the social security system in much the same way as are most private employer pension plans.

2. *Elimination of the current AFDC and food stamp programs, and their replacement by a federal negative income tax based on need rather than the categorical status of the family.* The core of a workable program would include an initial minimum benefit level of $2,400 for a family of four (the same as would be provided under H.R. 1) paid to all families with no other income, a reduction of benefits by no more than 50 cents for each dollar earned, and a requirement that states now paying more than the federal minimum benefit continue to pay the higher amount to beneficiaries. Variation of the national benefit level by area, in accordance with differences in wage levels, could also be introduced. As the national minimum was gradually increased over the years, the role of the states would gradually disappear, leaving a purely national system.

3. *Reform of the payroll tax.* Wage ceilings would be eliminated for tax purposes, and family exemptions would be introduced into the payroll tax, converting it from a regressive into a mildly progressive tax.

4. *Automatic cost-of-living increases for all major cash income support programs.* In addition, the Congress should periodically review benefit levels and structures and increase benefits in line with long-term improvements in real living standards.

These proposed changes suggest only the general lines of development. If adopted, they would result in three distinct systems: a retirement, survivors, and disability system, partly contributory in nature; a contributory unemployment insurance system for the experienced unemployed; and a noncontributory negative income tax, with substantial work incentives, for the non-aged poor.

Other cash income support systems would remain—veterans' pensions and compensation and farm price supports. As benefits under social security improve, the veterans' pension program could gradually be merged into it and eliminated as a special program. The farm price support program raises entirely different policy questions that are beyond the scope of this chapter.

The remaining programs would be those providing medical care, housing, and higher education subsidies to low-income families. Each of these has special objectives in the light of which they must be evaluated. Their integration with other income support programs does not seem feasible now.

7. Health Insurance

DECIDING WHAT is the appropriate federal role in providing health insurance and designing a system to carry it out pose some of the most difficult problems of social policy facing the government and the electorate today. The availability of medical services is critical to those who need it; the system that delivers these services is exceedingly complex and to those who use it often mysterious; the objectives that a federally subsidized insurance system seeks to accomplish often conflict with one another and must inevitably be compromised; and the clash of interests is sharp. Difficult substantive questions and acute political controversy combine to make health insurance an exceptionally thorny problem.

What is so special about health care that gives rise to these difficulties? Like food or clothing or TV sets, it can be bought by individuals in the marketplace. For those who want to buy health insurance—in effect paying for medical care through monthly premiums rather than meeting each medical bill as it occurs—private insurance is available just as it is against fire damage or automobile accidents. The poor do not have the money to buy high quality medical care, but neither do they have the money to buy high quality food, clothing, or appliances. Providing more cash to the poor would help them with all these purchases. Even when the government decides to provide goods directly to the poor, as in the case of food stamps, this raises far fewer problems of policy and program design than does the provision of health insurance. Moreover, unlike the food stamp program, all of the major proposals now being considered for expanding the federal role in health insurance incorporate some form of protection for

213

middle- and upper-income groups. Again, why are health care and health insurance different?

Characteristics of Health Care and Health Insurance

No single aspect of health care makes it unique; but a number of its features, when taken together, give it a special character that creates problems for government policy.

1. While medical care is only one factor contributing to health, it is often essential—sometimes a matter of life and death. Denying care to someone because his income is low is not the same as rationing cars or clothes or TV sets on that basis. For many years, however, care has indeed been denied to the poor or has been provided to them only as a matter of charity. In recent years, society has come increasingly to the view that adequate medical care is a basic right, neither to be denied nor treated as a charity to those who are poor.

2. Medical costs can take an excessively high portion of family income in two kinds of situations. For the poor, even when payments are spread over time and risks are shared through insurance, buying adequate health care is an excessive burden. For the middle class, average medical bills and standard health insurance coverage do not take an impossibly high share of income. But for those afflicted with major health catastrophes, medical expenses can suddenly bring financial distress or even ruin, and most private insurance does not offer adequate protection.

3. In the case of most goods and services the consumer polices the market by shopping around, searching for lower prices or higher quality, and making decisions whether or not to buy marginally useful quantities of the good or service. But if all his medical bills are paid by insurance, the consumer has little incentive to play this role. His physician is also less inclined to use restraint in the treatment he prescribes or the fees he charges. As a consequence, prices can escalate, and medical services can be used excessively and inefficiently.

4. The nature of health care imposes yet another obstacle to having the consumer act as market policeman. The consumer knows very little about the medical services he is buying—possibly less than about any other service he purchases. He can choose a low-cost instead of a high-cost physician, and to some extent he can influence the physician's prescription of the treatment he is to receive on the basis

of cost or his own preferences. But a very large part of the decision making is done by the physician; diagnosis, treatment, drugs and tests, hospitalization, frequency of return visits—all of these are substantially under the physician's control. Many basic choices are made not by the buyer but by the seller of medical services. Those who provide medical care can, to a very great extent, create the demand for their own services. While the consumer can still play a role in policing the market, that role is much more limited in the field of health care than in almost any other area of private economic activity.

5. More so than most other services that can be bought in the marketplace, medical care is available in widely varying amounts and quality in different parts of the United States. While it may be difficult to secure high-fashion clothing in a small rural community, supplies of most really essential goods and services are available in almost all areas of the nation. Inexpensive housing in the suburbs and medical care are the chief exceptions. In the case of medical services, rural areas and those parts of urban areas with a high concentration of poor families have far fewer medical resources available than does the rest of the country.

These features in combination give to health care services and to health insurance some unique aspects that distinguish them from most other goods and services and require the federal government to play a major role in improving the current system by which health care is provided and financed. But these same features make the choice and design of a specific federal program exceptionally difficult.

Numerous proposals have been advanced for expanding the federal role in financing medical care. Most of them are directed toward one or more of the following objectives: (1) assuring that the poor and near poor are not precluded from obtaining essential medical services either for financial reasons or because medical resources are not available where they live; (2) preventing financial hardship for middle-income families faced with extraordinarily large medical bills; and (3) checking the current rapid rise in medical care prices. Improving insurance programs is only one means for achieving these objectives; other federal policies and programs are necessarily involved.

As a prelude to examining alternative proposals for improving health insurance, a brief survey of the current status of the nation's health care system will be useful. Who is now covered by private and public health insurance? What is the current distribution and avail-

Table 7-1. Percentage Distribution of Total Personal Health Care Expenditures, by Source of Funds, and Private Insurance Benefit Payments as Percentage of Total Consumer Personal Health Expenditures, Selected Fiscal Years, 1950–71

| Fiscal year | Total personal health care expenditures (billions of dollars) | Percentage distribution by source of funds | | | | | | | Private insurance benefit payments as percentage of consumer personal health expenditures |
| | | Consumer expenditures | | | | Public expenditures | | | |
		Total	Private insurance benefit payments	Direct payments	Industrial in-plant services	Medicare	Medicaid[a]	Other[b]	
1950	10.4	100.0	8.5	68.3	3.0	0.0	0.0	20.2	11.0
1960	22.7	100.0	20.7	55.3	2.3	0.0	2.1	19.6	27.2
1965	33.5	100.0	24.7	52.5	2.0	0.0	4.2	16.6	32.0
1968	46.3	100.0	22.5	40.8	1.7	12.9	7.6	14.5	35.6
1971	65.1	100.0	25.5	37.2	1.5	12.1	10.0	13.7	40.6

Sources: Dorothy P. Rice and Barbara S. Cooper, "National Health Expenditures, 1929–71," *Social Security Bulletin*, Vol. 35 (January 1972), pp. 9, 13, 15; Rice and Cooper, "National Health Expenditures, 1929–68," *Social Security Bulletin*, Vol. 33 (January 1970), p. 9; U.S. Department of Health, Education, and Welfare, National Center for Social Statistics, *Medicaid and Other Medical Care Financed from Public Assistance Funds, Selected Statistics, 1951–1969*, NCSS Report B-6 (1970), p. 55.

a. Includes medical vendor payments under public assistance in 1960, 1965, and 1968.

b. Includes workmen's compensation medical benefits, general hospital and medical care (primarily mental and charity hospitals), Defense Department hospital and medical care, veterans hospital and medical care, maternal and child health services, school health, other public health activities, neighborhood health centers, and medical vocational rehabilitation.

ability of medical resources? What is happening to medical care prices?

Who Is Covered Now?

Total personal health care expenditures in the United States grew from $10 billion in 1950 to $65 billion two decades later. The share of these outlays paid directly by consumers dropped sharply over this period, from 68 percent of the total in 1950 to 37 percent in 1971, while the proportion paid by private insurance and by public programs, chiefly Medicare and Medicaid, rose. (See Table 7-1.)

Private Health Insurance

Private health insurance paid for 8.5 percent of the nation's medical bills in 1950 and 25 percent in 1971. In the latter year it paid for 41 percent of the medical bills not covered by public programs. Hospital care is extensively paid for by private insurance (73 percent of consumer outlays in 1971) and physicians' services less so (48 percent), while drugs and miscellaneous health services are only minimally covered (5 percent).

These averages conceal many important deficiencies in coverage. As is shown in Table 7-2, the amount of health insurance coverage varies widely according to income. In 1968 only one-third of the 16.3 million poor had some private insurance protection against hospital bills and surgical expenses, compared to more than nine-tenths of families with incomes over $10,000. The disparity is even greater in the case of children. Fewer than one-fourth of poor children had hospital insurance protection in 1968, compared to nine-tenths of the children from families with incomes of $10,000 or more.

Another major deficiency in private health insurance is the limited protection it offers against catastrophic expenses. Most basic insurance policies place limits on the extent of coverage, such as thirty days of hospital care or $5,000 of expenses. In 1970, only half the population was covered by major medical plans, which give protection against very large medical bills.[1] Even for persons with major medical insurance coverage, limits on covered expenses (such as $15,000) are

1. Marjorie Smith Mueller, "Private Health Insurance in 1970: Population Coverage, Enrollment and Financial Experience, A Review," *Social Security Bulletin*, Vol. 35 (February 1972), p. 4.

Table 7-2. Private Health Insurance Coverage by Family Income Class and Age, 1968

Family income class (dollars)	Percentage of persons under 65 years		Percentage of persons under 17 years	
	With hospital insurance	With surgical insurance	With hospital insurance	With surgical insurance
Under 3,000	36.3	34.8	23.3	22.9
3,000–4,999	56.8	54.6	49.0	47.3
5,000–6,999	78.5	76.7	74.6	72.9
7,000–9,999	89.3	87.8	88.4	87.0
10,000 and over	92.3	90.7	91.8	90.2

Source: Department of Health, Education, and Welfare, National Center for Health Statistics, *Hospital and Surgical Insurance Coverage, United States—1968*, Series 10, No. 66 (1972), pp. 18, 19.

frequently imposed, and such policies typically require the individual to pay up to 20 percent of all expenses, regardless of how large they are, and to pay the full cost of such services as private nursing, drugs, and dental care. Insured individuals, therefore, still face the possibility of extremely high out-of-pocket medical expenses. A study[2] made in 1963 found that only one-third of insured families with medical expenses of more than $500 received insurance benefits that covered half of their medical expenses, while another third received benefits amounting to less than one-fifth of their expenditures.

Medicaid

The major government effort to improve the access of the poor to medical care is the Medicaid program, initiated in 1966. Under this program, the federal government shares with the states the costs of providing medical care for welfare recipients and the medically indigent (the aged, blind, disabled, or families with dependent children and certain other families whose incomes are slightly above the cutoff point for public assistance). A few states, without federal assistance, extend medical care benefits to the working poor. Federal, state, and local expenditures under the Medicaid program have increased from $1.7 billion in fiscal 1966, to $6.5 billion in 1971, and to an estimated $7 billion in 1973. Approximately 40 percent of Medicaid expenditures go for hospital care, with nursing home care accounting for an-

2. Ronald Andersen and Odin W. Anderson, *A Decade of Health Services: Social Survey Trends in Use and Expenditure* (University of Chicago Press, 1967), p. 95.

other 30 percent of payments. More than 19 million persons were eligible for Medicaid benefits in 1972.

Although large sums of money are being spent under this program, there is wide variation among states as to eligibility and coverage. These variations result from the federal–state nature of the program, which is patterned after the existing welfare system. Eligibility requirements based on income and assets vary widely from state to state. Only half of the states provide coverage for the medically indigent, and the income cutoff point for a medically indigent family of four ranges from $2,448 in Oklahoma to $6,000 in New York State. Thus, near-poor families may have most medical expenses paid if they live in one state and be completely unprotected if they live in another.

The Medicaid program tries to encourage uniform benefits among the states by requiring coverage of basic services such as hospital care and physicians' services. The states have the option of covering such items as drugs, dental services, optometrists' services, and private nurses. Some states have added the full range of optional services, while others cover only a few. In addition, states are permitted to place limits on the extent of coverage of basic services. One state covers only fifteen days of hospital care, and other states place limits on the number of physicians' visits that are covered.

Because the states have considerable leeway in setting eligibility requirements and benefit coverage, some states have far more generous programs than others. The range of benefits among the states is very wide indeed, as is shown by the following estimate for fiscal 1972:[3]

Average medical vendor payment per family	*Number of states*
Less than $100	1
$100–249	7
250–399	5
400–549	16
550–699	5
700–849	9
850–999	6
1,000 and over	3

3. From U.S. Department of Health, Education, and Welfare, Social and Rehabilitation Services, unpublished tabulation prepared in 1971. Includes Guam, Puerto Rico, Virgin Islands, and Hawaii; excludes Alaska and Arizona.

The average medical payments on behalf of families eligible for aid to families with dependent children (AFDC) is estimated to range from $50 per family in Mississippi to $1,150 per family in California. Partly as a consequence of these differences, three states—New York, California, and Massachusetts—spend 50 percent of all Medicaid funds.

Serious inequities are also created by the limitation of federal benefits to categories of persons who are eligible for welfare—families with dependent children, the blind, disabled, and aged. In the twenty-six states in which a family headed by an unemployed male is not entitled to cash welfare assistance, it is also not entitled to Medicaid benefits.

In the past year and a half the combination of rapidly rising medical costs, large growth in the number of families claiming Medicaid benefits, and depressed state budget revenues resulting from general economic slack, have led a number of states to cut back on their Medicaid benefits. Eligibility rules have been tightened and covered services reduced, leading to a removal of some poor or near-poor families from coverage altogether and forcing others to pay a higher share of their medical bills. The administration has also proposed a series of amendments to the Medicaid law that would require recipients to pay a portion of their medical bills in an amount determined by their income.

Medicare

In addition to establishing the Medicaid program, the 1965 amendments to the Social Security Act created the Medicare program, providing for the elderly a basic hospital insurance plan and a voluntary supplementary medical insurance plan (SMI) that covers physicians' services and provides certain other benefits. By 1970, 20.4 million persons were entitled to hospital insurance, and 19.6 million of these (96.2 percent) had enrolled for SMI.

Beneficiaries must pay a deductible of $68 covering up to sixty days in the hospital; between the sixty-first and ninetieth days they must pay coinsurance of $17 a day; for the next sixty days they must pay $34 a day, after which hospital insurance ceases.[4] Under SMI they must pay

4. Under current law, the last sixty days of coverage constitutes a "lifetime reserve." Once that is used, no coverage is provided after the first ninety days. H.R. 1 would add coinsurance of $8.50 a day for the period between the thirty-first and sixtieth days and increase the lifetime reserve to 120 days.

Table 7-3. Estimated per Capita Personal Health Care Expenditures for Persons Aged 65 and Over, by Type of Service and Source of Funds, Fiscal Years 1966 and 1970
Dollars

		1966			*1970*	
Type of service	*Total*	*Private sources*	*Public sources*	*Total*	*Private sources*	*Public sources*
All services, total	426	293	133	791	257	534
Hospital care	179	93	86	372	58	314
Physicians' services	71	65	5	136	37	100
Nursing-home care	68	40	29	129	46	83
Other health services	107	95	13	153	117	36

Source: Barbara S. Cooper and Mary F. McGee, "Medical Care Outlays for Three Age Groups: Young, Intermediate, and Aged," *Social Security Bulletin*, Vol. 34 (May 1971), Tables 2 and 6. Figures are rounded and may not add to totals.

each year the first $50 of physicians' charges and 20 percent of the remainder. They also pay a monthly premium for SMI, now set at $5.60. Federal expenditures under Medicare reached $7.9 billion in fiscal 1971 and are expected to total $10 billion in 1973.

The Medicare program has been generally successful in providing older people with the financial means to pay a major portion of their large bills for hospital and medical care. Medicare expenditures in fact are concentrated on persons with large medical bills. Forty percent of Medicare reimbursements in 1967 were for services rendered to the 7.5 percent of Medicare beneficiaries who had expenses of $2,000 or more.[5]

Despite Medicare, the amounts paid for medical care by the elderly themselves have continued to rise. Private payments for personal health care averaged $293 in fiscal 1966, before the introduction of Medicare. (See Table 7-3.) In fiscal 1970, private payments of $257 plus SMI premiums of $48 a year totaled $305 per capita, a slight *increase* in private costs for the elderly despite the sizable benefits paid by the federal program.

In the four years from 1966 to 1970, per capita health care expenditures for the elderly grew least rapidly for those services that are not covered, or are covered to a very slight extent, by the Medicare program. Per capita outlays for hospital care and physicians' services, which are covered, rose by 108 percent and 93 percent, respectively.

5. Howard West, "Five Years of Medicare—A Statistical Review," *Social Security Bulletin*, Vol. 34 (December 1971), p. 27.

But spending on drugs and eyeglasses, which predominantly are not covered, rose by only 35 percent and 27 percent.[6] The degree of coverage under Medicare is by no means the only explanation of differences in the growth of per capita outlays, but it is an important one.

In summary, private insurance, Medicare, and Medicaid combined have taken over a substantial part of the nation's medical bills. But for the poor, public financing of health care varies widely among the states, and many poor or near-poor families who do not fall into one or another welfare category are completely excluded. Most middle-income families are covered by some form of private health insurance, but typically are exposed to the threat of financial distress and economic insecurity when they face very large medical bills.

Distribution of Medical Resources and Access to Medical Care

The geographical maldistribution of medical resources is relevant to a discussion of national health insurance in several ways. On the one hand, providing better medical insurance coverage to the poor is clearly necessary if more health care resources are to be attracted to areas of scarcity, most of which have high concentrations of low-income families. Medical personnel and facilities will not be available in areas where the bulk of the population cannot afford to pay for their services. But, at the same time, simply increasing the demand for medical care in these areas may not be enough to attract a supply of additional medical resources quickly. Unless other means of improving supply conditions are used, the benefits of expanded insurance coverage in shortage areas may in part be limited by a lack of medical resources and be partially dissipated by higher prices.

The uneven availability of medical resources in the United States is striking. In 1970 the 15 counties with the highest per capita incomes had seven times as many patient-care physicians per capita as did the 15 counties with the lowest per capita incomes, twenty-six times as many physician specialists per capita, and three times as many hospital beds per capita. The shortage of physicians is particularly acute in rural areas. In 1970, of the 3,100 counties in the United States, 132 had no active nonfederal physicians, an increase from 98 counties in 1963. Residents of counties with 5 million or more inhabitants had five times as many patient-care physicians per capita as did residents of

6. Eyeglasses and drugs are included in "other services" in Table 7-3.

counties with fewer than 10,000 inhabitants and fifteen times as many physician specialists per capita.[7]

Very little evidence is available on how rapidly, and how significantly, the supply of medical resources responds to changes in demand. It is quite likely, however, that supply responds slowly and in limited amount. Most physicians are unwilling to move their practices once they are established. Those most affected by changed financial conditions would be young doctors first entering practice. Even with improved pay for services in low-income areas, physicians may prefer to locate in higher-income areas with their many cultural and social amenities, low crime rates, good educational systems, and so on.

Although supply responses may be slow, subsidizing the purchase of medical care by the poor, as in the Medicaid program, may still significantly improve the ability of low-income groups to secure health services. For example, improved financing of medical care may enable poor people to pay for the transportation required to obtain care. Recent data published by the U.S. Department of Health, Education, and Welfare indicate that low-income groups have made important gains relative to other groups since the advent of Medicaid in 1966, as is shown in Tables 7-4 and 7-5.

Rates of hospital use by the poor have risen sharply, particularly among the aged poor. By 1968, the rates of hospitalization for all age groups among the poor were equal to, or larger than, they were for higher-income families. Physician visits per capita rose slightly for the poor, while they were falling among higher-income groups. Among children of the poor, however, physician visits were still much less common in 1969 than among children of higher income groups.

Although this preliminary evidence suggests that public programs that increase the demand for medical services on the part of the poor can lead to a significant increase in their access to care, several qualifications must be made. The rise in the rate of hospitalization for the poor, after the advent of Medicaid, partly reflects the fact that the poor are much less likely than the rich to receive medical care in doctors' offices or at home. Moreover, partly because of physician shortages in poverty areas, the poor are more likely to see a physician in the

7. J. N. Haug, G. A. Roback, and B. C. Martin, *Distribution of Physicians in the United States, 1970: Regional, State, County, Metropolitan Areas* (Chicago: American Medical Association, 1971), pp. 7, 10, 157–309.

Table 7-4. Persons Hospitalized per 1,000 Population, by Age and Family Income Group, Fiscal Years 1962 and 1966, and Calendar Year 1968

Age and income group[a]	1962	1966	1968
All ages			
Low income	94.7	106.6	114.5
Middle income	97.6	100.9	95.4
High income	86.7	88.9	81.8
Ratio, low income to high income	1.09	1.20	1.40
Under 15 years			
Low income	45.1	51.2	52.0
Middle income	53.8	60.2	53.2
High income	51.4	52.3	47.4
Ratio, low income to high income	0.88	0.98	1.10
15–64 years			
Low income	116.3	130.0	127.5
Middle income	123.7	122.3	113.8
High income	101.6	102.3	93.9
Ratio, low income to high income	1.14	1.27	1.36
65 years and older			
Low income	110.8	125.3	157.7
Middle income	110.7	132.3	155.4
High income	124.6	149.7	155.9
Ratio, low income to high income	0.89	0.84	1.0

Sources: Department of Health, Education, and Welfare, National Center for Health Statistics, *Persons Hospitalized by Number of Hospital Episodes and Days in a Year, United States, July 1960–June 1962*, Series 10, No. 20 (1965), and issues for *July 1965–June 1966*, No. 50 (1969), and *1968*, No. 64 (1971).

a. Low income is defined as under $4,000 in 1962 and under $5,000 in 1966 and 1968. Middle income is defined as $4,000–$6,999 in 1962 and $5,000–$9,999 in 1966 and 1968. High income is defined as $7,000 and above in 1962 and $10,000 and above in 1966 and 1968.

outpatient clinics of large city hospitals, often after long waits. Finally, the data presented earlier on the wide variation among states in per capita Medicaid expenditures suggest that the average increase in the use of medical services by the poor is very unevenly distributed across the nation. Removing the financial barriers to health care may still have to be supplemented by other measures if the poor are to have adequate access to medical services. Several alternatives are possible:

• Providing financial incentives to medical students, such as interest-free loans or forgiveness of part of loans if they practice for a specified number of years in ghetto or rural areas.

• Allowing physicians to practice in low-income areas in lieu of military service.

• Placing federal health personnel in medically under-served areas.

Table 7-5. Physician Visits per Capita by Age and Family Income Group, Fiscal Years 1964, 1967, and Calendar Year 1969

Age and income group[a]	1964	1967	1969
All ages			
Low income	4.3	4.3	4.6
Middle income	4.5	4.2	4.0
High income	5.1	4.6	4.3
Ratio, low income to high income	*0.84*	*0.93*	*1.07*
Under 15 years			
Low income	2.7	2.8	2.8
Middle income	2.8	3.9	3.6
High income	4.5	4.4	4.3
Ratio, low income to high income	*0.60*	*0.65*	*0.65*
15–64 years			
Low income	4.4	4.6	4.8
Middle income	4.7	4.1	4.1
High income	4.9	4.6	4.2
Ratio, low income to high income	*0.92*	*1.00*	*1.14*
65 years and older			
Low income	6.3	5.8	6.1
Middle income	7.0	6.7	5.8
High income	7.3	6.5	7.5
Ratio, low income to high income	*0.86*	*0.89*	*0.81*

Sources: 1964, 1967, Department of Health, Education, and Welfare, National Center for Health Statistics, *Volume of Physician Visits by Place of Visit and Type of Service, United States, July 1963–June 1964,* Series 10, No. 18 (1965), and issue for *July 1966–June 1967,* No. 49 (1968); 1969, National Health Statistics, unpublished tabulations.

a. Low income is defined as under $4,000 in 1964 and under $5,000 in 1967 and 1969. Middle income is defined as $4,000–$6,999 in 1964 and $5,000 to $9,999 in 1967 and 1969. High income is defined as $7,000 and above in 1964 and $10,000 and above in 1967 and 1969.

• Subsidizing medical schools that take minority students, in the expectation that a larger percentage of these students will return to low-income areas.

• Training residents of low-income areas as paramedical personnel to supplement existing medical manpower.

• Using guaranteed loans, interest subsidies, planning funds, and capital grants to subsidize group medical organizations—such as health maintenance organizations, neighborhood health centers, and hospital outpatient facilities—that locate in low-income areas.

• Paying higher rates for medical care provided in low-income areas.

• Providing adequate transportation to medical facilities, particularly in rural areas.

Programs have recently been created to pursue a number of these alternatives. The Comprehensive Health Manpower Training Act of 1971 established numerous programs designed to improve the distribution of medical manpower. The act authorizes the secretary of health, education, and welfare to give priority to health manpower shortage areas in awarding, and determining the federal share of, grants for the construction of medical research and teaching facilities. Other provisions authorize scholarships and loan forgiveness (up to 85 percent of professional educational loans) for students who agree to practice for a specified time in medically under-served areas. In addition, medical schools are encouraged to admit students from low-income backgrounds through direct scholarship payments to schools. The act also authorizes the establishment of a clearing house within HEW to provide information on areas needing health professionals and on prospective health workers interested in serving in such areas.

The recently created National Health Services Corps will place an estimated 600 health professionals paid by the federal government in approximately 200 medically under-served areas. Several area health education centers will be established to provide permanent bases for attracting health professionals. Many other programs give priority in funding to organizations that provide health services and that agree to be located in low-income areas.

Medical Care Inflation

Much of the concern with excessively burdensome medical expenses and the inability of some families to afford necessary care stems from the rapidly rising price of medical care. Medical care prices have increased much faster than those of other consumer goods and services. Inflation has been particularly acute in recent years, with the medical care component of the consumer price index (CPI) increasing by 6.6 percent annually from 1967 to 1971. Inflation in hospital services, one of the heaviest medical expenses, has been particularly marked. (See Table 7-6.) Hospital prices, as measured by the daily service charge in the CPI (the room and board charge), increased at an average annual rate of 13.5 percent from 1967 to 1971. In 1970 average hospital prices exceeded $100 a day in five states (Alaska, California, Connecticut, Massachusetts, and New York) and the District

Table 7-6. Average Annual Percentage Increase in Consumer and Medical Care Prices,
Various Periods, Fiscal Years 1946–71

Fiscal year periods	Consumer price index, all items	Medical care			
		Total	Physicians' fees	Hospital daily service charge	Drugs and prescriptions
1946ᵃ–60	3.0	4.2	3.4	8.3	2.3
1960–67	1.6	3.2	3.5	7.8	n.a.
1967–71	4.8	6.6	6.7	13.5	1.1

Source: Department of Health, Education, and Welfare, Social Security Administration, *Medical Care Costs and Prices: Background Book* (1972), p. 10.
n.a. Not available.
a. 1946 is calendar year.

of Columbia and were, of course, much higher in many hospitals in those states.

Many causes for the inflation of medical prices have been suggested. These can be classified into several categories that interact and reinforce each other.

One factor has been the rapidly increasing demand for medical care associated with rising incomes, the growing spread of private insurance, and, after 1966, the introduction of Medicare and Medicaid. The sharp rise in demand impinged on a limited and slow-to-expand supply of medical resources, giving rise to large price increases.

Several special factors also intervened. The increase in demand speeded the adoption of complex new medical techniques in hospitals and clinics, which often help save lives but are very costly. And, starting in 1966, the wages of hospital workers began to rise sharply from a level that had been very low compared to that of other workers. The wages of municipal employees, which influence the pay scales of hospital workers, began to increase rapidly after 1966, and in 1967 minimum wage laws were extended to cover hospital workers. All of these cost factors contributed to a sharp increase in prices.

Through the way it affects the demand for and costs of medical care, health insurance plays an important role in raising prices.

1. To the individual consumer, insurance lowers the price of using medical care. If it is covered by insurance, a physician's visit, a hospital stay, or a diagnostic procedure costs the consumer far less than the amount the physician or the hospital charges for the service. As insurance coverage is extended, the lower price to consumers leads to an increased use of services and, given a limited supply, to an inflation of

medical prices. Moreover, the fact that most private insurance gives better coverage for hospital stays than for physicians' visits encourages consumers and their physicians to use hospitals extensively, rather than services outside the hospital that are not covered—a practice that tends to raise the overall cost of health care.

2. A second explanation of how health insurance raises prices rests on the view that physicians take into account the financial situation of their patients in setting fees. As insurance coverage has been extended, physicians have been able to increase fees with less regard for the impact on their patients. And as Medicare and Medicaid became operative, fees charged for services to the poor and the low-income aged, which were often lower than other fees, were raised substantially. Closely linked to this is the belief that, within limits, a physician can create a demand for his services, since it is he, not the patient, who often decides how much service the patient receives. The United States, for example, has twice as many surgeons per capita as does England, and twice as many surgeries are performed. It is unlikely that there are so many necessary but unperformed surgeries in England, or that citizens of the United States have ailments needing twice as much surgery as do the English. The market power of physicians to create the demand for their own services, combined with insurance that reduces the financial restraints against raising fees, has been an important factor in recent medical price inflation.

3. In the case of hospitals and nursing homes, the way in which private and public insurance programs pay for medical services tends to encourage rising costs. Hospitals and nursing homes are reimbursed individually for the services they provide insured patients. Under the government and many private insurance programs, the amount each receives is based on the costs it incurs. Even when reimbursement is not directly tied to costs, the fact that a third party—not the patient and not the hospital—pays the bills encourages an escalation of costs. As a result, there is little or no incentive for those who operate these institutions to hold down costs, to avoid excessive delivery of expensive services, or to institute more efficient management practices. Higher costs are fully passed on to the private insurance company or the government. And since the provision of more technically advanced and expensive care raises the prestige of a hospital, doctors and administrators have a positive incentive to increase costs, with private and public insurance paying the bill.

There are several alternative ways to reduce the rate at which medical care prices have been rising. Each of them is relevant to the design of federal health insurance programs.

Price Controls

Of all the possible approaches to curtailing medical care inflation, the one most amenable to immediate use is price controls. Other policies could be expected to have substantial effects over longer periods of time, but the only policy that could have immediate direct consequences is one that sets limits on the rate at which physicians, hospitals, and other providers of medical care can increase their charges. When the Nixon administration froze all wages and prices for a ninety-day period and then imposed controls on the rates of increase in wages and prices, it also established specific controls for the medical care industry.

In December 1971, the Price Commission, acting on recommendations of a specially created Health Services Industry Committee, issued guidelines for institutional and noninstitutional health care providers. Noninstitutional providers such as physicians are limited to an average 2.5 percent price increase, and even this small amount must be justified by an increase in costs. Institutional providers such as hospitals and nursing homes may increase their prices up to 2.5 percent without reporting to the government. Price increases of more than 2.5 percent and up to 6 percent are allowed but must be reported to the Internal Revenue Service and the Medicare intermediary, with cost justifications. Wage increases in excess of 5.5 percent or price increases in other goods and services purchased by institutional providers above the 2.5 percent general economic target may not be used as the basis for a price increase by the institution. Any increase in institutional prices in excess of 6 percent must be applied for as an exception with the Internal Revenue Service and be approved before it can take effect. State advisory boards are required to evaluate applications for exceptions before they are submitted to the Internal Revenue Service.

It is too soon to judge the effectiveness of these controls. In the fourth quarter of 1971, during most of which the ninety-day freeze was in effect, medical care prices fell at an annual rate of 0.9 percent, after rising at a rate of 6.6 percent in the first three quarters. In the first two months of 1972, medical care prices rose again but at an annual rate of only 4.2 percent. Part of the rise may have reflected an initial spurt after the freeze was lifted.

While the current price controls may be effective in restraining medical care price inflation in the short run, the feasibility of such controls in the longer run is open to question. There are more than 7,000 hospitals, 20,000 nursing homes, and 300,000 physicians in the United States whose prices and charges would have to be controlled. The market for medical care is not national in scope but is distinctly local. Differing conditions in different cities may give rise to quite different prices. Since medical care is not homogeneous, the scope for quality differentials is great. Unlike industries in which productivity gains offset increases in the prices of labor and other inputs, the changing nature of hospital services has led to an increase in the use of these inputs. More than half of the inflation in hospital prices over the last decade has been attributable to an increase in labor and other inputs per day of care, rather than to an increase in the prices of those inputs. For all of these reasons, controlling medical care inflation requires substantially more administrative machinery than does controlling inflation in manufacturing industries.

Even if price controls were effective in holding down prices per unit of service, medical care providers would have substantial leeway to subvert the intent of such regulations by increasing the quantity or quality of services. Hospitals could encourage physicians to keep patients in the hospital longer. Physicians could increase their incomes despite fixed fee schedules by multiplying the procedures performed (additional tests, shots, and so on), by increasing the number of referrals and consultations, and by increasing repeat visits. All of these tactics would result in more revenue for hospitals and physicians, higher real resource costs, and little or no improvement in the health of patients.

Another drawback of medical care price regulation is its interference with the function of prices in attracting medical care resources to areas of greatest need. When prices are allowed to increase automatically in areas where there is an increasing demand for medical services or where there are shortages in medical manpower and facilities, the greater returns earned by personnel and institutions there can be expected to attract additional resources. Admittedly, medical care prices today act only imperfectly to perform this function. But if the price mechanism were abandoned entirely, a new and complex control apparatus would be needed to allocate medical resources.

The question of controls on medical prices is crucial to the evaluation of alternative national health insurance proposals. Those who propose a nationwide system of federal or federally supported insurance, not just for the poor and the aged but for all citizens, must wrestle with the problem of controlling medical care prices. Weak and imperfect as the private market is in maintaining some check on medical prices, it does provide a restraint. The more comprehensive the services offered by a national health insurance system are, and the larger the percentage of medical bills it covers, the less the reliance that can be placed on private market restraints and the greater the need for some form of government price-setting. The relationship between the structure of insurance programs and the control of medical care prices is discussed further below.

Medical Care Manpower

A long-run approach to reducing medical care inflation is to expand the supply of medical manpower. In addition to provisions for improving the distribution of medical resources noted above, the Comprehensive Health Manpower Training Act of 1971 provides institutional assistance to increase enrollment and to improve the quality of instruction in health profession schools, and student assistance in the form of scholarships and loans. A new feature of institutional support for health profession schools is payments to the schools based on the number of students enrolled. The payments are increased if students graduate in three years instead of four.

Over all, federal outlays in 1973 for health manpower training and education will be $1.5 billion. More than half of the budgets of the nation's medical schools will be financed by federal grants or contracts. In the academic year 1972–73, it is estimated that 22,080 medical students, 8,300 dental students, 45,500 nursing students, and 15,500 other health personnel will receive loans and scholarships from the Department of Health, Education, and Welfare. In addition, other federal agencies, such as the Department of Labor, support paramedical personnel training programs.

Increasing the supply of manpower, at least within foreseeable limits, will not ease the upward pressure on medical prices unless other measures are taken to create incentives for efficient delivery of services. As was noted earlier, consumer ignorance of medicine to some extent enables physicians to create a demand for their services through the diagnoses they perform, the referrals they make, and the advice they give their patients. The greater the proportion of medical bills paid by private or public insurance, the greater their ability to do so. If federally supported health insurance is adopted in some broad and comprehensive form, increasing manpower resources could not be relied upon as the sole means of checking price rises, even in the long run. Incentives would have to be developed for both suppliers and consumers of medical services to use resources more efficiently and to minimize price increases that are out of line with general economic conditions. The two sections that follow discuss alternative paths to this goal—establishing new kinds of health care organizations and restructuring insurance coverage.

Health Maintenance Organizations

One proposed solution to rising medical costs is to reorganize the delivery of medical care. The leading proposal of this kind encourages the growth of health maintenance organizations (HMOs), which agree to provide comprehensive medical services for a defined population in exchange for a fixed annual payment for each person served.

It is widely believed that the promotion of organizations that agree to provide services in exchange for a fixed annual fee, rather than on a fee-for-service basis, will have several cost-reducing effects. First, since the HMO earns a greater return when its members are healthy than when they are sick, the HMO has an incentive to prevent illness and to treat illness in its early stages. Second, since the annual fee is fixed, and the HMO cannot charge for each service provided, it has an incentive to use a minimum cost combination of medical resources— avoiding, when possible, expensive types of care such as hospitalization and specialist treatment. Third, it is easier to budget in advance and to control total medical care expenditures when reimbursement is on a fixed per capita basis than when it depends on an uncontrollable level of medical services provided. Fourth, the promotion of HMOs may increase competition in the medical care market by providing alternatives to the current forms of care. Fifth, economies of large-scale operation may be effected through the promotion of group practice. Finally, health maintenance organizations may improve the quality of care and reduce costs by reducing fragmentation and discontinuity of services, by central record keeping, and by integrating patterns of referral and consultation.

The administration has chosen to promote HMOs as its central strategy for reforming the way in which health care is delivered and for controlling the inflation in medical costs. It has proposed legislation to assist the establishment of HMOs through technical assistance, planning grants and contracts, direct loans, and loan guarantees. It is requesting $57 million in budget authority for 1972 and $60 million in 1973 to assist health maintenance organizations. These funds, it is hoped, will assist 284 HMOs in 1972, with potential subscribers of 8.5 million persons, and 348 HMOs in 1973, with potential subscribers of 10.4 million. Priority in funding would be given to HMOs located in medically under-served areas. Other legislation would make it easier for persons covered by Medicare, Medicaid, the proposed family health insurance plan (FHIP), and private insurance plans to join HMOs. Legislation has also been proposed to remove existing state and local barriers that prevent or hinder the creation of HMOs. And efforts will be made in 1972 and 1973 to convert federally funded health centers, such as neighborhood and family health centers, into HMOs. The funds requested would provide each HMO with an average of $200,000, or $7 per person served. Some supporters of the HMO concept, while agreeing with the administration's strategy, question whether these funds would be enough to enable the planned number of HMOs to begin operating and to survive their difficult first years.

Although the arguments extolling the merits of health maintenance organizations are quite convincing, several words of caution are in order. Most of the empirical evidence presented in support of the health maintenance form of organization is based on experience under prepaid group practices. These organizations are not common, and they differ in important ways. Some, for example, have direct control over hospitals associated with the plan; others do not. Moreover, these plans have been inadequately studied.[8] Experience under the Medicare program indicates that the major saving through HMOs comes from a reduced use of hospitals in plans that have their own hospital. Little difference is observed in the use of physicians as between prepaid groups and conventional practice. Further information is needed on the benefits of health maintenance organizations—perhaps through controlled experiments.

8. For a summary and appraisal of existing studies, see Herbert E. Klarman, "Analysis of the HMO Proposal—Its Assumptions, Implications, and Prospects" (revision of paper delivered at the Annual Symposium on Hospital Affairs, University of Chicago, April 30, 1971; processed).

The second concern about HMOs as proposed in the administration plan is their lenient definition. Basically, any organization that agreed to provide comprehensive health services to a defined population for a fixed annual fee would be able to qualify for federal support. The organization might contract with hospitals or groups of physicians not under its direct control to provide medical services under various payment arrangements. Conceivably a private health insurance firm might meet this definition of an HMO, since it accepts a fixed annual sum (premium) and in exchange agrees to pay for a wide range of health services for members enrolled in its plan. But private health insurance companies have been notably unsuccessful in curtailing inflation in medical care costs. If the benefits of HMOs are to be realized, much more stringent requirements over the way in which they reimburse physicians and control hospitals may be necessary.

The final concern about the HMO idea is that it may contain incentives to downgrade the quality of care or to neglect the provision of needed care. Since an HMO can increase its income by reducing the quality and quantity of its services, there is genuine concern that this opportunity may be abused. If consumers were able to judge the quality or adequacy of the care received, and if enough alternative opportunities for care existed, the HMO would presumably be constrained to avoid downgrading quality by fear of losing members. It remains to be seen, however, whether competition will be effective in assuring that quality levels are not reduced.

Restructuring Insurance Coverage

The earlier discussion of the impact of insurance on medical care prices pointed out two kinds of problems. (1) An insured consumer faces a reduced or even a zero cost when he, or his physician for him, decides to use medical services; as a consequence, services are used excessively, unnecessarily expensive treatments are prescribed, and providers of medical care find it easier to charge higher prices. (2) By paying hospitals and other institutional providers according to the costs each incurs, many insurance plans, including Medicare and Medicaid, encourage inefficiency and cost increases. These problems must be faced in designing an expanded federal health insurance program. Two lines of attack are available—providing incentives to consumers to avoid excessive use and resist higher prices by requiring them to pay part of the costs; and providing incentives to suppliers of medical care to deliver health services efficiently and at reasonable cost.

If all services were free to individuals, they and their physicians would have no incentive to select lower-cost medical resources. Patients might prefer specialists when family doctors would be sufficient. Physicians might place patients in conveniently located, but higher-cost, hospitals; or they might hospitalize a patient who could be cared for adequately at a nursing home, or at home with the aid of visiting nurses. The use of "deductibles" and "coinsurance" in insurance programs is the major device for giving consumers incentives to police the market for medical services. Under insurance plans with a deductible, the consumer must pay some initial part of the medical bill before the insurance coverage begins (for example, the first $50 of physicians' charges, or the cost of the first two days of hospital care). Coinsurance requires the consumer to pay some percentage of the remaining bills. The Medicare program provides for deductibles and coinsurance on both hospital and doctors' bills. The administration has submitted legislation adding deductibles and coinsurance to the Medicaid program.

Deductibles and coinsurance have two disadvantages as part of a federal health insurance program. In the first place, American families tend to buy private insurance with low deductibles and coinsurance on normal medical expenses, often called "low dollar coverage" insurance.[9] When covered by a federal insurance program that carries higher deductibles and coinsurance, they tend to buy low dollar coverage supplementary insurance, which picks up the deductibles and coinsurance on all but the largest medical bills. This has happened extensively under Medicare. Large-scale purchases of low dollar coverage supplementary insurance would, of course, defeat the basic objectives of deductibles and coinsurance in a federally supported

9. On a straight financial calculation, low dollar coverage is often not a good buy. It does not protect against the catastrophic expenses that hit some families and against which insurance is really needed. And for ordinary medical expenses, the total of premiums paid over a few years is larger than the medical expenses covered. One reason for the prevalence of low dollar coverage insurance is that it greatly aids the providers of medical service in collecting bills. Rather than having to worry whether a particular patient will be able to pay, an insurance company can be looked to for payment. As a consequence, medical societies and hospitals have had an interest in sponsoring and promoting low dollar coverage health insurance, and employers and unions have increasingly made its highly visible benefits part of workers' fringe benefits. Various tax provisions have also encouraged the growth of low dollar coverage.

health insurance program. In theory it would be possible to require as part of the federal program that consumers pay the deductibles and coinsurance out of their own pockets or to forbid the sale of low dollar coverage private insurance; but whether either of these steps is politically feasible is open to question.

The second problem with coinsurance or deductibles is that they have a much greater impact on the poor than on the well-to-do. The deductibles and coinsurance that might cause a $20,000-a-year white collar worker to avoid excessive use of medical care would often be a major barrier preventing the $3,000-a-year janitor from obtaining essential services. Special provisions must therefore be included to adjust the size of deductibles and coinsurance to family income, reducing them to zero for the very poor.

Another way of moderating the price-raising effects of health insurance would be to provide incentives for efficiency to medical care providers. Delivering medical care through HMOs is one way, and its incentive features were described above. But it is unlikely that HMOs will soon provide most of the medical care in the United States. Independent hospitals and nursing homes will continue to provide much of the institutional care. Therefore it is important that the way the government reimburses hospitals and other institutions be reformed to provide incentives to halt the escalation of costs. Several suggestions have been offered. Instead of paying each hospital on the basis of the actual costs incurred during the past year, the government could negotiate with the hospital in advance a budget within which the hospital must operate. It could pay a certain amount per capita for meeting the hospital needs of a given population. It could relate the reimbursement of each hospital to the average costs of similar hospitals in a given region, penalizing the high cost hospitals and rewarding the less costly ones. Because experience with such innovative methods of payment is limited, it would be desirable to experiment with various techniques before imposing across-the-board reforms. (See Chapter 15 for a discussion of social experiments.)

National Health Insurance Proposals

Several proposals have been introduced into the Congress to expand significantly the federal role in health insurance, including two programs submitted by the administration. They differ widely in scope and nature; and while none has been enacted, one or more measures providing broad federal support for health insurance are likely to become law within the next several years. In the following section, each of the major proposals is described and its pros and cons discussed. The proposals are listed beginning with the least comprehensive and ending with the very comprehensive Kennedy-Griffiths national health insurance plan.

Catastrophic Health Insurance Proposal

One of the national health insurance proposals specifically designed to solve the problem of inadequate protection against catastrophic medical expenses is the bill (S. 1376) introduced by Senator Russell B. Long. It would cover all persons under sixty-five who are covered by the social security system and would provide the same kind of medical benefits as the Medicare program, but with such large deductibles on hospital and other services that it would be, in effect, catastrophic insurance against the huge medical bills that accompany protracted illness.

Hospital services would be covered only after sixty days, and the beneficiary would pay approximately 25 percent of the cost of care beyond that point. Coverage for physicians' and other medical services would begin only after a deductible of $2,000, and individuals would pay a 20 percent coinsurance on expenses above $2,000. The program would be financed like Medicare, with a special payroll tax on wages and self-employed income subject to social security taxes.

This plan would help the many families who have inadequate medical insurance against large bills. But it would still leave many gaps in protection against catastrophic expenses. First, because it would be restricted to workers who are covered by social security, some groups —mainly welfare recipients and the unemployed—would receive no benefits. Second, by setting deductibles in terms of time spent in the hospital (sixty days of hospital care), the bill would not protect against large hospital bills incurred during shorter stays. An easy way to eliminate this anomaly would be to define all deductibles in dollar terms— for example, a $2,000 deductible on all medical expenses. The Long plan shares the weakness of existing major medical insurance plans in being open-ended—that is, there would be no limit on the amount that would have to be paid under the coinsurance feature. If a maximum were set, say $5,000, beyond which all expenses would be covered, the individual would have a guarantee as to his maximum out-of-pocket cost.

Finally, this approach fails to recognize that what constitutes a catastrophic expense varies according to a family's income. For a family with an income of $25,000, a medical bill of $2,500 might not be prohibitive. For a family with an income of $5,000, or even $10,000, such a bill would place a substantial strain on the family's financial resources. This shortcoming could be eliminated by stating the deductible in terms of family income. For example, the deductible could be 8 percent of income up to a family income of $25,000, and then a flat rate of $2,000 for all incomes above $25,000.

Any catastrophic insurance plan faces a major dilemma. If the coinsurance has a ceiling, so that once some dollar limit has been passed the insurance plan pays all remaining bills, then the program does offer full protection against catastrophic expenses. But at the same time, from the point of view of the individual and his physician, once the limit has been reached, further medical expenses are "free"—someone else is paying for them. And to the extent that people buy low dollar coverage insurance to pick up part or all of the deductibles and coinsurance, the financial constraints are reduced even further. Nationwide adoption of a catastrophic insurance program of this kind could dramatically encourage the already growing emphasis of the health care industry on highly publicized and expensive technology—open heart surgery, cobalt machines, organ transplants, intensive care units, and the like. This emphasis, many observers believe, absorbs enormous resources at the expense of more prosaic treatment oriented toward early diagnosis and prevention, which does more in the long run to save lives and improve health. On the other hand, to the extent that an insurance program provided for open-ended coinsurance as a financial constraint against excessive use of very expensive medical technology, it would fail to provide protection against crushing financial burdens for the small percentage of the population that unavoidably incurs very large medical bills.

In short, having people pay a significant fraction of large medical bills helps to prevent excessive recourse to expensive treatment but subjects a small fraction of the population to ruinous expense. Some checks against excessive use of high cost technology could be provided by requiring that the individual himself pay the deductible in the catastrophic plan (that is, any payments he received under private supplementary insurance would not count against the deductible). But even with this check, a nationwide catastrophic plan that paid all expenses above a certain limit would have to be accompanied by a non-market regulatory mechanism to monitor those practices and techniques that result in very large medical bills.

The Administration's Proposals: (1) Mandatory Employer-Employee Private Health Insurance

The administration's health insurance proposals were presented to the Congress last year. They have two components, the first being a legally specified minimum package of insurance benefits that all employers would have to provide their employees. This proposal is aimed essentially at providing certain basic benefits and catastrophic insurance protection to the great majority of American families with a full-time worker. Second, a federally financed health insurance plan would replace part of the Medicaid program.

The mandatory employer-employee program is contained in the proposed National Health Insurance Standards Act. This act would require employers to make available to employees a standard private health insurance plan with comprehensive benefits: hospital inpatient and outpatient care, physician services (including well child care to age five, and annual eye examinations for children under twelve), laboratory and X-ray services, outpatient physical therapy services, and medical supplies and appliances.

The standard plan would have an annual $100 deductible per person with a family maximum of $300, and 25 percent coinsurance on all expenses above the deductible. (The deductibles and coinsurance would not apply to preventive services for infants.) If a person received $5,000 of medical services in a year, all cost-sharing would be waived for him and his family for that year and the following two years. The standard plan would provide substantially greater protection against catastrophic expenses than would the more restricted Long proposal. However, it too would leave working families with low incomes subject to medical payments that could be very large relative to their income.

As in the Long plan, the deductibles and coinsurance rates are not related to income. A family could have out-of-pocket costs of as much as $1,500 to $2,000, which would pose an overwhelming financial strain on families with incomes in the $3,000 to $4,000 range and a substantial strain on those with incomes even as high as $10,000 to $15,000. As was suggested earlier, one way to eliminate this source of financial burden would be to scale deductibles and coinsurance rates with income and to make the ceiling apply to family medical expenses instead of individual expenses.

It would not be mandatory that employees accept the standard plan. They could decline to accept coverage, select an alternative plan offered by the employer, or purchase supplemental insurance in addition to the standard plan. As a consequence, it is not clear to what extent this proposal would change existing types of insurance coverage. While the standard plan would provide better protection against catastrophic expenses, it would offer less protection against normal medical outlays than do existing types of private insurance coverage, principally because it has higher deductibles and coinsurance. If given the choice of keeping existing types of coverage instead of switching to the standard plan, many employees might prefer insurance with low or zero deductibles and coinsurance for basic expenses but without adequate protection for catastrophic expenses. To the extent that this happened, several undesirable effects could result: substituting low dollar coverage for catastrophic insurance would remove the incentive for careful use of medical care that deductibles and coinsurance provide; and the minority of families that incurred crushing medical bills would be without adequate protection. These consequences could be avoided by requiring that any alternative plan offered by the employer must contain significant protection for catastrophic expenses and must provide for coinsurance and deductibles on moderate-sized medical bills at least equal to those in the standard plan.

Since most of the cost of this plan would be covered directly through premium payments by employers and employees, it would not result in significant federal budget costs. The employer would be required to pay at least 65 percent of the premium on the standard plan for the first two and one-half years of the program and at least 75 percent thereafter. The employer's health insurance premium would be, in effect, a flat tax on each worker hired. Since the premium would be the same for low-wage as for high-wage employees, it would be a higher fraction of the wage of the former than of the latter. In low-wage industries, the compulsory premium would be a fairly significant tax on the hiring of workers, and might adversely affect employment.[10] A modified version of the administration's proposal (the Byrnes bill) would provide a federal subsidy to pick up premium costs that exceeded 4 percent of the payroll for any employer and would require about $400 million a year from the federal budget.

The Administration's Proposals: (2) The Family Health Insurance Plan

The second part of the administration's proposals deals with financing health care for the poor who are not covered by the mandatory employer plan. First, families or individuals receiving welfare payments under the so-called adult categories (aid to the aged, blind, and disabled) would remain under the Medicaid program, but the program would be transferred to the Social Security Administration, probably as the first step toward integrating it with Medicare. Second, a new family health insurance plan (FHIP) is proposed to cover poor families with children which do not have a full-time employed member and therefore would not be helped by the mandatory employer program.

As was noted above, the current Medicaid program determines eligibility on the basis of welfare status. In the majority of states, families with children, headed by an unemployed male, are not eligible for welfare and therefore cannot receive Medicaid; eligibility requirements vary from state to state on other grounds; and the kinds of medical services covered also vary substantially. FHIP would eliminate most of this patchwork variation. All families with children that are not covered by an employer program (because no member is currently a full-time worker) and whose income and asset position are below a certain level—for example, $5,000 in income for a family of four—would be eligible for FHIP. The lowest-income families (under $3,000 for a family of four) would pay nothing for FHIP benefits. Higher-income families would pay insurance premiums, deductibles, and coinsurance graduated upward according to their income. A family of four with $4,000 income would pay a $50 annual premium, a

10. The premium would resemble a payroll tax, but with higher rates of tax for low-than for high-wage workers. Economists generally believe that a payroll tax nominally paid by the employer is ultimately borne by the worker in the form of lower wages than he would otherwise receive or in higher prices for what he buys. See, for example, John A. Brittain, "The Incidence of Social Security Payroll Taxes," *American Economic Review*, Vol. 61 (March 1971), pp. 110–25; and Brittain, *The Payroll Tax for Social Security* (Brookings Institution, forthcoming).

deductible of one day of hospital room and board, and a deductible of
$50 for all other services combined. A $5,000 family would pay twice
these premiums and deductibles. Coinsurance payments would not be
required until income reached $4,500. At the $5,000 income level, the
premium and coinsurance would be equal to those paid by the employee under the mandatory employer plan (but deductibles would be
lower).

FHIP would provide a nationally uniform package of basic benefits
covering a broad range of medical services, including thirty days of
hospital care, extended care in nursing homes, physicians' services
both in and out of the hospital (with a limit of eight non-hospital
visits), well child care, family planning and maternity care, and other
health services and supplies. It would not cover drugs, dental care,
private nursing, physical therapy and related services, and transportation required to obtain medical care—though these services are now
covered by many states in the Medicaid program. It is estimated that
FHIP would cover 3 million families containing 15 million persons,
and would cost $2.6 billion more than current Medicaid expenditures
for families with dependent children, which it would replace.

The proposed plan would eliminate many of the inequities of the
existing program among families in different states and between male-
and female-headed families. Moreover, the deductibles would help
impose some constraint on excessive and unnecessarily expensive use
of medical care, without placing an impossible burden on the very
poor. The graduation of premiums and deductibles as income rises
would mean that the subsidy benefits would be reduced gradually,
rather than ending suddenly as a certain income level was reached.
This would help to avoid work disincentive effects. Under Medicaid, a
family falling just below the income level that determines eligibility
continues to receive full Medicaid benefits. When its income exceeds
that level, the benefits stop altogether. The loss in Medicaid benefits is
larger than the added income, and the family is worse off for having
increased its earnings.

Several major criticisms have been leveled at FHIP. First, it would
not include poor childless couples and single persons; if they were unemployed they would not be covered by any plan. In a related vein,
families whose incomes were above the FHIP eligibility level, but who
earned their income by part-time work or self-employment, would receive no benefits. They could buy from a special insurance pool the
same mandatory plan offered to employees by paying a full-cost pre-

mium. But this could be as high as $700 a year—substantially more than the premiums paid by employees under the mandatory plan.

Second, FHIP and the mandatory plan are significantly different in many respects, so families with the same income but different employment status would not receive the same benefits. FHIP would be more generous in a number of respects—lower deductibles and, for families with incomes under $4,500, lower premiums and coinsurance and better coverage of maternity care, home health services, nursing home care, and family planning services. On the other hand, the mandatory plan would provide better coverage against very large medical bills than would FHIP.[11] The existence of different plans for those who work and those who do not may create a welfare stigma for FHIP. If the two plans were identical, with the government paying part or all of the premiums for those not covered by an employer plan, a single system could be created.[12] Under those circumstances it is less likely that a welfare stigma would become attached to the public plan.

Tax Subsidies

A quite different approach to financing medical care is the tax subsidy plan sponsored by the American Medical Association. This plan, called Medicredit and introduced by Representatives Richard H. Fulton and Joel T. Broyhill, would offer income tax credits for individuals purchasing a private health insurance plan that provides specified basic and catastrophic benefits.

The amount of credit against federal income taxes would be equal to the full premium cost of the catastrophic component of the insurance. An additional credit would be allowed for the premium cost of the basic benefits; the full credit would be given to families with no tax liability and would be gradually scaled downward to zero for families with tax liabilities of $891 or more. Families with little or no tax liability against which to offset the credit would receive a voucher for use in buying insurance. The prescribed plan for which the credit would be available is more liberal than most existing plans, and presumably most people holding private insurance would switch to the new plan because of the considerable tax savings they would enjoy.

11. In practice, if FHIP remains unchanged, many states will have to arrange to pay for extended illnesses of the unemployed poor.

12. Integrating the two plans would require the government to pay some of the deductibles and coinsurance under the employer plan for workers below the $5,000 income category.

This plan would result in a loss of about $8 billion in federal tax revenues but would eliminate the need for certain federal expenditures under the Medicaid program, so that the net additional cost to the federal government would be about $6 billion.

Because the plan would seek to induce the purchase of private insurance through the indirect mechanism of tax credits, its potential impact is uncertain. Although the advantages of switching to a private insurance plan of the prescribed type would be substantial, it is difficult to estimate how many persons who are currently without private insurance would respond to the indirect incentives by purchasing the plan. Among the poor, who could receive a voucher for 100 percent of the premium, many might be unaware of the option and fail to take advantage of it. The principal effect of the plan would probably be to change the kind of insurance coverage most people would buy and substantially reduce the taxes payable by insured families, but without greatly affecting the total number of people covered by insurance. The amount of the subsidy for medical care would be somewhat arbitrary, since it would depend on the amount of a family's tax liability, which is sensitive to all the loopholes in the tax laws. Because homeowners, for example, can deduct interest and property taxes, they have lower tax liabilities and would receive greater medical insurance subsidies than would renters.

Although the poor would receive a subsidy equal to the cost of the insurance premium, they would still have to pay the coinsurance (20 percent of non-hospital medical expenses up to $500) regardless of their income level. For the very poor this would be a substantial barrier to the use of needed medical services.

The primary problem with this plan, however, is the absence of any real incentive to curb inflation in the costs of medical care or to induce efficiency in the use of medical resources. Although the basic plan incorporates some deductible and coinsurance provisions, these are not structured in a way that would give them substantial influence on individual decisions. Hospital cost-sharing would consist of a fixed deductible for each stay and would not depend on the length of stay or on the costliness of the hospital selected. The maximum that any family would have to pay for physician, laboratory, or X-ray services combined would be $100 annually. It is unlikely that a 20 percent coinsurance, with a maximum direct family payment of $100, would cause families in middle- and upper-income groups to weigh the benefits of alternative medical resources against their costs or to go to physicians who charge less. The only significant constraints on hospital use would apply to stays beyond sixty days, and it is those stays that are least likely to be elective.

The plan specifically would prohibit federal supervision of medical fees or any control over the practice of medicine or the manner in which services are provided. Private insurance companies would be required to pay providers of medical services according to their customary charges. Since patients would have little financial incentive to use physicians who charged lower fees, physicians would have substantial market power to enforce high fees on private insurance companies.

Income-Related Health Insurance Benefits

A proposal that would protect middle- and upper-income groups against catastrophic expenses, while at the same time subsidizing the medical care expenditures of the poor, has been advanced by Martin S. Feldstein of Harvard University. He envisages a uniform plan for everyone (except the elderly, who would remain under Medicare), with the costs subsidized according to income level. All families with incomes above $12,000 would pay the full premium cost of the insurance, with a gradually increasing federal subsidy provided to lower-income families to the point where the premium cost was zero for a family of four with an income below $3,000. The Internal Revenue Service would be used to collect the premiums. Both deductibles and coinsurance would also vary with income, growing larger as income rose from $3,000 to $12,000. But no families, not even those in the $12,000-and-above income brackets, would have to pay more than $1,050 for medical expenses in any one year. Thus the plan would cover catastrophic expenses. It is so constructed that families with average medical expenses could expect to pay 3 to 5 percent of their income on medical care, while the maximum payments even with prolonged illness would seldom exceed 10 percent of family income. Table 7-7 indicates the major financial aspects of the plan, showing both the average and the maximum out-of-pocket medical expenses for a family of two adults and two children at different income levels.

To cover the entire U.S. population under age sixty-five, the cost to the federal budget would have been about $20 billion in 1971, before any premiums were collected from beneficiaries. If the special income

Table 7-7. Financial Aspects of the Feldstein Health Insurance Plan, Family of Two Adults and Two Children, by Selected Family Incomes, Annual Basis

Family income (dollars)	Amount deductible (dollars)	Coinsur- ance rate (percent)	Average insurance benefits (dollars)	Average out-of-pocket payments (dollars)	Maximum out-of-pocket payments	
					Total (dollars)	Fraction of income (percent)
3,000	150	20	441	170	400	13
5,000	250	28	377	234	572	11
8,000	400	40	307	304	800	10
10,000	500	48	278	333	932	9
12,000	600	56	258	353	1,048	9
15,000	600	56	258	353	1,048	7

Source: Martin Feldstein, unpublished estimates (Harvard University, 1971).

tax treatment of medical expenses and health insurance premiums were removed, and assuming that Medicaid were replaced by the new plan, the net additional cost would be $14 billion. A large part of this cost would be financed by compulsory premiums paid by middle- and upper-income groups as part of their federal income tax return.

The plan would realize many of the advantages of a full coverage plan in that it would create one system of medical care for all, provide protection against catastrophic expenses, remove gaps in coverage, and eliminate the disparate treatment of people who are working and those not working. It would not require the large budgetary outlays that a fully federalized health benefits plan would require, because middle- and upper-income groups would continue to pay the full premium cost of the benefits. It would achieve the two objectives of improving the financial access of the poor to medical care and of protecting all families against the financial burden of very large medical expenses.

With respect to the control of escalating medical prices, the proposal has both advantages and disadvantages. On the one hand, it would provide substantial deductibles and coinsurance for normal medical expenses, giving consumers and their physicians an incentive to avoid overusing expensive services. Moreover, since the deductibles and coinsurance would be graduated with income levels, they would not bar the use of needed care by the poor.

On the other hand, as was noted earlier in this chapter, the consumer is an imperfect policeman of the health care market because he lacks knowledge of medical diagnosis and practices and is not in a good position to shop around. In the long run, structural changes in the way health care is delivered (for example, through competitive HMOs) and in the way insurance companies reimburse hospitals would probably be a necessary supplement to this program. Moreover, the total absence of coinsurance for medical bills over $1,400 would raise the problem of excessive use of very expensive medical technology that was discussed above. As was suggested there, a non-market mechanism to monitor these areas of medical practice would have to be developed to accompany any plan that furnished good catastrophic protection.

A Comprehensive National Insurance System

The most comprehensive proposal is the Health Security Act introduced in the Congress by Senator Edward M. Kennedy and Representative Martha W. Griffiths. This bill would establish a national health insurance program covering the entire population and providing a broad range of health services. No payment would be required of the patient. In addition, the proposal includes provisions designed to reorganize the delivery of health services, improve health planning, and increase the supply of health care manpower and facilities.

The Department of Health, Education, and Welfare estimates that the federal cost of the program would be $90 billion annually if it were initiated in 1974. Half of the cost would be financed by the imposition of an additional federal payroll tax, which—according to the HEW estimate—would have to be about 6.3 percent on wages and salaries below $15,000. The other half of the funds would come from general revenues. Since the Kennedy-Griffiths program would replace current federal outlays to finance medical care (including Medicare and Medicaid), and since additional federal revenues would be generated by the elimination of medical expense deductions in the current income tax law, the net cost of the program to the federal government would be about $60 billion. About $52 billion, however, would represent replacement of privately financed expenditures; the other $8 billion would represent additional medical expenditures.

Because the Kennedy-Griffiths program would provide free medical care to all, with no deductibles or coinsurance, control of excessive use and medical care price inflation would have to be sought through a series of financial and regulatory devices. Each year a national medical care budget for the coming year would be established, based on the current year's cost and estimated changes in prices, population, and supply. That fixed budget would then be allocated to ten regions and within the regions to about 100 subareas. In turn, within each subarea an administrative agency would allocate funds between "practitioners" (physicians, dentists) and hospitals. The agency would calculate a "capitation" amount for each type of practitioner—the compensation a practitioner would receive for agreeing to take care of a patient for a year, whatever his needs. Practitioners could also elect to operate on a fixed salary or to charge fees for individual services rather than enter into capitation agreements, but the program is designed to discourage the fee-for-service option. HMOs providing all services on a capitation basis would be given preferential treatment. Each hospital in the subarea would have to operate within a fixed budget for the coming year, subject to certain provisions for budget revisions. Committees of professionals and consumers would be established to monitor the use of medical services in order to control excessive use.

This plan has many advantages. It would establish one system of medical care for all—with all the social and economic advantages of a single system. All families, regardless of employment status, would be entitled to the same benefits. The plan would provide protection against catastrophic expenses (indeed against nearly *all* medical expenses). It would remove gaps in coverage, since everybody would be eligible.

But the Kennedy-Griffiths program also raises problems. Because it would provide free medical care not only to the poor but to all of the population, it would move into the federal budget a huge component of private outlays for normal medical expenses that are now being made by middle- and upper-income groups with no major financial strain. Financing this would require large tax increases that would be devoted not toward accomplishing objectives attainable only in the public sector, but toward substituting public outlays for private outlays that would have been undertaken in any event. If the large tax increases necessary to finance the program were adopted, it is highly unlikely that additional taxes could be raised to meet the costs of other high priority public objectives.

Other difficulties would arise from the abandonment of private payments for most medical services and the introduction of complex regulatory mechanisms to control the prices and use of services. There are more than 7,000 hospitals in the United States, more than 20,000 nursing homes, and several hundred thousand physicians. The kinds of practice, costs, types of services, and quality of care vary greatly from area to area and within each area. The establishment by administrative bodies of equitable and appropriate fees and charges would be a task of Herculean proportions, particularly on a nationwide scale. Controlling costs would also require the control and monitoring of services rendered. Utilization review committees would have to be established to determine whether stays in institutions were unnecessarily long. Similarly, it would have to be determined whether physicians were ordering unnecessary tests as a means of increasing their incomes, requesting unnecessary repeat visits, referring patients unnecessarily to additional physicians, and so on. At present the technical capability for monitoring the entire health care system is simply not available.

Some of the controls proposed in the Kennedy-Griffiths bill are novel and imaginative—the concept of a fixed budget to be allocated among regions, and new methods of encouraging the capitation and HMO approach to financing and delivering medical care. But they are as yet untested. Experimenting with those approaches in existing federal health insurance programs in selected areas might yield valuable information. However, to carry them out all at once in a nationwide system of medical care could pose major risks.

The last major concern with the Kennedy-Griffiths plan is the impact it would have on the health care services provided to low-income people. Unlike other plans that specifically subsidize the care of the poor and the near poor, this plan would give everyone equal financial access to medical care—that is, care would be free for all. But this alone would not guarantee that everyone would have equal access to care. Instead, at least initially, the plan might widen the disparity among income classes in the use of medical services. A changeover to free care would represent a greater reduction in the price of care to higher-income persons. Many of the poor currently receive free care or reduced-cost care through Medicaid or charity. The largest increases in demand therefore might come from higher-income groups. Moreover, medical manpower and facilities are much more abundant in higher-income areas. Unless deliberate steps were taken to increase the supply of these resources in low-income areas, the poor would have less physical access to care. While these problems might be overcome in time, the result of providing free care to all might paradoxically be to increase care most for those who can already afford it.

Conclusions

Without government assistance, the poor cannot afford to meet even the normal cost of adequate medical care. Middle-income families can handle normal medical bills but are faced with severe financial crises if they must pay the abnormally high medical costs that accompany prolonged illness. Dealing with these two problems should be the central task of federal health insurance. But in so doing it should meet several other major tests:

• It should provide checks on the escalation of medical prices and excessive use of services.

• It should avoid the creation of a two-class medical system in which one group of the population receives different benefits and treatment, depending on its welfare, employment, or other status.

• It should minimize the transfer to the federal budget of normal medical bills paid by middle- and upper-income consumers in order to save scarce tax resources for high priority public expenditures.

A single program that would provide both basic benefits and catastrophic protection for all the population, but that would scale premiums, deductibles, and coinsurance to family income, would largely meet these criteria. The poor would receive financial resources to secure medical care; middle-income families would be protected against catastrophic expenses, but the cost of their normal medical bills would not be transferred to the federal budget; the coinsurance and deductibles would provide a check against price escalation and excessive use but, being scaled according to income, would not place undue burdens on the poor.

Three important problems would remain in this approach. First, if families or their employers and unions bought supplementary insurance to cover the deductibles and coinsurance, the check on inflation and excessive use would be dissipated. Hence the federal plan's deductibles and coinsurance would have to be so applied that they could not be picked up by private insurance. Second, if the catastrophic component of the federal plan covered all expenses above a certain limit, as it must to provide good protection, a regulatory mechanism would have to be set up to monitor the excessive use of very high cost technology. Third, scaling premiums, deductibles, and coinsurance with income would require a "means test," not just for the poor but for families with incomes up to perhaps $10,000 or $15,000. While this test is commonly used with federal loans and scholarships for higher education, it could prove unpopular—initially at least—when applied to medical care, and in the case of deductibles and coinsurance it could be difficult to administer.

No insurance program, however ideal, could solve all the problems of the nation's health care system. Improving the supply of medical manpower, encouraging more medical resources in shortage areas, and restructuring the medical delivery system to provide suppliers of medical care with greater incentives for efficiency are all areas for public policy intervention. But they are not inconsistent with, and can to some extent be furthered by, well designed federal health insurance policies.

8. Child Care

THIS CHAPTER RAISES TWO QUESTIONS whose answers could have a sizable impact on the federal budget over the next few years: (1) What responsibility should the federal government take for day care for children of working mothers, and (2) what should it do about the education and development of children before they reach school age? These questions are related, but they are not the same. Day care need not be educational, and preschool programs need not be limited to children whose mothers work.

At present, day care and early childhood programs are relatively small items in the federal budget. The administration's proposed budget for fiscal 1973 allocates about $1 billion for this range of programs, about $100 million more than in fiscal 1972. (See Table 8-1.) Most of this money is for day care of children on public assistance whose mothers are in training programs and for the Head Start program, which provides preschool education for poor children. These programs reach only a fraction of their potential participants.

If the federal government were to take on a major responsibility in these areas, budgetary costs could mount rapidly. For example, operating a free public preschool program for all three- and four-year-olds at federal expense might cost about $5 billion a year.[1] Federal provision of free day care for children from poor and moderate-income families could easily cost $12 billion to $15 billion by 1977.[2]

1. This estimate is based on the assumption that 75 percent of eligible children would participate and that costs would average $1,000 annually per child.

2. The estimate assumes 50 percent participation of children under fourteen in families with incomes below the Labor Department's lower living standard budget ($7,214 for a family of four), at a cost of $2,000 per child for those up to five years old and $700 per child for before- and after-school and vacation care of those six to fourteen.

Table 8-1. Federal Spending for Day Care and Other Early Childhood Programs, Fiscal Years 1970–73

Millions of dollars

Program	1970	1971	1972 Estimate	1973 Estimate
Day care	164	233	404	507
Head Start	330	363	364	369
Preschool programs under Elementary and Secondary Education Act, Title 1	26	92	98	93
Total	520	688	866	969

Sources: Day care, 1970: *Child Care Data and Materials*, Senate Committee on Finance, 92 Cong. 1 sess. (1971), p. 32; other 1970 data: *Special Analyses, Budget of the United States Government, Fiscal Year 1972*, pp. 120–21; other data: *Special Analyses of the United States Government, Fiscal Year 1973*, pp. 123, 144.

Decisions about day care and early childhood programs are likely to provoke a heated national debate over the next few years, not only because the budgetary consequences might be large, but because sensitive emotional issues are involved. How should the responsibility for children be divided between the family and society? Should mothers of small children work? The spectrum of views is wide: some people believe that liberating women from the burden of child care would lead to happier families; others fear that putting children in day care centers would destroy family life and lead to a collectivized society.

Responsibility for Children

Traditionally in the United States, the responsibility for the care and supervision of children has rested squarely with parents. Only when a child reached age six did society at large take a major hand by insisting that he attend school and by providing schools at the taxpayers' expense. But even at school ages, public concern is limited primarily to the child's intellectual development and to a few hours a day on school days. What happens to the child the rest of the time is his parents' business. Society intervenes only if he is severely abused or neglected or runs afoul of the law.

Public services offered to help parents with their responsibilities for children have been far from comprehensive. Some health services are provided—well-baby clinics, measles vaccine, Medicaid for some poor families—but there is no comprehensive program for meeting the health expenses of children comparable to Medicare for the aged. Many communities, though not all, provide free public kindergarten for five-year-olds, but few provide public nursery school for the three- and four-year-olds or any kind of infant care, except in emergencies. The mother who needs or wants to take a job normally has to make her own arrangements for child care without public help. Indeed, welfare programs have been designed to reduce the need for women to go to work, by paying them to stay at home and look after their children if there is no male breadwinner in the household.

Until recently, this division of labor between the family and the public was widely accepted as being in the best interest of all concerned. That mothers stayed home and cared for their children before school age and after school hours was considered good for children, good for mothers, and good for society at large. But now this division of responsibility is being challenged from several directions at once. Pressure for public provision or subsidization of day care and preschool programs of various sorts arises from at least three concerns:

1. *Concern with reducing welfare rolls by enabling welfare recipients to work.* The number of mothers and children receiving public assistance has grown rapidly in recent years, causing widespread interest in ways of reducing the welfare rolls. Some believe that mothers on welfare should be required to work; others think that they should simply be encouraged to work. In either case, lack of day care facilities for their children is seen as one of the major impediments to increasing the employment of welfare mothers.

2. *Concern with the children of working mothers generally.* The number of mothers at all income levels who are in the labor force is rising rapidly, causing concern about the large number of children who need care while their mothers work. Little is known about how these children are cared for now, but there is reason to believe that the care is not adequate—that "latchkey" children, left to their own devices, may get into trouble and that low quality day care may be harmful to children. The women's liberation movement is arguing more and more vocally that the public has a responsibility to provide adequate child care arrangements so that mothers will have a genuine choice between staying at home and going to work.

3. *Concern with early childhood development, especially for low-income children.* Children develop intellectual skills and capacities very rapidly at early ages. By age three, poor children on the average already lag behind children from more affluent homes. These observations have led to the hope that early intervention could reduce the

handicaps of the poor and might increase the capabilities of all children.

These different concerns all point in the direction of wider public responsibility for children outside the usual school hours and ages and have greatly increased the pressure on the federal government to provide new and expanded day care and preschool programs.

In considering how the federal government should respond to these concerns—if at all—at least three sets of issues need to be resolved:

1. *What kinds of programs are desirable?* The possibilities include "custodial" day care, aimed primarily at keeping children from harm; child development services, including preschool education, nutrition, and health care (in day care settings or elsewhere); and parent education in nutrition, health, and child development.

2. *What should be the government's role?* The government could confine itself to setting standards; it could subsidize parents by giving them vouchers or tax relief for child care; or it could finance or even operate programs directly.

3. *Who should benefit?* Government-supported child care programs could be made available to everyone or limited to the needy. If the latter course is chosen, the problem becomes one of defining who is "needy."

This chapter will focus mainly on day care for children of working mothers and on preschool education in a day care setting. It first describes what is known about the demand for, and supply of, day care of various sorts. The discussion then turns to an evaluation of the case for public subsidization of day care—for the poor and for the non-poor. The final sections deal with proposed federal programs and the options facing the government in the future.

The Demand for Day Care

If consideration is being given to a large-scale day care program, the first question is: What is the demand for various kinds of day care? The answer depends on how many children are likely to need care because their mothers work, on what kind of child care arrangements parents want, and on what they are willing to pay.

Available information indicates (1) that the proportion of young children with working mothers is rising rapidly and seems likely to continue to do so whether the government provides day care or not;

(2) that most working mothers arrange to have their children cared for in their own homes or someone else's and that they do not pay much for child care; and (3) that the demand for more elaborate and educational forms of day care appears to be very sensitive to price. Hence, if the government were to offer an expensive variety of day care, it would also have to provide a large subsidy to parents, or they would not enroll their children.

The Increase in Working Mothers

In this generation a dramatic change has taken place in American family life. Two or three decades ago, it was unusual for mothers to work outside the home, especially if they had young children. (See Table 8-2.) Now it is not unusual. More than half the mothers of school age children are in the labor force, and about one-third of those with children under six. In the past decade, the rise in labor force participation has been especially rapid among mothers of very young children—those with children under six or even under three years old. (See Table 8-3.) This increase is not a reflection of the breakup of families; it has occurred mainly among wives living with their husbands. Separated, widowed, and divorced women bringing up children on their own have had relatively high labor force participation rates for some time. This group is increasing, but it is not large and does not account for the increased labor force participation rate of mothers.

Mothers are much more likely to be in the labor force if they are black than if they are white, and the difference is not attributable to the fact that black women are more likely to head families. Labor

Table 8-2. Labor Force Participation Rates of Mothers, by Age of Children, 1940, 1950, 1960, and 1970
Percent

Year	All mothers	Mothers with children 6 to 17 years only	Mothers with children under 6 years
1940	9[a]	n.a.	n.a.
1950	22	33	14
1960	30	43	20
1970	42	52	32

Sources: 1940: U.S. Department of Labor, Women's Bureau, *Women as Workers: A Statistical Guide* (1953), p. 74; other data, from Women's Bureau as given in *Child Care Data and Materials*, Senate Committee on Finance, p. 19.
n.a. Not available.
a. Estimate.

Table 8-3. Labor Force Participation Rates of Mothers[a] by Age of Children, Color, and Marital Status, March 1960 and March 1970
Percent

Age of children, and color	All ever-married mothers		Married, husband present		Widowed, divorced, or married, husband absent	
	1970	1960	1970	1960	1970	1960
All ever-married mothers	42.0	30.4	39.7	27.6	60.6	55.5
Children 6 to 17 years only	51.5	42.5	49.2	39.0	67.3	66.2
Children under 6 years	32.2	20.2	30.3	18.6	50.7	39.8
Children 3 to 5 years, with none under 3 years	39.2	27.4	37.0	25.1	58.8	51.7
Children under 3 years	27.3	16.5	25.8	15.3	43.6	32.4
Nonwhite	53.8	n.a.	53.4	n.a.	54.9	n.a.
Children 6 to 17 years only	62.0	n.a.	62.6	52.6	60.8	n.a.
Children under 6 years	47.2	n.a.	46.9	27.0	48.1	n.a.

Sources: Elizabeth Waldman and Anne M. Young, "Marital and Family Characteristics of Workers, March 1970," U.S. Bureau of Labor Statistics, Special Labor Force Report 130 (1971; processed), Table F; Jacob Schiffman, "Marital and Family Characteristics of Workers, March 1960," Bureau of Labor Statistics, Special Labor Force Report 13 (1961; processed), Tables G, K.
n.a. Not available.
a. Mothers who have children under 18 years of age and who are or have been married.

force participation rates of black mothers living with their husbands are also high and have increased markedly in the past decade among those with young children. (See Table 8-3.)

Some working mothers work part-time, but a majority have full-time jobs. (See Table 8-4.) Also some work only part of the year. It follows that the proportion of mothers who seek work at some time during a year is higher than the proportion in the labor force at any one time. As is shown in Table 8-4, in a March 1970 survey, 44 percent of all wives with preschool children and 58 percent of those with school age children reported that they had worked during the previous year. Comparable figures for black wives were 63 percent for those with children under six and 73 percent for those with school age children.

The chances that a mother will be working are related not only to her race, her marital status, and the ages of her children, but to several other factors. The chances are higher if she

- has more education
- lives in a city

Table 8-4. Work Experience in 1969 of Married Women with Husband Present, by Age of Children, and Color, March 1970

Age of children, and color	Percentage of civilian non-institutional population with work experience	Percentage distribution of wives with work experience				
			Worked at full-time jobs			Worked at part-time jobs
		Total	Total	50 to 52 weeks	1 to 49 weeks	
All wives[a]	50.4	100.0	69.5	40.8	28.8	30.5
With children under 18 years	51.0	100.0	64.5	32.5	31.9	35.5
Under 6 years	44.3	100.0	63.8	21.9	41.9	36.2
Under 3 years	41.9	100.0	66.3	15.6	50.7	33.7
6 to 17 years only	57.5	100.0	65.0	40.6	24.3	35.0
White[a]	49.2	100.0	69.0	40.8	28.3	31.0
With children under 18 years	49.5	100.0	63.1	31.9	31.2	36.9
Under 6 years	42.3	100.0	62.0	21.0	40.9	38.0
Under 3 years	40.2	100.0	64.8	15.0	49.8	35.2
6 to 17 years only	56.3	100.0	63.8	39.6	24.2	36.2
Black[a]	64.3	100.0	74.2	40.3	33.8	25.8
With children under 18 years	66.9	100.0	75.8	36.6	39.2	24.2
Under 6 years	62.6	100.0	75.0	26.2	48.8	25.0
Under 3 years	57.9	100.0	75.5	17.9	57.6	24.5
6 to 17 years only	73.0	100.0	76.7	49.3	27.4	23.3

Source: Elizabeth Waldman and Kathryn R. Gover, "Children of Women in the Labor Force," *Monthly Labor Review*, Vol. 94 (July 1971), p. 21. Figures are rounded and may not add to totals.
a. Includes wives with no children under 18 years.

- has a small number of children
- believes her family needs the money.

At any level of education, mothers are more likely to work if the rest of the family's earnings are low than if they are high; and wives are more likely to work if their husbands are unemployed. Indeed, when asked why they work, most mothers give economic reasons.

Reasons for the Increase

Although differences exist among population groups in the extent to which mothers work, the striking fact is that the proportion of working mothers is rising in all groups. Mothers may say that they work for money, but family incomes have never been higher, so explanations for the increase must lie elsewhere. At least six sets of reasons may be offered, though all of them seem as likely to be results of the phenomenon as causes of it.

1. *The declining birth rate.* The two- and three-child family has become typical, while larger families are becoming rarer. A mother with fewer children has less housework to do and is more likely to be able to earn enough to cover the cost of buying child care outside the home. Moreover, even if she drops out of the labor force until her children reach school age, a mother with two children is likely to have many more years left for working than has a mother of six. The longer work

span makes it more worthwhile for the mother of two to invest in the education and on-the-job learning that make work remunerative.

2. *Changing technology in the home.* Taking care of children in the home requires a full-time adult presence but does not require the complete attention of the adult all of the time. So long as mothers have other economic activities to perform at home (cooking, cleaning, canning, laundry), they can look after children at relatively low extra cost. Labor saving devices and convenience foods, however, have made it far less necessary for women to stay in the home for reasons other than child care and have made it more important to earn income to cover the cost of these conveniences. Thus, women have greater incentives to seek employment outside the home, even if they have to purchase child care from someone else.

3. *Changing technology outside the home.* The mechanization of manufacturing and the growth of service industries have reduced the proportion of jobs for which physical strength is required and have greatly increased job opportunities for women, albeit usually at lower wage levels than men. Many occupations traditionally considered almost exclusively "women's jobs" (teaching at the elementary and secondary school level, nursing, secretarial work) have expanded dramatically in recent years.

4. *Increasing educational levels of women.* Young mothers have substantially more education now than they did a generation ago. Hence, the economic cost to a mother of staying home—the wages she gives up by not entering the labor market—are appreciably higher than they used to be.

5. *Changing attitudes toward "woman's place."* Although attitudes may not be changing fast enough to suit the more militant leaders of the women's liberation movement, the idea that women should be individuals with lives and careers of their own—not exclusively wives and mothers—is clearly gaining ground, especially among the young.

6. *Changing attitudes about what is good for children.* To an increasing extent, kindergarten and nursery school are considered—by educators and parents alike—to be desirable experiences for children, even if their mothers do not work. Most children now go to kindergarten, and preschool enrollment of three- and four-year-olds is rising rapidly, especially among middle- and upper-income groups. In 1970, nearly half of the three- and four-year-olds from families with incomes over $10,000 in 1969 were enrolled in some sort of preschool program (compared with 23 percent from families with incomes under $3,000).

Since all of these factors seem likely to continue operating in the same direction, there is every reason to expect a continuing increase in the proportion of mothers who work—even if no major new day care programs are undertaken by the government. If the proportion of mothers in the labor force increases at the same rate in the 1970s as in the 1960s, one would expect that about 59 percent of all mothers will be in the labor force by 1980—51 percent of those with preschool children and 63 percent of those with school age children, and even higher percentages will work at least some time during the year. Increased availability of subsidized day care would probably increase these proportions somewhat and enable some mothers to shift from part-time to full-time work. Nevertheless, a substantial proportion of mothers, especially those with young children, will continue to choose not to work, so one would not expect these proportions to approach 100 percent. Hence, the main effect of more subsidized day care is likely to be not an increase in the proportion of mothers working, but a change in the kind of care available for children whose mothers have decided to work.

Children of Working Mothers: What Happens Now?

A mother who works can arrange for the care of her children in a variety of ways, depending on their ages, her income and the hours she works, her family situation, and where she lives. Perhaps her husband, an older child, or another person living in the household can take over while she works. She may have a relative with whom she can leave the children or who can come to her home to look after them. If she thinks the child is old enough, she can let him look after himself, perhaps asking a neighbor to keep an eye on him. If she can afford it, she can hire a maid or a sitter, or she can find a woman who earns money by taking care of other people's children in her home. Or she can enroll her child in a day care center if there is one within feasible commuting distance of where she lives or works.

Of the 70 million children under age eighteen in 1971, 26 million had mothers in the labor force. Of these, nearly 6 million were under six years old. Another 18 million were between six and fourteen, presumably in school but requiring some kind of supervision after school or on nonschool days. When one considers the large number of children involved, it is remarkable how little is known about what happens to them. Several recent surveys agree, however, on the main outlines of the situation.

The most striking fact is that most children of working mothers are cared for in their own homes or someone else's; only a small proportion are in day care centers. A government survey of child care arrangements of working mothers in 1965 revealed that about half the children under six were cared for in their own homes, usually by their father or another relative, less often by a nonrelative, such as a sitter or a maid. (See Table 8-5.) Some were looked after by the mother while she worked, presumably in a small business or on a farm. About 30 percent were cared for in someone else's home, about half by a relative, and the rest by a nonrelative, a situation often described as "family day care." A very small group, only about 6 percent, were in day care centers. For school-age children the predominance of home and family arrangements was even greater. Roughly two-thirds were cared for in their own homes, and a substantial proportion were described as looking after themselves.

A survey made by the Westinghouse Learning Corporation in 1970, while not entirely comparable, confirmed these general findings. Westinghouse found somewhat greater use of day care centers than did the earlier survey, perhaps reflecting the growth of public pro-

Table 8-5. Percentage Distribution of Child Care Arrangements of Working Mothers, by Age of Children, 1965 and 1970

	Age of children			
	Under 6 years		6 to 14 years	
Child care arrangement	1965[a]	1970[b]	1965[a]	1970[b]
Care in own home	48.0	49.9	66.0	78.7
By father	14.4	18.4	15.1	10.6
By other relative	17.5	18.9	22.6	20.6
By a nonrelative	15.3	7.3	6.8	4.5
Mother worked during child's school hours	0.8	5.2	21.5	42.9
Care in someone else's home	30.7	34.5	9.2	12.6
By a relative	14.9	15.5	4.7	7.6
By a nonrelative	15.8	19.0	4.5	5.0
Day care center	5.6	10.5	0.6	0.6
No special care[c]	15.7	5.0	24.3	8.3
Total	100.0	100.0	100.0	100.0

Sources: 1965, Seth Low and Pearl G. Spindler, *Child Care Arrangements of Working Mothers in the United States*, U.S. Children's Bureau and U.S. Women's Bureau (1968), pp. 15, 71, 72; 1970, Westinghouse Learning Corporation and Westat Research, Incorporated, "Day Care Survey—1970: Summary Report and Basic Analysis," Prepared for Evaluation Division, Office of Economic Opportunity (1971; processed), pp. 175, 178–80. Figures are rounded and may not add to totals.

a. When several kinds of care were used for the same child, the predominating and most recent child care arrangement is given.

b. Child care arrangements on the last day the mother worked.

c. Includes child looked after self, mother looked after child while working, and other.

Table 8-6. Percentage Distribution of Children for Whom Some Payment for Care Was Made, by Family Income and Amount Paid per Year, 1964

Family income (dollars)		Amount paid per year[a]		
	Total	Under $250	$250–$450	$500 and over
Under 3,000	100	47.2	28.1	24.7
3,000–5,999	100	26.0	43.2	30.7
6,000–9,999	100	20.9	46.1	33.0
10,000 and over	100	17.1	30.0	52.9

Source: Seth Low and Pearl G. Spindler, *Child Care Arrangements of Working Mothers in the United States*, p. 106. Figures are rounded and may not add to totals.
a. The amount paid is per child in the family.

grams for low-income children. Nevertheless, the survey found only 10 percent of the preschool children—and a negligible proportion of school age children—enrolled in day care centers.

Since so many of these arrangements are within the family, it is not surprising that few mothers pay much for child care. Indeed, most get it free. The 1965 survey estimated that only 21 percent of the arrangements for care of children under fourteen and 34 percent for children under six involved a money payment.

While most mothers do not pay, those who do, pay widely differing proportions of their income. As may be seen in Table 8-6, families with higher incomes tend to pay higher dollar amounts, but some low-income families pay significant proportions of their income for child care. The figures in the table are for *each* child, and some families have several children needing care.

Day Care Centers

Although day care centers enroll a small proportion of children of working mothers, more is known about them than about the less formal but more usual arrangements for child care. Two surveys confirm these general findings:[3] (1) Day care centers vary tremendously in size, staffing, equipment and facilities, the range of services they offer, the groups they serve, and the quality of their product. (2) Most centers are low budget operations, largely because their staffs have little training and receive low wages. (3) To a significant extent, a two-class

3. Westinghouse Learning Corporation and Westat Research, Incorporated, "Day Care Survey—1970: Summary Report and Basic Analysis," Prepared for Evaluation Division, Office of Economic Opportunity (1971; processed); and Mary Dublin Keyserling, *Windows on Day Care, A Report On The Findings of Members of the National Council of Jewish Women on Day Care Needs and Services in Their Communities* (New York: National Council of Jewish Women, 1972).

system has evolved in day care, with a small proportion of the poor getting more comprehensive and costly care in subsidized day care centers than is available to the nonpoor in unsubsidized centers.

According to the Westinghouse survey, there were 17,500 day care centers in 1970 that provided full day care for at least seven children. Almost all were licensed by their states. About 60 percent of the centers were proprietary—run by individuals or by companies for profit. The rest were nonprofit operations—run mostly by churches, community action agencies, united funds, and other charitable groups, and a few by public schools.

Most day care centers are small—half enroll fewer than thirty children—and most are in residential neighborhoods. Day care at the mother's place of work is infrequent, although the survey took note of some day care centers run by hospitals for children of their staff members.

The Westinghouse survey divided the centers in the sample into three categories, depending on the type of services they offered, without making a judgment of the quality of services. (See Table 8-7.) Category A centers were "custodial." They offered food, shelter, and adult supervision, but no educational programs or health or other services. The category A centers were mostly proprietary (79 percent). They had an average of twelve full-time children per staff member if all staff were included, and fifteen per staff member if only those that dealt directly with the children were counted.

Category B centers offered food, shelter, supervision, and some sort of educational program. These centers were also mostly proprietary (68 percent), though some were operated by nonprofit groups—one-fourth by churches. The average child-to-staff ratios were about the same as in the category A centers, but a higher percentage of the staff were certified teachers, and the average pay level was higher. There was more equipment for art, music, and indoor and outdoor play activities in the B than in the A centers.

Finally, there were category C centers described as "developmental." These centers offered not only an educational program, but also a range of other services, usually including health, family counseling, and some parent participation in the activities. The C centers were generally nonprofit (83 percent), and nearly half of them were operated by community action agencies. They had much lower child-to-staff ratios—four children for each member of the total staff and six children per staff member dealing directly with children. The staffs

Table 8-7. Characteristics of Day Care Centers and Users, by Category of Service Offered, 1970

Characteristic	Category of service offered[a]		
	Custodial (A)	Educational (B)	Developmental (C)
General characteristics			
Number of children per center	33	49	52
Percent proprietary	79	68	17
Percent operated by community action agencies	0	2	46
Percent operated by churches	12	25	8
Percent with waiting lists	30	52	78
Examination programs and services			
Percent offering physical examinations	5	8	73
Percent offering dental examinations	3	7	70
Percent offering vision tests	8	19	86
Percent offering psychological testing	2	7	67
Percent offering social work	4	14	74
Staffing			
Percent with any certified teachers	5	43	62
Number of certified teachers per center (all centers)	0.06	0.82	1.19
Full-day equivalent children per child-related staff persons (median)	15	14	6
Monthly salary of child-related staff per full-day equivalent child (median in dollars)	14	26	44
Users			
Percent of families with incomes under $4,000	18	16	59
Percent of families with incomes of $8,000 and over	28	45	17
Ratio of one-parent to two-parent households	0.33	0.37	0.93
Percent of minority group children	45	34	61

Source: Westinghouse Learning Corporation and Westat Research, Incorporated, *Day Care Survey—1970: Summary Report and Basic Analysis*, pp. 12–20.

a. The categories are described as follows: custodial, offers food, shelter, and adult supervision, but makes no attempt to provide education or other services; educational, offers food, shelter, adult supervision, and some kind of educational program; developmental, same as educational, and in addition provides one or more services such as health care, parent participation, counseling, and social and creative activities.

had more training than did those of the B centers, though the C centers did not seem to have more equipment.

As may be seen in Table 8-7, the category C centers are offering a more costly service, primarily to the poor and the near poor. Over half the parents of children in C centers are estimated to have incomes of less than $4,000, and only 17 percent above $8,000. The proportion of one-parent families is high. Many of these centers are funded by Head Start and other federal programs and serve welfare mothers who are working or in training. In contrast, the category A centers, which are mostly unsubsidized, offer a much less costly service, primarily to lower middle-income families. Over half the families of children in A centers are reported to have incomes in the $4,000–$8,000 bracket. Most of these families have two parents, presumably both working at fairly low-wage jobs. The B centers serve a slightly higher income group than do the A centers, but offer a less costly service than the C centers.

Another survey of day care, carried out in 1970 by the National Council of Jewish Women, confirms the Westinghouse findings that nonprofit centers offer more costly service to a lower-income population (Table 8-8). Unlike Westinghouse, the Council survey attempted to evaluate the quality of care provided by the centers, assigning each one a rating of "superior," "good," "fair," and "poor" on the basis of a combination of objective factors and interviewers' impressions. In general, the nonprofit centers scored higher, though half were rated only "fair" and 11 percent "poor." Half the proprietaries rated "poor" and 35 percent "fair." The "poor" centers were dirty, dismal, crowded, understaffed, and sometimes inhumane. Descriptions of the worst of them make depressing reading, though it is not clear how many children are subjected to the worst conditions described.

Although both surveys found considerable variation in fees charged to parents, the charges of proprietary centers were typically $15 to $20 a week per child. Most proprietary centers charge a flat fee regardless of income, though many charge less for a second or third child from the same family. The nonprofits charge somewhat lower fees (normally $10 to $15 a week), and most adjust the fee to the parents' income.

According to the Westinghouse survey, the proprietary centers depend almost entirely on parents' fees to meet their costs, while the nonprofits depend on other sources, as is shown below (in percent):

	Proprietary centers	*Nonprofit centers*
Parent fees	99	22
Federal government	1	44
State and local government	...	18
Other	...	17

Table 8-8. Characteristics of Nonprofit and Proprietary Day Care Centers, 1970

Characteristic	Nonprofit	Proprietary
Percent serving only or mainly families with incomes under $5,000	66	21
Percent of centers with 75 percent of children from one-parent homes	47	15
Percent of centers with 75 percent and over white children	20	74
Percent of centers with 75 percent and over black children	45	15
Percent charging:		
No fee	20	—
Sliding scale	58	27
Flat fee	22	73
Percent in which lowest professional salary was:		
Under $3,000	8	28
$3,000–$4,999	34	52
Over $5,000	58	19
Percent in which highest professional salary was:		
Under $5,000	19	71
$5,000–$7,999	48	22
Over $8,000	33	7
Percent in which director had college degree	75	47
Percent in which there were:		
9 or fewer children per adult	75	45
From 10 to 14 children per adult	18	39
15 or more children per adult	7	16
Percent rated by interviewers as:		
Good or superior	38	15
Fair	51	35
Poor	11	50

Source: Mary Dublin Keyserling, *Windows on Day Care, A Report On The Findings of Members of the National Council of Jewish Women on Day Care Needs and Services in Their Communities* (New York: National Council of Jewish Women, 1972), pp. 40–129.

Black families are disproportionately large users of day care centers both because black mothers are more likely to work and because those who work are more likely to use day care centers. About one-third of the children in day care centers are black (more than half of them in nonprofit centers), though blacks make up only 14 percent of preschool children.

The basic fact to keep in mind, however, is that very few working mothers—black or white, rich or poor—use day care centers. Moreover, subsidized centers serve only a small proportion of the poor. Child care arrangements of welfare mothers who are working or are in training are shown in Table 8-9. These arrangements are not very different from those of mothers at higher income levels. Most children are taken care of in their own homes or by a relative, and substantially more are in family day care than in day care centers. Even among mothers enrolled in the Work Incentive Program (WIN), center care was unusual. Only 14 percent of their children under six were in day care centers.

Family Day Care Homes

Family day care homes serve far more children than do day care centers, but much less is known about them. Many are simply informal arrangements among friends and neighbors, and most—perhaps 90 to 95 percent—are unlicensed.

Family day care is primarily a by-product operation. Women with children of their own take in other children to supplement the family income. Often they are "filling the empty nest," taking in young children who need day care after their own have reached school age.

Surveys indicate that the typical family day care home is in a single-family dwelling with an outdoor play area and some equipment for children. Most serve only one or two children besides the caregiver's own family. (The Westinghouse survey found an average of 1.6.) The proportion of infants and toddlers in day care homes is higher than in day care centers. Users of day care homes come from somewhat lower income groups than do the users of proprietary centers, and the fees charged appear to be somewhat less than those of proprietary centers, though higher than those of nonprofit day care operations. The Council survey found the average fee for day care homes to be $16.50 a week, about $2 less than it found for proprietary centers. Licensed homes tend to be larger and to serve an even lower-income population because welfare agencies will normally pay for care only in licensed homes.

Caregivers typically have little education or special training in child care. The Council survey found that two-thirds of the operators of family day care homes in their sample were not high school graduates, and only 9 percent had college training. Although some real horror stories turned up, interviewers' impressions were that most of the women were warm and responsive to children but not trained for an educative role. Most thought of themselves as babysitters, not teachers.

What Mothers Want

When asked if they are "satisfied" with their child care arrangements, most working mothers reply that they are. More probing questions, however, frequently turn up serious problems, complaints,

Table 8-9. Number and Percentage Distribution of Child Care Arrangements of AFDC Mothers[a] Who Are Enrolled in WIN or Who are Employed or Enrolled in Work or Training Programs, by Age of Children, 1971

Numbers in thousands

Child care arrangement	Mother is enrolled in work incentive program (WIN)				Mother is employed or enrolled in work or training programs (including WIN)						
	Children under 6 years		Children 6 to 14 years		Children under 3 years		Children 3 to 5 years		Children 6 to 14 years	
	Number	Percent	Number	Percent	Number	Percent	Number	Percent	Number	Percent
Care in own home or home of relative[b]	39.1	62.3	47.0	67.5	67.9	54.9	78.4	50.8	97.8	41.9
Care in home of nonrelative[c]	9.5	15.1	7.4	10.7	32.7	26.4	33.3	21.6	25.1	10.8
Group care center[d]	9.1	14.5	3.8	5.5	6.9	5.6	22.1	14.3	8.1	3.5
Other or unknown	5.1	8.1	11.4	16.4	16.2	13.1	20.4	13.2	102.2	43.8
Total	62.8	100.0	69.6	100.0	123.7	100.0	154.2	100.0	233.2	100.0

Sources: U.S. Department of Health, Education, and Welfare, National Center for Social Statistics, "Child Care Arrangements of AFDC Recipients Under the Work Incentive Program as of the Last Day of the Quarter Ended June 30, 1971" (February 9, 1972; processed), Tables 2, 2B, 2C; HEW, National Center for Social Statistics, "Findings of the 1971 AFDC Study, Pt. 1, Demographic and Program Characteristics" (December 22, 1971; processed), Tables 25, 26, 27. Percentages may not add to 100 because of rounding.
a. Mothers receiving assistance under the aid to families with dependent children program.
b. Includes cases in which a caretaker works during school hours.
c. The WIN study calls these family day care and group day care homes and includes all arrangements outside the home for fewer than twelve children. The AFDC study does not have a precise definition.
d. The WIN study includes any arrangement for twelve or more children. The AFDC study does not define precisely.

and anxieties. Some mothers are concerned about abuse and neglect of their children, especially by babysitters or day care homes. Some worry about the safety of children left alone or with siblings. There are many complaints about the high cost of day care, about the difficulty of making satisfactory arrangements for children under three years old, about the problem of transporting children to distant locations for care and picking them up after work, about the inflexible hours of day care centers and homes and the refusal of many of them to take care of even mildly ill children.

Surveys indicate that more mothers would use good day care centers if they were available at an acceptable cost. On the other hand, substantial numbers of mothers appear to prefer care in their own home or in another home in the neighborhood. Transporting children long distances lengthens the mother's working day and is tiring for both mother and child. There is evidence that mothers place a large premium on closeness to home when choosing child care arrangements. When a Massachusetts survey asked parents whether they would prefer day care next door at $15 a week (for all children) or free care one-half hour away, 58 percent said they would prefer to pay for the care next door.[4] Surveys to determine what parents are seeking in child care arrangements indicate that they give high priority to convenience and to the child's well-being and social development (getting along with each other) and generally lower priority to educational aspects. The Westinghouse survey found that users of day care centers tended to rate education higher than other mothers do.

Some nonworking mothers say they would work if cheaper or better day care were available, but it is not clear how seriously these statements should be taken. In the Westinghouse survey, 18 percent of the nonworking mothers said they did not work because they could not find satisfactory day care or could not earn enough to pay for it. When asked what kind of care they would prefer if they went to work, more than half the mothers said they would prefer care in their own home or in another's home, but 27 percent indicated they would prefer day care centers. Preferences for day care centers were substantially higher among blacks than whites, possibly because blacks are already heavy

4. Richard R. Rowe (ed.), *Child Care in Massachusetts: The Public Responsibility*, a Study for the Massachusetts Advisory Council on Education by the Massachusetts Early Education Project, Harvard Program in Public Psychology (The Council, 1972), Table 3-B.

users of day care centers and are more familiar with this kind of arrangement.

It is clear from the surveys that the demand for day care is highly sensitive to price. The Westinghouse study asked working mothers with children under age ten and annual incomes under $8,000 what they would be willing to pay for the kind of day care arrangements they would most like to have. Sixteen percent said they could pay nothing. Of those who would be willing to pay something, the median response was $10 a week. Less than one-fourth of all the families responding said they could pay more than $13 a week, and only 7 percent said they could pay as much as $23 a week per child. There was particular reluctance to pay for care of school-age children.

On the basis of survey evidence, Mary P. Rowe has concluded: "It can be expected that fewer than 5% of all families in all ordinary populations will pay over $20 per week per child and fewer than 1% of all such families would now pay $40 per week. As [a rule] of thumb, families ordinarily will not pay more than 20–30% of family incomes for child care for all children."[5]

In sum, information about the demand for day care suggests the following: (1) the number of working mothers seeking care for their children is likely to increase; (2) many mothers would like "better" day care for their children—more convenient, more reliable, more conducive to the child's educational development and well-being; (3) some of these mothers would prefer day care centers to their present arrangement; (4) most mothers, especially those at low income levels, are unwilling or unable to pay much more than they are now paying. Hence, more expensive forms of day care would have to be subsidized if they are to be used by families in the lower- and middle-income groups. These results are hardly surprising. If large numbers of families were willing to pay more for day care than they are now paying, the private market would surely have responded to this unsatisfied demand.

Supply of Day Care

Shifting the focus from demand to supply raises the question, What would it cost to supply various types of day care if the federal govern-

5. Mary P. Rowe, "The Economics of Child Care," in *Child Care*, Hearings before the Senate Committee on Finance, 92 Cong. 1 sess. (1971), p. 270.

ment were to undertake to do so? Combing the day care literature for answers to the question "What does day care cost?" yields answers ranging from $300 a year per child to $3,000. On closer examination, however, it appears that these widely divergent estimates are actually answers to different questions. To give a useful answer to the question "What does day care cost?" it is necessary to specify (1) how many hours a day one is talking about—half day, full day, after school, and so on; (2) whether the program is carried out in a home or in an institution, such as a day care center; (3) what kinds of services are to be provided—custodial care, an educational curriculum, or a full range of developmental services that include psychological testing, health examinations, social work counseling, and so on; (4) whether the costs to be measured are the operating costs of an existing program or the start-up costs of a new program; and (5) whether a relatively small program operating now is at issue or a major national program operating in the future that might be expected to raise the wages of day care workers.

Despite these difficulties of definition, however, two major facts about day care costs are clear. First, day care, however defined, is a process in which adults look after children. Hence, the cost of day care per child depends primarily on two factors: (1) the ratio of adults to children and (2) the wages paid to these adults. The wage level in turn depends mainly on the educational background and training required for the staff. College graduates, certified teachers, and specialists in child development obviously command higher wages than do non-specialists with lower educational qualifications.

Second, the cost of child care depends in part on whether it is regarded as a by-product of the ongoing operation of households, or whether it is a separate economic activity whose full costs must be met. So long as the care of children of working mothers is kept largely within the family, as it is now, the additional costs are low. It involves the labor of mothers and other family members who would have stayed at home anyway and the use of a facility (the home) that is being used also for other purposes. Once day care becomes a separate economic activity, staffed by people who must be paid what they could be earning in other jobs outside the home, and located in facilities devoted solely to day care, costs tend to rise. The higher wage and facility costs of institutional day care, however, may be more than offset by higher ratios of children to adults.

The cost estimates collected by the Westinghouse survey for full-day care in day care centers were astonishingly low. Operators of the category A "custodial" centers estimated their average annual cost for a "full-time equivalent" child to be $324. Operators of the category B centers, described as "educational," gave average costs of $540, and the comparable figure for the category C, or "developmental" centers, was $1,368 per year per full-time equivalent child. There is reason to think, however, that costs were substantially underestimated in all categories. The proprietary centers appear not to have included in their costs the proprietor's income or the labor of unpaid family members. These items are likely to be substantial, since proprietary day care centers tend to be small family operations often run in the family home, much like a "ma and pa" grocery store, with the family living over the store and family members taking their turns behind the counter. The nonprofit centers probably also underestimated their costs by failing to include the costs of facilities and equipment donated by churches and others and the value of volunteer work. In some centers, parents and other volunteers make up a substantial part of the staff. But biased as it is, the Westinghouse study makes clear that the costs of existing day care centers are kept relatively low by two factors: high ratios of children to staff, at least in the A and B category centers, and low wages paid to staff even in the nonprofit centers.

As was shown in Table 8-7, category A and B centers had staff ratios averaging fourteen to fifteen children per child-related staff member. Most of these centers would not have met the federal interagency day care standards, which require that there be no more than 5 children per child-related staff member. In the A centers, more than three-fourths of the full-time staff received less than $300 a month and 92 percent less than $400 a month. Salaries in the category B centers were slightly higher, but 77 percent of the full-time staff earned less than $400 a month. Even in the category C centers, where higher wages and more staff per child contributed to higher costs, the staff could hardly be described as "highly paid."

Nonprofit day care centers often have moderately paid professionals with some child care training supervising aides who have little education or professional experience with children. This may well be an effective way to run a day care center, especially if one of the objectives is to provide employment for women in poverty. Even the supervising professionals, however, earn relatively little compared to elementary school teachers. In 45 percent of the nonprofit centers surveyed by the Council, the highest professional salary paid was less than $7,000. If a major national day care program were financed at the federal level, one would expect the wages and salaries of day care workers, both professional and nonprofessional, to rise.

Estimates of what it would cost to provide "good quality" day care in the future vary greatly, but tend to be substantially above the Westinghouse estimates because they assume lower ratios of children to staff and higher wage levels.

A frequently quoted study made in 1968 by Jule Sugarman and Lawrence Feldman gave the following estimates of the costs of day care per child per year (in dollars):[6]

	Minimum	Acceptable	Desirable
Day care center (preschoolers)	1,245	1,862	2,320
Family day care (to age six)	1,423	2,032	2,372
Before and after school, and summer	310	653	653

The "minimum" standard was defined as care sufficient to maintain the health and safety of the child, with little attention to his development. "Acceptable" quality included what the authors considered to be a "basic program of developmental activities" in addition to custodial care, while the "desirable" included a broader range of specialized services, especially health care and parent education. Differences among the three levels were associated primarily with staff ratios. It was assumed that day care center professionals would be paid $6,600 a year, while family day care mothers and center nonprofessionals would receive $4,400 a year. The minimum budget for day care centers was based on one professional and two nonprofessionals for each twenty children, while the desirable budget assumed one professional and three nonprofessionals for each fifteen children. Family day care was deemed more costly because the number of children per adult is lower, and this outweighs the lower wages and facility costs.

A study by Abt Associates was based on the actual budgets of twenty day care centers offering educational and developmental as

6. U.S. Department of Health, Education, and Welfare, Children's Bureau, and Day Care and Child Development Council of America, "Standards and Costs for Day Care" (1968; processed), as given in Rowe, "Economics of Child Care," p. 280.

well as custodial services and recognized as "among the better centers of their kind in the country."[7] Model budgets derived by Abt from this study gave an annual cost per child of $2,349 in a center of twenty-five children, $2,223 for a center with fifty children, and $2,189 for a center with seventy-five children.[8] In other words, economies of scale were modest and were possibly offset by impersonality and a decline in "warmth" in the larger centers. The high cost was due to low ratios of children to total staff, not to high salaries. The day care teachers were assumed to earn $6,000 a year.

Another set of cost estimates was prepared recently for the Office of Economic Opportunity (OEO) by David Weikart for a proposed experiment to test the effect on children of various staffing ratios and the extent of training of staff. Weikart divided day care into two basic types: "inexplicit," in which staff time was devoted primarily to care of children, not to teaching, and "explicit," in which staff members had more training in early childhood education and devoted 40 percent of their time to teaching. A basic cost of $295 per child for health, social services, and related items was assumed in all categories. Salaries were taken from the Abt study. The following are the cost estimates (in dollars per child per year) made in the Weikart proposal:[9]

Type of program and staff/child ratio	Inexplicit	Explicit
Day care home 1:6	2,351	2,656
Day care center 1:6	2,247	2,552
Day care center 1:10	1,784	2,039
Day care center 1:15	1,553	1,783

The impression that emerges from these studies is that $2,000 per child per year is a typical estimate of the cost of full-day care in a center with an education curriculum and moderate medical and other developmental services. Costs might be less if lower ratios of staff to

7. Stephen J. Fitzsimmons and Mary P. Rowe, "A Study in Child Care, 1970–71." Prepared for the Office of Economic Opportunity by Abt Associates (1971; processed), Vol. 1, p. 5.

8. *Ibid.*, Vol. 3, as given in Rowe, "Economics of Child Care," pp. 285, 287.

9. David P. Weikart, "A Design for a National Day Care Cost-Effectiveness Experiment," Prepared for Division of Research and Evaluation, Office of Economic Opportunity, by High/Scope Educational Research Foundation (Ypsilanti, Michigan: The Foundation, March 1, 1972; processed), pp. 2-9 and 7-8.

children were assumed, but they might also be appreciably higher if more elaborate services were provided or if wages and salaries of day care workers should rise appreciably above the levels now paid in the better day care centers. If the salaries of day care teachers, for example, were to rise to the public school level, costs would be increased appreciably.

These typical estimates do not support the notion that carrying out such a program in day care homes rather than day care centers would save money. They assume that the lower wages paid to caregivers in day care homes would be offset by the lower ratio of children to adults.

Should Day Care Be Subsidized?

If these studies are correct, full-day "developmental" day care for preschool children outside their own homes may be expected to cost about $2,000 per child per year, or $40 a week. Most families are not paying this much at present—indeed, few are paying as much as $20 a week—nor could they afford to do so. It follows that substantial subsidies would be required to make developmental care available to the majority of working mothers. This section examines the arguments for subsidizing day care for the poor—either to enable welfare mothers to work or to benefit low-income children—and then turns to the argument for subsidizing the nonpoor.

Subsidizing the Poor: The Welfare Argument

In about 1966, welfare rolls began rising rapidly despite a generally prosperous economy and low unemployment rates. The number of recipients of aid to families with dependent children (AFDC) climbed from 4.5 million in 1966 to 6.7 million in 1969, while expenditures on the AFDC program rose from $1.8 billion to $3.5 billion over the three-year period. The rapid rise had no obvious single explanation. Many people believed that it was caused by migration of the poor from rural areas to cities and from the South to the North and West, where welfare benefits were higher. This migration in search of jobs and better living conditions had been going on for some time, however, and there is no evidence that it contributed much to the upsurge of welfare recipients in the late sixties. More plausible explanations seem to be that states changed their rules to make a higher proportion of the poor eligible for welfare, and that higher proportions of the eligible poor began applying for benefits.

Whatever the reasons, legislators, both in state capitals and in the Congress, became concerned about the mounting costs of the welfare system and the specter of an ever-increasing dependent class in the population and began looking for ways to cut the welfare rolls, either by tightening eligibility rules or by finding ways of making welfare recipients self-supporting. In 1967, the Congress enacted a freeze on welfare rolls—which was never brought into force, however, and was later repealed. It also passed the Work Incentive Program (WIN), which was designed to provide training, job placement, and day care to help welfare recipients become self-supporting.

But WIN geared up slowly, apparently because of organizational and administrative difficulties. More money was appropriated than could be spent, though more mothers volunteered for the program than could be accommodated. By mid-summer of 1969, only 62,000 welfare recipients were enrolled out of a projected 102,000; 49,000 children were receiving care, about half of whom were in their own homes.

Undiscouraged by the slow buildup of WIN, President Nixon in the summer of 1969 announced his welfare reform proposals, which laid heavy emphasis on getting welfare recipients to work by providing training and day care. In his August 1969 speech announcing welfare reform, the President called for 150,000 new training "slots" and 450,000 new day care spaces.

But there are strong reasons to doubt whether training and day care can, in fact, reduce the welfare rolls appreciably and whether it would be in the taxpayer's interest if they could. Whether it is cheaper to encourage a mother to work rather than remain on welfare depends partly on what she could earn if she were employed, partly on her chances of finding and holding a job, and partly on the cost to the taxpayer of providing the day care and other services that she needs to continue working. This, in turn, depends on what type of day care is thought to be appropriate.

Even if welfare recipients were employed, the earnings of most of them would be low because of their limited education and skill levels, lack of work experience, and other barriers to high earnings. In 1971, 31 percent of the AFDC mothers had no more than an eighth grade education, and 72 percent were not high school graduates. About one-fourth had never worked. A study of welfare recipients made in 1968 divided them into groups with "high" and "low" employment potential based on education and experience. Welfare mothers who had either graduated from high school or had experience in skilled blue-collar or white-collar jobs were classified as having "high" potential. Fifty-six percent met neither criterion in 1968, though this proportion had dropped from 75 percent in 1961. Even the high potential group, however, had many problems that were barriers to employment. Many of them had health problems, some of which were serious. Others had psychological difficulties, and some were needed at home to care for sick relatives.

Even for the high potential group, moreover, labor market conditions are discouraging. Unemployment rates for women have been rising relative to those for men for some years, and black unemployment rates are consistently above those for whites. In ghetto and rural poverty areas, high unemployment rates are the rule, and for women with the kind of handicaps that put them on welfare in the first place, the chance of finding employment is low. But the main problem is that if child care is provided in day care centers or licensed day care homes, the cost to the taxpayer may well be more than the cost of continuing welfare payments to enable the mother to stay at home. A state that pays a welfare mother with three children $60 a week is, in effect, purchasing day care for $20 a week, which is less than it would cost to take care of the child in a good nonprofit day care center. If such a mother participated in a training program and found a job that paid $90 a week, she might be able to support herself without welfare assistance, but she would not be able to contribute much to the costs of child care. The welfare department would probably find that it was paying more for keeping three children in day care than it had been paying the mother in welfare benefits.

A recent study in New York City indicates that it might not benefit the taxpayer to require a welfare mother to work even if she had only one or two children.[10] In New York, a mother and two children on AFDC would receive $3,272 a year, or about $65 a week. If she obtained an $80-a-week job paying $4,160 annually, her welfare benefit would not drop to zero. In determining her benefit, she would be allowed to deduct her payroll and income taxes and work expenses

10. Peter Kihss, "Letting Welfare Mothers Work Is Said to Increase City Costs," *New York Times*, Aug. 17, 1971.

(assumed to amount to $832 a year) from her income and she would be allowed to keep a $360 incentive allowance and one-third of her remaining earnings, with no deduction from her welfare payment. Her welfare payment would be reduced under these assumptions to $1,671 a year, or about $32 a week. The welfare department would thus save a little over $30 a week by her having a job, but the cost of day care in publicly supported day care centers in New York is about $2,500 a year, or $50 a week. At these prices, the city would be paying more for the mother to go to work even if only one of her children were in day care. And should two children require day care, the city's taxpayers would be worse off unless day care could be bought for less than $15 a week.

Both welfare benefit levels and day care costs differ from state to state, but in general if a mother has more than two children, it is unlikely that the taxpayers will benefit, at least in the short run, by paying day care costs rather than welfare benefits to the mother. This of course does *not* mean that encouraging work and day care is a bad idea. It means only that such a policy has to be justified on grounds other than saving money—for example, on the grounds that day care is beneficial to children.

The Child Development Argument

A different argument for subsidizing day care for the poor relates to the benefits poor children would derive from early childhood education and child development services that could be delivered in a day care setting. Those who advocate subsidized day care for low-income groups usually have in mind either day care centers or supervised networks of family day care homes in which caregivers have special training and some special teaching equipment.

The argument rests on two sets of widely acknowledged facts. First, children learn extremely rapidly in the first few years of life; they acquire powers of observation and expression and muscular control that they will be using all their lives. Second, children from poor families, on the average, begin to fall behind middle-class children in IQ and other measures of intellectual skills long before they reach school age. These differences are not observable in infants, though of course it is very difficult to get a good measure of the intellectual development of a child who cannot speak. Such tests as can be given, however, do not show significant differences among income levels before about eighteen months or two years. By four years, however, the differences are marked, and by school age the children from lower-income families, on the average, are already considerably behind. These facts have led to the hypothesis that much of the handicap of the disadvantaged child is not genetic, but is attributable to lack of stimulation and education at home during the preschool years, and that intervention at an early age would help overcome these deficiencies.

This hypothesis led to the creation in 1965 of the Head Start program by the federal government and to a number of smaller preschool projects designed to test theories about preschool education. Most of the work so far has been with four- and five-year-olds. The evidence is incomplete and relates mainly to strictly cognitive measures of development like IQ, not to other measures of the child's emotional or psychological health or his general ability to function. The accumulating evidence seems to indicate the following: (1) Preschool programs *can* raise the IQs of disadvantaged children, sometimes dramatically. Intensive experimental programs frequently report gains of ten to twenty-five IQ points on an average for children in the preschools. Children in the full-year Head Start program have shown IQ gains of five to ten points on an average. (2) The test score gains that the children make in preschool, however, tend to fade when they enter regular school. The children who have been in the preschool program may show a drop in IQ in grades one to three, and the control children who did not go through preschool tend to catch up. For most programs, few significant differences between the experimental and control children remain after a couple of years either in IQ or in achievement tests, such as reading. More lasting differences in a few measures have been observed in some projects, but the "fading out" of initial gains is a general result. (3) There seems to be no clear evidence that early intervention is more effective—that is, that children who started preschool at the age of three or four gained more from the experience than those who started at five.

In sum, preschool for four- and five-year-olds appears to have some immediate positive results, and it certainly has not been shown to do children any immediate or lasting harm. By itself, however, it may not be a particularly good investment if the objective is to increase children's ability to function well in school. It is still an open question whether funds should be concentrated on preschool education, on improving the schools themselves, or on other programs—income maintenance, housing, public employment, parent education—that would improve the child's home environment.

Moreover, if the primary motive is to provide preschool education and child development services for disadvantaged children, it is not necessary to go to the expense of providing a full-day program. Half-day programs would meet the needs of the children, though such programs would be less convenient for working mothers. Television programming, visiting nurses and "teachers" and special education for mothers might also be effective and less costly ways of providing preschool stimulation for low-income children.

What about even younger children? There is some reason to think that reaching disadvantaged children in infancy or as toddlers might be even more effective than reaching them at four or five, but the evidence is scanty. In an interesting project in Milwaukee, children of mentally retarded low-income mothers have received intensive all-day care and mental stimulation since infancy. After several years, the difference between experimental children and the controls was dramatic. Babies in an infant care program in the children's center at Syracuse, New York, have also shown more rapid development than control children. These are isolated examples of highly intensive experiments, however, and the most that can be said about infant day care at present is that research indicates that it does not necessarily have harmful effects on children, as was once thought.

Subsidizing Day Care for the Nonpoor

Many who favor subsidizing day care believe that the subsidies should not be limited to the poor, but should be extended to middle- and upper-income groups as well. Some argue for making day care freely available at public expense to everyone, and others for a sliding scale of payments based on income that would extend at least a partial subsidy to families well above the median income level.

The case for making day care free to all income groups is similar to the case for free public schools. First, it is argued that children benefit from good quality day care, but that parents—even middle- and upper-income parents—may not understand how valuable the experience is to the child and may not be willing to pay for it. The same could be said of higher education, but the college student whose parents are unwilling to pay for his education is old enough to earn money, or to apply for a loan or a scholarship himself. The preschool child has no such option, so society should encourage his parents to provide him with good care by making the service available free.

Second, it is contended that society at large, not just the children, benefits if children have a satisfactory preschool experience. It is argued that a good child development program can reduce failures in school—which may cause problems for others than the ones who fail —and can avert health or psychological difficulties that would be costly to others later on. The hypothesis is that much antisocial behavior stems from early failure and frustration and that some of this can be avoided with good preschool programs. Society, of course, has to balance the alleged benefits of preschool against the benefits of other alternatives, such as using an equivalent amount of money to improve the public schools themselves.

Both kinds of benefits—those to children and those to society at large—are very difficult to assess. Their magnitude, however, is likely to be much greater for the poor than for the nonpoor.

A third argument for a universal day care subsidy is that limiting the subsidy to the poor would subject applicants for day care to a means test and that means tests are inherently undignified and demeaning. Hence, day care should be free and universally available without a means test. This is what society believes is appropriate for elementary and secondary education, though not necessarily for higher education. Few objections are raised to means tests for scholarship assistance at the college level.

Fourth, it is claimed that mixing racial and socioeconomic groups is desirable and that day care centers are particularly good places to do it because young children have fewer prejudices than do older children. One might hope that mixing socioeconomic groups in day care centers would raise the performance of poor children, since children learn a great deal from each other, and children from middle- and upper-income groups have larger vocabularies and more readiness for reading and other intellectual skills than do poor children. Moreover, a common interest in the welfare of children might get parents working together and communicating across racial and economic lines. Of course, it would be possible to achieve some mixing in day care centers without actually making day care free; high-income families could be allowed to use public day care centers if they were willing to pay all or part of the cost. On the other hand, making day care free by no means would guarantee a substantial mixing of racial and economic groups in day care centers so long as neighborhoods were primarily segregated on racial and economic lines. As has been seen, parents have a strong preference for conveniently located neighborhood day care centers, and parental objections to busing would doubtless be even stronger for toddlers than for school age children.

A final argument for free and universal day care is made by advocates of high quality programs for small children who believe that the only way to build political support for such programs is to extend them to all income groups. Programs limited to the poor, they fear, would receive inadequate support from taxpayers and the Congress.

Representative Shirley A. Chisholm has put the case this way:

> We know from our experience with the poverty program that programs exclusively for the poor—no matter how well justified—are not popular. We have seen time and time again how popular resentment has generated enough political pressure so that poverty appropriations are hacked to smithereens on the floor of this House.
>
> All of us are vividly aware of the splits and tensions in this country between the poor and the working class. The lazy bums on the welfare dole vs. us middle Americans of the silent majority is the jargon this battle is currently cast in.
>
> Let's not aggravate those tensions. The poor and the working class have the same needs and the same problems. Low wages, inflation, lack of job opportunities, poor educational resources, frustration with the impersonal bureaucracy, and the lack of day care facilities—they are the same problems. Do not pit these people against each other like starving packs of dogs fighting over the same meager scraps.[11]

Finally, it is alleged that the only way to achieve real equality for women is for society to take over the financing of child care for those who want to work outside the home. If this does not happen, women will either have to stay at home to take care of their children or feel guilty about subjecting their children to the inferior care that all but the rich must make do with in the private sector. Men do not have to make this choice. They can pursue careers while their wives worry about the children, and the argument is that women should have equal freedom.

11. "Statement of Congresswoman Shirley Chisholm before the Select Subcommittee on Education of the House Committee on Education and Labor on Preschool Education and Day Care" (March 4, 1970; processed), p. 6.

The primary argument against subsidizing day care for everyone is its tremendous expense. Providing day care costing $2,000 a year per child for all children under six would cost $28 billion, even if one-third of them did not participate. It seems extremely inefficient to subsidize all families when a substantial proportion could afford to buy the service for themselves. Of course, the same argument could be made about public schools and public kindergartens. In effect, society has decided that sometime about the age of five the case for a universal subsidy outweighs the case against it. There is no magic about the age of five, and universal day care advocates are asking, "Why not at four, or three, or even at birth?"

Another argument against a universal subsidy for day care, especially for the very young, is that it might encourage people to have more children at a time when there is a fairly general belief that a lower rate of population growth would be in the national interest. At present, most of the responsibility, financial and otherwise, for rearing children in the first five or six years of life falls on parents, and this may deter many people from adding to their families. If free day care and preschool for infants and toddlers were available to all parents, they might be less cautious about having more children.

Many who admit the difficulties of a universal free program argue that day care should be at least partially subsidized well into the middle-income range. A family with an $8,000 income cannot afford a $2,000 day care center. Even those with $12,000 cannot afford such care if they have two or three children. The argument is that if these middle-income families are not at least partially subsidized, they will buy inferior care. The two-class day care system, of which there is already considerable evidence, will be perpetuated—with poor children receiving substantially more costly care than is available to children from middle-income families. While this might be justified as compensating for the handicaps facing poor children, it might also generate resentment of the poor by the moderate-income group.

A partial subsidy to the middle-income group could be accomplished by making day care free for families with incomes up to about $4,000 (for a family of four) and then charging families with higher incomes 25 percent of their income over $4,000 for the first child and 10 percent for additional children. Thus, a family with an $8,000 income would pay $1,000 for the first child and $400 for additional children. If one assumes that the day care costs $2,000, a $12,000 family with one child would pay the full cost. However, a family with three children and an income up to $17,333 would get some subsidy. The cost of such a program would be roughly $17 billion, assuming a 75 percent participation rate.

This very substantial subsidy would have to come out of someone's taxes. How the cost was shared among income groups would, of course, depend on what tax was chosen to finance it (see Chapter 14), but the net losers would clearly be those with older children or no children at all. The cost could be reduced by having the payment rise more steeply with income, but even the illustration just given would subject people in the middle-income groups to a substantial "tax" on additional income that might impair their incentive to work. In the illustration, a family with three children would be subject to a 45 percent "tax" on their additional earnings. Since they would also have to pay income and social security taxes out of these additional earnings, their take-home pay would probably go up by less than one-third of any raise they achieved. If they were also subject to higher health insurance premiums, coinsurance, and deductibles, as was discussed in Chapter 7, they might find that additional earnings brought them no benefits at all.

Issues To Be Decided

It is difficult to defend subsidizing day care solely on the grounds that it would save taxpayers money by enabling welfare mothers to work. If a mother has little education or work experience, or if she has more than two children, the training–work–day care option may be more costly than paying her to stay home. For this group, a day care subsidy has to be defended either on the grounds that there are noneconomic benefits to the mother—such as the self-respect she gains from holding a job—or to the child. The benefits to poor children of developmental day care, in turn, are difficult to assess. Many persons would weight heavily the immediate benefit to the child of being in a safe, attractive environment, getting attention from adults who consider his well-being their job, eating balanced meals, and receiving routine medical attention. Others believe that a subsidy can be justified only on the basis of long-run benefits, such as permament increases in IQ or reading scores. At the moment, there is little reason to hope that preschool education *alone* will yield these permanent benefits. Whether preschool plus improved education in elementary school would constitute a permanent breakthrough for low-income children is an open question.

If a decision is made to subsidize developmental day care for the poor in general (not just to ration it to a minority as at present), serious questions arise about the treatment of moderate-income families. As we have seen, day care charges for families in the $4,000 to $12,000 range could be adjusted to income. If, however, the charges rose steeply as income increased in this range, middle-income parents would either seek less costly alternatives in the private sector— presumably resenting the fact that better care was available to the poor—or would make less effort to increase their earnings. On the other hand, if charges rose gradually as income increased, the public cost would mount, rapidly approaching the cost of universal free day care.

If the developmental day care option is chosen, it seems likely that the costs will be large because political pressure to extend the subsidy in the middle-income range will be heavy. Some would argue that these costs to the taxpayer are fully justified. Others would argue that developmental day care should not be subsidized, even for the poor, but that emphasis should be placed on less costly ways of reaching low-income children, either in their own homes or in whatever day care arrangements their mothers choose to make for them. Options that have been suggested include more educational television programming for preschool children, educational programs for mothers and family day care providers, and visiting nurse arrangements.

Child Care Legislation: The Administration versus the Congress

In a message to the Congress early in his administration, President Nixon said, "So crucial is the matter of early growth that we must make a national commitment to providing all American children an opportunity for healthful and stimulating development during the first five years of life."[12] The administration and the Congress, however, have been in sharp disagreement over the form that the commitment should take.

The administration has continued to fund the Head Start program,

12. "The Nation's Antipoverty Programs," The President's Message to the Congress, February 19, 1969, in *Weekly Compilation of Presidential Documents*, Vol. 5, No. 8 (February 24, 1969), p. 285.

which it moved from OEO to the new Office of Child Development in the Department of Health, Education, and Welfare (HEW), and some research on early childhood. The major administration emphasis, however, has been on day care in the context of welfare reform—day care for children of welfare mothers to enable those mothers to go to work. In his message proposing welfare reform in August 1969, the President said he was requesting authority and funds for additional day care, and emphasized that it would be developmental care: "The child care I propose is more than custodial. This Administration is committed to a new emphasis on child development in the first five years of life. The day care that would be part of this plan would be of a quality that will help in the development of the child and provide for its health and safety, and would break the poverty cycle for this new generation."[13] The exact nature of the administration's day care proposals, however, remained vague for about two years.

Meanwhile, the Congress, not waiting for action on welfare reform, pushed ahead with its own child development bill. With the strong backing of organized labor and many civic organizations interested in child welfare, two similar bills passed the Congress in 1971 attached to the economic opportunity amendments of that year. The Senate version, sponsored by Senator Walter F. Mondale, was designed to provide comprehensive child development services to all children. Although sponsors of the bill stressed the need for developmental day care for children of working mothers, the list of activities for which funds were authorized was extremely broad, including, among other things, "comprehensive physical and mental health, social, and cognitive development services," food and nutrition, programs designed to meet the special needs of minority, Indian, and migrant children, prenatal care, and "special activities designed to identify and ameliorate identified physical, mental, and emotional handicaps and special learning disabilities. . . ."[14]

Though all children were to be eligible to participate, priority was given to children whose families had incomes below the Department of Labor's minimum living standard (then $6,960 for a family of four). Services to this income group were to be free, and 65 percent of the spaces were to be reserved for these families. The rest would be

13. "Reform of the Nation's Welfare System," The President's Message to Congress, August 11, 1969, in *ibid.*, Vol. 5, No. 33 (August 18, 1969), p. 1130.

14. *Economic Opportunity Amendments of 1971*, Report of the Senate Committee on Labor and Public Welfare, S. Rpt. 92-331, 92 Cong. 1 sess. (1971), p. 115.

available for persons with higher incomes, who would pay fees on a sliding scale based on their income.

The bill stressed parent participation in decision making and local control of the services. Any city or county, regardless of size, could be a "prime sponsor," applying directly to the federal government rather than going through the state. Governments that were prime sponsors would have to create child development councils—half of whose members would be parents of participating children and at least one-fourth of whom would represent the poor—to develop plans for the use of the money. Individual projects would have to have parent and community councils as well. Provision was made for nongovernmental prime sponsors in areas where the governmental unit refused to participate or where the secretary of health, education, and welfare thought the area would otherwise be inadequately served.

The Mondale bill passed the Senate by more than a two-thirds majority in September 1971. Meanwhile, a similar measure was being shepherded through the House by Representatives John Brademas and Ogden Reid. The House version laid somewhat less emphasis on local control. As the bill was reported out of committee, prime sponsorship was restricted to governments of 100,000 people or more, though this was reduced to 10,000 on the floor of the House. In an attempt to avoid an administration veto, the income level for free day care was lowered on the House floor to $4,320, the point above which a family of four would be ineligible for assistance under the administration's welfare reform proposal. The House-Senate conference committee accepted this compromise, specifying that care would be free to families with incomes of less than $4,320, with small charges specified for families between $4,320 and $6,960. Families above that level would pay according to a sliding scale to be set by the secretary of HEW. Localities with a population of more than 5,000 were to be eligible to be prime sponsors. The compromise bill passed both houses by large majorities but was vetoed by the President. An attempt to override the veto failed.

In his veto message of December 10, 1971, the President stressed his view that allowing small communities to be prime sponsors would create serious administrative difficulties and relegate the states to an "insignificant role." He pointed out that to some extent, the bill duplicated his own welfare reform proposal for "day care centers to provide for the children of the poor so that their parents can leave the welfare rolls to go on the payrolls of the nation." He also declared that the congressional bill would be too expensive and, perhaps reacting to extreme right-wing pressure, charged that it would undermine the authority of the family over children: "For the Federal Government to plunge headlong financially into supporting child development would commit the vast moral authority of the National Government to the side of communal approaches to child rearing over against the family-centered approach."[15]

On May 3, 1972, the Senate Committee on Labor and Public Welfare approved a bill modified to meet most of the President's objections. The population limit for prime sponsors would be raised to 25,000. Fee schedules would be similar to those in the vetoed bill, but only $1.2 billion would be authorized for the first year of operation, and full-day services would be limited to children whose parents were already out of the home or to handicapped children—in order to avoid the charge that the bill was encouraging mothers to go to work.

In his veto message, the President also pointed out that he had supported the increased tax deductions for child care in the Revenue Act of 1971, which "provide a significant Federal subsidy for day care in families where both parents are employed, potentially benefitting 97 percent of all such families in the country and offering parents free choice of the child care arrangements they deem best for their own families."[16] The increases in child care deductions are indeed substantial. Under the old law, a two-parent family with a joint income of less than $6,000 was allowed to deduct up to $600 for one child and up to $900 for two or more children. Under the Revenue Act of 1971, two-parent families are allowed to deduct employment-related child care expenses up to $2,400 a year for one child, $3,600 for two, and $4,800 for three or more, provided their joint income is no more than $18,-000. Partial deductions are allowed for incomes up to $27,600. The Treasury estimates that this new provision will cost the government about $150 million in 1972 and $300 million in 1973, even if it does not induce mothers to spend more for child care than they are now spending.

The new provisions, however, do nothing for the poor who do not pay income tax, and almost nothing for the near poor. Treasury De-

---

15. *Veto Message—Economic Opportunity Amendments of 1971*, Message from the President of the United States, S. Doc. 92-48, 92 Cong. 1 sess. (1971), pp. 4, 5.
16. *Ibid.*, p. 3.
17. *Congressional Record*, daily ed., February 17, 1972, pp. S1972, S1990.

partment estimates[17] show that the tax savings for child care under the Revenue Act for families in the $4,000 to $7,000 range are negligible because their marginal tax rate is so low:

Family income	*Assumed spending for child care*	Tax saving
$ 5,000	$ 500	$ 0
7,000	700	77
10,000	1,000	190
18,000	1,000	250

The higher the family income (up to $18,000), the greater the potential reduction in taxes.

In the meantime, the administration has clarified its intentions with respect to day care if welfare reform is enacted substantially along the lines of H.R. 1. Under H.R. 1, $750 million would be allocated to day care in the first year. Of this amount, $50 million would be for construction to be administered directly by HEW. The remaining $700 million would pay for 291,000 day care spaces for preschoolers and 584,000 day care spaces for school age children. The initial emphasis on school age children presumably reflects both the priority to be given to mothers of school age children in work and training programs (mothers of children aged three to five would not be required to register for work and training until after the program had been in effect for a year) and the lower cost of providing before- and after-school care for these older children.

The day care money would be allocated to states, though cities of more than 500,000 population and Indian reservations could be "prime sponsors." Governors and big-city mayors would have to appoint child development councils, one-fourth of whose members would be parents of children in day care. Governors and mayors could designate whatever agency they wished to run day care—perhaps public school systems for before- and after-school care and state welfare agencies for the preschool care.

In administering its work and training programs, the Labor Department would be required to use HEW day care if it were available. Otherwise it could use any public, private, nonprofit, or proprietary day care that was available for the children of its trainees. Federal interagency day care requirements would govern the care provided by HEW under H.R. 1, but not the care purchased separately by the Labor Department.

It is not entirely clear what control a mother would have over the day care arrangements for her children. The administration has stated that a mother would not be encouraged to work "where there was a risk of the abuse or neglect of her child."[18] But it is not clear that she would be able to refuse training or employment because available day care did not meet HEW's or her own standards. As the House committee put it, "Child care for the pre-school child . . . should include educational, health, nutritional, and other needed services whenever possible. However, the lack of child care of that level would not be good cause for failure to take training, if other adequate and acceptable care is available." It is not clear to whom such care must be "acceptable."[19]

Day care under H.R. 1 would be free for welfare mothers taking part in work training or vocational rehabilitation if their earnings were less than $4,320 a year. A sliding scale of fees would apply above that level. Others could use HEW's day care or buy it elsewhere, deducting some part of the cost up to $2,000 from income in determining eligibility for family assistance. H.R. 1 is ambiguous about the amount to be deductible: "Such part (and according to such schedule) as the Secretary may prescribe, of the cost . . ."[20] of child care. If the full $2,000 were deductible from earnings in determining eligibility for family assistance, the effect would be to extend the benefits of family assistance to families with somewhat higher earnings. For example, a family earning $6,200 and paying $2,000 for day care would be counted as having earnings of $4,200—just below the breakeven point for family assistance—and hence would be eligible for a small assistance payment.

Congressional action on these bills will begin to resolve some of the issues raised in this chapter. Is day care to be thought of primarily as a mechanism for persuading welfare mothers to work? Is it to be subsidized only for the very poor, or should the subsidies continue into the middle-income range? What standards will be applied? How much choice will mothers have? Is the primary emphasis to be on mothers and their work, or on children and their development?

18. Testimony of Secretary of HEW Elliot L. Richardson, in *Child Care*, Hearings, p. 107.

19. *Social Security Amendments of 1971*, Report of the Committee on Ways and Means on H.R. 1, H. Rpt. 92-231, 92 Cong. 1 sess. (1971), p. 193.

20. "H.R. 1," 92 Cong. 1 sess., Passed by the House (June 22, 1971), and Read in the Senate (June 28, 1971), p. 364.

9. Fiscal Problems of Cities

WHILE THE NATION'S LARGE CITIES are plagued by many specific problems—crime, pollution, congestion, and poverty—the overriding urban problem of the coming decade may well be the general inability of large city governments to make ends meet. Although total federal aid to state and local governments has expanded dramatically in the past ten years—from $8.8 billion in 1963 to the $43.5 billion proposed in the 1973 federal budget—it has not been sufficiently concentrated in the central cities to deal effectively with their fiscal problems. As a consequence, pressure has mounted for some form of increased federal commitment to beleaguered urban governments. Revenue sharing, if enacted, will help, but will not channel substantial amounts of funds into central cities. It is clear that a basic decision must soon be made about the nation's interest in preserving the public services and long-run viability of the older central cities.

The cities' fiscal crisis stems from the interaction of two developments. First, the levels of per capita local expenditures are higher and are generally growing faster than those of the surrounding suburbs. While some of the reasons for this lie in deliberate choices made by central city governments, others spring from demographic, economic, and social developments that are outside their control. Second, although the revenue base in most central cities is still somewhat higher than in surrounding suburbs, this advantage is steadily eroding. Retail sales, personal incomes, and property values, which form the basis for taxation, have been growing more slowly in the central cities than in the suburbs.

The interaction of these two developments intensifies the fiscal

291

squeeze on central cities. Public services appear to be deteriorating while tax rates climb. Compared with the suburbs, the central city is becoming a less desirable place to live, to shop, and even to work, especially for middle- and upper-income groups. The resulting change in the city's economic and demographic structure increases its need for public expenditures—for welfare, crime control, and social programs—while reducing its ability to pay for them. Not every central city faces these problems, but virtually every older one does.

There are several possible approaches to dealing with the growing financial plight of cities. Could the central cities become more efficient in delivering public services and discover new sources of public revenue? Would a dispersal of low-income population into the suburbs and a return of high-income residents to the city be a desirable way of reducing financial problems; and even if it were, is it likely to occur? Would a change in jurisdictional boundaries and a move toward metropolitan government provide a solution, and is such a development foreseeable? Should the federal government assume a larger share of the financial burdens of the central cities, and, if so, how—through revenue sharing, increases in current grant programs, or new types of financial aid? Can and should the federal government play a role, through financial incentives or otherwise, in encouraging the development of metropolitan-wide governments and finances?

This chapter analyzes the two major causes of the central cities' financial dilemma—rapid expenditure growth and an eroding revenue base. It evaluates the possibility that these problems could be handled without federal intervention, and then considers alternative federal approaches to the fiscal problems of the cities.

Big-City Expenditures

Two facts stand out from the welter of statistics on urban government expenditures. First, the level of spending is high in central cities —considerably higher, in general, than it is in surrounding areas. Second, central city expenditures have been growing rapidly—usually faster than those of the suburbs.

Level of Expenditures

As may be seen in Table 9-1, local government expenditures per capita are significantly higher in the central city than in the suburbs.[1]

1. The expenditures and revenues referred to in this chapter are computed on a per capita basis to allow useful comparisons between cities and suburbs of unequal and chang-

Indeed, in only eight of the nation's seventy-two largest metropolitan areas were expenditures higher in the suburbs than in the central city in 1970. The two major explanations for this are the greater needs and the higher costs in the cities. Cities have much greater concentrations of persons with high needs for public help—especially the aged and the poor—than do suburbs (see Table 9-2). Crime rates are much higher, and the streets and air are dirtier. Density and congestion make the needs for such services as traffic control, sidewalks, street lighting, and street repair far greater than they are in the suburbs. Some of the congestion and need for services is generated by commuters who work and shop in the city, thus increasing its population by day, but go home to the suburbs at night. The higher cost of providing public services in the city is due both to higher wages and to the difficulties of providing certain services under crowded conditions. For example, the sanitation truck in the city may waste a great deal of time stopped in traffic jams or driving to distant disposal locations.

Of course, not all of the indices of need for services show the central city to be on the short end of the stick. For example, although the core areas' children may be more costly to educate, a far smaller fraction of the cities' population is of school age, and an even smaller proportion generally attends public schools than in the suburbs (Table 9-3). Also, dense housing patterns may make certain services easier to provide.

Another source of the expenditure disparity between city and suburbs is that some of the public services of the cities are privately provided in suburban areas. Trash collection is more likely to be in the hands of private carters, houses more likely to have septic tanks rather than municipal sewers and waste treatment facilities, and volunteer fire companies more likely to provide fire protection. Expenditure differences may also result from the fact that a greater proportion of city revenues comes from nonresidents than is the case in the suburbs. Residential property tends to account for a smaller fraction of the total assessed value of property in the city; retail sales tax receipts in the city come partly from purchases of nonresidents; and where local income or payroll taxes are levied, taxes are often imposed on com-

---

ing populations. The data refer to the consolidated general expenditures and revenue of all of the local governments that operate within an area, whether municipalities, school districts, county governments, or special districts. Where the boundaries of a local government do not lie wholly within either the central city or the suburbs, its revenues and expenditures have been apportioned between the city and the outlying area.

Table 9-1. Level in 1970 and Growth, 1957–70, of Local Government Expenditures, per Capita, in Central Cities and outside Central Cities of Selected Metropolitan Areas

Region and standard metropolitan statistical area	1970 Per capita total expenditure (dollars) Central city	Outside central city	Per capita state and federal aid (dollars) Central city	Outside central city	Percentage increase in per capita expenditure, 1957–70 Central city	Outside central city
Northeast						
Washington, D.C.	1,006	425	358	118	321	224
Baltimore	638	349	329	127	221	146
Boston	531	365	224	73	95	102
Newark	735	441	276	102	202	144
Paterson-Clifton-Passaic	381	418	131	56	146	124
Buffalo	528	520	207	226	174	148
New York City	894	644	385	216	248	148
Rochester	699	548	235	238	250	180
Philadelphia	495	325	134	88	200	136
Pittsburgh	450	309	111	95	139	141
Providence	392	265	111	71	145	168
Midwest						
Chicago	478	346	146	86	137	144
Indianapolis	355	306	85	93	99	186
Detroit	474	462	189	131	135	131
Minneapolis-St. Paul	540	520	177	228	192	177
Kansas City	485	347	90	100	161	210
St. Louis	463	292	99	83	211	135
Cincinnati	761	262	171	79	209	124
Cleveland	512	368	187	66	180	91
Columbus	398	290	75	77	140	86
Dayton	456	291	108	83	173	126
Milwaukee	562	486	199	224	145	131
South						
Miami	481	387	137	129	113	129
Tampa-St. Petersburg	372	289	119	108	134	225
Atlanta	554	315	97	95	251	215
Louisville	508	302	108	94	214	165
New Orleans	334	325	100	116	105	171
Dallas	352	279	54	70	91	158
Houston	305	307	61	73	97	64
San Antonio	252	288	89	96	123	177
West						
Los Angeles-Long Beach	624	529	209	227	134	161
San Bernardino	624	529	278	215	111	176
San Diego	484	472	194	202	153	150
San Francisco-Oakland	768	596	298	201	244	159
Denver	502	306	149	94	135	108
Portland	486	328	125	102	139	150
Seattle-Everett	524	471	137	162	201	232

Source: Seymour Sacks and John Callahan, "Central City–Suburban Fiscal Disparities in the 72 Largest Metropolitan Areas" (unpublished paper, January 1972), Tables 14, 28.

Table 9-2. Family Characteristics and Crime Rates in Metropolitan Areas, 1970

Item	Central city	Outside central city
Percentage of persons below poverty level[a]	13.4	6.3
Percentage aged 25–29 with less than high school education	25.3	19.2
Percentage of population over 65	11.1	7.4
Female-headed families as a percentage of all families[b]	17.0	8.8
AFDC families as a percentage of all families[b,c]	9.8	2.4
Crime rate (per 1,000 inhabitants)	45.6	21.4

Sources: Poverty level, education, and population data, U.S. Bureau of the Census, *Current Population Reports*, Series P-23, No. 37, "Social and Economic Characteristics of the Population in Metropolitan and Nonmetropolitan Areas: 1970 and 1960" (1971), pp. 15, 51, 76; female-headed families data, Bureau of the Census, *Current Population Reports*, Series P-20, No. 233, "Household and Family Characteristics: March 1971" (1972), pp. 12, 33; AFDC data, U.S. National Center for Social Statistics, *Findings of the 1971 AFDC Study*, Pt. 1, *Demographic and Program Characteristics*, NCSS Report AFDC-1 (1971), p. 13; crime rate, U.S. Federal Bureau of Investigation, *Uniform Crime Reports for the United States—1970* (1971), pp. 104–05.
a. 1969 data.
b. 1971 data.
c. AFDC = aid to families with dependent children.

Table 9-3. Public School Enrollment as a Percentage of Population, Central Cities and Suburbs in Selected Metropolitan Areas, 1969–70 School Year

Standard metropolitan statistical area	Central city	Outside central city
Boston	14.6	26.6
New York	14.3	23.4
Philadelphia	15.1	20.3
Pittsburgh	14.0	21.1
Syracuse	15.4	26.7
Columbus	20.0	26.0
Minneapolis-St. Paul	15.5	27.5
Omaha	16.9	28.9
Louisville	14.5	25.6
Richmond	16.5	27.5
Tulsa	20.9	30.3
Denver	18.8	27.6
Phoenix	20.0	28.3
Salt Lake City	19.7	33.3
San Francisco-Oakland	15.1	24.3
Seattle-Everett	16.0	27.1

Source: Seymour Sacks and Ralph Andrew with Tony Carnevale, "School State Aid and the System of Finance: Central City, Suburban and Rural Dimensions of Revenue Sharing" (Syracuse University, no date; processed), Table 3.

muters. Moreover, state and federal grants often make up a larger proportion of revenues in the city than in the suburbs. The net effect may be to make the city voter less reluctant to increase city expenditures than is the suburban taxpayer-voter, who knows that he himself will have to pay a higher share of the bill.

Growth of Expenditures

While expenditures by all local governments increased rapidly during the past decade, those in central city areas tended to grow more rapidly than those in the suburbs (Table 9-1). There were many exceptions to this pattern, especially in the South, but there were also many instances (for example, in New York, St. Louis, Cleveland, and San Francisco) where per capita local government expenditures in the central city area increased over 50 percent faster than those of their suburbs.

Of the many factors that contributed to the rapid growth of big-city expenditures during the past decade, inflation was probably the most important. The price index for the goods and services purchased by local governments rose at twice the rate of that for consumer expenditures between 1960 and 1971. This exceptional increase was attributable largely to rising labor costs, which make up more than half the current budgets of local governments.

By any measure, the recent rise in the compensation of local government employees has been spectacular. (See Figure 9-1.) Through the mid-1960s, municipal wages roughly kept pace with those in manufacturing, but beginning in about 1966 the rate of increase appears to have been much greater for municipal workers. Along with wage increases, liberalized pension benefits and health plans also contributed to the rising cost of labor. Reductions in the length of the average workday and more generous provisions regarding sick leave, lunch breaks, vacations, and paid holidays further pushed up the hourly cost of labor in the public sector. The importance of such fringe benefits should not be underestimated. For example, the city administrator of New York reported that although the number of policemen increased from 16,000 to 24,000 between 1940 and 1965, the total number of hours worked by the entire force was less in 1965 than it had been a quarter of a century earlier.

There are many possible explanations for the rise in the relative wages of public employees during the past decade. In the generally

Figure 9-1. Average Monthly Earnings of All U.S. Manufacturing Employees and of Municipal Employees[a] in Chicago and in Cities over and under 50,000, 1960-70

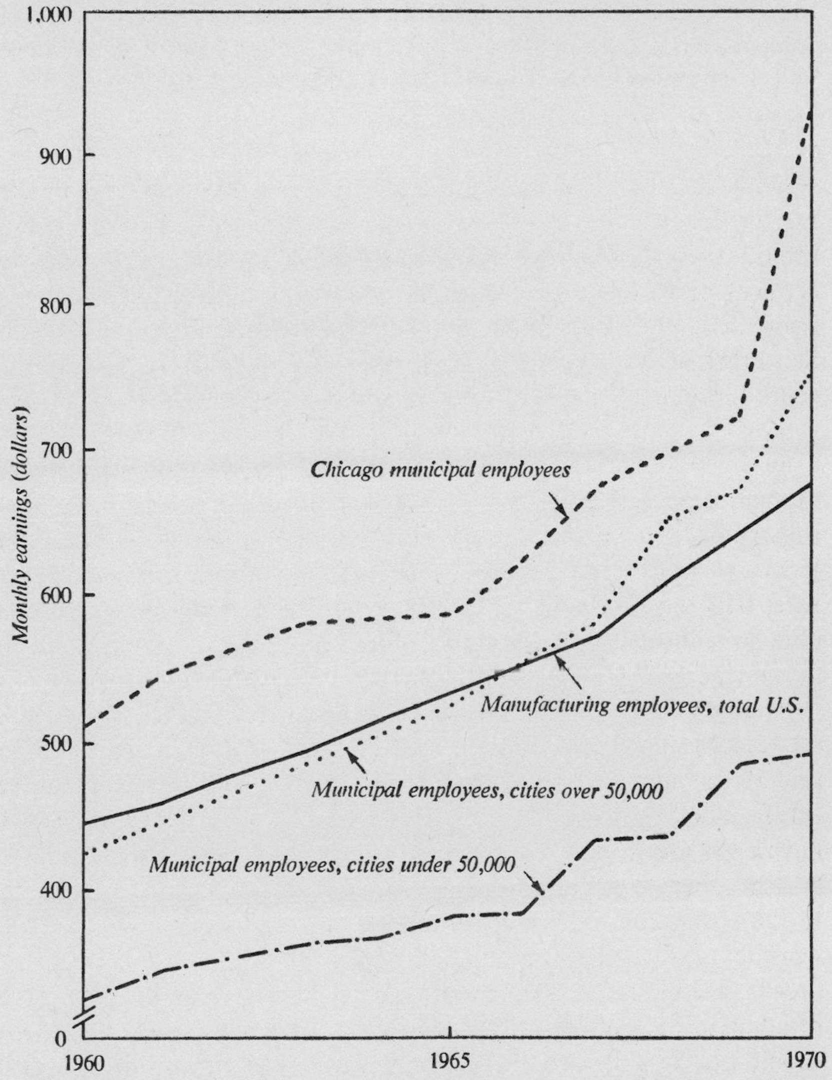

Sources: U.S. Bureau of the Census, *City Employment in 1970*, various issues, Tables 2, 3, and 4; U.S. Office of Business Economics, *Survey of Current Business*, Vol. 51 (July 1971), Table 6.5; Office of Business Economics, *U.S. National Income and Product Accounts, 1964–67* (1971), Table 6.5; Office of Business Economics, *The National Income and Product Accounts of the United States, 1929–1965: Statistical Tables* (1966), Table 6.5.
a. Includes highway, police and fire, sewerage and other sanitation, water supply, parks and recreation, library, financial administration, and general control employees.

tight labor market that characterized the 1965–69 period, most wages were rising, but the public may have been disposed to accept greater-than-average wage increases for public employees, who were regarded as being in some sense "underpaid." A more important reason was the increased unionization that made it possible for local government employees to obtain large settlements. Until recently, public employees were largely unorganized. Although professional associations existed, they had few powers. In general, cities, counties, and school districts unilaterally dictated contract terms and wage rates. All of this has changed in the past twenty years as unionization has spread into the public sector. The new unions and the old associations in many areas have gained many of the prerogatives of unions in the private sector. Most important, they often represent their members in collective bargaining. Along with this ability to organize has come an increased willingness on the part of public employees to engage in "job actions" or strikes—even in violation of the law. During the past five years, teachers, policemen, firemen, and sanitation workers have walked off their jobs in ever increasing numbers. (See Table 9-4.) The sudden acceleration of public employee strikes in 1966 coincides dramatically with the sharp upsurge in relative wages of municipal employees that began in the same year.

Finally, political factors probably have played an important role in the wage increases offered to city employees. Racial violence and the shifting base of power have created an uncertain political environment in most large cities. Faced with this situation, politicians have

Table 9-4. Work Stoppages by Local Government Employees, 1958–70

Year	Number of stoppages	Number of workers involved (thousands)	Man-days lost (thousands)	Workers involved as percentage of total
1958–63 average	24	11.3	24.4	0.24
1964	37	22.5	67.7	0.40
1965	42	11.9	145.0	0.20
1966	133	102.0	449.0	1.70
1967	169	127.0	1,230.0	1.90
1968	235	190.9	2,492.8	2.70
1969	372	139.0	592.2	2.01
1970	386	168.9	1,330.5	2.36

Sources: Harry H. Wellington and Ralph K. Winter, Jr., *The Unions and the Cities* (Brookings Institution, 1971), pp. 212–13; U.S. Bureau of Labor Statistics, "Government Work Stoppages, 1960, 1969, and 1970" (1971; processed), p. 3.

tried to keep the support of municipal employees, who represent a potent political constituency in many big cities. With the emergence of blacks and Spanish-Americans as a political force, local governments have expanded employment opportunities for these groups. Often this has meant hiring the "new minorities" in jobs that once were the prerogatives of the older ethnic groups—the Irish cop, the Italian sanitation man, and the Jewish teacher. Large wage increases in some cases may have been designed to placate these groups for their loss of hegemony over public service employment.

The net effect of all of these forces has been that local government employees—at least in the nation's largest cities—are no longer at the end of the pecking order. In the cities for which there are data, it appears that local government workers earn as much per hour as, and often considerably more than, their counterparts in private industry.[2] In addition, they usually enjoy better pension and health insurance plans, more liberal holiday and vacation provisions, and greater job security than do comparable workers in the private sector.

Population changes have been a second major cause of the rapid growth in the expenditures of central city areas. Although the aggregate population of most large cities declined or grew only marginally during the past ten years, there were important shifts in the population mix of most core cities. Persons who rely heavily on services provided by local governments while contributing little to their support—that is, school age children, families with below average incomes, and the aged—became an ever-increasing fraction of the central cities' residents. In some cities, such as Newark and Cleveland, which have been all but abandoned by the middle class, these shifts have been profound.

Stagnant or declining productivity is often mentioned as another cause of the rising expenditures of big cities. Since reliable measures of the output of public employees are lacking, most of the discussion of productivity in the cities is speculative. Many have the impression that, although employment has increased rapidly, the quality of municipal services has improved little or has even deteriorated. Local government employment has indeed expanded considerably in many big cities; in New York there is now one full-time local government employee for every twenty residents of the city. But despite the grow-

2. Stephen H. Perloff, "Comparing Municipal Salaries with Industry and Federal Pay," *Monthly Labor Review*, Vol. 94 (October 1971), pp. 46–50.

ing work force, many believe that the sidewalks are dirtier, the streets more dangerous, the schools poorer, and city services less reliable than in the past.

While all this may be true, it is not clear that outmoded work rules, labor militancy, or other factors related to the attitudes or effort of the workers are primarily responsible. Increased street congestion and aging equipment may explain why a sanitation crew collects less trash per hour now than a decade ago; the growing proportion of children in the schools who are from disadvantaged homes may present more of an educational problem than even the expanded number of teachers and teacher aides can deal with; the added deterrence of enlarged police departments possibly does not offset the changes brought about by new social mores, the changing economic patterns of the city, and the congested legal process. In short, while output per worker in the public sector may be growing only marginally, or even falling, this may be primarily attributable to changes in the environment in which these services are provided. Furthermore, one should not overlook the "outputs" of public employment other than the provision of services. Traditionally such jobs have served as a kind of antipoverty program —a road for advancement for workers who suffer discrimination in the private job market. They also are used in some instances as mechanisms for keeping the political machine of a city operating smoothly. Perhaps the rapid growth of public employment in the past few years should be interpreted partly as a way of keeping the lid on an otherwise volatile racial and political situation.

Another factor responsible for the growth in big-city expenditures is the proliferation in the number and kind of services provided by urban governments. For example, local programs for pollution control, consumer protection, drug rehabilitation, family planning, day care, and community colleges were almost nonexistent a decade ago. Many such innovations have been spurred by federal legislation. In the case of the Model Cities program, federal dollars were pumped into the central city's budget for new or expanded poverty-related services. Compensatory educational programs are another new service that is financed largely by the federal government. The rapid growth in municipal hospital and health expenditures was undoubtedly stimulated by the Medicare and Medicaid programs, which allowed local governments to expand their facilities and care for the poor and aged while charging most of the costs to the state and federal governments. Thus, although all of these programs increased local government expenditures, not all of the burden for raising the necessary revenues fell on the local taxpayer.

Expenditures by Function

The division of responsibility between state and local governments differs greatly from state to state. In many states, welfare is largely a state function, but in some (notably New York and California) a substantial part of the burden is carried by local governments. Some states make major contributions to education; others leave education primarily to the localities. Hence, big cities differ considerably in the distribution of funds by function within their budgets and in the relative growth of expenditures by function over recent years.

If one consolidates the per capita expenditures of the nation's largest metropolitan areas and cities for the period 1962–70, welfare, health, and education emerge as the fastest growing functions. (See Table 9-5.) Although welfare expenditures have risen sharply, they continue to account for a relatively modest proportion of total budget

Table 9-5. Increase in per Capita Local Government Expenditure and Revenue in the 72 Largest Standard Metropolitan Statistical Areas and in 41 Large Cities, 1962–70

	72 largest SMSAs			41 large cities and their school districts[a]		
Item	Percentage increase, 1962–70	Percentage of 1962–70 increase	Percentage of 1970 budget	Percentage increase, 1962–70	Percentage of 1962–70 increase	Percentage of 1970 budget
Direct general expenditure, total	90	100	100	112	100	100
Education	99	45	43	109	37	36
Highways	24	2	5	14	1	4
Public welfare	258	13	10	264	16	11
Health and hospitals	106	7	6	101	7	7
Police and fire protection	78	8	8	94	11	12
Sewerage and sanitation	55	4	5	56	3	5
Financial administration and general control	75	3	4	81	2	3
Interest on general debt	79	4	4	92	3	3
Other	87	16	16	135	20	18
General revenue, total	94	100	100	108	100	100
Intergovernmental	154	43	35	217	46	36
Property taxes	61	33	42	57	24	35
Other taxes	103	10	9	108	16	16
Current charges and miscellaneous revenues	95	15	15	90	12	13

Sources: Four publications from U.S. Bureau of the Census: *Local Government Finances in Selected Metropolitan Areas and Large Counties: 1969–70*, Series GF70—No. 6 (1971), Table 1; *City Government Finances in 1969–70*, Series GF70—No. 4 (1971), Table 7; *Compendium of City Government Finances in 1962*, Series G-CF62—No. 2 (1963), Table 7; *Census of Governments: 1962*, Vol. 5, *Local Government in Metropolitan Areas* (1964), Table 14. Figures are rounded and may not add to totals.

a. Includes 41 of the 43 largest cities in 1962, and the matching cities in 1970, and 32 matching school districts with budgets independent of their city budgets.

spending in most central cities, mainly because city governments usually finance only a small fraction of welfare costs. New York City is the outstanding exception; welfare costs accounted for almost one-third of the increase in expenditures from 1962 to 1970 and were 23 percent of total city outlays in the latter year. Similarly, although the rate of increase in health and hospital expenditures has been very rapid in most cities, they still constitute a small fraction of total expenditures and contributed only a modest amount to the overall expenditure rise. Expenditures for education, by contrast, grew somewhat less rapidly in most cities than did those for either health or welfare, but accounted for a larger share of the total increase because they were already typically the largest item in the local budgets.

The Revenue Base

For the reasons given above, city expenditures are generally higher and are rising more rapidly than those of the suburbs. If the ability of big cities to raise revenues were commensurably high and rising there would be no problem. But this does not appear to be the case.

In the past, the revenue raising capability of cities far exceeded that of their suburbs—a fact that goes far in explaining how they were able to sustain higher expenditure levels with little assistance from the state or federal government. This superiority stemmed from the fact that real property, sales, payrolls, incomes, and the other bases from which local government revenues are derived were disproportionately concentrated in the central city. Even today, big cities do not appear to be resource-poor in these terms. As the first column of Table 9-6 indicates, their per capita capacity to raise revenue, as measured by an index of the value of their revenue bases, is at least equal to that of their suburbs. In many cases—for example, Boston and Denver—the financial capacity of the city is considerably greater than that of the surrounding areas. Nevertheless, whatever advantages central cities may have in revenue raising capacity are generally outweighed by their greater need for revenue. This can be seen by comparing the first two columns of Table 9-6. Thus, while Atlanta's revenue raising capacity is some 42 percent greater than that of its suburbs, the city area raised 63 percent more revenue per capita in 1969–70 than did its suburbs. Thus the burden was relatively much greater in the city than in the suburbs.

Table 9-6. Per Capita Revenue-Producing Capacity, Revenue Collected, and Growth of Revenue Bases of Selected Cities Relative to Their Suburban Areas, Various Dates, 1950–70

	Ratio, central city to suburban area, per capita basis				
City	Revenue capacity, 1966–67 (1)	Local revenues, 1969–70 (2)	Growth of equalized real property values, 1950–70 (3)	Growth of retail sales, 1954–67 (4)	Growth of income, 1964–70 (5)
Atlanta	1.42	1.63	n.a.	0.34	0.67
Baltimore	1.06	1.19	0.30	0.32	0.35
Boston	1.67	1.48	0.16	0.59	0.65
Chicago	1.05	0.93	6.42	0.49	0.84
Cincinnati	1.31	2.65	0.98	0.49	0.93
Cleveland	1.01	1.26	0.76	0.09	1.06
Columbus	1.00	1.31	0.99	0.26	1.51
Dayton	1.30	1.59	0.62	0.37	0.68
Denver	1.68	1.70	0.75	0.44	0.68
Kansas City	1.12	1.64	n.a.	0.41	0.36
Los Angeles– Long Beach	1.15	1.23	1.03	0.88	0.69
Louisville	1.15	1.63	0.37	0.36	0.86
Miami	1.11	1.33	n.a.	0.11	0.78
New Orleans	1.19	1.42	n.a.	0.39	0.74
New York	1.30	1.23	0.69	0.67	1.22
Philadelphia	1.06	1.39	0.57	0.40	0.93
Pittsburgh	1.33	1.53	0.81	1.07	0.94
Portland, Oregon	1.41	1.87	2.96	0.59	0.62
San Diego	1.06	1.07	0.82	0.41	0.74
St. Louis	1.49	1.78	0.50	0.42	0.75
Seattle	1.12	1.42	0.10	0.42	0.54
Washington, D.C.	1.06	2.01	n.a.	0.47	0.92

Sources: Col. 1, Advisory Commission on Intergovernmental Relations, *Measuring the Fiscal Capacity and Effort of State and Local Areas* (ACIR, 1971); col. 2, Seymour Sacks and John Callahan, "Central City–Suburban Fiscal Disparities in the 72 Largest Metropolitan Areas," Table 25; col. 3, based on unpublished data from state boards of equalization; col. 4, U.S. Bureau of the Census, *U.S. Census of Business, 1954*, Vol. 2, *Retail Trade–Area Statistics*, Pts. 1, 2 (1956), and Bureau of the Census, *U.S. Census of Business, 1967*, Vol. 2, *Retail Trade–Area Statistics*, Pts. 1, 2, 3 (1970); col. 5, *Sales Management*, Vol. 94 (June 10, 1965), and Vol. 107 (June 10, 1971).
n.a. Not available.

Moreover, the advantages the cities now seem to have in revenue raising ability are rapidly eroding, just when their needs for additional revenues seem to be rising most rapidly. Property values, sales, and incomes, which are the ultimate source of local government revenues, are growing far faster in the suburbs than in the cities.

In the past, cities had higher property values per capita than did their suburbs. Indeed, the flight to the suburbs was partly a flight from the high cost of owning or renting property in the city. However, with the movement of middle- and upper middle-income families to the suburbs and the recent suburbanization of industry, per capita property values—and with them the property tax base—in the suburban ring have grown considerably faster than those in the core areas. (See column 3 of Table 9-6.) Some suburban areas now have higher per capita property values than do their central cities. In a few older cities, such as Newark and Trenton, New Jersey, the aggregate value of taxable property has actually begun to decline. There are of course exceptions to these trends. For example, in Chicago and Portland, where there has been a lot of new construction activity in the core area, the per capita value of property has increased much more rapidly in the city than in the surrounding areas in recent years.

Cities in the past have also had higher volumes of retail sales per capita and hence a greater capacity to raise revenue through the sales tax. Per capita sales are still higher in most cities than in their suburbs, but this advantage is also declining rapidly. (See Table 9-6, column 4.) The suburbanization of higher-income families, the growing use of the automobile in shopping, and the proliferation of large shopping malls used by central city residents have caused the retail sales tax base in the suburbs to grow far faster than in the city. In New York, Detroit, and Philadelphia, per capita sales in the suburbs have already surpassed those of the city.

Income taxes do not play a major role in local finance because the states and the federal government have largely preempted this form of taxation. Even here, however, the cities that tax the incomes of their residents face a growing disadvantage vis-à-vis the suburbs. In most older cities, per capita personal incomes have been lower than in the suburbs for some years. Even in the newer cities, per capita incomes are growing far more slowly than in the suburbs. (See Table 9-6, column 5.) Many middle- and upper-income suburban residents, of course, work in the city. If local governments imposed payroll taxes or commuter taxes to tap income where it is earned rather than where the earner resides, the cities would still have the advantage. However, states have not generally permitted cities to tax the incomes of commuters at the same rate as they tax their city residents.

This relative deterioration of the central cities' ability to raise revenue has meant that these areas have had to rely on increased tax rates and on aid from higher levels of government to cover their rising expenditures. While the property tax continues to be the workhorse of the local government revenue system, cities have generally tried to diversify their revenue structures. Many cities have increased their reliance on sales and income taxes. As can be seen in Table 9-5, in the forty-one largest cities per capita property tax revenues grew only half as fast as total revenues during the past decade. Other taxes, many charges, and intergovernmental grants all grew faster. Intergovernmental grants have become especially important. As Table 9-5 shows, roughly half of the recent increase in general revenues came from state or federal grants. Such aid now constitutes more than one-third of the general revenue of local governments in metropolitan areas.

What Can Be Done?

The fiscal dilemma of big cities is quite simply that their expenditures for the public services their citizens want and need are outrunning their revenues. Moreover, the situation seems likely to get worse. Obviously, one could attack this problem from either side—by finding ways of reducing expenditures or by finding new revenue sources in the city itself or outside it. The rest of this chapter will be devoted to considering (1) the prospects for reducing city expenditures by cutting back services, by making them more efficient, or by "exporting" some of the cities' more costly problems; (2) the prospects for raising more revenues from nonfederal sources by revitalizing the cities' own tax base, sharing in the growth of suburban revenues, or obtaining state help; and (3) alternative mechanisms for federal assistance to the cities. A final section discusses ways in which the federal government could provide incentives for metropolitan areas to take collective action to solve the fiscal crisis of their central cities.

Reducing Expenditures

The most direct way of reducing city expenditures is to curtail public services by repairing the streets less often, allowing pupil–teacher ratios to rise, or hiring fewer policemen. Although many large municipalities and school districts recently have cut employment and eliminated certain services, this strategy is likely to be self-defeating, especially if higher expenditures are a function of greater needs. In such cases, service reductions will make the city a less attractive place in which to live or to establish an industry. To be sure, such reductions may often seem preferable to tax increases, but they will surely impair the city's position relative to the suburbs.

The possibility of cutting costs by increasing the efficiency of municipal services has received a good deal of attention in recent years. New management systems, decentralization, technological innovations, and contracts with private firms for the provision of public services have all been proposed as possible ways of cutting costs. Strenuous efforts should certainly be made to improve efficiency, but so far there is little hard evidence that any of these innovations would save significant amounts of money and be politically palatable. For example, although private carters can collect trash in New York for about half what it costs the City Department of Sanitation, this differential would probably not persist if private carters became major suppliers of sanitation services to the city. The sanitation workers union would do its best to eliminate the private sector's lower wages and more onerous working conditions that account for virtually all of the existing cost differential. Similarly, experiments with performance contracting in education—arrangements by which school systems contract with private industry to teach children certain skills—have not offered much hope that this technique will either increase children's performance or save the schools money.

Another way to reduce the level of city expenditures would be to disperse some of the problems that give rise to high expenditures. Since a substantial part of the city's extraordinary expenditures are associated with its concentration of low-income residents, a dispersal of the poor throughout the metropolitan area could help the cities considerably. At least two factors, however, suggest that this is unlikely to happen.

First, there is opposition in the suburbs to the dispersal of low-income families throughout the metropolitan area. While some of this hostility is racial, much of it has an economic basis. Suburbs do not want families who consume more in the way of services than they are able to pay for through taxes. To exclude such families, many have resorted to "fiscal zoning"—that is, restricting the use of their vacant land to single family homes on large lots or to "clean" industry. Any suburb's opposition to low-income housing derives partly from a fear that it would reduce its attractiveness vis-à-vis other communities. If all suburbs were required to accept some low-income housing, the opposition might be reduced. Unless the state or federal government provides an incentive, however, such agreements are hard to obtain. Only in the Dayton and Washington, D.C., areas have area-wide plans to decentralize public housing been approved; and even in these instances, most of the new low-income housing still will be located within the central city.

The second factor working against the decentralization of low-income families is the various advantages the city holds for the poor. First, there is the availability of old and hence cheap rental housing in the core. Of course, this advantage could be reduced if all of the new subsidized housing for low-income families were built outside the city; but even if this occurred, most low-income housing would still be in the city for a long time to come. A second advantage of the city is its accessibility to low-skill jobs. Although this accessibility is declining, it is still superior to that of most suburbs. Finally, the availability of public transportation also makes the city a more rational location for many low-income families.

Increasing State and Local Revenue

Some cities could increase their tax rates or impose new kinds of taxes; but, as was pointed out above, the tax effort of the cities is generally high already. Higher tax rates might accelerate the flight to the suburbs of business and middle-income families.

The ability of large cities to revive their failing tax bases by attracting either higher-income residents or new industries is also very limited. This is because the city has little new left to offer. The forces that once attracted business and people to the center of the metropolitan area are fading away; the accessibility and centrality of the core are no longer as vital to industry as they once were. The truck has allowed manufacturers to locate far from railroads, wharves, and suppliers, while new methods of production and material handling demand a great deal of ground space, a scarce commodity in the congested core. Communication advances and the formalization of business practices have reduced the need for the face-to-face contact that downtown alone could provide. With its dwindling population, the city can no longer even offer service industries and retailers the richest market in the metropolitan area.

For the prospective middle- or upper-income resident, the central city is even less inviting. The automobile has freed him from the need to live close to his job or to leisure time activities, and a rising income has allowed him to express his taste for the newer and less dense housing that is more readily available in the suburbs. The city's public services are heavily skewed toward meeting the needs of the poor, its schools are inferior, and it is beset with problems of crime and dirt. By moving to the suburbs, the middle-income person can avoid the burden of supporting the local public services that are consumed by the poor and be assured of a more problem-free existence. Virtually the only new incentive that the city could use to attract industry or upper-income residents is tax relief. While there is no evidence that either would respond to this lure, it would constitute giving away the very reason for drawing such persons and firms back into the city.

The problem of revitalizing the city and its tax base should not be dismissed as hopeless, but it clearly cannot be done gradually or piecemeal. Massive efforts to rebuild whole sections of cities and provide first-rate services, especially schools, might reverse the exodus to the suburbs. But the funds needed to do this cannot come from the cities themselves.

Although cities may not be able to do much by themselves, most metropolitan areas as a whole do have the capability for dealing with the growing imbalance between the resources and the needs of their core cities. One way is to expand the city's resource base by annexing surrounding areas or consolidating the central city with a larger unit of government, such as the county. In effect, this would allow the city to share in the growth occurring in the suburbs and would shift its demographic makeup toward families that are less in need of local government services. Except in the Northeast, where city boundaries have been fairly static for several decades, annexation and consolidation have been used fairly effectively. In the past decade, such cities as Sacramento, San Jose, Tulsa, Memphis, Toledo, and Omaha have annexed considerable parts of their surrounding areas. City–county consolidation of one sort or another has occurred in Nashville (1962), Jacksonville (1967), and Indianapolis (1969).

Unfortunately, expanding the city cannot be regarded as a likely solution to the fiscal crises of most of the largest metropolitan areas because it has little political appeal. Since annexation usually must be approved by state legislatures or by the residents of the affected jurisdictions, it can easily be blocked by suburbanites who see no reason for giving up their service and tax advantages to help solve the urban problems they have often just managed to escape. Minority residents of the central cities also have begun to oppose annexation and consolidation efforts out of fear that their growing political power base in the core will be diluted by suburban whites. Annexation has generated the least opposition in areas such as the South, where a degree of consolidation already exists because many local public services are provided at the county level. But in such areas, the need for consolidation is least. Elsewhere the effect of annexation often has been seriously blunted because the most important local government service—education—has been excluded from the unification effort. Kansas City, for example, which has annexed so much territory that it now has rural areas within the city boundaries, has preserved a balkanized school system of seventeen separate districts; San Jose has fifteen school districts operating within its current boundaries. While the municipal governments may have solved their fiscal problems through annexation, the school districts that include the poorer sections of the city are still unable to provide adequate education.

Some of the benefits of consolidation or annexation could be obtained, possibly with less opposition, through tax-sharing schemes. A metropolitan-wide tax could be imposed, similar to those that now finance the operating deficits of some urban transportation systems, and the receipts could be distributed in accordance with some measure of fiscal need. While the likelihood that suburban residents would accept such a plan is slight in most areas, an area-wide tax has recently been levied in the Minneapolis–St. Paul metropolitan area. There each locality is required to contribute to a common pool 40 percent of its property tax receipts that are attributable to increases in the value of commercial and industrial property within its borders. This common revenue will be distributed among the various communities on the basis of their population and per capita property wealth. This distribution formula will provide the central cities of Minneapolis and St. Paul with only an average share of the common fund. Whether they are net beneficiaries, therefore, will depend solely on the patterns of growth of commercial and industrial property within the metropolitan region. In any case, the central cities' gain from intrametropolitan revenue sharing schemes will depend on the tax base used to raise the revenue and the formula chosen for distributing the receipts.

The same political forces that have thwarted efforts at generating metropolitan solutions to the fiscal problems of central cities are likely to preclude action at the state level as well. Although the one man–one vote ruling has effectively ended the rural domination of most state legislatures, representatives of suburban areas are now in control. Several decades ago, when the cities and suburbs were joined in a strong symbiotic relationship, suburban legislators might have supported efforts to have the state aid the central city. However, now that they are increasingly independent, self-sufficient economic and political entities, the suburbs often act as though their interests were opposed to those of the core cities. With the continuation of those trends and the declining population of the core, the political power of the nation's large cities is likely to decrease in state legislatures. Since states have given little in the way of special aid to large cities in the past, there is little reason to expect a sudden change in the near future.

The Federal Government's Response

The federal government could respond in a number of ways to the growing fiscal imbalance of large cities. It could expand and modify those grant-in-aid programs that are oriented toward the problems afflicting cities; it could implement new programs, such as general revenue sharing and welfare reform, that are expected to have an important impact on urban areas; or it could provide incentives to induce states and metropolitan areas to come to grips with the problems of the cities in their own ways.

EXISTING GRANT PROGRAMS. Federal grants to state and local governments have been increasing rapidly in recent years—by more than 19 percent annually since 1965—and a substantial portion of these funds goes to big cities. For two reasons, however, it seems doubtful that a simple expansion of existing grant programs will do much to alleviate the fundamental fiscal problems of the cities.

First, many of the existing grant programs that channel federal funds into the cities are aimed at alleviating the poverty of individuals rather than that of governments. Of course, higher welfare benefits, better health care, more generous food stamp allowances, and an expansion in the number of public housing units would alleviate the poverty of many low-income city residents; but only in the long run would this alter the city's need for more police, sanitation services, compensatory education facilities, and other municipal services. In the short run, the city would be no more able to support these needs than it is today.

The second reason why a simple expansion of existing grants would probably not help is that many of the programs that are intended to assist local governments in providing services are encumbered by stringent regulations that preclude their use for the support of basic services. Usually these grants were intended to stimulate the provision of new or additional services; in many cases, they require that the recipient government match some fraction of the federal contribution. Hence, rather than providing relief from the fiscal burden of running basic city services, they tend to add to that burden (as well as to the level of services).

Several major federal grant programs are specifically oriented toward big city problems (see Table 9-7), but these have not been growing rapidly in recent years, nor does the administration's budget propose major increases in fiscal 1973. While the urban mass transit program is expected to expand by two-thirds, and there is a moderate increase in public housing programs, the Model Cities program remains at its current level, while urban renewal decreases. The legislative and administrative changes the administration has proposed are potentially far more significant for the future of cities than are the budget changes of recent years. They represent an attempt to make the existing federal contribution more effective in dealing with problems of large cities by reducing the red tape, spending constraints, matching requirements, and uncertainty that have come to characterize the current grant system. The "planned variations" activity within the Model Cities program is one move in this direction. Under it, twenty cities will be given additional money to strengthen the "planning and man-

Table 9-7. Levels of City-oriented Grant-in-Aid Programs, Fiscal Years 1971-73
Millions of dollars

Program	1971	1972	1973
Model Cities	521	620	620
Urban renewal	1,029	1,450	1,000
Community action	410	353	384
Urban mass transit	334	606	1,000
Public housing	626	886	1,105
Open space land	75	100	100
Neighborhood facilities	40	40	40
Total	3,035	4,055	4,249

Source: *The Budget of The United States Government, Fiscal Year 1973*, p. 128; *The Budget of the United States Government—Appendix, Fiscal Year 1973*.

agement capacity of the local chief executive." Sixteen of these cities will also receive new Model Cities program funds with which to implement their plans on a city-wide basis. These cities will also be given broad discretion in deciding how to spend their Model Cities money. In the President's words, they will be encouraged to "address priority needs which they themselves have identified and which cannot be met through other Federal, State, and local funding sources."[3]

The Law Enforcement Assistance Administration (LEAA) grants—in particular the impact program—are another effort to give the lower levels of government greater freedom in determining how to use federal money to solve their problems. Under the impact program, eight cities will be given $20 million each over a three-year period to demonstrate what they can do to reduce crime. Like other LEAA grants that the states are required to share with their localities, few restrictions and reporting requirements are attached to this money. The cities will be able to devote the funds to improving their basic law enforcement activities.

The major initiative in this area, however, is the administration's request for an urban community development revenue sharing program. This proposal, which was unveiled last year, calls for the consolidation of a number of urban aid programs into a single grant, which would be distributed among metropolitan areas and cities on a formula, rather than a project application, basis. Few restrictions would be placed on the use of the money by the recipient government. In March 1972 the Senate passed a modified version of this proposal, which combined the urban renewal, water and sewer, and neighborhood development and facilities programs with some smaller grants. The total amount will be distributed on the basis of each metropolitan area's relative need as measured by its total population, its poor population, its relative amount of overcrowded housing, and its previous experience with the consolidated programs. In contrast to the administration's proposal, the Senate bill requires that the recipient governments file applications, plans, reports, and performance statements, as well as share at least 10 percent of the cost. Even with these restrictions, however, there is a significant increase in the discretion left in the hands of the recipient governments. This should allow most large cities to divert a portion of their grant toward meeting the

3. Office of the White House Press Secretary, "Statement of the President," July 29, 1971.

needs for basic municipal services. While both the administration's plan and the Senate version request a significant increase in budget authority over that of the consolidated programs, few large cities would receive more than they do today under the existing programs. The new money that has been added as a "sweetener" will be used up by the many smaller cities that will receive money for the first time or that have received only small amounts in the past from the programs that were consolidated.

NEW INITIATIVES. Two major administration initiatives now being debated by the Congress—general revenue sharing and welfare reform —have both been promoted as means of easing the fiscal plight of large cities. With respect to revenue sharing the claim is clearly valid. No matter how the revenue sharing funds are distributed, a considerable sum would be given to central cities. Since few if any restrictions will be placed on the recipients' use of this money, cities could apply their share to meeting their day-to-day revenue requirements. The degree to which general revenue sharing would relieve the cities' crisis would, of course, depend on both the total amount of federal funds to be shared and the priority accorded to cities in the distribution mechanism.

The administration's proposal calls for the distribution of approximately $5 billion among the states on the basis of their populations and their revenue raising efforts. Each state would be required to share its grant with its general purpose local governments (cities, towns, counties, and so on). The fraction remaining with the state government would be equal to the ratio of state revenues to all state and locally raised revenues. Local general purpose governments would divide the rest in proportion to their locally raised revenues.

The administration's proposal in theory is neutral with respect to the city–suburb problem. Since the funds would be distributed among local general purpose governments in proportion to their locally raised revenues, the size of each grant would be in effect a flat percentage of the taxes, fees, and charges of both the cities and the suburbs. In practice, however, the administration formula would tend to favor cities over their surrounding areas because a larger part of the revenues in city areas are raised by general purpose governments than is the case in the suburbs, where school districts are often separate units of government. The necessity of using in the distribution formula data that are several years old further favors the cities, since their locally raised revenues are generally growing less rapidly than are those of the suburbs. Much of the relative advantage of the cities could be expected to be eliminated as the data base improved and as suburbs incorporated school and other special districts into their general purpose governments so as to maximize the size of their revenue sharing grant.

An alternative revenue sharing plan introduced by Senator Edmund S. Muskie would be more favorable to large cities. Its formula for distributing funds among local general purpose governments would give more to those with large populations and more to areas with high concentrations of welfare recipients and poor families. On the other hand, a plan recently approved by the House Ways and Means Committee, while giving more money to local governments than the administration's proposal, would favor suburbs relative to central cities. This plan would distribute money among the municipalities within a county on the basis of population and relative incomes. The per capita grants received by a city under this plan would thus differ little from those received by its suburbs. Since suburban expenditures tend to be lower than those of the city, however, the suburbs would normally receive more aid relative to their expenditures than would the cities.

WILL THESE MEASURES HELP? Revenue sharing will certainly help cities deal with their fiscal problems, but the amounts of money under consideration will not put the cities on easy street. The plans now receiving serious consideration would give large cities an amount equal to between 5 and 10 percent of the revenues they now raise locally. While this contribution is significant, it should be noted that locally raised revenues have been increasing by roughly this amount every year. In effect, then, general revenue sharing would be equivalent to one year's normal growth in revenues.

Revenue sharing is an inefficient means of dealing with the special plight of large cities because much of the money will be distributed among suburban governments that are not facing critical fiscal problems. Of course, such a general distribution may be the price necessary to persuade a nation of suburbs to support increased aid for its cities. Providing resources that allow the city to maintain its existing services, however, will do nothing to enhance the position of the cities relative to that of the suburbs. Unless indices of need are included in the distribution formula, large cities will continue to have a harder time than their suburbs in balancing their budgets while maintaining comparable services and tax rates.

It is clear that welfare reform would do little to ease the fiscal problems of large cities. This is because at present little of the financial burden for supporting the programs that would be replaced by the welfare reform proposals is borne by local governments. In seventeen states, localities contribute nothing to financing the categorical public assistance programs, and in seventeen other states less than 5 percent of total expenditures on such programs derives from local taxes.

Of course, in a few states where welfare expenditures are large, local governments are required to bear a significant share of the costs. New York, New Jersey, California, and Wisconsin fall in this category. But even in these areas the local contribution for supporting the categorical assistance programs is raised at the county level, which generally means that the suburbs within the central county must share the burden of supporting the welfare population that resides primarily within the central city. Only in San Francisco and New York, where the city and county are coterminous, is this not so.

In any case it is not clear that welfare reform as it is being discussed today would relieve the burden even of those localities that do contribute to the support of public assistance programs. Most of these cities and counties are in states that have payment standards considerably above the contemplated federal support level. If, as seems likely, the states either choose, or are forced, to maintain their current levels of assistance through state supplementation, there is reason to expect that they will ask their local governments to continue contributing. If this happened, then the main benefit to the cities of welfare reform would be the federal government's guarantee that the current contribution of states and localities would not rise in the future.

In summary, it is unlikely that welfare reform will provide substantial direct aid for cities; it would not free a major source of funds, primarily because today cities and local governments devote little of their locally raised revenue to welfare. Of course, substantial indirect benefits could flow from welfare reform, but predictions in this area are hazardous. Higher benefit levels would improve the lot of the low-income city residents, and this eventually might alleviate the cities' need for certain compensatory municipal services; a more equal distribution of welfare benefits might reduce the migration of low-income, high-need families into the nation's largest cities; and finally, states might be more willing when their contribution to welfare is frozen to channel their growing revenues into their deteriorating cities.

New Incentive Structures

The preceding section of this chapter concluded that metropolitan areas have the capability of dealing with the fiscal problems of their central cities but lack the necessary will and organization. An appropriate role for the federal government therefore would appear to be that of providing incentives to induce either state action or metropolitan area-wide efforts. To date the federal government has placed little emphasis on this approach. Metropolitan agencies are eligible for federal planning grants and certain other programs, but rarely, if ever, do they receive preferential treatment. Similarly, some capital projects must obtain the approval of area-wide planning agencies to be eligible for federal financing, but such requirements have not touched off major efforts to achieve the coordinated planned development of metropolitan areas.

If the federal government decided to take this approach, several options are available. First, it could provide larger special revenue sharing grants to those areas that were attempting to deal with their problems on a metropolitan-wide basis. In cases where the recipient agency had area-wide authority, the matching requirements and other restrictions of existing grant programs could be reduced or eliminated.

A second possibility would be for the federal government to contribute to any intrametropolitan area revenue sharing scheme or to supplement any state's distribution of urban aid. Another approach would be to underwrite a more balanced distribution of needs within metropolitan areas. This could be done by providing an incentive for suburbs to accept low-income housing or added burdens. Communities could be given grants to cover the cost of the public services consumed by residents of low-income public housing. Suburban school districts that accepted children from the central city ghetto could be provided with bonuses.

Finally, the federal government could provide incentives for full state financing of certain functions that may weigh heavily on cities. For example, the reimbursement formulas for the existing categorical welfare systems could be altered to include bonuses to states that paid the entire nonfederal portion of the welfare bill. Another example of this approach is contained in the report of the President's Commission on School Finance, which suggested that a federal incentive payment be made to states that increased their relative contributions to financing elementary and secondary education.[4]

The difficulty the cities are experiencing in balancing their growing needs with their dwindling resources is likely to intensify in the future. By default the federal government will be required to come to the rescue. Although recent federal initiatives—general and special revenue sharing—will certainly help, the fiscal problems of large cities are not likely to be eradicated by these programs. The basic choice that the federal government now faces is whether to enlist the cooperation of the states and suburbs in improving the condition of the cities or to face the problem alone.

4. The President's Commission on School Finance, *Schools, People, & Money: The Need for Educational Reform*, Final Report (1972).

10. Financing Elementary and Secondary Education

THE FISCAL 1973 BUDGET for elementary and secondary education as originally presented by the President would not by itself justify a chapter in this book. The budget reflects a continuation of the present limited federal role in education: it keeps the major federal program for disadvantaged children at last year's level; slightly increases the emphasis on research, development, and training programs; continues the administration's efforts to consolidate categorical aid programs; and renews last year's request for emergency school assistance to alleviate the problems of desegregation. Outside the budget, however, the President has made two major proposals affecting education. First, in the State of the Union Message, he promised a "revolutionary" new federal program of school finance designed to replace the residential property tax as a source of funds for education. This proposal is currently under study by the Advisory Commission on Intergovernmental Relations (ACIR). Second, in his school busing speech of March 16, 1972, the President proposed not only a moratorium on new school busing orders, but also new federal legislation aimed at improving educational opportunities for disadvantaged students. Both these presidential statements raise basic questions about the federal role in education that could profoundly affect the budget over the next several years.

318

The Present Federal Role and the 1973 Budget

Although federal spending for education grew rapidly in the 1960s, the federal government still pays less than 10 percent of the costs of elementary and secondary education. None of the existing federal programs was designed to provide basic financial support for schools, but rather to provide a federal stimulus for specific educational activities. Thus, there are programs to support such "categorical" purposes as vocational education and school libraries; targeted aid programs, such as Title I of the Elementary and Secondary Education Act, designed to aid disadvantaged children; and aid to "impacted areas," which are school districts containing substantial numbers of children of federal civilian and military employees. In the present administration, the central budgetary questions have concerned the relative emphasis to be given to each of these programs and how to consolidate them.

The administration's past elementary and secondary education budgets have pursued four objectives. First, they have placed an emphasis on holding down expenditures; only very modest increases were requested in 1971 and 1972. Second, last year the administration made a major effort to consolidate certain categorical aid programs by combining them into a special educational revenue sharing grant that was to have been distributed on a formula basis to states and school districts. Third, this administration, like its predecessor, has persistently and unsuccessfully tried to reduce the impacted areas aid program. Finally, the Nixon administration's budget requests have attempted to increase emphasis on research, training, and innovation in order to improve the effectiveness of schools.

The Congress, on the other hand, has ignored the aims of the administration and instead has tended to maintain past emphases while increasing the total amount spent on education. In both fiscal 1970 and 1971, it enacted appropriations for education that the President vetoed because he considered them both too large and misdirected. The administration's special revenue sharing program for education, which was to have consolidated more than thirty programs into five block grants, was not acted on by the Congress last year. Instead it passed a 1972 appropriation for the Office of Education (separate from the appropriation of the Department of Health, Education, and Welfare in order to speed it along) that reflected its usual priorities. Funds for impacted areas and vocational education, which the Presi-

dent wished to reduce, were substantially increased. Aid for disadvantaged and handicapped children exceeded the administration's
request, as did a number of categorical aid programs that the administration wanted to consolidate and reduce.

Table 10-1 shows the administration's budget request for the Office
of Education for fiscal 1973. The highlights are:

• A renewed request for special revenue sharing for education. The
administration is proposing a major cutback in the impact aid portion
of special revenue sharing to reduce the level of assistance in school
districts where federal employment has negligible effects on the taxing
capacity of the district. The proposed "new money" for the consolidated program would just about make up for the proposed cutbacks,
leaving the total to be allotted about the same as in fiscal 1972.

**Table 10-1. Appropriations to the U.S. Office of Education for Elementary and
Secondary Education, by Type of Program, Fiscal Years 1971–73**

Millions of dollars

Type of program	1971 Actual	1972 Estimate	1973 Requested
Special revenue sharing			
Educationally deprived children	1,500	1,598	1,598
Aid to impacted areas	505	566	370
Education for the handicapped	34	38	38
Vocational education	425	475	475
Other[a]	540	560	532
Additional amounts for special revenue sharing	...	...	224
Total, special revenue sharing	3,004	3,237	3,237
Emergency school assistance and civil rights education	94	520	1,000
Education renewal	301	314	363
Research and development			
National Institute of Education	...	3	125
Existing programs	68	87	...
Total, research and development	68	90	125
Other[b]	235	256	264
Total, all Office of Education appropriations for elementary and secondary education[c]	3,477	4,192	4,765

Sources: *The Budget of the United States Government, Fiscal Year 1973; The Budget of the United States
Government—Appendix, Fiscal Year 1973; Special Analyses of the United States Government, Fiscal Year
1973; Congressional Record*, daily ed., August 6, 1971, pp. S13444–48.

a. Includes library programs, state agency assistance, supplementary centers, and other programs (including the U.S. Department of Agriculture school lunch program) that would be consolidated into special
revenue sharing.

b. Includes those parts of impacted areas, handicapped, vocational education, and library resource programs that are not scheduled for consolidation into special revenue sharing.

c. Total does not equal sum of components because it excludes the Department of Agriculture school
lunch program included in Other under revenue sharing (see note *a*).

• A renewed request of $1 billion for emergency school assistance. The budget states that these funds will be used for "project grants to local school districts that are desegregating under court order or voluntarily attempting to overcome the educational disadvantages of minority group isolation."[1] On March 16, 1972, the President changed his request and said that funds provided under this program should be channeled into districts with high concentrations of low-income students.

• Two new ventures are proposed to stimulate educational change.

First, a number of separate programs have been gathered together in a single appropriation called "educational renewal." Under this rubric increases are proposed for the collection of statistics about education, the distribution of information on successful educational innovations, and the stimulation of new techniques. Funding is also requested for a new effort called education "renewal sites." This program will provide funds for selected school districts to enable them to improve planning and coordination in a limited number of schools so as to increase the effectiveness with which federal moneys are used to meet the needs of these schools.

Second, the administration supported the creation of a National Institute of Education (NIE), which is part of the 1972 higher education bill. It proposes to transfer some $87 million in existing research programs to the institute, as well as adding about $38 million in new money. The NIE would have a broad mandate to further educational research, development, demonstration, and dissemination.

In total, the administration proposes a 1973 appropriation for elementary and secondary education of $4.8 billion, up $600 million from 1972.

Three Problems of Education

There has been rising pressure on the federal government to play a more important role in financing elementary and secondary education. This pressure comes from three sources. (1) There is widespread concern about the overall fiscal problem of education—the difficulty of financing education adequately from state and local revenues, particularly from property taxes. (2) There is concern about equalizing educational opportunity for children who live in different jurisdic-

1. *The Budget of the United States Government, Fiscal Year 1973*, p. 132.

tions. This concern has been brought sharply to the fore by recent court decisions declaring it unconstitutional for states to allow large differences in per pupil expenditures among jurisdictions when these differences are related primarily to the wealth of the individual school districts. (3) There is bitter controversy over the equalization of opportunity for education among racial and economic groups, dramatized by recent desegregation cases and the widespread debate over busing. This chapter will examine these three problems in turn and then discuss alternative solutions and possible roles for the federal government.

The Fiscal Problem

The financial problem of elementary and secondary education results from a combination of two factors. First, the cost of providing education is rising rapidly. Second, the heavy reliance of school finance on the property tax, which taxpayers appear to find especially painful, makes it difficult to raise more revenue at the local level.

RISING COSTS OF EDUCATION. Total outlays on public elementary and secondary education have risen dramatically over the past few years, tripling since 1957–58 to a level of $43 billion a year. They now represent 14 percent of all domestic government spending and 47 percent of the outlays of local governments.

One reason for the rise in school expenditures is the increase in the total school population in the United States from 33 million students in 1957–58 to 46 million in the 1970–71 school year. Only about one-fourth of the rise in expenditures, however, can be attributed to the larger number of students. The rest is a result of an increase in the amount spent per pupil, which rose from $335 a year in 1957–59 to $867 in 1970–71. As may be seen in Table 10-2, almost two-thirds of the increase in per pupil outlays was related to increases in the amount spent for teachers and "other instructional personnel" such as librarians and guidance counselors. These outlays increased both because the number of instructional personnel per pupil was rising and because their salaries and other benefits were increasing. During this period, the number of pupils per teacher fell from about 26 to 22, and the number of pupils per "other instructional" employees dropped from 325 to 160. These changes accounted for just under one-fifth of the rise in per pupil outlays for instructional personnel. The rest resulted from rising salaries and benefits.

Table 10-2. Public School Expenditures per Pupil, by Purpose, 1970-71
School Year, and Increase over 1957-59 Average

| Purpose | 1970-71 school year | | Percentage increase, 1970-71 over 1957-59 average | Percentage contribution to increase in total expenditures |
	Amount of expenditures (dollars)	Percentage of expenditures		
Administrative and miscellaneous services	63	7	236	8
Salaries and fringe benefits of instructional personnel	554	64	162	64
Other instructional services	38	4	209	5
Plant operation and maintenance	90	10	129	10
Transportation	32	4	157	4
Capital outlays and debt service	90	10	124	9
All purposes	867	100	159	100

Source: Computed from Orlando F. Furno and Paul K. Cuneo, "Cost of Education Index, 1970-71," *School Management*, Vol. 15 (January 1971), p. 14. Figures are rounded and may not add to totals.

Teachers as a group have fared somewhat better as to salary than the average American worker during the past twelve years. While the average wage for full-time employees in all industries was rising by 74 percent, teachers' salaries went up by 90 percent, and the salaries of other instructional personnel grew by more than 100 percent. Since 1966, average teacher salaries have increased at an annual rate of almost 8 percent—about one-third faster than wages in general.

Several explanations have been suggested for this rise in the relative salaries of teachers. Among these are the increasing militancy and unionization of teachers, the expansion of federal aid programs, and the "teacher shortage" that prevailed until a few years ago. Some contend that teacher salaries were rising rapidly to "catch up" to a level consistent with the importance of the profession and the level of education required. Whatever the reasons, the relative rise in wages of teachers has played a crucial role in the growth in expenditures for education. Had the rate of increase of instructional wages not exceeded the average for other occupations over the past twelve years, school expenditures in 1970-71 would have been some $3.3 billion, or 8 percent, less than they actually were.

RAISING THE MONEY. While expanded federal and state aid have helped, school districts have had to rely on local revenues to finance roughly half of the recent rise in educational expenditures. In the aggregate, local revenues supply 53 percent of the funds spent on elementary and secondary education, while 41 percent comes from state sources and the remainder is contributed by the federal government. This division of responsibility has changed little over the past decade; in 1959–60, local sources accounted for 57 percent of the total, state sources amounted to 39 percent, and the federal share was 4 percent. Of course, financial arrangements vary considerably from state to state. For example, in Hawaii and Delaware a large fraction of school expenditures comes from state sources, while in New Hampshire and Nebraska local revenues dominate. (See Table 10-3.)

Recently in many areas, resistance to further increases in the local contribution to education has mounted. This "taxpayers' revolt," as it has been labeled by the media, is reflected in the refusal of local voters to approve school construction bond issues and property tax hikes for increases in current school expenditures. Roughly half of all school bond issues were turned down last year, whereas more than 70 percent were approved during the 1958 to 1966 period. Similarly, about half of the requests for school tax rises were rejected in 1970. This "revolt" has not visibly slowed the national rise in school budgets, but in some places it has resulted in shortened school years, re-

Table 10-3. Distribution of State, Local, and Federal Financing of Public Schools, by States with the Four Highest and Lowest State Proportions, 1970–71 School Year
Percent

State	Percentage distribution			
	State	Local	Federal	Total
States with highest proportion of state financing				
Hawaii	89.4	2.9	7.7	100
Delaware	71.2	21.7	7.1	100
Alaska	69.7	12.8	17.5	100
North Carolina	66.2	18.8	15.0	100
States with lowest proportion of state financing				
Oregon	19.6	74.5	5.9	100
Nebraska	17.6	75.8	6.6	100
South Dakota	15.1	73.9	10.9	100
New Hampshire	9.6	86.2	4.3	100
U.S. average	41.1	52.0	6.9	100

Source: National Education Association, *Rankings of the States, 1971*, Research Report 1971-R1 (NEA, 1971), Tables 86, 88, 90. Figures are rounded and may not add to totals.

duced offerings of academic programs, teacher layoffs, and the abolition of sports and other special activities. Some large school districts, such as Chicago and Philadelphia, have sustained substantial budget deficits.

The taxpayers' revolt may be a temporary phenomenon associated with the economic recession or the impact of recent court decisions. Many educators fear, however, that it reflects a more permanent negative shift in the taxpayers' attitudes toward education and the way it is financed. There seems to be widespread feeling among taxpayers that school expenditures have been rising "too fast" and that the increases have not produced any overall improvements in the quality of education but instead have been eaten up by increases in the salaries and benefits of school district employees. There is considerable dissatisfaction with the schools, ranging from concern over the relevance of the educational program to a fear and dislike of the lifestyles of the students. In some areas, opposition to busing may be adding to citizen reluctance to spend for schools.

Another explanation for the possible shift in public attitudes is the changing structure of the population. In many communities the fraction of voters with school age children is dropping, while single, childless, and aged voters are forming an increasingly large segment of the electorate. In some places private school enrollments are quite large. When bond issues or tax increases must be approved by more than a simple majority, a small decline in the relative numbers of persons having a direct stake in the school system may be an important determinant of the election's outcome.

DISLIKE OF THE PROPERTY TAX. The final and most often cited cause of the taxpayer revolt is the widespread dislike of the property tax—the source of 84 percent of locally raised school revenues. Apparently many people believe that property taxes have been rising at an uncontrolled pace, although, in fact, compared with other state and local taxes, property tax growth has been quite modest. As may be seen in Table 10-4, property tax receipts have risen in the postwar period at a slightly faster rate than national income, but they have grown considerably more slowly than other state and local taxes.

Several factors explain why taxpayers may believe that the property tax is rising faster than other taxes, even though this is generally not true. First, the property tax is paid in large lumps—most communities bill taxpayers annually or semiannually. Even the taxpayer who pays

Table 10-4. Property and Other State and Local Tax Receipts, and Property Taxes as Percentage of Potential Gross National Product, Selected Fiscal Years, 1927-71

Taxes in millions of dollars

Fiscal year	Property taxes	Other state and local taxes	Property taxes as percentage of total state and local taxes	Property taxes as percentage of potential GNP
1927	4,730	1,357	77.7	4.9ᵃ
1956	11,749	14,619	44.6	2.6
1962	19,054	22,500	45.9	3.2
1967	26,047	34,953	42.7	3.3
1971	38,260	56,019	40.6	3.4

Sources: Tax receipts, 1927–67, U.S. Bureau of the Census, *Census of Governments, 1967*, Vol. 6, Topical Studies, No. 5, *Historical Statistics on Governmental Finances and Employment* (1969), Table 4; and 1971, Bureau of the Census, "Quarterly Summary of State and Local Tax Revenue, April–June 1971," GT71 No. 2 (September 1971), p. 1; potential GNP, estimated by authors.
a. Percentage of actual GNP.

his property tax monthly with the mortgage payment may be more conscious of this tax than he is of a sales tax that he pays almost continuously, a few pennies at a time. Second, reassessments of property values are made infrequently and may involve large amounts. Unlike sales and income taxes, property tax yields do not rise automatically as incomes rise. Property values do generally go up as income increases, but this does not generate more revenue for the community unless property is reassessed or the millage rate is raised—both actions of which the taxpayer is likely to be conscious and resentful. He will be especially resentful of an increase in his property tax bill if his own income is not rising—a situation typical of older people, who have a tendency to remain in housing that is large and valuable relative to their needs and income. A widow living alone in an eight room house after her family is gone does not feel wealthier because the house is increasing in value, and she may have a hard time paying the tax out of her income.

Discontent with the property tax also relates to inequities in its administration. Assessment of property values is a judgmental process. Unless the property has recently been sold, its value is a matter of guesswork. This leaves a lot of room for favoritism, corruption, and careless administration. The result is that the ratios of assessed valuations to objectively determined market values often vary greatly. For example, one study of Boston showed that in 1962 the ratio of assessed value to market value for single family homes ranged from 0.28 in East Boston to 0.54 in the Roxbury ghetto, while assessment ratios on commercial property ranged from 0.59 in Hyde Park to 1.11 in South Boston. This suggests that some Boston homeowners were paying double the tax rate that others paid, while owners of some commercial property were paying at a rate four times that of the most fortunate homeowners.

The final source of discontent with the property tax stems from the belief that it hits the poor harder than the rich. This judgment rests on the assumption that property taxes are borne by homeowners and renters in proportion to their expenditures on housing and on the fact that the poor spend a greater fraction of their incomes on housing than do the rich. Recently some economists have argued that the burden of the property tax, rather than falling on the homeowner or renter, is actually borne by the owners of capital. (See Chapter 14.) This theory implies that the burden of the property tax rises with income because wealthier persons tend to own more capital relative to their incomes than do the poor. It is safe to say that for economists, if not for politicians, the issue of who ultimately pays the property tax is still very much up in the air.

Looking Ahead

The past decade has been a difficult one for school finances, but what of the future? There are several reasons to expect the severity of the fiscal problems of school districts to decrease. In the first place, the growth in school enrollment that choked the system during the 1950s and continued into the 1960s has all but ended. As a result of the fall in the birth rate during the past decade, the number of children aged five to seventeen has already begun to decline, and projections of public school enrollments indicate that starting next year the number of students in public schools should begin to decrease. This drop will reduce the need for more classrooms, books, instructional personnel, and other educational inputs. A second factor that should ease the fiscal plight of school districts is the drastic change that has occurred in the market for teachers. The shortage of the 1960s has become the glut of the 1970s as growing numbers of newly trained teachers continue to swell the ranks of those seeking positions. This excess supply should damp if not eliminate the relative wage increases of instructional personnel. Also, if the general rate of inflation declines, the rates of increase in the prices of the materials, supplies, and capital construction purchased by school districts will slacken.

On the revenue side it is more difficult to see change that will lessen the financial predicaments of school districts. As long as local governments are required to bear the main responsibility for financing education, the shortcomings of the property tax will continue to plague school finance. If, as many analysts have suggested, a greater share of the responsibility for financing education were put at the state and federal levels, the situation would brighten considerably. While state and federal taxes are by no means popular, they are more responsive to economic growth.

Inequality: Disparities among Jurisdictions

The second major concern about elementary and secondary education that has prompted a reevaluation of the federal role is the inequality of the education offered children who live in different locations. While it is difficult to compare the quality of education received in different jurisdictions, it seems reasonable to assume that it is at least roughly related to the amount of resources devoted to it. It is clear that the resources differ immensely, both among and within states.

Disparities in Expenditures

Average per pupil expenditures vary widely among states, as may be seen in column 3 of Table 10-5. New York spends about three times as much per child as does Alabama. Moreover, disparities within states are typically at least as great as disparities among them. (See columns 1 and 2 of Table 10-5.) In most states the highest per pupil expenditure levels are found in a few wealthy suburbs. Central cities tend to spend above the statewide average as well, while suburban areas as a whole generally have expenditure levels slightly below those of the central city. At the bottom of the spectrum are the school districts in nonmetropolitan areas, which spend substantially less per pupil than do those in metropolitan areas.

Sources of Expenditure Disparities

The variation in per pupil expenditures *among* states is related both to differences in the capacity of states (and their constituent localities) to raise money and to their willingness to do so. States with low per capita income tend to have low per pupil expenditures for education, but there is also wide variation among states in the proportion of per-

Table 10-5. Expenditures per Pupil in Ninety-fifth Percentile and Fifth Percentile School Districts and State Averages, by State, 1969–70 School Year
Dollars

State	*Expenditure per pupil*		
	95th percentile district	*5th percentile district*	*State average*
Alabama	520	369	438
Alaska	1,454	868	1,083
Arizona	1,681	552	766
Arkansas	631	324	534
California	1,250	504	922
Colorado	1,394	574	695
Connecticut	1,034	565	882
Delaware	826	661	793
District of Columbia	n.a.	n.a.	977
Florida	881	597	710
Georgia	598	421	600
Hawaii	544	434	851
Idaho	1,197	565	629
Illinois	1,283	595	803
Indiana	716	436	624
Iowa	1,026	652	890
Kansas	1,111	539	721
Kentucky	538	391	612
Louisiana	891	537	620
Maine	784	404	685
Maryland	819	676	882
Massachusetts	1,286	556	753
Michigan	893	539	842
Minnesota	809	503	883
Mississippi	627	346	476
Missouri	848	393	714
Montana	2,544	623	822
Nebraska	1,357	388	527
Nevada	1,612	746	764
New Hampshire	814	373	692
New Jersey	1,112	573	963
New Mexico	962	497	724
New York	1,410	761	1,237
North Carolina	681	492	609
North Dakota	1,100	530	621
Ohio	834	488	680
Oklahoma	1,063	445	540
Oregon	1,499	562	891
Pennsylvania	1,471	687	876
Rhode Island	986	568	904
South Carolina	562	426	555
South Dakota	1,513	422	657
Tennessee	594	376	560
Texas	1,198	426	581
Utah	1,022	534	600
Vermont	947	433	934
Virginia	723	489	691
Washington	1,632	627	743
West Virginia	706	527	626
Wisconsin	968	584	875
Wyoming	3,820	681	810

Source: *Review of Existing State School Finance Programs*, Vol. 2, *Documentation of Disparities in the Financing of Public Elementary and Secondary School Systems—By State*, a Commission Staff Report submitted to the President's Commission on School Finance (1972), pp. 19ff.
n.a. Not applicable.

sonal income devoted to education. At present, federal programs do little to reduce interstate disparities, both because federal funds are relatively small and because (except under Title I of the Elementary and Secondary Education Act) they are not concentrated in low-income areas.

Similarly, the variation *within* states in per pupil spending is related primarily to differences in local capacity and willingness to spend for education. State aid to education is substantial, especially in some states, but it is usually not distributed in a way that does much to offset differences in local fiscal capacity. Since locally raised revenues derive almost exclusively from property taxes, the value of property per pupil may be used as a measure of ability to pay. Within any state there is a tremendous variation in this index of fiscal capacity. For example, the range of per student property values among the school districts of California is $103 to $952,156, or about 1 to 10,000. Extreme cases like these are usually either rural districts with little taxable property or districts with great industrial wealth and only a handful of students. Yet even within a single county without these anomalies the discrepancies are considerable. For example, in Los Angeles County the tax base of Beverly Hills is $50,885 per pupil, while nearby Baldwin Park's is a meager $3,706. In effect, this means that Beverly Hills may tax itself at less than one-fourth the rate of Baldwin Park and still generate more than three times as much revenue per student as the poorer district. Table 10-6, which indicates the relationships among district property wealth, tax rates, and expendi-

Table 10-6. Relation of School District Wealth to Tax Rates, Local Revenue per Pupil, and Total Expenditures per Pupil, 110 Texas School Districts, 1966–67 School Year

Market value of taxable property per pupil (dollars)	Number of school districts	Equalized tax rates per $100 valuation (dollars)	Local revenue per pupil (dollars)	Total expenditure per pupil by local, state, and federal governments (dollars)
Above 100,000	9	0.31	610	856
100,000–50,000	26	0.38	287	610
50,000–30,000	29	0.55	224	529
30,000–10,000	41	0.72	166	546
Below 10,000	5	0.70	63	441

Source: Joel S. Berke, Affidavit, U.S. District Court, Western District of Texas, San Antonio Division, Civil Action 68-175-SA (1971), Tables 2 and 5.

ture patterns for a representative sample of 110 Texas school districts shows what is apparently the typical pattern: wealthier school districts tax themselves at lower rates and still raise more per pupil than do poorer districts, while state and federal aid does little to reduce these local disparities except for the extremes of the distribution.

Local revenues, of course, depend on the willingness as well as the ability to spend on education. Some communities place much greater emphasis on education than do others and are willing to tax themselves more heavily to ensure that their children receive a good education. A community's taste for education may be influenced by its values and the structure of its population. Districts with a large proportion of retired or single voters may put education fairly far down on their lists of desirable local public expenditures as might communities with large parochial school attendance. Willingness to spend on education also depends on the alternative needs for a community's funds. Central cities with pressing problems such as crime, congestion, or poverty may not accord the priority to education that a tranquil middle-class suburb would. The voters of both districts may have identical feelings about education, but they face radically different sets of public expenditure alternatives.

RECENT COURT DECISIONS. The expenditure patterns resulting from the interplay of ability and willingness to pay have led to landmark court decisions in California, Minnesota, Texas, and New Jersey. In each of these states the judges ruled that the existing systems of school finance violated the equal protection clause of the Fourteenth Amendment. The basic line of argument in these decisions was that public education is a "fundamental interest" for which the state has the chief responsibility; as such, access to education should not be conditioned upon local wealth, any more than it should be conditioned on race. Since state aid does little to equalize the disparities arising out of differences in the amounts raised locally, and since these amounts reflect primarily the wealth rather than the willingness of residents to tax themselves for education, it was found that the system of school finance of those states "invidiously discriminates against the poor because it makes the quality of a child's education a function of the wealth of his parents and neighbors."[2] These court decisions, if upheld, could lead to radical changes in the current methods of financ-

2. *Serrano* v. *Priest*, California Supreme Court 938254, L.A. 29820 (1971), p. 1.

ing elementary and secondary education that would greatly reduce the existing expenditure disparities.

COST DIFFERENCES. Expenditure differences, of course, may fail to reflect true differences in resources because a dollar of spending on education may buy different amounts of inputs in different places. There are great variations in the price of land and school construction and in the salary needed to attract teachers of equal quality. For example, the asking wage for teachers with similar training is higher in the industrial Northeast and West than in the Midwest or South, and higher in the central cities than in the suburbs or rural areas. One estimate is that this salary differential is about $4,000 between the Detroit metropolitan area and Michigan's upper peninsula, which would account for a difference of about $160 in per pupil spending. Differences in the cost of living, the level of wages in alternative occupations, the strength of unions, and general working conditions all contribute to determining these disparities in salary levels. Some inner city areas must give teachers "combat pay" to induce them to leave the safety and pleasant surroundings of the suburbs. Rural areas and small towns in the past have held little attraction for college-trained people, and may have to offer "boredom pay" to attract teachers.

Furthermore, in a state such as New Hampshire, resources must be devoted to heating the schools and shoveling snow from the sidewalks—expenses that are minimal in Miami. Inner city schools must spend more to protect themselves. In 1970, Newark spent $2 million, or $25.90 per pupil, to guard its buildings from vandalism. In rural areas or low-density school districts, per pupil transportation costs tend to be higher.

Differences in costs among jurisdictions also reflect differences in their history. School plant operation and maintenance tend to be more expensive in the old decaying schools of the central cities than in the modern, efficiently designed plants found in many new suburbs. Similarly, older communities with stable or shrinking enrollments tend to have higher teacher costs, because salaries rise with the number of years on the job, and the proportion of the teaching force in such communities that has been working in the school system for a long time is higher than in the rapidly expanding districts.

In general, interstate and urban–rural expenditure disparities probably overstate the differences in real resources for education. The gap in educational spending per pupil between the predominantly urban industrial states of the North and the predominantly rural states of the deep South is explained partly by cost differences. On the other hand, a comparison of expenditures probably masks real differences between cities and suburbs within the same region. The high expenditure levels in central cities should be discounted considerably to reflect the greater costs of running a school system in the central city.

DIFFERENCES IN NEED. Equality of real resources per child between two districts, of course, would not necessarily indicate that children in those districts were receiving education of equal quality. One school system might be far more effectively organized than the other, and the needs of the children might be very different. In general, younger children are less expensive to teach than older children, who need more expensive equipment and more highly specialized teachers. Students with severe physical or mental handicaps require more expensive education. Moreover, children from low-income or deprived homes learn less from their families that will help them in school. If the schools are to compensate these children by helping them learn in school what middle class children learn at home, greater resources will clearly be required in districts with high concentrations of deprived children.

Equality: Race and Poverty

Even if a more satisfactory way of financing education were found and disparities among jurisdictions in resources for education were greatly reduced, two big problems would remain for American education: the problems of race and poverty as they relate to the schools. Obviously, these are not the same problem. Schools have never been legally segregated on the basis of income, as they have on the basis of race, though de facto segregation of the poor is widespread. Moreover, members of minority groups are by no means all poor, and a large proportion of the poor are white. Nevertheless, the two problems are related, and they have recently come together in the public mind because the President, among others, has described improving the education of poor children as a major policy alternative to racial integration of the schools by means of busing.

Race, Poverty, and School Performance

It has long been obvious to anyone familiar with the schools that poor children do not do as well in school as children from higher-income families. There are tremendous variations within any income group in school performance, as in other characteristics, and many glaring exceptions—brilliant scholars from poor families and rich children who cannot learn. But, on the average, the children of the poor come to school with fewer skills and more limited vocabularies, make lower grades, and drop out sooner than the children of the affluent. Black, Chicano, Indian, and other minority children—many of whom are poor—do not perform as well on the average as white children in school, and they drop out earlier.

These observations were confirmed and given national publicity by the large-scale Educational Opportunities Survey, on which the Coleman Report of 1966 was based. As may be seen in Table 10-7, the survey found that a child's performance on standardized tests was related both to race and to social class.

Performance in school, in turn, is closely related to a student's chances of finishing high school and getting further education, and to his future income prospects. Hence, if different racial and economic groups are to have equal chances of success in later life, it is important to find out why such large differences in school performance occur and what can be done about them.

Unfortunately, it is very difficult to sort out how much of the lower school performance of minority and poor children is attributable to inferior schools, how much to poorly trained, hostile, or unsympathetic teachers, how much to the damaging psychological effects of racial and economic segregation, past and present, and how much to a

Table 10-7. Grade Level Equivalents Based on Verbal Achievement of Sixth Grade Students, by Social Class and Ethnic Group, 1965–66 School Year

	Social class group[a]		
Ethnic group	Low	Medium	High
Negro	4.1	4.7	5.3
White	5.6	6.5	7.3
Puerto Rican	3.1	3.6	4.6
Mexican	4.1	4.8	5.7
Indian	4.4	5.1	6.0
Oriental	4.7	6.1	7.0

Source: Frederick Mosteller and Daniel P. Moynihan, "A Pathbreaking Report," in Frederick Mosteller and Daniel P. Moynihan (eds.), *On Equality of Educational Opportunity*, Papers Deriving from the Harvard University Faculty Seminar on the Coleman Report (Random House, 1972), p. 23.

a. Social class groups are based on father's and mother's educational level and father's occupational level.

failure of the schools to compensate for the deprivations of the child's home and neighborhood. Moreover, since there has been little sustained or systematic effort to experiment with educational innovations or major increases in educational resources for the poor, it is difficult to say what solutions are possible or what they would cost.

In the mid-1960s, when the United States rediscovered the poor and declared war on poverty, there was considerable faith that compensatory education held the key to breaking the cycle of poverty. Title I of the Elementary and Secondary Education Act (ESEA) of 1965 gave funds (now about $1.6 billion a year) to school districts for special compensatory programs for poor children. Head Start set up preschool programs to give poor children a better start in school.

But compensatory education proved no quick panacea. Funds were spread thin, and results proved disappointing. (For a more detailed evaluation, see pp. 355–58, below.) The lack of demonstrable results made both the administration and the Congress cautious about increasing funds for compensatory programs. It also led some to believe that integration of the schools across racial and economic lines— rather than compensatory education—was the key to better educational performance for the poor and minorities.

Desegregation and the Courts

In 1954, the Supreme Court rejected the "separate but equal" doctrine and ruled that racially segregated schools were inherently unequal and violated the Fourteenth Amendment to the Constitution. The ruling did not rest on findings about children's performance on tests, but mainly on evidence that segregation is psychologically damaging to minority children.

Today, some eighteen years later, the ramifications of this ruling are still making themselves felt. A major debate now rages over how far it is necessary to go in order to wipe out racially segregated schools. What is required in those areas that once maintained officially sanctioned dual school systems? What is required in districts where racial isolation was maintained and perpetuated, not by a dual school system, but by such policies as gerrymandering school attendance zones, selective abandonment of buildings, or school site selection? What is required in areas where school segregation is the product solely of economic forces and housing patterns?

In several recent cases the Supreme Court has ruled that segregation

Table 10-8. Patterns of Public School Segregation by Geographic Area, Fall 1968 and Fall 1971

Numbers in millions

Area and year	Total number of pupils	Negro pupils				
		Total number	Attending predominantly white schools[a]		Attending racially isolated schools[b]	
			Number	Percent	Number	Percent
North and West						
1968	28.6	2.7	0.75	27.6	1.55	57.4
1971	29.3	2.9	0.81	27.8	1.66	57.1
South						
1968	11.0	2.9	0.54	18.4	2.32	78.8
1971	11.6	3.1	1.38	43.9	1.01	32.2
Border states and District of Columbia						
1968	3.7	0.6	0.18	28.4	0.41	63.8
1971	3.8	0.7	0.21	30.5	0.41	60.9

Source: U.S. Department of Health, Education, and Welfare, "HEW News," January 13, 1972, p. 5. Percentages are calculated from data before rounding.
a. White enrollment, 50–99 percent.
b. Minority enrollment, 80–100 percent.

within a school district that is the result of past or present operation of dual school systems is unconstitutional and must be corrected at once. Busing that does not "risk the health of the children or significantly impinge on the educational process"[3] has been sanctioned by the courts as a permissible, and possibly even necessary, tool for removing the vestiges of the dual school system. Other methods of achieving this end include voluntary majority-to-minority transfer programs, pairing and grouping of schools, redrawing school attendance zones, and construction of schools in areas accessible to both blacks and whites.

These rulings have resulted in a dramatic reduction in the proportion of southern blacks attending racially isolated schools. (See Table 10-8.) In some places, the implementation of desegregation has resulted in increased busing, but in many areas students have simply continued to be bused, sometimes for shorter distances than in the past, to integrated rather than segregated schools.

In most areas outside the South, segregation is largely the result of

3. *Swann* v. *Charlotte-Mecklenburg Board of Education*, 402 U.S. 30, 31 (1971).

housing patterns. Whites and blacks live in different sections of school districts or in different school districts altogether. In some instances subtle discriminatory policies of school boards also have fostered segregated schools. The Supreme Court has yet to rule on such a case, involving what is called de facto segregation. Lower courts, however, generally have found that the Fourteenth Amendment has been violated if the deliberate policies of public officials have perpetuated racial isolation. In such cases the remedies can be financially and administratively more difficult to achieve than is true in the South. One reason for this is that, unlike the South, which has large consolidated county school systems, the school districts of the rest of the nation tend to be fragmented subcounty units. Generally a smaller fraction of their students are bused, which means that integration within districts could result in considerably increased expenditures for transportation.

Attempts to achieve racial balance are further constrained by the fact that white public school children are concentrated in suburban school districts, while the minority children are concentrated in the central city. Unless school district lines are radically changed, there may be little potential for integration. (See Table 10-9.) While there are court suits pending in Detroit, Indianapolis, and Hartford that request a merging of the central city and suburban school districts to permit genuine integration, only in Richmond, Virginia, has such a case been decided. In this instance, the judge ordered that the predominantly black central city school system be merged with the primarily white systems in the surrounding two counties. Per pupil expenditures would be equalized, which would help the rural-suburban counties that now spend less than Richmond, and the proportion of children being bused would increase from about 65 percent to 75 percent. While many of the factors in the case were peculiar to the circumstances in Virginia, if similar rulings were made for all of the metropolitan areas in which the races are isolated in separate school districts, there would be increases in two-way busing and reductions in the expenditure disparities that now exist.

The current situation can only be characterized as emotional, complicated, and uncertain. The uncertainty relates not only to what the courts will ultimately decide is in accord with constitutional guarantees, but to what would be the best way to organize the schools to improve academic performance and racial tolerance.

Table 10-9. Racial and Ethnic Composition of School Districts, Selected Large Cities and Surrounding Counties, Fall 1968

City and surrounding counties	Total public school enrollment	Percentage white	Percentage minority[a]
New York City	1,063,787	43.9	56.1
Nassau County	331,349	93.5	6.5
Westchester County	169,081	85.4	14.6
Chicago	582,274	37.7	62.3
Cook County[b]	397,842	92.3	7.7
Detroit	296,097	39.3	60.7
Wayne County[b]	276,495	92.3	7.7
San Francisco	94,154	41.2	58.8
San Mateo County	118,572	82.7	17.3
Marin County	40,304	94.6	5.4
Oakland	64,102	30.9	69.1
Alameda County[b]	164,473	79.8	20.2
Baltimore	192,171	34.9	65.1
Baltimore County[b]	123,717	96.5	3.5
Anne Arundel County	65,745	85.9	13.1
District of Columbia	148,725	5.6	94.4
Prince Georges County, Maryland	146,976	84.8	15.2
Montgomery County, Maryland	121,458	93.6	6.4
Arlington County, Virginia	25,934	85.9	14.1
Cleveland	156,054	42.5	57.5
Cuyahoga County[b]	182,184	94.6	5.4
St. Louis	115,582	36.2	63.8
St. Louis County[b]	191,953	94.9	5.1

Source: Department of Health, Education, and Welfare, Office for Civil Rights, *Directory of Public Elementary and Secondary Schools in Selected Districts: Enrollment and Staff by Racial/Ethnic Group, Fall 1968,* OCR-101-70 (1970).

a. Includes American Indians, blacks, Orientals, and Spanish surnamed individuals.
b. Does not include central city.

Unfortunate Facts and Conflicting Objectives

To deal with the three major problems just discussed calls for (1) easing the fiscal problem of education by reducing reliance on the property tax, (2) equalizing resources for education among jurisdictions, and (3) improving educational opportunities for minorities and the poor.

Some unfortunate circumstances make it hard to achieve these goals. First, reliance on the property tax is uneven, but it is generally higher in high-spending districts. It follows that efforts to relieve the property tax necessarily conflict with the objectives of equalizing resources among jurisdictions.

Second, the poor and minority groups are heavily concentrated in central cities and in rural areas, and generally do not live in the more affluent suburbs surrounding metropolitan areas. Central cities generally spend relatively high amounts per child for education, though their costs are higher and there is more competition for their limited tax resources. It follows that equalizing expenditures for education among jurisdictions may make it more difficult to improve the education of low-income and minority groups in the city.

The concentration of the poor and minorities in central cities also makes it more difficult and expensive to improve the quality of their education either by busing or by other means. If cities were ordered to consolidate with suburbs, to balance the schools racially, and to equalize spending over the whole metropolitan area, a major source of spending disparities would be removed. But in many urban areas the amount of pupil transportation needed to achieve racial balance would be large. Some people fear that if massive two-way busing were ordered by the courts, many families would opt out of public schools. This would surely have some impact on the willingness of communities to provide adequate financing for public education. On the other hand, one-way busing (out of "low-quality" schools), which seems to be more acceptable to the white population, could give rise to substantial needs for new school construction, since the capacity of "high-quality" schools would not be adequate to absorb the influx.

Alternative Solutions to the Fiscal Problem

The fiscal problem of elementary and secondary education results largely from heavy use of the unpopular and relatively unresponsive local property tax to finance the nation's schools. Given this situation, there would seem to be two possible solutions: (1) reform the property tax to make it more acceptable to taxpayers or (2) find some other source of funding for the schools.

Reforming the Property Tax

The reform approach would improve administration of the tax through training and certification of assessors, annual reassessment, and improved notification and appeals systems. In addition, the special problems of property taxpayers who are elderly and have low incomes could be addressed by allowing them relief from excessive tax burdens. Unequal assessments within a taxing jurisdiction could be discouraged by mandatory public disclosure requirements. Some areas have already taken steps to reform the property tax and to relieve the burden on elderly taxpayers with low incomes.

Federal legislation to improve property tax administration and relieve elderly taxpayers was proposed by Senator Edmund S. Muskie in January 1972. Muskie's proposal calls for reforms in the administration of the property tax and for a housing security system whereby $1 billion would be distributed to the states in proportion to the number of people over sixty-five years old living in each state. Funds would be used to make "direct housing assistance payments to all citizens over 65 who on the basis of their total financial resources . . . could not afford the cost of minimum decent housing in their area."[4] Thus, funds would be limited to relatively poor elderly families (although the funds would be distributed among states without regard to need). The proposed reform would ease the fiscal problems of the schools to the extent that the elderly poor are now generating the pressures against property tax increases.

State Financing of Schools

An alternative to reforming the local property tax would be to stop using it for schools and instead have the states take over the burden of financing elementary and secondary education. States currently vary tremendously in the extent to which they rely on the local property tax to support education. The ACIR, which favors a state takeover of education finance, has estimated what it would cost for each state to assume 90 percent of school costs by simply replacing local expenditures with state funds with no attempt to reduce disparities among localities. (See Table 10-10.) In states where the local share is small, little additional state financing would be necessary. (In Hawaii, the state already provides more than 90 percent of the money.) In others, however, such as New Jersey, New Hampshire, and South Dakota, considerable state money would be required to replace the local property tax even if the state did nothing to reduce differences in local spending. It is hardly realistic, however, especially in view of recent court cases, to

4. "Muskie Proposes New Housing Security System," press release from office of Edmund S. Muskie, Jan. 31, 1972.

Table 10-10. Additional Revenue Required for State to Assume 90 Percent of Public School Financing, Selected States, 1969–70 School Year

	Additional state revenue required		
State	Amount (millions of dollars)	Per capita (dollars)	As percentage of total state taxes
States requiring high additional proportion of state revenue			
South Dakota	81.9	123	72.7
New Hampshire	65.8	91	69.4
Nebraska	152.8	104	58.5
Oregon	244.2	118	56.7
New Jersey	750.3	106	56.3
Ohio	861.3	82	50.1
States requiring low additional proportion of state revenue			
North Carolina	23.0	5	1.9
Mississippi	18.0	8	3.7
New Mexico	11.1	11	4.1
Alabama	43.0	12	6.5
Delaware	13.0	24	6.6
Florida	114.0	17	8.0

Sources: Additional revenue, Advisory Commission on Intergovernmental Relations, *State-Local Revenue Systems and Educational Finance* (ACIR, 1971), Table 18; population data, U.S. Bureau of the Census, *Statistical Abstract of the United States, 1971*, p. 14; state taxes, Bureau of the Census, *State Government Finances in 1970*, GF70 No. 3 (1971), p. 19.

assume that states could take over school finance without equalizing local expenditures. Nor is it politically realistic to suppose that equalization could be carried out by cutting school expenditures in districts that now spend large amounts per child. The only feasible approach to reducing differences in local spending for education would be for states to spend the additional sums necessary to raise expenditure levels in all communities closer to the levels of those that spend the most. This would require substantially more money than would be necessary simply to replace local financing.

Indeed, in most states, a substantial new revenue source would probably be required. The Fleischmann Commission in its report for New York State advocated a statewide property tax in its state assumption proposal.[5] Similarly, the ACIR has advocated such a tax, at least on a provisional basis. Large new state taxes, however, are unlikely to prove more popular or politically acceptable than the local property tax. Hence, advocates of local property tax relief and state

5. See "A Plan to Narrow that Dollar Gap," *New York Times*, Oct. 24, 1971.

education funding have turned to the federal treasury as the remaining source of new funds for school finance.

The Administration Proposal

In his State of the Union Message in January 1972, the President announced that he was considering a "revolutionary" proposal to eliminate the local residential property tax as a source of funds for schools. In a subsequent letter to the ACIR, the President asked the commission to study a proposal for a new federal value added tax (VAT). In a later elaboration the administration suggested a VAT to yield about $12 billion to $13 billion for the support of schools, to be distributed to states that agreed to eliminate all residential property taxes, both local and state, used to support the public schools. Property taxes on commercial and industrial property for supporting education would not be permitted at the local level, but it is assumed that states would levy a uniform tax on such property.

As is shown in Table 10-11, residential property taxes used to support schools amounted to about $10.2 billion in 1970. If one assumes that such taxes have grown at the same rate as local school revenues over the past two years, their 1972 level would be about $12 billion. Thus, the President is proposing a federal VAT that would be just about enough to offset the aggregate revenue lost nationally from the abandonment of residential property taxes used for education. Such a plan involves grave difficulties relating both to the distribution of funds *among* states and to their distribution *within* states.

DISTRIBUTION AMONG STATES. As has been seen above, states differ greatly in the extent to which they rely on the residential property tax to finance schools. Hence, if the federal government were simply to replace the amount each state now raises for schools through the residential property tax, it would be forced to make grants of very different amounts per pupil to various states. As is seen from column 2 of Table 10-11, New Jersey would get $445 per pupil, Alabama $32, and Hawaii nothing. It is inconceivable that the Congress would accept a program with such wide and erratic disparities, whose main effect would be to reward states for having been heavy users of the property tax in the past.

The President, of course, did not suggest such a formula for distribution of the VAT. His proposal to the ACIR suggested, by way of example, that federal VAT funds be distributed among the states on a matching basis—$1 of federal aid for each $2 of state expenditure—

Table 10-11. Yield on Residential Property Taxes for Education Compared to Federal Matching Grants, by State, 1970

State	Residential property tax for education		Federal matching grants of $1 for each $2 of state expenditure		Change required in state expenditures per pupil under matching grants to maintain same expenditure level (dollars)
	Total (millions of dollars)	Per pupil (dollars)	Total (millions of dollars)	Per pupil (dollars)	
Alabama	25	32	105	135	−103
Alaska	3	54	17	300	−246
Arizona	98	246	104	260	−14
Arkansas	35	87	65	159	−72
California	1,513	323	1,304	278	45
Colorado	130	259	113	226	33
Connecticut	238	359	170	257	102
Delaware	15	128	40	340	−212
District of Columbia	24	159	61	409	−250
Florida	205	156	320	243	−87
Georgia	161	158	215	210	−52
Hawaii	...	...	55	309	−309
Idaho	13	79	29	171	−92
Illinois	663	319	671	323	−4
Indiana	341	307	314	283	24
Iowa	120	184	155	237	−53
Kansas	102	205	129	260	−55
Kentucky	79	122	134	207	−85
Louisiana	50	64	137	177	−113
Maine	41	170	40	165	5
Maryland	259	300	222	257	43
Massachusetts	386	339	252	221	118
Michigan	587	273	576	268	5
Minnesota	203	206	280	283	−77
Mississippi	24	45	72	138	−93
Missouri	229	255	217	242	13
Montana	29	181	36	219	−38
Nebraska	64	196	70	213	−17
Nevada	20	173	25	219	−46
New Hampshire	58	386	31	206	180
New Jersey	655	445	448	305	140
New Mexico	17	62	52	189	−127
New York	1,130	337	1,352	403	−66
North Carolina	52	47	205	186	−139
North Dakota	12	81	25	171	−90
Ohio	774	323	569	237	86
Oklahoma	88	157	100	178	−21
Oregon	143	309	121	263	46
Pennsylvania	522	228	612	267	−39
Rhode Island	51	290	42	237	53
South Carolina	43	71	116	194	−123
South Dakota	24	146	35	209	−63
Tennessee	82	97	130	156	−59
Texas	247	102	474	196	−94
Utah	41	141	59	206	−65
Vermont	15	130	21	184	−54
Virginia	146	147	175	176	−29
Washington	151	191	229	288	−97
West Virginia	42	112	69	186	−74
Wisconsin	272	293	243	261	32
Wyoming	22	262	20	232	30
U.S. total	10,244	235	11,056	254	−19

Sources: Residential property tax for education was calculated by multiplying property tax for schools (Advisory Commission on Intergovernmental Relations, *State-Local Revenue Systems and Educational Finance*, Table 23) by the percent of property that is residential nonfarm (Bureau of the Census, *Census of Governments, 1967*, Vol. 2, *Taxable Property Values* [1968], Table 5); school enrollment data are from *Review of Existing State School Finance Programs*, Vol. 2, Report submitted to the President's Commission on School Finance: federal matching grant = ⅓ × (total property tax for education from ACIR, *State-Local Revenue Systems...*, Table 23, + school revenue from state sources, from National Education Association, *Estimates of School Statistics, 1970–71*, Research Report 1970-R15 [NEA, 1970], p. 34); col. 5 = col. 2 − col. 4.

up to a maximum per pupil grant of $400. Such a formula would have distributed about $11 billion to the states in 1970, or, allowing for growth, roughly the same amount the President suggests raising from the VAT. As may be seen in columns 3 and 4 of Table 10-11, per student grants resulting from this matching formula would vary considerably among states, although not as much as grants based strictly on present residential property taxes.

Two features of such a matching formula should be noted, however. First, distributing funds in this way would accentuate existing disparities in spending levels among states. New York would get more than twice as much per child as Tennessee. Second, although the total amount distributed would be as much as was collected in residential property tax for schools, not all states would get enough to provide total relief from the property tax without raising state taxes. States such as North Carolina, Alabama, South Carolina, and Hawaii would receive more than enough from the VAT fund to replace their low school property taxes, while high property tax states such as New Hampshire, New Jersey, and California would receive insufficient VAT funds to replace the yield on their outlawed residential property tax. Thus, the matching formula would force some states not only to replace residential property tax losses but also to raise new revenues at the state level to replace the excess of residential property taxes over the VAT receipts. Indeed, distribution of the VAT funds on *any* basis other than strict replacement of current property tax yields would require either that some states take on a substantial new financial burden or that the VAT be adjusted to yield substantially more revenues than the property tax it is replacing. Thus a matching formula of the type suggested would raise both an equity problem (because disparities among the states would be accentuated) and a financing problem (because some states would have to increase taxes to replace lost revenues).

DISTRIBUTION WITHIN STATES. An equally serious problem arises when one considers how states would distribute the money within their borders, because reliance on residential property taxes to finance schools varies greatly within states as well as among them. Table 10-12 shows an estimate of the per capita amount of residential property taxes used to support schools in several major cities and surrounding suburban counties in 1966–67. Even a state like New York, which would receive enough VAT funds to replace in the aggregate the resi-

Table 10-12. Revenue Available for Public Education from the Residential Property Tax and from a 2.5 Percent Value Added Tax, and the Corresponding Value Added Tax Burden, Selected Areas, 1966–67 School Year

Dollars per capita

City and surrounding area	Estimated residential property tax revenue used for education	Equal per pupil distribution of 2.5 percent value added tax revenue[a]	Estimated value added tax burden
New York City	29[b]	31	55
Nassau County	112	52	70
Suffolk County	86	57	51
Westchester County	83	42	77
Philadelphia	29	31	47
Bucks County	65	43	52
Chester County	47	52	55
Delaware County	52	35	59
Detroit	29	42	57
Wayne County (except Detroit)	42	56	62
Macomb County	43	57	54
Oakland County	60	60	67
Chicago	37	36	58
Cook County (except Chicago)	61	50	72
Du Page County	103	59	69
Lake County	79	54	66
St. Louis	36	39	48
St. Louis County	79	39	67
Denver	58	43	55
Adams County	36	73	41
Arapahoe County	78	73	54
Boulder County	63	61	49
San Francisco	40	35	63
Contra Costa County	81	69	54
San Mateo County	116	59	64
New Orleans	15	38	45
Jefferson Parish	5	41	48
St. Bernard Parish	16[c]	59	42

Sources: Residential property tax was calculated by multiplying property tax revenue of school districts (Bureau of the Census, *Census of Governments, 1967*, Vol. 5, *Local Government in Metropolitan Areas* [1969], Table 13, and [for Chicago and Detroit] Vol. 4, No. 1, *Finances of School Districts* [1969], Table 8) by percent of property that is residential nonfarm (*Census of Governments, 1967*, Vol. 2, *Taxable Property Values*, Table 19). Population, public school enrollment, and personal disposable income are from U.S. Office of Education, Office of Program Planning and Evaluation, unpublished tabulations. The 2.5 percent value added tax burden was computed at 1.87 percent of personal disposable income to account for the exclusion of housing expenditures and savings from the VAT base.

a. Estimated as $232 per public school enrollee.
b. Total residential property tax per capita × (education expenditures/total expenditures).
c. State average was used for percent of property that is residential.

dential property taxes used for schools, would have to decide what to do about the enormous property tax reductions in wealthy suburban Nassau County ($112 per capita in 1966–67) and the small losses of New York City (only $29 per capita). New York State could in principle simply replace Nassau's tax loss and give much less to New York City. But it is hard to imagine a state allocating funds to preserve current spending disparities associated with wealth—for that is what replacement of school tax losses means—when all the recent court decisions call for the elimination of wealth-related expenditure differences. Alternatively, New York State could allocate receipts from a federal VAT on an equal per pupil basis to all counties. However, as may be seen by comparing columns 1 and 2 of Table 10-12, such a distribution would prove inadequate to replace the residential property tax for schools in the high-tax suburban counties. So under equal per pupil allocations, suburban school districts in Nassau County in New York, Bucks County in Pennsylvania, and San Mateo County in California would have to cut back school spending, even if their states as a whole received enough VAT funds to replace the statewide total of residential property taxes used to support the schools. Such cutbacks are not likely to be politically feasible. Hence, state governments would have to face up to the problem not only of "replacing" forgone residential property taxes, but of raising additional money to increase expenditures in low spending districts toward the level of the higher ones. These state-level financing requirements would be in addition to the burden of the VAT, an estimate of which is shown in the last column of Table 10-12. Of course, property taxes would be reduced.

In summary, a federal VAT of about $12 billion in 1972 would be enough to replace residential property taxes for school support only in the sense that the total sum indeed covers the amount of such taxes levied across the nation. Any realistic formula for distributing such funds—for example, the matching formula used as an illustration by the administration—would leave some states with more than enough to replace residential school taxes and other states with too little. Even states that got enough VAT money to replace the statewide total of residential property taxes for schools would not be able to "replace" them with the federal funds in each district without running afoul of the courts and political opposition. Therefore, in the end, a much larger total of federal or state-level revenues would be required to replace the present aggregate amount of local residential property taxes for schools. The excess would depend on the degree to which states attempted to equalize intrastate differences in spending. Property tax relief itself would do nothing to reduce expenditure disparities either within or among states, although it might provide an opportunity for enactment of a new and more equalizing way of financing education if enough additional funds could be found.

Inequality among Jurisdictions: Alternative Solutions

As has been seen, there are currently large disparities in per pupil expenditures for education, both within and among states. These disparities create a prima facie case that educational opportunities for students in various jurisdictions are unequal, although it is certainly not clear that equal expenditures per pupil would mean equal educational opportunity. In the first place, costs differ, so it is more justifiable to equalize real resources than expenditures. Unfortunately, however, valid cost comparisons are hard to make, and hence it is much easier to equalize expenditures. Second, school districts with high concentrations of poor children need more resources than districts with mostly middle-class children if equal opportunity is to be provided. If one carried this approach to its logical conclusion, one would try to distribute resources so as to equalize the *results* of education (for groups of students, not individuals) rather than the inputs. At present, however, little is known about the relationship between inputs and results or how one would go about ensuring this kind of equality. It therefore seems reasonable to concentrate mainly on ways of reducing disparities in expenditures, with adjustments to allow for the fact that some districts have higher costs or greater needs.

Whether one is attempting to equalize within or among states (or both), at least three approaches are possible:

1. *Setting a minimum level.* This approach assumes that equality of opportunity means that no child is to be denied a minimum standard of education and that the role of the central government is to ensure for all children at least the minimum by putting a floor under educational spending. If individual jurisdictions exceed the minimum, that is their business.

2. *Subsidies to offset differences in wealth or income.* This approach is based on the premise that it is undesirable to allow disparities in education spending to arise from the fact that some jurisdictions have

fewer taxable resources than others and therefore find it more painful to raise money for education. It holds that disparities should arise only out of differential willingness of communities to tax themselves for education, not out of differences in their capacity to raise money. Under this approach, therefore, the central government would try to offset (or at least reduce) the effect of differential resources by providing a larger subsidy to districts with low wealth and income than to those with high wealth or income. In effect, this approach would operate by changing the price of education facing districts with differential resources. Because they would get a larger subsidy from the central government, poorer districts could undertake a given amount of education spending without taxing themselves at a higher rate than richer districts.

3. *Full equalization.* Either a state or the federal government might decide that educational opportunities are too important to be left to the judgment of lower levels of government and that equality of opportunity means that every child should be treated equally regardless of where he lives. This approach would still leave room for argument about the extent to which additional resources should be devoted to handicapped or disadvantaged children, but it would not allow variations attributable either to local wealth or to local preference for education.

Interstate Equalization

Over the years a great many proposals have been made for federal grants to the states for education ("general aid to education") that would reduce disparities among the states in spending for education. Some have taken the minimum guarantee approach, putting a federal floor under state spending for education. For example, the federal government could provide enough money to each state to bring that state's spending up to a certain minimum level, say, the current median spending level for all states. Alternatively, the federal government could provide a flat grant per student—say, $500 per pupil—and allow the states to spend whatever they wanted over that amount. The cost of such a proposal would be substantial, about $23 billion annually. The minimum level approach would only reduce disparities at the low end of the education spending scale. Disparities among states whose spending was already above the minimum would remain.

An alternative approach to interstate equalization would be for the federal government to give to the states grants that would pay a larger share of the education expenditures of poor states than of rich states. This could be accomplished by having the federal government match state spending for education but varying the matching ratio in accordance with personal income per pupil, or some other measure of fiscal capacity. The effect would be to reduce the cost of raising education funds to all states, but to reduce it more for poor states than for rich states, with "poor" and "rich" defined in terms of personal income per student in each state. Two examples of such an approach are shown in Table 10-13. The first is a variable matching formula designed to offset entirely the effect of differences in state capacity measured by personal income per student. Under this formula, each

Table 10-13. Effect of Variable Matching Formula on Public School Expenditures, Selected States, 1969–70 School Year

	Full offsetting formula[a]		Partial offsetting formula[b]		
State	*Federal grant per student (dollars)*	*Grant as percentage of state and local spending*	*Federal grant per student (dollars)*	*Grant as percentage of state and local spending*	*State personal income per student (dollars)*
High spending states					
New York	0	*0*	143	*12.0*	25,976
Connecticut	111	*11.4*	135	*13.9*	23,166
Vermont	726	*77.1*	236	*25.1*	14,565
New Jersey	139	*14.8*	136	*14.5*	22,470
Wisconsin	411	*48.5*	172	*20.3*	17,432
Iowa	532	*63.3*	192	*22.8*	15,806
Low spending states					
Alabama	467	*119.4*	126	*32.2*	11,731
Mississippi	624	*157.9*	153	*38.9*	9,977
Arkansas	521	*116.2*	142	*31.8*	11,983
Texas	355	*72.9*	119	*24.4*	14,988
North Carolina	448	*90.9*	135	*27.5*	13,610
Oklahoma	429	*86.1*	133	*26.7*	13,948
U.S. average	306	*42.6*	137	*19.1*	17,615

Source: National Education Association, *Rankings of the States, 1971*, Tables 15, 56, 89, 108.

a. Grant = state and local spending for education × ([1.47/state's relative fiscal capacity] − 1), where 1.47 is the highest relative fiscal capacity of any state (calculated by dividing the personal income per pupil in each state by the overall national average).

b. Grant = state and local spending for education × ([0.25/state's relative fiscal capacity] − 0.05). This formula is taken from Russell B. Vlaanderen and Erick L. Lindman, *Intergovernmental Relations and the Governance of Education*, A Report to the President's Commission on School Finance (Denver: Education Commission of the States, 1971), App. C, p. 1.

state would be allowed to spend for education as if it were as wealthy as New York State—the state with the highest income per student. The federal grants in this approach would supplement each state's own tax capacity to bring it up to the New York level. New York itself would receive no grants at all, since its own taxing capacity would be used as the standard, while Mississippi, a low-capacity, high-effort state, would get federal grants in excess of its current spending levels. The data in the table are based on the assumption that each state would continue to spend as much from its own funds as it did in 1969–70. Under these circumstances, the federal cost of such an equalizing program would be $306 per student, or about $14 billion.

The second is a partially offsetting formula under which the federal government would match 20 percent of state and local spending in the average state, less (12 percent) in the state with the highest income per pupil, and more (39 percent) in the poorest state. While this formula would reduce the differences among states in tax effort required to achieve any given spending level, it still would allow New York to spend more than other states that exert the same tax effort. The federal cost of such a program would be less than $6 billion—again assuming that states and localities maintain their own spending at the 1969–70 level.

Finally, the federal government might undertake full equalization of state spending for education by providing enough funds to bring each state's spending up to, say, the New York state level. This would cost about $25 billion if the federal government simply handed out enough funds to make up the difference between what each state is now spending and the New York level. Alternatively, states might be required to maintain a common level of effort—perhaps to keep their education spending at 4.8 percent of their personal income (the current national average). The federal government would then add the amount required to reach the New York level. This alternative would cost only slightly less—about $23 billion in federal funds.

None of these federal-to-state grant plans, however, could be said to equalize opportunity for education unless it also addressed the more difficult problem of intrastate disparities.

Equalizing within the States

Intrastate disparities in spending for education have been drawn to the public's attention by recent court rulings in several states. The courts have not specified, however, exactly how the states should go about reforming education finance. They have simply said that present systems are unconstitutional because they allow large disparities in expenditures on education that seem to be related primarily to local wealth. The courts have left it to the states to devise better systems; none of the three approaches listed above—minimum level, wealth-offsetting, or full equalization—has been either specified or rejected.

Many state aid-to-education programs already undertake to provide a minimum guaranteed expenditure per pupil in each district, but in general the minimum is very low, and local add-ons are relatively large, with the result that substantial spending differences exist between wealthy and less wealthy districts. If states are to retain the minimum-level approach to equalization without running afoul of the courts, they will presumably have to raise the minimum expenditure and find a way of limiting local add-ons so that major disparities among districts do not result. Three ways of limiting local add-ons are to make the minimum level so high that no district wants to add to it, to put a ceiling on local expenditures for education, or to make wealthy districts pay more for each supplementary dollar of school expenditure than poor districts.

If states take the minimum-level approach to equalization, they will probably be forced by political pressure to raise the minimum close to the level of the highest-spending districts in the state ("leveling up"). The alternative—choosing a lower minimum and forcing high-spending districts to cut back so as not to be too far out of line—hardly seems feasible. It follows that this approach would certainly be expensive. Many states would probably choose to impose mandatory property tax rates on communities, or institute state-level property taxes as well as expand existing state income and sales taxes. In some states, where the cost of leveling up is a high fraction of current expenditures, all three might be necessary. An illustration of what such an equalization program might entail is given in Table 10-14, which shows the costs of raising all districts in each state to the spending level currently enjoyed by the ninetieth percentile student in each state. (Only 10 percent of the students would be receiving higher levels of expenditure than the minimum.) If all states undertook such a program, the aggregate extra cost to education budgets in the whole nation would have been on the order of $7 billion in 1970. This sum has probably grown to between $8 billion and $9 billion in 1972. Equalization to the eightieth, seventieth, and fiftieth percentile levels would cost approximately $5.3 billion, $3.9 billion, and $2.4 billion, respectively, in 1972.

Table 10-14. Cost of Equalizing School Expenditures to the Ninetieth Pupil Percentile, by State, 1969–70 School Year

State	Total cost (millions of dollars)	Cost per pupil (dollars)	Percentage of 1970 state taxes
Alabama	44.2	56.88	6.7
Alaska	11.3	197.75	13.2
Arizona	96.7	242.18	20.4
Arkansas	40.9	100.84	11.6
California	828.1	176.83	15.1
Colorado	72.0	143.89	15.3
Connecticut	141.3	213.42	19.0
Delaware	34.8	295.89	17.8
Florida	132.1	100.63	9.3
Georgia	177.1	173.73	18.8
Hawaii	9.6	53.32	2.8
Idaho	36.5	213.55	23.4
Illinois	457.0	220.10	15.9
Indiana	129.2	116.34	12.9
Iowa	93.9	143.84	14.9
Kansas	76.1	152.58	17.7
Kentucky	63.1	97.38	9.0
Louisiana	61.1	78.79	7.3
Maine	26.2	107.79	12.6
Maryland	190.8	221.32	17.6
Massachusetts	259.1	228.01	18.6
Michigan	364.1	169.29	15.5
Minnesota	120.7	122.12	11.8
Mississippi	45.7	87.55	9.4
Missouri	125.8	139.92	15.3
Montana	68.5	421.69	53.2
Nebraska	54.8	166.75	21.0
Nevada	9.1	79.91	6.1
New Hampshire	19.6	131.32	20.7
New Jersey	317.7	216.08	23.8
New Mexico	27.3	99.80	10.0
New York	610.2	181.89	10.0
North Carolina	95.0	86.03	8.0
North Dakota	19.5	133.66	16.0
Ohio	518.9	216.33	30.5
Oklahoma	61.5	109.77	12.2
Oregon	62.7	135.82	14.6
Pennsylvania	504.3	220.26	18.2
Rhode Island	49.5	278.61	21.6
South Carolina	32.3	53.84	5.9
South Dakota	22.8	137.20	20.2
Tennessee	99.5	119.02	14.5
Texas	292.7	120.71	14.8
Utah	14.5	50.45	5.8
Vermont	24.1	208.14	17.8
Virginia	145.1	145.74	15.2
Washington	121.2	152.92	11.8
West Virginia	34.1	91.60	8.9
Wisconsin	101.6	109.22	7.6
Wyoming	29.1	340.65	34.4
All states, total	6,973.0	159.96	14.5

Sources: Cost and enrollment data, *Review of Existing State School Finance Programs*, Vol. 2, Report submitted to the President's Commission on School Finance, pp. 22ff (cost data include an estimate of the costs associated with the lowest 5 percent of students); state tax data, U.S. Bureau of the Census, *State Government Finances in 1970*, GF70 No. 3 (1971), p. 19.

An alternative approach to intrastate equalization would seek to eliminate entirely the influence of local wealth on education spending in the same way that the full offsetting formula corrects for interstate income differences. Variations in expenditures would arise only because of differences in local preferences for education. This approach —often called "power equalizing"—would work as follows:

1. All districts in a state would be assigned the same hypothetical tax base per pupil—say, $10,000 of taxable property per pupil— regardless of their actual tax base.

2. Each district could decide what level of spending per child it wanted and set its tax rate accordingly. A district that wanted to spend $1,200 per child would set a 12 percent tax rate, and one that wanted to spend $500 would set a tax rate of 5 percent.

3. Each district's chosen rate would then be applied to its *actual* tax base. All taxes collected would be paid into a state fund, from which payments would be made to each district to cover its chosen level of expenditures per child. High-wealth districts would end up making net contributions to the fund. For example, if a rich suburb wanted to spend $1,200 per child, it would have to set a tax rate of 12 percent. However, 12 percent applied to its actual tax base of, say, $50,000 per student would yield $6,000 per school child. The excess of the amount raised over the amount the rich district spends would be its net contribution to the state fund to be used to supplement revenues in low-wealth districts. Similarly, if a low-wealth ($4,000 of property value per student) area were to choose a 10 percent tax rate, it would be entitled to spend $1,000 per student. The local base would yield only $400 per student (10 percent tax on $4,000); thus, the state would transfer $600 per student from the state fund, which would have been built up by the contributions of the surplus districts.

The effect of "power equalizing" is to change the "price" of education facing a locality. If a wealthy locality wanted a $1,200-per-pupil school system, it would have to raise considerably more than $1,200 per pupil to get it. If a poor district wanted the same spending level, it could have it without having to contribute $1,200 per pupil from its more limited resources.

Whether the state fund would break even or not would depend on the level at which the hypothetical common tax base was set. If it were set low, there would be plenty of money coming in from wealthy districts to cover the cost of net payments to poor districts. If it were set high, which seems the most politically feasible approach, new state-level funds would be required to supplement the insufficient property tax yields in low-wealth districts. How much would have to be added at the state level would depend on how strongly the low-wealth districts responded to the reduced costs of education.

"Power equalizing" is appealing in that it would effectively eliminate local wealth as a factor in determining the amount spent, and this is what the courts seem to be calling for. It would also retain the maximum amount of local choice. Disparities in educational expenditures would spring from differences in tax effort, not differences in wealth. By itself, however, it would not reduce the reliance of education finance on the property tax. Moreover, no one can predict by exactly how much "power equalizing" would reduce existing disparities in spending on education. Would cheap education induce low-wealth communities to spend a lot more while high prices drove down spending in high wealth districts? If so, would high-income residents of high-wealth districts shift their children to private schools? Or is the preference for education in some high-wealth communities so strong that they would continue to have the best public schools, while the low-wealth districts chose less education for their children? Some districts—perhaps those with sizable elderly populations—might attach a low priority to education and might keep their spending levels very low, while others spent far more. It would, however, be possible to put a floor under education spending, thus combining the minimum-level and power-equalizing approaches.

A third approach to equalization would be for the state to assume full responsibility for education on the grounds that, since local communities are unable to provide equal education, it is the state's responsibility to assume all the costs of education and distribute funds equally. No local add-on would be permitted. Adherents to this view strongly urge that education be treated differently from cabbages and cars, about which individual choice may be appropriate, and be considered more like voting—a basic right.

Assumption by the states of full responsibility for education would still leave open some choices, but they would be exercised at the state level. One set of choices is whether to equalize spending per pupil throughout a state or to try to adjust expenditures for differences among school districts in the cost of education. Variations in cost among districts due to differences in teacher salaries would probably be reduced by full state assumption, since statewide collective bargaining would probably become commonplace and would tend to raise salaries where they are currently low. Another set of choices involves the question whether need, as determined at the state level, should be a factor in the distribution of funds. The state could determine, for example, where the educationally disadvantaged students are enrolled and allocate extra amounts to their districts. The President's Commission on School Finance recommended that both factors—cost differences and need differences—be a part of any state's formula for distributing funds to school districts.

Another set of choices has to do with how much control should be left in local hands. Fully state-financed education would imply that a local school district has no power to set its expenditure level. This would mean an obvious erosion of local control of education. However, most advocates of this approach envision a considerable role for local school boards in hiring and firing, establishing curricula, choosing textbooks, and other purely educational matters.

The problem of equalizing expenditures in all school districts is similar to that of finding an acceptable minimum level of state guarantee. It is unlikely that political forces would allow a state to equalize much below the ninetieth-percentile student. Thus, realistically, the $8 billion to $9 billion that would be required in 1972 to raise all students to the ninetieth percentile is a minimum budget for state assumption. This sum might be reduced if states adjusted for cost-of-education differences (and thus did not have to raise every district to the ninetieth percentile); but adjustments for educational need, if realistically funded, would undoubtedly raise the total required.

Race and Poverty: Alternative Solutions

There are currently three general approaches to the problem of improving education for racial minorities and the poor: compensatory education, integration of the schools, and community control. It is probably a mistake to regard these approaches as alternatives, since all three may be necessary; but each has its strong proponents and opponents.

Compensatory Education

The case for compensatory education is based on the fact that children from deprived homes get less intellectual stimulation and motivation at home, so they need more help in school if they are to have educational opportunities approaching those of middle-class children. This means that more resources are needed by schools that educate children from disadvantaged homes.

Almost any theory of how schools facilitate learning would lead one to the proposition that spending more money is necessary to improve learning. Whether one emphasizes small class size, or quality of faculty, or equipment that allows individualized instruction, money is a necessary resource for the school system seeking to use these resources to help all children, especially those with learning disadvantages. But money alone is almost certainly not enough to upgrade education. Many stories that are unfortunately true have been told of school districts that have spent funds intended for compensatory education on visual aid equipment that was immediately stored in a closet or on additional administrative personnel whose job it was to keep tabs on the closets. Thus, those who advocate upgrading inner-city schools with money have to confront the problem of incentives or controls to ensure that funds are used for plausible educational purposes.

The evidence on the relation of money to learning is decidedly mixed and inconclusive. There are two basic kinds of studies of money and learning. The first uses evidence from large-scale surveys, such as the Coleman Report. These studies attempt to estimate the importance of various influences on learning. All such studies show, first, that most of the variation in test scores occurs within a school, rather than between schools. For example, a re-analysis of the Coleman Report shows that 85 to 90 percent of the variation in verbal achievement occurs within schools.[6] Since survey studies must, for lack of data, assume that within a school, expenditure levels are the same for all students, this means that money differences can at best explain only 10 to 15 percent of student achievement, that is, the portion of variation that is attributable to between-school differences. When these between-school test score differences are analyzed, it turns out that most of the variation (52 percent for whites, 35 percent for blacks, both in the sixth grade) is accounted for by "home background" factors—the incomes and education of the families, the expectations of

6. Marshall S. Smith, "Equality of Educational Opportunity: The Basic Findings Reconsidered," in Frederick Mosteller and Daniel P. Moynihan (eds.), *On Equality of Educational Opportunity*, Paper Deriving from the Harvard University Faculty Seminar on the Coleman Report (Random House, 1972), p. 248.

the parents, the structure of the family—and very little is attributable to school facilities, curriculum, or teacher characteristics. Unfortunately, both for the statistical exercise and for society, the school resources are so closely associated with the home background factors (for example, higher paid teachers are found mainly in schools with students from wealthier homes) that it is difficult to ascertain the unique effects of money, as such. The statistical tests that have been performed seem to indicate that school resources do not have much independent effect on school achievement, after controlling for other factors. The fact is that if these studies were to be relevant to the policy question at hand—will increasing funds for inner-city schools improve their pupils' achievement?—they would have had to focus on ghetto schools that had varying amounts of funds applied to them. This has not been done in any of the surveys, so the survey analysts' conclusion that money makes little difference—makes little difference.

Another major group of studies has focused on evaluating the results of special programs—notably Title I of ESEA and Head Start—under which additional "compensatory" education has been provided to children in low-income areas. The evidence from broad evaluations of these programs is that for the most part they either have had no significant effect on pupil achievement, or that significant effects were lost within a year or two after the child left the program. These conclusions, however, are suspect on at least three grounds. First, many of the projects surveyed were funded at such low levels that no measurable effect could have been expected. Title I has just this year reached about $200 per child. Second, analysts cannot say that a program makes no difference unless they know how well the pupils participating in the program would have scored without the program. Since this "what if" condition cannot be observed, analysts try to find a control group of children similar to those who receive compensatory services, but who themselves do not receive them. Then the test scores of the control group are contrasted to those of the treatment group to ascertain differences. There is evidence, however, that the treatment groups and control groups are often different, with the latter group being better off to begin with. Thus, comparisons of the test scores of the two groups are biased against finding significant improvements. Third, many of the studies were marred because the weakest projects were selected and the results of the start-up years of new projects were analyzed, showing small improvements in test scores that may be more the result of inadequate planning than of anything else.[7]

Some recent studies of certain compensatory programs have discovered more successful outcomes. For the most part, these successful compensatory programs featured tightly structured approaches with constant supervision and guidance from a staff that had been trained well and had engaged in considerable planning. The program costs for these effective programs vary widely. A recent study prepared by the RAND Corporation for the President's Commission on School Finance reviewed the cost of various compensatory education projects for which success had been reported and came to the conclusion that "per pupil costs of successful educational intervention vary anywhere from $200 on up." They concluded that $250-$350 per pupil (in addition to regular expenditures) was a "feasible range" for a successful compensatory program—meaning that an appreciable number of programs funded in this range had been successful. The study noted, however, that "numerous interventions funded at these levels have failed. Clearly the level of funding is not itself a sufficient condition for success."[8]

One major unknown in estimating the likelihood of success of compensatory programs is whether the small-scale experiments that have succeeded in producing dramatic results can be replicated and put into widespread use, and if so, what costs will be incurred when the programs become widespread. A great many of the successful pilot projects have been sponsored by leading educators who have had highly competent manpower available to do the necessary training of teachers and aides. How much money would be needed to attract enough such people to inner-city programs is not known.

Integration

The case for mixing racial and economic groups in the schools has been made on several grounds, both legal and educational. Perhaps the simplest reason for doing so is that education is supposed to equip children to live in a multiracial society, and the best way to do that is

7. Harvey A. Averch and others, "How Effective is Schooling? A Critical Review and Synthesis of Research Findings," Final Report to the President's Commission on School Finance (RAND Corporation, 1971), pp. 100–108.

8. *Ibid.*, p. 125.

to give them experience in interracial schools. In recent years, the arguments for integration have turned away from the psychological to the more intellectual effects expected from integration and have stressed economic as well as racial integration. The proposition is that children learn a great deal from each other, and thus majority children whose home environments and earlier schooling are more verbal will help their minority schoolmates. Another theory is that what teachers expect in the way of performance from children strongly affects that performance; if teachers even subconsciously believe that an all-black classroom will not do well, they will teach down to the students or assign busywork to them. Only by bringing white children together with minority children will the teachers' expectations be raised. Another variant of the integration theory is that racially isolated schools are always shortchanged in facilities, or in adequately trained teachers, or in more subtle ways. From this point of view, the only way for black children to get adequate resources is to make sure that the snow blowing through broken windows falls on white kids, too.

Does integration in fact help minority children psychologically? Does it change the attitudes of teachers toward minority students? Does it guarantee that school districts will devote adequate resources to educating minority children? Does it improve educational attainment? The answer to these questions is that nobody really knows. A recent comprehensive review of the literature prepared for the President's Commission on School Finance concludes as follows:

1. There is no evidence that the racial composition of a student body affects the performance of individual members of that student body.
2. There is no strong evidence to the contrary.

The problem is that most studies like the Coleman Report, which observe the higher verbal achievement of black and poor students in predominantly white schools, are measuring the achievements not of a random selection of black students but of those who chose to attend such schools. It is impossible to tell whether it was the integration of the school itself that produced the somewhat better test results or whether it was that children from poor or black families who chose to attend predominantly middle class white schools are more likely to be academically talented or motivated to begin with.

In too few instances have specific children been observed after being moved from all-black schools to predominantly white schools to draw any conclusions about integration. In school districts where integration has "worked well," there is some evidence that more resources were put into the schools to prepare them for the new situation. In that case, integration and more funds were not alternative, but complementary, routes to the improvement of education for minority children.

Community Control

Another approach that has received fairly short shrift from all but the minority groups themselves is community control of the schools. The argument for this approach is that blacks, Puerto Ricans, and other minorities have received an inferior education, not because they were in segregated schools but rather because the responsibility for running those schools was in the hands of white middle-class educators who neither respected the minorities nor understood their culture and problems. The answer to the problems of predominantly minority schools, according to this view, is to turn the keys over to people in the community itself so that the neighborhood can exercise its own theories of child development, and can hire minority teachers and administrators who will understand the children's needs and provide adequate role models for the students to emulate. Racial balance, which would disperse most black and Spanish-Americans to schools in which they were a minority, it is argued, would never allow them to develop the pride and self-confidence that comes from being a member of the dominant group in a school.

What little experience there is with neighborhood control, as exercised for example in the smaller suburban communities that have active parent groups, has been favorable. But those communities have all the advantages of a motivating home background and generous financing as well. In the central cities and ghettos, neighborhood control has rarely been tried.

Administration Proposals

In an attempt to make racial integration of the schools more palatable by easing its financial burden, the administration proposed the Emergency School Assistance Act (ESAA) two years ago. This bill, which in a slightly revised form is now in conference in the Congress, would provide $1.5 billion over a two-year period to school systems that are trying to establish or maintain "stable, quality integrated schools." The major issue originally surrounding this piece of legislation was whether some paths to integration should be particularly encouraged and others discouraged. The Senate version of the bill places heavy emphasis on educational parks and the stimulation of a limited number of "quality integrated schools" to serve as a magnet for middle-class students. The House bill is less specific in its encouragement of particular activities and would insist on district-wide programs not targeted on a few high-quality projects.

Of more importance politically is what the federal legislation should say about busing as a means of achieving integrated schools. The Senate bill originally contained few restrictions on the use of funds for busing, but the House version contains very strong anti-busing language. It provides that ESAA funds cannot (1) be used for busing "to overcome racial imbalance in any school or school system" or (2) be used to "carry out a plan of racial desegregation of any school or school system." Moreover, it states that officials of the Department of Health, Education, and Welfare (1) cannot "urge, persuade, induce, or require" any school district to bus students, even when state and local funds are used, nor (2) "condition the receipt of Federal funds under any Federal program" on action by state or local officials to bus students.[9]

In response to the House action, the Senate passed the Mansfield-Scott amendment, which also prohibits the use of federal funds for busing "except on the express written request of appropriate local school officials," and then only if the time and distance of busing are not "so great as to risk the health of the children or significantly impinge on the educational process." Federal officials also would be prohibited from urging school districts to bus children to schools where educational opportunities would "be substantially inferior" to their neighborhood school.[10]

Responding to these congressional initiatives and to popular opposition to busing to achieve integration, the President made several proposals in mid-March 1972 that would severely curtail further school integration. First, he suggested a one-year congressionally imposed moratorium on new court-ordered busing. Second, he instructed the Department of Justice to intervene in selected cases "where the lower courts have gone beyond the Supreme Court's re-

9. *Congressional Record*, daily ed., Nov. 4, 1971, p. H10475.
10. *Congressional Record*, daily ed., Feb. 23, 1972, p. S2448.

quirements in ordering busing."[11] Finally, he proposed permanent legislation—the Equal Educational Opportunities Act of 1972—that would both explicitly define what constituted a denial of equal educational opportunity and set down the order in which remedies for rectifying such a denial must be considered. *Increased* busing to achieve a better racial balance would be ruled out below the seventh grade, while in higher grades it could be used only temporarily and only as a last resort.

Both the actions of the Congress and the President's proposals are likely to bring integration efforts to a grinding halt. This is because busing is often the only way to achieve racial desegregation in a society of segregated housing patterns. Already HEW has withdrawn its threats to cut off federal funds from several districts that have been recalcitrant about implementing desegregation plans (for example, Prince George's County, Maryland). Elsewhere districts have begun to defy state demands that they desegregate (for example, Buffalo, New York). Since the President's proposed Equal Educational Opportunities Act would permit modification of existing desegregation orders to bring them into compliance with the provisions of the act, there is a distinct possibility that passage of the act would result in considerable resegregation. The bill also stipulates that busing can be required for only a five-year period and that other provisions are limited to a ten-year time span. Hence, unless a district were found guilty of a *new* denial of equal education opportunity, it could do pretty much as it pleased after a decade. If housing patterns were not drastically changed in the interim, considerable resegregation might be allowed to occur in the future.

The Equal Educational Opportunities Act's proposed alternative to racial integration is to increase the resources available to some schools that educate children from disadvantaged homes. The President, in his mid-March statement, suggested that the current $1.6 billion contained in the Title I program be combined with part of the $1 billion of the money in the Emergency School Assistance Act to provide beefed-up programs of compensatory education. The actual specifications in the Equal Educational Opportunities Act for doing this are extremely vague.

In the fact sheet and the presidential message that accompanied the

11. *Weekly Compilation of Presidential Documents*, Vol. 8 (March 20, 1972), p. 592.

Equal Educational Opportunities Act, the administration spelled out the actions that the commissioner of education would be expected to take to concentrate the compensatory education money. It suggested that roughly $300 per disadvantaged pupil be provided to target schools—those where more than 30 percent of the student body are from disadvantaged homes. The uses to which this money could be put would be tightened beyond the requirements of the Title I regulations. The money would have to be spent on "basic instructional programs for language skills and mathematics, and on basic supportive services such as health and nutrition."[12] An incentive would be provided to disperse disadvantaged children among schools with few such children. This would be accomplished by allowing the child to carry his $300 grant with him if he transferred to a better school. The sending school, however, would also retain a sizable grant for that student, even though he was no longer enrolled in the target school. This may provide an impetus to socioeconomic integration in the long run.

While the President's effort represented a renewal of public concern over the plight of the disadvantaged—stimulated largely by a desire to placate those interested in busing for racial integration—congressional critics were quick to point out that it was largely a repackaging of existing funds. The $300 per disadvantaged student represented only a $100 increase over the amount being spent now under the Title I program, and this added $100 came out of the ESAA authorization that would have gone to many of the same school districts.

The congressional response to the President's proposals has centered around providing significant *new* money for compensatory education programs. The President's proposals to concentrate the effort where the need is greatest and his plan to provide incentives for dispersing disadvantaged children among middle class schools have met with support. With respect to more money, a proposal sponsored by Representative Carl D. Perkins would add $2.5 billion to the $1.5 billion already requested for the existing Title I program. This would increase the amount spent per disadvantaged child from $200 to about $500. The ESAA money would be left intact to help districts overcome the problems of desegregation and of racial isolation in their schools. After all, desegregation is not the same problem as providing a better education to disadvantaged children. Many minority children

12. *Ibid.*, p. 603.

in racially isolated schools are not from disadvantaged homes, and many poor children in inferior schools are not members of minority groups.

The Basic Choice

The federal government faces a difficult choice among several alternative objectives. It could strengthen its present commitments to help disadvantaged students and to provide financial aid to desegregating or racially isolated school systems; it could put federal dollars into interstate equalization; it could give money for property tax relief; it could provide the states with incentives for taking over the financing of education from localities; and it could provide incentives for intrastate equalization.

If any of these objectives are pursued, a decision must also be made as to the amount to be spent. The recommendations that have been made vary greatly. For example, while the administration has proposed an increase of $1 billion a year from the ESAA for helping disadvantaged students and facilitating desegregation, the proposal of Representative Perkins involves an increased expenditure of $2.5 billion a year in the Title I program plus the $1 billion in the ESAA. The President's Commission on School Finance suggests that a short-term incentive of no more than $6 billion distributed over five years is needed to facilitate state takeover and intrastate equalization, while Senator Muskie has proposed a continuing grant of $5.2 billion a year for these purposes. Finally, while some do not favor using federal money to relieve local property taxes, the proposal being considered by the administration would spend for this purpose $12 billion to $13 billion raised from a value added tax.

After settling on the appropriate objectives for federal programs and the amounts to be devoted to achieving them, there remains the problem of deciding how to distribute the money among the states and school districts of the nation. This involves not only choosing a distribution formula but also deciding on the appropriate restrictions and conditions that should be placed on the states. For example, as suggested by the White House staff's proposal, federal grants for tax relief could be conditioned on states' abolishing residential property taxes used for school support; on the other hand, states could be left free to maintain such levies at reduced levels. Federal programs for in-

Table 10-15. States Gaining Most and Least on a per Pupil Basis under Various Programs for Federal Aid to Public Education

Program	States gaining most on a per pupil basis	States gaining least on a per pupil basis
Aid to disadvantaged children[a]	Mississippi New York Arkansas South Carolina Kentucky	Nevada New Hampshire Utah Indiana Idaho
Financial assistance in school desegregation[b]	District of Columbia Mississippi New Mexico Louisiana South Carolina	Vermont New Hampshire Maine North Dakota Iowa
Equalization of expenditures among states[c]	Utah New Mexico Vermont South Carolina Montana	New York Illinois Connecticut New Jersey Massachusetts
Financial incentive for state assumption of school expenditures[d]	Oregon New Jersey South Dakota Nebraska Connecticut	Hawaii North Carolina Mississippi New Mexico Alabama
Replacement of residential property tax	New Hampshire Connecticut Massachusetts New York California	Hawaii Alabama Mississippi North Carolina Alaska
Financial incentive for intrastate equalization of school expenditures[e]	Montana Wyoming Delaware Rhode Island Arizona	District of Columbia Utah Hawaii South Carolina Alabama

Sources: Aid to disadvantaged, *Office of Education and Related Agencies Appropriations for Fiscal Year 1972*, Hearings before a Subcommittee of the Senate Committee on Appropriations, 92 Cong. 1 sess. (1971), pp. 956–57, and National Education Association, *Rankings of the States, 1971*, Table 15; school desegregation program, Department of Health, Education, and Welfare, "HEW News," June 18, 1971, Table 1-E; equalization program, NEA, *Rankings of the States, 1971*, Tables 89 and 108; state assumption of expenditures, see Table 10-10, col. 1, and NEA, *Rankings of the States, 1971*, Table 15; replacement of residential property tax, see Table 10-11; intrastate equalization, see Table 10-14, col. 2.

a. Based on allocation of Title I funds in fiscal year 1971.
b. Based on percentage of minority enrollment in public schools.
c. Based on full-offsetting variable matching formula of Table 10-13.
d. Based on per pupil expenditure required for state to assume 90 percent of school expenditures.
e. Based on data in Table 10-14.

terstate equalization could require that all states maintain their current tax effort for education or raise their effort to the national average. If federal funds are devoted to reducing intrastate expenditure disparities, the federal government could require equal per pupil expenditures in every district, or it might demand only that expenditures in any district not deviate by more than 10 or 20 percent from the statewide average. Decisions made on these kinds of issues will greatly influence the ultimate outcomes of such programs.

The particular federal focus selected will determine how any new funds are distributed among the states. As Table 10-15 shows, the states that would gain the most from one type of federal program may benefit least by another plausible federal role. There is little question that a state's ranking on such lists will have much to do with the political debates surrounding the school finance question.

Major changes in financing elementary and secondary education are almost surely going to be made in the next decade, and the federal government will play a significant role in them. However, federal money, incentives, regulations, and conditions are in the end only attempts to change the behavior of state and local officials and parents, who will continue to play the dominant decision-making roles in elementary and secondary education programs. The efficiency of various federal programs in changing such behavior is a subject about which little is known.

11. The Environment

IMPROVING THE QUALITY of the environment is a national goal that is reflected only imperfectly in federal budgetary decisions. In fiscal 1973 the federal government will spend $2.4 billion for environmental control, principally for research and development and financial assistance to local communities for constructing waste treatment plants. But most of the sources of air and water pollution lie in industry. Consequently, most of the costs of cleaning up pollution will be added not to the federal budget but to the prices consumers pay for the goods and services they buy from industry. The federal government has, and must have, a major role in requiring industries to reduce pollution, but it is not primarily a budgetary role.

Controlling pollution is both technically and politically a very complex problem of public policy, and it is necessarily the subject of much controversy. An understanding of the problem and an evaluation of alternative public policies must start with four central facts:

1. *The environmental qualities of air and water are valuable assets to a society.* Yet for most of history, societies—including our own—have treated these assets as if they were limitless, allowing individuals, municipalities, and industries to use them freely. Because no charge was made, no one felt any need to economize on their use. Why assume the expense of reducing the pollutants from an industrial process when the air and water are free "dumps" for such wastes? In short, pollution arises because the institutional arrangements of society have positively encouraged the waste of environmental assets.

2. *The nation now wants cleaner air and cleaner water, and looks to the federal government as the principal agent to secure them.* Whatever disagreement there is as to how ambitious the objectives of environ-

367

mental control policy should be, there is a wide consensus that pollution must be reduced below its present level and that future growth in production and population should not be allowed to undo the initial efforts.

3. *Reducing pollution is expensive.* The cost of constructing and operating municipal waste treatment plants adds to the tax bill. Reducing industrial pollution of air and water adds to the cost of production and ultimately to prices paid by consumers. Moreover, the costs of pollution removal rise very steeply as the targets for environmental cleanliness become more ambitious.

4. *Both air and water pollution are exceedingly complex phenomena.* Control policy must wrestle with the very great technical difficulty of tracing pollution in the air or water back to specific sources. It must take account of the fact that in almost every industry and every situation there are alternative ways to reduce pollution and that they vary widely in effectiveness and cost. And it must recognize that reducing one kind of pollution sometimes increases others. The air pollution generated by conventionally fueled power plants, for example, can be avoided by switching to nuclear power generation, but only at the environmental cost of creating long-lived radioactive wastes and an attendant disposal problem.

For all of these reasons, federal policies designed to deal with pollution should meet two essential criteria. In the face of a very complex situation, control policy should be effective and enforceable so as to achieve swiftly the reduction in pollution that the nation clearly wants. And since most of the costs of pollution control will ultimately be paid by consumers, poor as well as rich, control policy should be efficient— that is, it should seek the least-cost means of achieving whatever environmental standards the nation decides on.

Alternative Approaches to Pollution Control

The question of how the government can best go about securing a sharp reduction in industrial air and water pollution suggests two alternative approaches—the route of regulation and the route of economic incentives. The regulatory approach, in which the government specifies what each firm must do to limit pollution, has been the chief line of attack to date. With some exceptions, it has not proved very effective. The Congress now has before it several proposals to expand dramatically the powers of the federal government in the area of industrial water pollution control by strengthening the regulatory approach. Many economists, joined recently by a coalition of conservation groups, have urged that economic incentives be given a major role in controlling pollution through the imposition of "effluent charges" (or taxes) on each unit of pollution released by industry into the air or water. This would provide business firms with an incentive to reduce pollution in order to lower their tax burden. The issue between proponents of the two approaches is not merely a technical problem of secondary importance. It goes to the heart of the question whether, and at what cost to the nation's standard of living, the pollution that accompanies abundant production can be controlled and reduced.

Several technical aspects of the pollution problem have an important bearing on the choice between these two alternatives. As was mentioned briefly above, many means are available to reduce pollution, and the appropriateness of each depends on a wide variety of factors. Firms can treat the pollution they have generated to reduce its harmful effects on the quality of air or water; they can change the fuels or raw materials they use from those that pollute heavily to those that do not; they can modify their production process to generate less pollution per unit of output; they can recirculate water and thereby minimize the cost of treating waste water; they can change the kinds of products they produce from ones that cause a great deal of pollution to ones that create little. For example, the manufacture of white or pastel colored household paper products, because of the bleaching process required, causes much more water pollution than does the production of unbleached paper.

The range of available alternatives and the costs of pollution reduction vary widely from firm to firm and industry to industry. Cutting back pollution by, say, 90 percent would be relatively inexpensive in some industries but very costly in others. Moreover, the most appropriate means of pollution control from the point of view of a single firm may not be appropriate for many firms taken together. The substitution of low-sulfur coal for high-sulfur coal may be an inexpensive way for a particular electric utility to cut down on the sulfur oxides it pours into the air. But the supplies of low-sulfur coal are limited. What seems a practical and inexpensive way for one firm to limit pollution would be an expensive, and indeed impossible, means for the economy as a whole.

The costs of reducing pollution tend to grow very rapidly as the percentage removed from an industrial process rises. In a typical case, when 30 percent of the pollutant BOD[1] has been removed from an industrial process, it costs 4 cents per pound of BOD to remove 1 additional percentage point; after 90 percent has been removed, it costs 30 cents a pound to remove another percentage point; and after 95 percent has been eliminated, removing an additional percentage point costs 50 cents a pound.[2]

It follows that a control policy that simply requires each firm to reduce pollution by the same percentage will be unnecessarily costly and will not yield the maximum possible reduction in pollution for a given cost. In the case of water pollution, for example, suppose that all firms were required to eliminate 90 percent of the major oxygen-demanding waste (BOD) from their water discharges. For one industry the cost of eliminating the last 1,000 pounds of waste under this standard might be 50 cents a pound. For another industry, the cost of removing the last 1,000 pounds might be only 10 cents a pound. Clearly, the total costs of reaching a 90 percent standard would be lowered if the second industry were required to eliminate more pollution and the first industry less. More generally, the least-cost approach to achieving any given standard for pollution control requires that each firm remove wastes to the point where the cost of removing an additional pound is the same as that for every other firm.

Cost differences between the uniform reduction and least-cost approaches to pollution cleanup are very large. According to one estimate, achieving current targets for controlling sulfur emissions into the atmosphere would cost two to three times as much under the former as under the latter.[3] A study of water pollution in the Delaware River basin estimated that current water quality standards would be

1. Many waste materials discharged into water absorb oxygen in the natural process of decomposition. This demand for oxygen is called BOD (biochemical oxygen demand). Untreated wastes reduce the supply of oxygen, thus impairing the quality of the water, frequently to the point where the natural process of purification breaks down, making the water unfit for human use and damaging to both fish and wildlife.

2. While these particular costs relate to the removal of BOD from the wastes generated by an ice cream and frozen dessert plant, they are a fair illustration of how rapidly marginal costs increase as pollution reduction targets become more ambitious. Ivars Gutmanis, "The Generation and Cost of Controlling Air, Water, and Solid Waste Pollution: 1970–2000," an analysis prepared for the Brookings Institution (April 1972; processed).

3. U.S. Department of the Treasury, Press Release, "Pure Air Tax Act of 1972: Background and Detailed Explanation" (Feb. 8, 1972; processed), p. 5.

roughly 50 to 100 percent more costly to achieve with uniform reductions than with a least-cost approach.[4] A similar estimate of the costs of controlling BOD discharges in the Great Lakes region comes to the same conclusion.[5]

To require a uniform percentage reduction of all firms would be inappropriate for other reasons. It would come to grips only imperfectly with the complexities of pollution control. Requiring a smelter that uses virgin ore to reduce the pollutants it generates by 85 percent might leave far more pollution in the environment than would a 50 percent cutback applied to a smelter using scrap as raw materials. Inducing consumers to switch from bleached to unbleached household paper products would reduce water pollution much more than would requiring producers of bleached paper to eliminate 80 percent of the pollutants from their bleaching process.

What is needed, therefore, is a variable standard that would concentrate the reduction in pollution where the costs of reduction are least. Different firms should cut back pollution by differing amounts, depending on the costs. Each firm should reduce pollution to the point where the cost of removing an additional unit is the same as that for every other firm. Moreover, the standards should encourage the substitution of raw materials that are less pollution-generating and the production of less polluting kinds of products.

In theory, a regulatory agency could establish for each firm rules and pollution limits that meet these criteria. The limits would have to be different for each firm and would have to be based on a consideration of the cost and effectiveness of all of the available alternatives for reducing pollution, including the possibilities of changing raw materials and switching product varieties. In practice, however, this is an impossible task. There are some 40,000 individual industrial sources of water pollution alone. A regulatory agency cannot know the costs, the technological opportunities, the alternative raw materials, and the kinds of products available for every firm in every industry. Even if it could determine the appropriate reduction standards for each firm, it would have to revise them frequently to accommodate changing costs and markets, new technologies, and economic growth.

Under the alternative approach, a tax could be levied on each unit

4. Edwin L. Johnson, "A Study in the Economics of Water Quality Management," *Water Resources Research*, Vol. 3 (second quarter, 1967), p. 297.
5. Gutmanis, "Generation and Cost."

of each kind of pollutant discharged into the air or water. Faced with these taxes or "effluent charges," each firm would find it in its own interest to reduce pollution by an amount related to the cost of reduction and through the use of the least-cost means of doing so. It would compare the cost of paying the effluent charge with the cost of cleaning up pollution, and would choose to remove pollution up to the point where the additional cost of removal was greater than the effluent charge. The larger the effluent charge, the greater the percentage of pollutants a firm would find it advantageous to remove. Firms with low costs of control would remove a larger percentage than would firms with high costs—precisely the situation needed to achieve a least-cost approach to reducing pollution for the economy as a whole. The kinds of products whose manufacture generated a lot of pollution would become more expensive and would carry higher prices than those that generated less, and consumers would be induced to buy more of the latter.

The effluent charge approach has another advantage. In the case of regulations that require the removal of a specific percentage of pollutants, once a firm has achieved that point, it has no incentive to cut pollution further. Indeed it has a positive incentive *not* to do so, since the additional reduction is costly and lowers profits. With effluent charges, however, firms are taxed for every unit of pollution they have not removed. They would have a continuing incentive to devote research and engineering talent toward finding less costly ways of achieving still further reductions. This continuing incentive is important. The quantity of air and water available to the nation is fixed, roughly speaking. But as economic activity grows over time, the volume of pollution discharged into the air and water will rise unless an ever-increasing percentage of pollutants is removed.

Objections have been raised against the effluent charge approach. Some have called effluent charges "licenses to pollute," since firms paying the charge are not subject to prosecution for causing pollution. But payment of the effluent charge is no more a license to pollute than is a permit or a pollution limit established by a regulatory agency. Effluent charges can be set high enough to reduce overall pollution by whatever degree the nation wants. A regulatory agency can similarly set pollution limits designed to achieve that goal. Under neither approach is pollution likely to be reduced to zero: the costs are too great. In a sense, the remaining pollution does result from a license to pollute. But the license will be there under either method of pollution control.

It has also been argued that large firms with substantial market power would simply pass on the effluent charge to their customers and not make the effort to clean up pollution. This might indeed occur, but there is overwhelming reason to believe that it would not be the response of the majority of firms. Effluent charges can be set high enough that the cost of removing a substantial percentage of pollution is less than the cost of paying the charge. Firms could then reduce costs by reducing pollution, just as they can now lower costs by reducing the amount of labor used per unit of output. Despite the fact that many firms do have substantial market power, the drive to lower costs has produced in the American economy an average increase in productivity that *halves* labor requirements per unit of output every twenty-five years. Firms do not as a rule pass up opportunities to cut production costs. And with a stiff effluent charge, the reduction of pollution becomes a way to cut costs.

In the case of toxic and highly dangerous pollutants, such as mercury, effluent charges are not suitable. Even a small amount of such pollutants causes severe damage, and thus prohibition is in order. But for the vast majority of pollutants, effluent charges offer a means of harnessing self-interest and the profit motive in the direction of environmental control.

The Goals of Environmental Policy

Whatever the method or combination of methods chosen to control pollution, a decision must also be made as to the goals of environmental policy. How clean should the environment be? Should the federal government make these decisions on a uniform basis for all river basins, coastal areas, and airsheds, or should the decision be left principally to states or regional groups of states? Much of the controversy over environmental control policy revolves around these questions.

If reducing air and water pollution cost nothing—if it could be accomplished with no reduction in living standards—the answer to the first question would be easy. The appropriate goal would be zero discharges—no pollutants of any kind should be allowed to be emitted into the air or water. But as was pointed out at the beginning of this chapter, reducing pollution is expensive, and the cost grows sharply as the target becomes more ambitious. As a result, the nation has to decide what balance it wants to strike between the benefits of clean air and water and the costs of achieving them.

There is no way at present to estimate very precisely how much it would cost nationwide to achieve various levels of environmental cleanliness, assuming that the most efficient means of reducing pollution were adopted. But some rough estimates have been made under various assumptions about the means used to reduce pollution.

In the case of water pollution, current policies generally call for "secondary treatment or its equivalent." This standard implies the removal of 85 to 90 percent of the major water pollutants from waste discharges. On the assumption that removal is accomplished chiefly by treating wastes already generated, one estimate has placed the annual cost of achieving this standard at $23 billion to $27 billion by 1980.[6] These estimates include the costs of dealing with municipal sewage and urban runoff, industrial wastes, and wastes from livestock feeding operations. Using the same approach, it was further estimated that achieving waste reductions equivalent to tertiary treatment—95 to 99 percent of major wastes removed—would cost $60 billion to $70 billion a year in 1980. Like the earlier estimate, this one also assumes that wastes are treated rather than reduced by changes in internal industrial processes. Since in many cases changing an industrial process to reduce the generation of wastes is a cheaper way of reducing pollution than treating the wastes once they are generated, an efficient water pollution control policy could achieve the same goals at a lower cost than the estimate cited above. Thus, the costs are overstated compared to the most efficient pollution control methods. But the costs would still be very high. In the case of air pollution, one estimate puts the cost of achieving current air quality standards at $14 billion annually by 1980. And this estimate assumes significant improvements in industrial technology, which helps to keep the costs down.

However imperfect these measures of cost may be, they indicate that reducing pollution will be expensive. There is no way in which technical or economic analysis can determine at what point the costs to society of cleaning up pollution begin to outweigh the advantages

6. Gutmanis, "Generation and Costs." Costs are expressed in dollars of 1971 purchasing power.

of a cleaner environment. This must ultimately be a political decision. However, several points can be made clear.

In the first place, nothing in the nature of air or water pollution suggests that the best way to halt it is to stop economic growth. If the estimate of $23 billion to $27 billion is accepted as the annual cost of achieving current goals in the case of water pollution, and $14 billion as the annual cost in the case of air pollution, the total cost in 1980 would be approximately $40 billion a year, in contrast to the approximately $4 billion that was spent to control air and water pollution in 1970. Also by 1980, if a prosperous, growing economy can be achieved, the nation will be producing $550 billion a year more than in 1970. Thus if less than 10 percent of this increase is devoted to pollution control, sizable reductions in air and water pollution can be achieved. Even if the estimate of $60 billion to $70 billion is accepted as the annual cost of achieving the stringent "tertiary treatment" standard for water pollution control, and the $14 billion devoted to air pollution control is doubled, to achieve even more ambitious air quality standards, the total would still be less than one-fifth the added output yielded by economic growth. In other words, by devoting only a fraction of the increase in GNP over the next eight years to environmental control purposes, the nation could achieve stringent control standards and still have very substantial gains in living standards, as conventionally defined. Stopping growth is an unnecessary and excessively costly means of controlling pollution.

The problem of setting goals for clean air and water also involves the question of federal–state relations. Until recently, the establishment of air and water quality standards was mainly a responsibility of state governments. As the nation has become increasingly concerned about the environment, the federal government has undertaken a larger role. If stringent standards are ever to be applied, this is an inevitable development. Individual states are necessarily reluctant, on their own, to apply rigorous standards to industry, for fear that other states will be more lenient and will thereby attract the lion's share of industrial development. Over the past decade, the task of setting air and water quality standards has passed to the federal government, at least in terms of imposing a minimum set of standards that usually leave the states free to set more stringent standards if they wish. Basically this is no longer a major controversy. The question of federal–state relations in the *enforcement* of these standards is now a center of political debate. On the one hand, lax enforcement of federally approved pollution control standards is a means by which a state can gain a competitive advantage in attracting industry. On the other hand, complete centralization of enforcement authority in the federal government, given the large number of pollution sources in the United States, could result in unwieldy and ineffective controls. In general the Congress has tended to attack this question by leaving the basic responsibility for enforcement in the hands of the states, but giving federal authorities the power of oversight and review. The final division of authority is still fluid and in the process of development.

None of this discussion answers the question how far environmental control should be pushed, either by federal or by state authorities. But it is clear that the nation wants substantially cleaner air and water than it now enjoys. While the complete elimination of air and water pollution is not a realistic target, recent experience has shown that even the achievement of more modest goals will challenge the political, technical, and economic inventiveness of the nation. All of this suggests that the central issue for public policy at present is to determine how best to reduce pollution significantly from current levels. Controversy about the choice of ultimate goals should not be allowed to obscure the important practical problems of moving swiftly and efficiently to improve the current situation.

The problems that arise in determining the best means of securing a substantial reduction in air and water pollution can be illustrated by a review of current federal policy and the legislative proposals that are now before the Congress.

Controlling Water Pollution

Current federal programs to control water pollution stem from the Water Pollution Control Act amendments of 1956 and the strengthening amendments contained in the Water Quality Act of 1965. Under these acts the federal government makes grants to local communities to cover up to 55 percent of the construction cost of municipal waste treatment plants, and both regulates and helps enforce water quality standards set by state govenments.

Solid information about the amounts of various pollutants discharged in waterways in the United States is woefully inadequate. Indeed, this lack of data is one of the major shortcomings of the existing control program. A 1969 report by the comptroller general of the United States analyzed pollution in eight river basins between 1957 and 1968. While conditions varied widely, the report generally showed that the reduction in pollution from municipal sources as a result of the construction of new waste treatment plants was more than offset by increases in industrial pollution.[7] In 1971 the federal Environmental Protection Agency (EPA) made a valiant effort, given the scarcity of data, to estimate what had happened to several industrial water pollutants in the nation as a whole. EPA estimated that during the entire period 1957–68, the discharge of BOD increased by 10 percent, whereas the discharge of plant nutrients (phosphorus and nitrogen), which cause the growth of algae, doubled.[8] In the past several years, the EPA report suggests, the discharge of BOD has declined, while the discharge of plant nutrients has continued to grow. In sum, though progress has been made in controlling water pollution, it has been painfully small, and there are aspects of the problem that have barely been touched.

This disappointing performance and experience in trying to carry out the current control program have convinced the administration, the Congress, and most outside observers that there are serious weaknesses in the present approach. During the waning months of 1970 and throughout 1971, the administration and the Congress wrestled with the problem. Both the Senate and the House committees concerned have drafted new legislation on which the Congress will be asked to vote in 1972. Both are far-reaching measures that would substantially increase the regulatory authority and the grant funds of the federal government. The administration, which had submitted its own set of proposals, has been critical of the congressional legislation, particularly the Senate bill, on grounds that it sets excessively ambitious and unrealizable goals and that it centralizes too much authority in the federal government.

Industrial Pollution

The control of industrial pollution currently hinges on the development and enforcement of "ambient water quality standards." The

7. "Examination into the Effectiveness of the Construction Grant Program for Abating, Controlling, and Preventing Water Pollution," Report to the Congress by the Comptroller General of the United States (U.S. General Accounting Office, Nov. 3, 1969; processed).

8. Environmental Protection Agency, Water Quality Office, *Cost of Clean Water*, Vol. II (March 1971), pp. 29, 34.

term *ambient* refers to the quality of water in the stream rather than the quality of the wastewater as it emerges from a particular industrial plant. Each state draws up water quality standards, which, for interstate waters, must be approved by the federal government. The standards are in two parts. They first specify the *uses* for which various parts of a river or stream should be suitable—swimming, boating, supporting wildlife, and so on. Second, they specify chemical and biological *characteristics* of the water that are consistent with the uses, such as the amount of dissolved oxygen or the tolerable number of coliform bacteria.

Having developed water quality standards, states must then set up "implementation schedules." These specify the actions that must be taken by both municipalities and industrial firms along a river to reduce pollutants sufficiently to meet the water quality standards. The standards and the implementation schedules must be approved by EPA. While the states are the primary enforcement agents, EPA can, under certain conditions, step in and enforce the standards.

There are several fundamental difficulties with this approach. In the first place, because of the very complex nature of the problem and the lack of technical information, states cannot explicitly relate their water quality standards to the pollutants discharged by a particular firm, especially when there are many firms along a river. As a result, the states have tended simply to specify that each industrial firm must provide secondary treatment, or its equivalent, to the wastes it generates. While the implications of this requirement vary from one pollutant to another, it generally calls for the removal of 85 to 90 percent of most polluting wastes.

Even more important, the lack of connection between water quality standards and the specific effluent limits applied to individual firms emasculates the possibility of strict enforcement. EPA cannot directly enforce a set of effluent limits applied to individual polluters. Enforcement proceedings provided by the current law are in any event time-consuming and difficult. But the difficulties are greatly increased by the need for EPA to prove that a particular polluter is responsible for reducing the water quality of a stream below approved standards. The previously cited difficulties in tracing water pollution along a stream back to individual firms makes it exceedingly hard to win a case in court, particularly in view of the stringent rules of evidence normally required in the judicial system. In testimony before the House Public

Table 11-1. Percentage of Industrial Waste Water Treated in Municipal Plants, and Percentage of Cost Borne by Industry, Selected Sectors, 1964 and 1970

Industrial sector	Percentage of industrial waste water treated in municipal plants		Average charges paid by industry as a percentage of total cost of treatment, 1970
	1964	1970	
Food and kindred products	35	50	55–60
Textile mill products	33	60	35–40
Paper and allied products	4	15	30–35
Chemicals and allied products	4	10	40–45
Primary metals	4	4	35–40

Source: Ivars Gutmanis, "The Generation and Cost of Controlling Air, Water, and Solid Waste Pollution: 1970–2000," an analysis prepared for the Brookings Institution (April 1972; processed).

Works Committee, the comptroller general strongly questioned the extent to which the current enforcement program against industrial polluters could be made to work.[9] Ralph Nader's Task Force on Water Pollution concluded that because the links between stream water quality standards and effluent limitations are so tenuous, the current program is probably unenforceable at law against individual firms discharging waste.[10]

Another major problem with the current program has been the impact on industrial polluters of government subsidies for the construction of municipal waste treatment works. Because of the federal subsidy, it has become increasingly profitable for industrial firms to channel their wastes into municipal treatment plants. The federal subsidy enables municipalities to charge industry less than the economic costs of this service. The waste treatment approach to pollution control thereby becomes an artificially attractive solution for industry, as compared to other approaches that are often more effective or cheaper from a national standpoint—recycling water, recapturing by-products, and so on. Table 11-1 shows the growing importance of municipal treatment of industrial wastes and provides some rough estimates of the subsidy involved.

This is not to say that industrial wastes should never be treated in

9. Testimony of Elmer B. Staats in *Water Pollution Control Legislation—1971* (*Oversight of Existing Programs*), Hearings before the House Committee on Public Works, 92 Cong. 1 sess. (1971), pp. 11, 12.

10. Nader Water Pollution Task Force, "Water Wasteland" (Washington, D.C.; Center for Study of Responsive Law, 1971; processed), Vol. 2, Chap. 14, pp. 26–28.

municipal plants. In many instances this may be the most efficient approach to pollution control. But the choice should not be artificially biased in this direction by making a federal subsidy indirectly available to industrial firms. Rather, firms should be required to choose the method of pollution control they will use in the light of the full costs of each alternative.

While attempts to control water pollution were proceeding under the acts of 1956 and 1965, a parallel effort was recently begun with the rediscovery of an obscure and previously unenforced law, passed in 1899 as part of an appropriation act for construction and repair work on rivers. This law prohibits a firm from dumping material into navigable waters without securing a permit from the Army Corps of Engineers. In 1970 the administration began to use the 1899 law by enforcing the permit requirement. Precisely what effluent limits or effluent reductions would be required to secure a permit was not made clear. Many states had been in the process of developing permit systems that included effluent limits as a means of implementing their water quality standards. EPA, for the federal government, was developing specific effluent limits that could presumably be used as the basis for granting permits under the 1899 act. By the end of 1971 some 20,000 permit applications had been received, but fewer than two dozen had been granted. Permit issuing was brought to a complete halt by a court order based on a suit that challenged the validity of the government's permit-issuing procedures.

Municipal Waste Treatment

The federal program of grants-in-aid for municipal waste treatment plants faces difficulties in addition to those cited above in connection with the treatment of industrial wastes. In many cases, local communities have no direct incentives to treat their wastes effectively. The chief benefits of cleaner water usually accrue not to their own citizens but to those who live farther downstream. The availability of federal grants does not itself induce a community to build a waste treatment plant. While the grant reduces the financial burden, the local community still has to bear part of the cost; it is cheaper to continue dumping inadequately treated wastes into the water. Under current strategy, enforcement is the "stick" that provides motivation. Consequently the grant program should be tied in with an enforcement strategy. Along each river basin, priority should be given to those communities in which waste reduction would cause the greatest improvement in water quality. But as last year's *Setting National Priorities* pointed out, this is not the way grants are allotted.[11] They are distributed among the states principally in accordance with population. Within states, priority in practice is given to the communities that the state water pollution control authority has persuaded to build additional treatment facilities. Predominantly these have been smaller municipalities, in part because it has been politically more feasible to proceed against them than against the larger, more politically powerful ones.

The operating efficiency of municipal treatment plants has been another major problem. Water pollution problems do not necessarily end when a treatment plant is built. Unless the plant is operated efficiently, substantial pollution can still be discharged into the water. The General Accounting Office in 1970 reported on a survey of sixty-nine municipal sewage treatment plants in six states, and found that forty of them had operational, mechanical, or structural problems and that twenty-eight of them bypassed some sewage wastes into the streams without treatment.[12] Again, there is no incentive for the municipalities to bear the costs of operating their treatment plants effectively, and thus the control program must rely on constant inspection and harassment by already overburdened state and federal enforcement staffs.

Pending Legislation

During 1971, the Senate Public Works Committee developed new water pollution control legislation in an effort to deal with the weaknesses of the current program. The Senate passed the bill unanimously on November 2, 1971. While the new bill incorporates major changes in the federal government's approach, essentially it reinforces the existing strategy. That is, it greatly extends the federal government's regulatory authority over industrial pollution and sharply increases the size of the construction grant program for municipal treatment plants. The bill is opposed by the administration as going too far in both areas. The House Public Works Committee in March 1972 re-

11. Charles L. Schultze and others, *Setting National Priorities: The 1972 Budget* (Brookings Institution, 1971), Chapter 12.
12. Testimony of Elmer B. Staats in *Water Pollution Control Legislation—1971*, p. 8.

ported its own bill, which resembles the Senate bill in many respects but differs in others.

The Senate bill declares as a goal the *elimination* by 1985 of the discharge of pollutants into navigable waters. The bill also establishes as an interim standard the achievement by 1981 of water quality suitable for swimming and for the protection and propagation of fish, shellfish, and wildlife. Much controversy has arisen over these proposed standards, especially the 1985 "no-discharge" goal. Administration spokesmen have pointed out that eliminating the last 5 percent of most pollutants is very expensive.

Stating goals in a piece of legislation, however, does not ensure their achievement. If experience shows that reaching the goals would be prohibitively expensive and would lead to major industrial dislocation, then most assuredly the goals will be modified. Of much greater importance is the question whether the complex regulatory approach provided in the legislation will substantially reduce industrial water pollution, and what the costs will be.

The proposed legislation recognizes the essential difficulty of enforcing state water quality standards arising from the hazy relation between stream water quality and specific sources of pollution. Instead of trying to enforce ambient water quality standards, it would give EPA direct authority to set and enforce (by the issuance of permits) specific effluent limits on all individual sources that discharge pollutants into navigable waters. This authority would supersede the regulations in the 1899 act. More specifically, the legislation would require the following:

• By 1976, all industrial sources must be limited to an amount of effluent consistent with "the best practicable control technology currently available."

• By 1981, each industrial source must cease any pollution of the water (zero effluent) unless the owner can demonstrate to EPA that this is "not attainable at reasonable cost," in which case the effluent limit would be that consistent with "the best available technology, taking into account the cost of such controls."

• The "best available" standard is made applicable to new industrial plants within a year, rather than in 1981.

• By 1976, all publicly owned treatment plants must provide secondary treatment, and by 1981, the "best practicable treatment."

Both Senate and House committee reports set the same 1976 goals for industry—effluent limitations on each firm that are consistent with the use of "best practicable technology." In most cases these would require a reduction in pollution consistent with that obtainable from secondary treatment of wastes. In effect, this means that the effluent limitations on individual firms now typically incorporated in state implementation schedules would be made part of federal law to be achieved by 1976. The 1981 goal, achieving effluent limits consistent with "best available technology," is more difficult to interpret. Essentially it would require pollution reductions that can be achieved through the most advanced technology that has been developed for use at reasonable costs, whether that involves treatment plants, recycling of water, recapture of by-products, industrial process change, or other techniques.

The Senate bill charges the EPA administrator with establishing for various classes of polluters specific effluent reduction targets that are attainable through the use of "best practicable" (1976) and "best available" (1981) technology. In establishing these targets, the legislation instructs him to take into account "the age of equipment and facilities involved, the process employed, the engineering aspects of the application of various types of control techniques, process changes, the cost of achieving such effluent reduction, and such other factors as the Administrator deems appropriate."[13] If a state satisfies the administrator that it has a system for enforcing specific effluent limits that meet his guidelines, he may delegate his enforcement powers to the state; under the Senate bill he would retain the right to review state actions on a permit-by-permit basis.

In both the House and Senate bills the administrator is charged with setting specific effluent limits for each of the 40,000 sources of water pollution in the United States. In setting the limits, particularly those for the 1981 goals, he must determine industry by industry and process by process what are the alternative means of control—and as the earlier discussion pointed out, the available alternatives are numerous. He must determine which are the most effective and efficient for each class and category of plant, after somehow determining what is an appropriate cost for each to bear. Since many large firms undertake a host of different processes at one plant, he must often make several individual determinations for each plant. Nothing in the Senate bill

13. "S. 2770," 92 Cong. 1 sess., passed by the Senate, Nov. 2, 1971, p. 81.

says that the administrator could tell a firm what varieties of a product to produce. But the discussion above emphasized the fact that the choice of product variety is an important aspect of pollution control and that somehow this must play a part in his determination. Similarly, in setting effluent limits, the administrator must presumably determine which raw materials are appropriate for various plants in different locations throughout the country.

Technology and product design are continually changing in American industry. In some cases the changes reduce pollution or make it cheaper to control; in others they increase pollution. Moreover, pollution will rise with economic growth unless the percentage of wastes removed is steadily increased. Consequently, the detailed effluent limits issued by the administrator would have to be revised continually to take account of technological change, new products, and economic growth. The legislation recognizes this and instructs the administrator to review his guidelines at least annually and to revise them as appropriate.

To carry out the law efficiently—in the sense of achieving a given reduction in pollution at the lowest cost—the administrator and his staff would have to be omniscient, knowing the engineering details, cost relationships, competitive situation, raw material availability, and future technological potential of the 40,000 plants involved. One of the major tasks facing the administrator would be to determine what is a "reasonable cost" to force a firm to bear. Since the circumstances that affect costs are different in each industry and indeed in many different classes of firms within an industry,[14] the regulatory authority—whether it be the EPA administrator or state agencies to which he has delegated the responsibility—would have to make a very large number of cost determinations. General guidelines could presumably be developed. But individual firms or industry associations might challenge in the courts the effluent limits applied to them, or the guidelines on which they are based, on the ground that the costs imposed were unreasonable. Thus, it would not only be difficult to make regulation efficient, it might also be difficult to make it prompt and effective.

While many other features of the Senate bill deal with industrial

14. For example, where a change in raw materials is an important means of reducing pollution, the costs of making such a change may vary from one firm to another, depending on their distance from the source of the materials.

water pollution (the committee print of the bill covers 192 pages), the regulatory process described above forms the core of the legislation. With respect to municipal waste treatment facilities, the bill authorizes federal grants of $14 billion over a four-year period (starting at $2 billion in 1972 and rising to $5 billion in 1975). The maximum federal share of construction costs is increased from the current 55 percent to 70 percent. The bill recognizes the problems created by the fact that federal grants currently provide an indirect subsidy to industrial firms whose wastes are treated in municipal sewage plants. It would require firms to pay charges for the municipal treatment service sufficient not only to cover local costs but also to repay the federal government for that part of its grant that is allocable to the services rendered the firm. If, for example, an industrial firm used 20 percent of the capacity of a sewage treatment plant that was constructed with a federal grant, it would have to repay, through service charges, 20 percent of the grant. This charge would help correct the distorted incentives of the current program that tend to push firms in the direction of a treatment approach to pollution control.

The House bill differs from the Senate bill in a number of respects. It does not make a final judgment about the 1985 "no-discharge" goal or the 1981 "best available technology" goal. It declares them to be desirable objectives, but commissions a two-year study by the National Academy of Sciences of the benefits and costs of these goals, and postpones a final decision on them until the study is complete. Compared to the Senate bill, the House bill gives the states more authority in enforcing EPA-determined effluent limits against individual firms.

Because of these two differences, much controversy has arisen about the relative merits of the two bills. Conservationists generally believe the Senate bill to be much the stronger. But despite the differences the two bills share the same general approach. Recognizing the weaknesses inherent in trying to enforce ambient (in-stream) water quality standards, the bills give the federal government power to establish specific effluent limits on individual firms. Both carry the concept of pollution control by regulatory agencies to its logical conclusion.

Incentives for Pollution Control: Effluent Charges

Under the "effluent charge" approach outlined earlier, a stiff tax would be imposed on each unit of pollution discharged into the nation's streams. An example of pollution removal costs when various percentages of the pollutant are removed is shown below:

Percentage of pollutant removed	Cost of removing an additional pound of BOD
40	$0.03
60	0.05
80	0.07
90	0.10
95	0.15
99	0.40

In these circumstances, if an effluent charge of 10 cents were imposed on each pound of BOD discharged, the firm would find it profitable to remove 90 percent of the BOD from its effluent—that is, the cost of removal would be less than the effluent charge for removal up to 90 percent. It would choose to discharge the remaining 10 percent of BOD, however, since for this last 10 percent the cost of removal would be greater than the charge. If the effluent charge were raised to 15 cents, the firm would find it profitable to remove 95 percent of the BOD, since the cost of removal of the additional 5 percent would now be less than the effluent charge. In other words, an effluent charge can be set high enough to accomplish any desired degree of pollution removal.

If effluent charges were imposed on each of the major water pollutants, economic factors would begin to work for, rather than against, a reduction of pollution. As was pointed out above, unbleached household paper products cause 85 to 90 percent less pollution (in the form of dissolved solids) than do bleached products. If an effluent charge were imposed, the price of bleached products would have to be raised relative to that of unbleached products, promoting a shift in consumer purchases toward the less-polluting good. Similarly, choices of raw materials and manufacturing methods would shift in favor of those that cause less pollution. A central regulatory authority would not have to undertake the exceedingly complex job of trying to decide, industry by industry and process by process, what pollution limits were consistent with the use of "best practicable" and "best available" technologies. Nor would primary reliance have to be placed on the government's ability (which is notoriously weak) to enforce complex regulations against industry.

The use of an incentive approach could also help minimize the very substantial costs of environmental control. A common charge would be set for a given pollutant, high enough to accomplish any desired average level of reduction. It might initially be set, for example, with the objective of removing 90 percent of the pollutant. Firms whose removal costs were quite low would have an incentive to reduce pollution by more than the average amount, while those with very high costs of reduction would remove a smaller than average amount. Pollution reductions thus would tend to be concentrated where the costs of removal were lowest—precisely what is needed to achieve a given reduction at lowest costs. Determining how the burden of pollution reduction should be distributed among individual firms in order to minimize costs would be an impossible task for a regulatory agency.

While, in theory, effluent charges could be designed to achieve any desired degree of overall pollution reduction, the technical information required for this to be done precisely is not available. Enough information and analytical techniques exist, however, to make a solid beginning. A good deal is known about the costs of reducing pollution by various degrees in different industries, using standard treatment techniques. The study of the Delaware River basin mentioned above estimated that an effluent charge of 8 to 10 cents a pound of BOD would lead to a reduction in pollution of the river that would equal and possibly exceed current standards for secondary treatment.[15] Since in some cases more efficient alternatives than the standard treatment techniques are available, a 10-cents-a-pound effluent charge would probably lead to even better results.

A graduated schedule of effluent charges could be enacted, starting at a low level and increasing each year until the desired level had been reached. In the case of BOD, for example, the charge could start at 2 cents the first year and be increased by 2 cents a year until it reached the 10-cent level. This would give notice that a stiff charge would shortly be in effect and would allow time for control measures to be adopted. If, after the 10-cent level were reached, more ambitious water quality standards should be adopted, the charge could be increased further, leading to still further pollution removal. Enforcement of effluent charges would be somewhat similar to enforcement of the tax laws. The major problem would occur in making certain that

15. Johnson, "A Study in the Economics of Water Quality Management," p. 304.

pollution discharges were accurately metered. Thereafter, assessment of the charge would be easy. But metering would also be necessary under the regulatory approach.

A single nationwide effluent charge would produce different results in different river basins, as would adoption of the 1976 and 1981 nationwide effluent limitations specified in the House and Senate bills. On a waterway with very little industrial activity, a given effluent charge would result in cleaner water, everything else being equal, than would the same effluent charge levied in a river basin in a highly industrialized area. This problem of differential impact is inherent in any approach to control. One possible way to handle the problem would be to apply different effluent charges to different river basins. So long as a basin met certain high standards of quality, the effluent charge might be set lower than in river basins with water of low quality. To achieve any given water quality standards, the latter basins need a greater reduction in current levels of pollution discharges than do the former and hence require the imposition of higher effluent charges.

Effluent charges should also be levied on municipal sewage. In particular, this would provide an incentive for municipalities to operate their treatment plants efficiently, since every pound of pollutant removed would pay for itself in reduced charges. However, there are obviously major political obstacles in the way of any procedure that taxes financially hard-pressed local communities and turns the proceeds over to the federal government. This problem could be avoided by placing the proceeds from municipal effluent charges in a common fund, which would be returned to local communities in inverse relationship to their per capita pollution levels. They would then have a double incentive to clean up pollution, first to avoid paying the charge, and second to receive a larger share of the common fund. Postponing the date when the charge would be imposed would give communities time to build the necessary sewage treatment facilities.

Air Pollution

Air pollution is even more difficult to control than water pollution. Air moves about more freely than does water in streambeds. As a result, tracing the causes of pollution in the air over a particular city or region to particular points of emission is very difficult. It is possible to define "airsheds" within which the quality of air is influenced predominantly by sources of pollution within the defined area. But though the boundaries of an airshed can be, and have been, defined for purposes of administering pollution control, in the real world they change, which means that pollution originating in one airshed can affect the quality of the air in surrounding airsheds.

A more important cause of difficulty in controlling air pollution is that much of it comes not from a limited number of stationary sources but from the more than 110 million autos, trucks, and buses that use the nation's streets and highways. This not only poses technical problems but also raises potential political difficulties. Politically it is one thing to impose controls on a limited number of business firms; it is quite another to restrict the use of automobiles on city streets, thus affecting the convenience and commuting habits of millions of voters. Yet such restrictions might well be necessary to achieve national air quality standards, even if major improvements are made in controlling pollution from auto exhausts.

Current National Policy: Air Quality Standards

National policies and programs to curtail air pollution are governed by the Clean Air amendments of 1970, which substantially modified and strengthened earlier federal legislation. Unlike the case of water pollution, there are no municipal treatment plants to be subsidized; national policy is concerned principally with regulatory problems. Air pollution control under the Clean Air amendments follows the same basic approach as that for water pollution control. Ambient air quality standards are set, which specify maximum allowable amounts of various kinds of pollutants in the air. In the case of air pollution, there is a common national standard for each pollutant, applicable in each of the 247 airsheds in the United States. Each state must develop implementation plans and schedules specifying what emission limits and other controls it will apply to the sources of pollution in each airshed to achieve the national air quality standards.

Under the Clean Air amendments the administrator of EPA was given a mandate to set national air quality standards. Those standards were announced in April 1971 for the six most important air pollutants: sulfur oxides, particulate matter, photochemical oxidants, hydrocarbons, carbon monoxide, and nitrogen dioxide. The first two are generated mainly by stationary sources—power plants, smelters, sulfuric acid plants, and the like. Vehicles are important sources of the other pollutants, particularly carbon monoxide, hydrocarbons, and nitrogen oxides. Two standards were issued for each pollutant: a primary standard specifying the pollutant concentrations low enough to prevent impairment of human health, and a stricter secondary standard sufficient to prevent damage to vegetation and materials.

By January 30, 1972, the states were required to submit to EPA their implementation plans, designed to reduce the six air pollutants to the primary standard by the middle of 1975 and to achieve the secondary standard within a "reasonable" time. In airsheds where the application of reasonably available technology can reduce pollution to the secondary standard within three years, the deadline is the same as for the primary standard. Where the application of such technology cannot accomplish this in three years, the deadline will depend on "the social, economic, and technological" problems involved. Almost all of the states have submitted implementation plans. The EPA administrator has until May 30, 1972, to approve them. If he disapproves any, he has two additional months in which to substitute a control plan of his own devising.

Proposed Tax on Sulfur Emissions

Designing and improving regulations to control air pollution at individual stationary sources encounters the same kinds of problems as those discussed above for water pollution. Applying a uniform percentage reduction to pollution from each source is likely to be particularly inefficient in the case of air pollution. As noted earlier, the application of a uniform reduction to sulfur emissions from every source in an airshed could be two to three times as costly in achieving the sulfur air quality standards as would an efficient approach that concentrated the reduction where the costs were lowest. Moreover, enforcement of emission limits is likely to be subject to extensive court proceedings and delays in the many cases where there are uncertainties about the feasibility, or the commercial availability, of control devices.

As a major step toward using the alternative incentive approach to pollution control, the administration early this year proposed to the Congress a tax on sulfur emissions. Sulfur oxide is one of the most important pollutants from stationary sources. Most of it arises from high-sulfur coal and residual oil burned in power plants and from certain smelting, chemical, and petroleum refining processes. An estimated 37 million tons of sulfur oxides are now poured into the atmosphere each year, and without control this amount would nearly quadruple to 126 million tons by the year 2000. A number of alternative approaches are available to reduce sulfur emissions: using fuel with lower sulfur content (the supply of which is limited at the present time); removing the sulfur from fuel by various processes, including potentially the production of liquefied or gaseous fuels from coal; "scrubbing" the sulfur from smokestack gases; and attaching recovery systems to manufacturing processes. With the proper incentives, there is every reason to believe that these approaches to reducing pollution can be improved and new ones designed.

The administration's proposal contemplates three levels of taxes to be imposed beginning in 1976, the year after the deadline for achieving primary air quality standards. In airsheds that have not attained the primary standard, the tax would be 15 cents per pound of sulfur emitted;[16] in airsheds that have attained the primary standard but not the stricter secondary standard, the tax would be 10 cents a pound; and in airsheds that have met or exceeded both primary and secondary standards, no tax would be levied.

There is an economic logic for the three levels of tax. The higher the tax, the greater the percentage of sulfur emissions it will pay each polluter to remove. Where air quality is very low—in airsheds with heavy concentrations of sulfur-emitting plants—individual polluters must make a large percentage reduction in order to bring the sulfur content of the air within the secondary standard. Where an intermediate quality of air has been achieved—meeting the primary but not the secondary standard—a significant but somewhat lower percentage reduction in pollution emissions is needed in order to achieve the secondary standard. A positive, but lower, emissions tax is therefore necessary. And where the air quality already exceeds the secondary standard, no reduction is necessary; hence, no tax is needed.

Studies of the costs of reducing sulfur emissions suggest that a 15-cent tax is high enough to induce substantial cutbacks in sulfur emissions, though it is impossible to prove that in all airsheds with poor quality air, this level of tax will suffice to reduce emissions enough to

16. The actual proposal is somewhat more complicated. Where a pollution source is too small for economical measurement of sulfur emitted from the smokestack, the tax would be imposed according to the sulfur content of the fuel used.

meet secondary quality standards. The administration's submission to the Congress on the sulfur tax cited estimates that sulfur pollution is now causing economic and social damage equal, on the average, to 20 cents per pound of sulfur emitted. An argument can therefore be made that a tax higher than 15 cents a pound might well be imposed. A 20-cent tax would not exceed the cost of the damages caused and would probably ensure that enough reduction would be forthcoming to meet secondary quality standards.[17] Or a 15-cent tax might be imposed initially, with a notice to industry that in areas where this failed to produce air quality meeting secondary standards within five years, the tax would be raised to 20 cents. Similarly, areas with a 10-cent tax would be put on notice that an additional 5-cent tax would be forthcoming under the same conditions.

Under the administration's proposal, an airshed that meets secondary standards would have no tax imposed. But with no sulfur tax, this area would be particularly attractive to heavy sulfur-emitting firms. If several of them decided individually to locate in the area, the overall effect of their investment decisions could cause air quality to fall below secondary standards—and it could take several years to correct the situation. For this reason it might be desirable to limit the tax exemption to areas whose air quality *exceeded* secondary standards by a specified percentage. Thus, there would be some "insurance" that the zero-tax areas would not eventually—through a burst of industrial development—exceed the secondary standard. Similar safety zones could be set up in defining areas subject to the 10-cent and 15-cent tax.

Pollution from Motor Vehicles

The Clean Air amendments required that by 1975 manufacturers must have available motor vehicles whose carbon monoxide and hydrocarbon emissions are 90 percent lower than present standards and whose warranties state that the vehicles will continue to meet the standard for five years, or 50,000 miles. A similar 90 percent reduction in nitrogen oxides emission was imposed, with a 1976 deadline. The EPA administrator was authorized to postpone those deadlines by one year under certain stringent conditions.

In the immediately foreseeable future, the cost of producing an internal combustion engine that meets these requirements will add sub-

17. If the *average* damage per pound of sulfur is 20 cents, then in areas that already have large sulfur concentrations in the air, the damage per additional pound of sulfur is much greater than 20 cents.

stantially to the price of automobiles. Estimates vary over a wide range, but it is unlikely that the cost increase will be less than several hundred dollars. Automobile manufacturers have already petitioned the EPA administrator for the one year delay allowed by law. It appears that it might be possible to produce an engine within the deadline that would meet the standards. But according to the manufacturers, it has so far been impossible to design an engine that could also meet the warranty requirements. As the time for enforcing the deadline approaches (and that is not far off, given the long planning and engineering period involved in auto production), a major confrontation and political issue is likely to develop. Are the automobile companies correct in their assertion that it is impossible to meet the deadlines? When the chips are down, will the government bring automobile production to a halt, rather than allow cars to be built that violate the standards?

An alternative to the rigid deadline approach is the imposition of a tax on each make of new automobile, graduated according to the amount of pollution it emits and to the length of the warranty it provides. Each year the tax could become higher. Rather than a once and for all showdown, characterized by claims and counterclaims as to what the automakers can and cannot produce, the tax would provide a steadily increasing incentive for the manufacturers to reduce pollution. The lower the pollution content of a particular make of car and the longer lasting the pollution control devices, the greater its price advantage. And that advantage would grow each year. A tax on new cars is not a technically or economically perfect approach to pollution control, in view of the very complex way in which the automobile affects the environment. But it has some distinct advantages over the built-in problems contained in the current showdown approach.

Even if the automobile manufacturers meet the 1975 and 1976 deadlines, for a number of years thereafter the bulk of the motor vehicles on city streets will be of older vintage, with much higher pollution emissions. Given this fact, it is unlikely that many urban areas will be able to meet the 1975 air quality standards imposed by current federal law, without sharply limiting motor vehicle traffic in downtown areas. If federal standards are maintained at their present level, some important political battles are likely to occur a few years hence as city governments grapple with this problem.

12. What Happened to the Fiscal Dividend

HISTORICALLY, peacetime economic growth has tended to generate increases in federal revenues that outstripped the rise in expenditures needed to carry out existing programs. The resulting "fiscal dividend" was available to reduce taxes or to launch new federal programs. Recent changes in tax rates and expenditure policies, however, have produced a situation in which economic growth can no longer be counted on to produce a fiscal dividend, at least not in the immediate future. This chapter examines the events of the past decade that have led to this change in the fiscal outlook.

Some Fiscal History

From the beginning of the Republic until the 1930s, federal spending was confined chiefly to providing military forces and to paying for past wars (veterans' benefits and interest on war debts). Spending for civilian purposes accounted for less than 1 percent of gross national product (GNP), a ratio that remained remarkably constant over the years. (See Table 12-1.) The New Deal measures of the 1930s for the first time expanded the federal role, and civilian outlays rose to 5 percent of GNP. That level continued throughout the postwar period into the late 1950s.

During most of the past history of the United States, the federal budget has been characterized by a tendency of revenues to grow faster than expenditures. Taxes have been increased during wars. (Indeed, major tax increases for reasons other than social security have seldom occurred except in wartime.) After each war, tax rates were reduced

394

Table 12-1. Federal Expenditures as a Percentage of Gross National Product, Selected Periods, 1869–1973[a]

Period	Total expenditures	Spending on defense or past wars[b]	Other spending
1869–73	4.5	3.3	1.2
1877–81	2.8	2.0	0.8
1889–93	2.5	1.6	0.9
1902–06	2.3	1.5	0.8
1912–16	1.8	1.1	0.7
1925–29	3.0	2.2	0.8
1935–39[c]	7.7	2.8	4.9
1947–49	15.7	10.2	5.5
1955–57	17.7	12.6	5.1
1961–63[c]	18.1	10.9	7.2
1973[c]	20.5	8.4	12.1

Sources: 1869–1939, M. Slade Kendrick, *A Century and a Half of Federal Expenditures* (National Bureau of Economic Research, 1955), pp. 75–77; 1947–49, Office of Management and Budget, Budget Review Division, unpublished tabulations (December 4, 1970); 1955–73, *The Budget of the United States Government*, relevant years. Potential GNP, 1935–39, U.S. Bureau of the Census, *Long Term Economic Growth, 1860–1965* (1966), p. 167; 1961–73, Council of Economic Advisers, unpublished tabulations (no date). Actual GNP, U.S. Office of Business Economics, *The National Income and Product Accounts of the United States, 1929–1965: Statistical Tables* (1966), Table 1.1; Office of Business Economics, *U.S. National Income and Product Accounts, 1964–67* (1971), Table 1.1; *Survey of Current Business*, various July issues.

a. Calendar years, 1869–1939; fiscal years thereafter.

b. Outlays for military purposes plus veterans' programs and net interest on the debt.

c. Potential GNP rather than actual GNP is used to avoid the effect of depression or recession on the ratios. For the same reason, federal expenditures have been adjusted to exclude the added federal unemployment compensation resulting from unemployment rates in excess of 4 percent.

but usually not to the level that prevailed before the war. In immediate postwar periods the additional taxes were needed to pay the interest on war debts. As economic growth occurred, tax collections grew apace. But military spending and interest payments did not grow. And the limited role of the federal government in the social and economic life of the nation prevented civilian outlays of the federal government from absorbing the growth of revenues. As a result, during many peacetime periods in the nineteenth century, the federal government was "embarrassed" by continuing budget surpluses and cast about for means to dispose of the fiscal dividend. Since a large part of the revenues came from tariffs imposed for protectionist reasons, tax cuts did not appeal politically as a way of eliminating the surplus. In 1837, faced with budget surpluses, the federal government distributed a revenue sharing "bonus" to the states. Three installments were paid, but the depression of 1837 led to a fall in government revenues and a cancellation of the scheduled fourth installment. When prosperity was later restored, revenues again persistently ran ahead of expenditures.

The problems posed by this surplus were clearly recognized by Secretary of the Treasury James Guthrie in his annual report for 1856:

There has been expended, since the 4th of March, 1853, more than $45,525,000 in the redemption of the public debt. This debt has been presented from time to time, as the money accumulated in the national treasury and caused stringency in the money market. If there had been no public debt, and no means of disbursing this large sum, and again giving it to the channels of commerce, the accumulated sum would have acted, fatally, on the banks and on trade. The only remedy would have been a reduction of the revenue, there being no demand and no reason for increased expenditure.[1]

In every year from 1866 to 1893 the federal government ran a surplus in its budget. When in 1887 there were no government bonds falling due for redemption, the Treasury was forced to go into the open market and buy bonds "as the only way of releasing for the uses of business its large surplus revenues."[2] When in the 1920s the same phenomenon occurred, the director of the U.S. Bureau of the Budget, General H. M. Lord, lamented the situation:

Despite persistent efforts to reduce revenue by cutting taxes to a point barely sufficient to meet our actual demands we seem helpless in the face of the country's continuing prosperity. Reduction in taxes has come to be almost synonymous with increase in revenue. At the end of each year we are called upon to determine what to do with surplus millions.[3]

Because the federal budget was such a small fraction of national economic activity, the tendency of revenues to rise faster than expenditures did not seriously threaten national economic stability until the end of the 1920s. The depression of the 1930s, the Second World War, and the Korean war obscured the problem for another twenty-five years.

By the late 1950s, however, the problem had reappeared. By then, federal expenditures accounted for 18 percent of GNP. The tax system channeled about one-fifth of economic growth into additional

1. Harvey E. Fisk, *Our Public Debt: An Historical Sketch with a Description of United States Securities* (New York: Bankers Trust Company, 1919), p. 32.
2. *Ibid.*, p. 45.
3. *Addresses of the President of the United States and the Director of the Bureau of the Budget at the Twelfth Regular Meeting of the Business Organization of the Government* (1927), p. 11.

federal revenues. On the expenditure side of the budget, however, defense and defense-related spending amounted to 12.6 percent and civilian spending to only 5.1 percent of GNP. Normal growth in civilian outlays would absorb only a small fraction of the annual increase in revenues. In the absence of a steadily rising defense budget, therefore, the potential increase in revenues each year was substantially larger than the likely increase in expenditures. And unlike the situation in earlier years, the potential excess of revenues was large enough to exert an important influence on the economy. Unless this fiscal dividend was returned to the income stream, in the form of either reduced taxes or increased expenditures, it would significantly reduce the level of economic activity. Economists, becoming aware of the phenomenon in the late 1950s, coined the term "fiscal drag" to represent the potential impact on economic activity of failure to distribute the fiscal dividend and its tendency to keep the economy operating at less than full employment. This analysis, and a political judgment that new expenditure programs could not be enacted in sufficient magnitude to absorb the revenue surplus, led to the major tax reduction of 1964.

The Fiscal Drag Reversed

The historical tendency of federal revenues to outrun expenditures during periods of prosperity has apparently been halted in recent years. In the budget for fiscal 1973, the rise in federal expenditures under existing programs, and those proposed by President Nixon in fiscal 1972, will absorb most of the growth in full employment revenues, leaving little room for major new program initiatives. And, as Chapter 13 spells out in detail, the budgetary outlook for the next three to five years is for more of the same—built-in expenditure increases more or less keeping pace with revenue growth under conditions of high and growing prosperity.

Instead of the fiscal drag foreseen a decade ago, which raised the problem of what to do with potentially excessive revenue growth, it appears increasingly difficult under existing tax rates to accommodate the fulfillment of admittedly high-priority national objectives. What has happened? Why this reversal of the budgetary outlook?

In summary, the answer is simple. First, in the space of ten short years, federal civilian expenditures as a percentage of GNP almost doubled; even if no new programs are added, the annual growth in existing expenditure programs now absorbs a much larger fraction of the growth in revenues than was the case ten years ago. Second, the American people and their political representatives have accepted a greatly broadened concept of the appropriate role of the federal government in dealing with the nation's social problems; there is a large backlog of unmet demands for new or sharply expanded federal programs addressed to those problems—assuming a share of the burden of local educational finance, providing day care centers for children of working mothers, and financing a large part of the cost of environmental cleanup, to name but a few. Third, and paradoxically, over the same decade the nation has also chosen to reduce federal income and excise taxes in a number of successive steps and by a large amount. In combination, these developments have radically altered the nature of the budgetary problem and have transformed the historical problem of fiscal drag into its opposite, the problem of "fiscal squeeze." The rest of this chapter examines the magnitude and implications of these developments.

Expenditure Growth, 1955–73

From 1955 to 1960 and again from 1960 to 1965, total federal expenditures grew quite modestly. In dollars of constant purchasing power they rose by 2.5 percent a year in the first period and 3.5 percent in the second, somewhat more slowly than the economy grew as a whole. Adjusted for inflation, defense outlays grew little over the ten-year period. While they rose sharply during the early sixties, when the U.S. strategic missile force was being rapidly put in place, by 1965 they had been reduced to a level little higher than they were in 1955. Real civilian outlays (expenditures for federal programs other than defense, space, and foreign affairs) advanced at 7.6 percent a year in the 1955–60 period and by slightly less than 6 percent in the subsequent five years, but they still remained a relatively modest proportion of GNP.

In the next five years, however, from 1965 to 1970, the rate of real increase in civilian outlays speeded up to an average of 9.1 percent a year and in the subsequent three years to 10.3 percent a year.[4] (See Table 12-2.) Civilian expenditures were 8.8 percent of GNP in 1965.

4. Expenditures have been adjusted to exclude the added federal outlays for unemployment compensation that occur when the unemployment rate exceeds 4 percent. In this way the expenditure growth comparisons are not distorted by the element of cyclical variability.

Table 12-2. Growth in Federal Civilian Outlays,ª Price Level, and Population, Selected
Periods, Fiscal Years 1955–73

Percentage growth per year

Period	Total outlays	Price level	Real outlays	Population	Real outlays per capita
1955–60	9.9	2.1	7.6	1.8	5.8
1960–65	7.3	1.4	5.8	1.5	4.1
1965–70	13.0	3.6	9.1	1.1	7.9
1970–73	15.2	4.5	10.3	1.2	9.0

Sources: Outlays, *The Budget of the United States Government*, relevant issues. Price deflators, Office of Business Economics, *The National Income and Product Accounts of the United States, 1929–1965; U.S. National Income and Product Accounts, 1964–67*, and *Survey of Current Business*, various July issues. Population, *Economic Report of the President, January 1972*, p. 219.

a. Civilian outlays include all federal expenditures except those for defense, space, and international affairs. Expenditures have been adjusted to exclude the effect of sales of financial assets and timing shifts discussed in Chapter 1. They also exclude the additional federal unemployment compensation outlays that accompany unemployment rates in excess of 4 percent.

By 1973 they will have jumped to 13.4 percent of GNP. Since the rate of growth in population has been slowing down, the contrast between the earlier and later periods in terms of per capita growth in expenditures is even more pronounced.

When civilian expenditures are only a small fraction of GNP, even a sharp rate of growth in those expenditures will not result in large dollar increases relative to the annual growth of GNP and to the federal revenues that growth produces. For example, if civilian outlays are 5 percent of GNP, even a 10 percent annual growth in those expenditures will amount to only 0.5 percent of GNP, which in turn is about one-ninth of the annual full employment growth in GNP. But if civilian outlays are, say, 15 percent of GNP, then a 10 percent rate of growth in those outlays equals 1.5 percent of GNP, which is one-third of the annual growth in full employment GNP.

The increase in the rate of expansion of federal civilian expenditures that occurred after 1965 therefore had a dual importance. Since civilian expenditures grew much more rapidly than GNP, their ratio to GNP also increased. The higher rate of growth in expenditures is now applied to a higher base, so that the resulting annual addition to expenditures represents a sharply expanded fraction of the annual growth in GNP and of the increment in federal revenues that accompanies GNP growth. If federal civilian expenditures were now the same fraction of GNP as they were in 1955, and if, on a per capita basis, they grew annually at the same rate as they did in the 1955–60 period, their annual growth would absorb about one-ninth of the yearly increase in full employment GNP and about one-half of the annual gain in revenues. In sharp contrast, starting with the 1973 ratio of civilian expenditures to GNP, continuation of the 1970–73 expenditures growth rate would absorb one-third of the annual growth in GNP. This is *larger* than the annual gain in revenues yielded by economic growth.

Sources of Expenditure Growth

In the eight years between 1955 and 1963 federal expenditures, expressed in dollars of constant 1973 purchasing power, rose by $39 billion. (See Table 12-3.) Civilian expenditures accounted for about three-fourths of this increase; outlays for defense and related purposes also rose temporarily during the rapid buildup of U.S. strategic forces in the early 1960s. More than half of the growth in civilian expenditures was concentrated in two areas—social security benefits and the newly enacted federal-aid highway program. Expenditures for all other civilian programs taken together grew by only $1.5 billion a year.

Although expenditures did not grow sharply in the next two years, a large number of new federal programs were enacted by the Congress. During the first year or so after enactment, expenditures on the programs were small. But after 1965, civilian expenditures began to rise

Table 12-3. Major Components of Federal Spending, Selected Fiscal Years, 1955–73[a]
Billions of fiscal year 1973 dollars

Component	1955	1960	1963	1965	1970	1973
Civilian expenditures, total	42.5	61.4	72.3	81.2	125.5	168.3
Social security, including Medicare	6.8	15.1	21.1	22.8	42.6	55.1
Other income maintenance	16.1	17.5	22.1	21.7	30.1	39.5
Highways	1.2	5.5	5.2	6.6	5.5	5.1
Other civilian programs	18.4	23.3	23.9	30.3	47.3	68.6
Military expenditures, total	82.2	79.4	91.3	86.2	103.0	88.0
Defense, space, foreign affairs (excluding Vietnam war)	82.2	79.4	91.3	85.6	82.6	84.5
Vietnam war costs	...	...	...	0.6	20.4	3.5
Total federal expenditures	124.7	140.8	163.6	167.6	228.5	256.3

Sources: Expenditures, except Vietnam war, *The Budget of the United States Government*, relevant issues. Vietnam war, 1973, authors' estimate; other years, based on U.S. Department of Defense data. Price deflators, same as Table 12-2.

a. Totals and components have been adjusted to exclude timing shifts, the effect of financial asset sales of the federal government, and excess unemployment benefits discussed in Chapter 1.

sharply, increasing over the next eight years more than twice as much as they had in the previous ten years. Social security outlays continued their rapid growth. And, in contrast to the earlier period, federal expenditures in other areas also climbed sharply. By the end of the period, federal civilian outlays, even apart from price increases, were rising at 10 percent a year.

Table 12-4 shows in more detail the composition of the expenditure increases from 1963 to 1973. (Unlike the previous table in this chapter, Table 12-4 is *not* expressed in constant dollars, but shows expenditures in current prices.) Defense and defense-related expenditures fell from 53 to 34 percent of the total budget over the period, while civilian outlays grew from 47 to 66 percent. The major impetus to the rapid growth in civilian budget outlays came from three sources: a continued sharp rise in cash social security benefits; the introduction and subsequent rapid expansion of new social programs; and President Nixon's newly proposed revenue sharing and welfare reform initiatives. The label "Great Society programs" in Table 12-4 may be misleading. The category includes those new social programs launched during the 1960s and a few older programs that were sharply modified and expanded during the period. Under the Nixon administration

Table 12-4. Changes in the Composition of Federal Expenditures,[a] 1963–73

Component[a]	Billions of current dollars		Percentage of total		Percentage of full employment GNP	
	1963	1973	1963	1973	1963	1973
Defense, space, foreign affairs	58.9	88.0	53	34	9.7	7.0
Civilian, total	52.6	168.3	47	66	8.7	13.5
Older income maintenance programs	28.4	75.0	25	29	4.7	6.0
Social Security (excluding Medicare)	(15.8)	(44.7)	(14)	(17)	(2.6)	(3.6)
Other	(12.6)	(30.3)	(11)	(12)	(2.1)	(2.4)
Major "Great Society" programs	1.7	35.7	2	14	0.3	2.9
Transfers in kind	(0.7)	(19.9)	(1)	(8)	(0.1)	(1.6)
Other	(0.9)	(15.8)	(1)	(6)	(0.1)	(1.3)
President Nixon's new programs	...	6.4	...	3	...	0.5
All other	22.5	51.2	20	20	3.6	4.1
Total	111.5	256.3	100	100	18.4	20.5

Sources: *The Budget of the United States Government, Fiscal Year 1965; The Budget of the United States Government, Fiscal Year 1973;* full employment GNP, Council of Economic Advisers, unpublished tabulations.

a. Figures are rounded and may not add to totals; 1973 components and total are adjusted for financial transactions and timing shifts and excess unemployment benefits discussed in Chapter 1.

these programs as a whole have continued to expand, and in several cases their growth has been accelerated—pollution control and law enforcement assistance being the outstanding examples. In total, civilian outlays rose from 8.7 to 13.5 percent of GNP, and most of the increase was accounted for by the three elements listed above.

In the past decade, the federal government took on several new responsibilities that are reflected in the growth of federal expenditures for new programs. Chapter 15 discusses the characteristics of these programs from the standpoint of their performance and the challenges they pose for effective management. But they have another aspect that has a marked impact on the rate at which federal expenditures grow. There are literally hundreds of these new programs, each providing funds for particular purposes—grants for community libraries, mental health centers, and sewer and water systems; medical services for the poor and the aged, family planning services, manpower training courses, and preschool day care centers; scholarships and loans for students and grants to colleges. In each case, particular organizations, often composed of professionals in a given field, become intensely concerned with the program, most often seeking to expand its coverage and its appropriation. By no means is this all self-interest. Once the federal government has taken on a major role in a particular area of national life, interested groups can point legitimately to how much of importance remains undone. Local librarians write to their congressman asking his support for higher appropriations for community libraries; eye doctors and physical therapists testify before the Congress seeking to expand Medicare benefits to cover their specialties; conservation organizations conduct a major campaign to increase federal grants for waste treatment plants; presidents of land grant colleges seek direct grants for their institutions, while presidents of private colleges urge expanded support for student scholarships. This is not a new kind of activity. Local chambers of commerce have been lobbying for federal flood control or navigation projects for generations. But the recent expansion in the areas of national life affected by federal programs has enormously multiplied the sources of demand for additional federal expenditures.

Changing Level and Structure of Federal Taxes

The past ten years have seen not only a sharp increase in federal civilian expenditures but also a significant change in the level and structure of federal taxes. A series of reductions has been made in the federal tax rates applied to income and corporate profits and in several major excise taxes. Simultaneously, the payroll taxes used to finance social security and Medicare have risen substantially.

The personal income tax has a progressive structure—that is, as a taxpayer's income increases, the tax rates on the successive increments of that income also rise. Moreover, as his income grows, the portion of it covered by deductions and exemptions declines, while the portion subject to taxation increases. Although the effect of this rate progression is moderated by various special provisions that give favorable tax treatment to certain forms of income received chiefly by high-income taxpayers, it is still true that as the income of a taxpayer grows, the percentage of his income taken by the personal income tax increases. As a consequence, when GNP rises and the total income of taxpayers increases, federal income tax revenues will respond more than proportionately. The ratio of personal taxes to GNP will rise, even if tax rates remain constant.

If federal personal income tax laws had remained unchanged in the period since 1963, personal income tax revenues would have increased from 8.4 percent of full employment GNP in that year to 10.2 percent in 1973. Income tax revenues would have risen by 151 percent while the GNP (in current dollars) grew by 107 percent. But personal income taxes were reduced in 1964, in 1969, and again in 1971. Because of these reductions, personal income tax collections in 1973 (at full employment levels of income) will be $28 billion less than they would have been at the 1963 income tax rates. The effect of income tax progression in raising the ratio of personal taxes to GNP has been wiped out, and indeed personal taxes will fall from 8.4 percent to 8.0 percent of GNP over the period.

Corporate income taxes are, roughly speaking, a flat percentage of corporate profits. While profits fluctuate sharply in a cyclical fashion, their proportion of full employment GNP remains more or less constant. As a consequence there is no tendency for corporate profit taxes as a percentage of GNP to rise or fall in the long run, given unchanged tax rates and depreciation regulations. But corporate tax rates were also reduced in successive steps. Part of the reduction took the form of liberalized depreciation allowances, which lower the effective rate of taxes on corporate earnings. As Table 12-5 shows, corporate tax revenues were cut by $7 billion and their ratio to GNP re-

Table 12-5. Federal Revenues in Fiscal Years 1963 and 1973 under 1963 Tax Rates, in 1973 under Current Rates, and as a Percentage of Full Employment Gross National Product

| | 1963 tax rates | | 1973 tax rates |
| | 1963 Actual | 1973 Estimated | 1973 Estimated |
Tax			
	Billions of dollars		
Individual income taxes	51.1	128.2	100.2
Corporate income taxes	25.8	53.4	46.8
Excise taxes	14.3	29.1	19.1
Other, except social security	10.0	19.3	19.4
Subtotal	101.2	230.0	185.5
Social security	15.2	41.0	59.5
Total	116.4	271.0	245.0
	Percentage of full employment GNP		
Individual income taxes	8.4	10.2	8.0
Corporate income taxes	4.3	4.3	3.7
Excise taxes	2.4	2.3	1.5
Other, except social security	1.7	1.5	1.5
Subtotal	16.8	18.3	14.7
Social security	2.5	3.3	4.8
Total	19.3	21.6	19.5

Sources: Full employment GNP, same as Table 12-4. Other data: *The Budget of the United States Government, Fiscal Year 1965; The Budget of the United States Government, Fiscal Year 1973; Reports of the 1971 Advisory Council on Social Security,* Communication from Secretary of Health, Education, and Welfare, H. Doc. 92-80, 92 Cong. 1 sess. (1971), p. 98; Council of Economic Advisers, unpublished tabulations (no date); Social Security Administration, unpublished tabulations (Dec. 30, 1971).

duced from 4.3 percent to 3.7 percent. Excise taxes were also reduced during the last decade, by $10 billion. Their ratio to GNP fell from 2.4 percent in 1963 to 1.5 percent in 1973.

While these tax reductions were taking place, payroll taxes were being raised. The legislation that establishes the benefits to be paid under social security also sets forth the payroll tax rates that finance the benefits. Historically, the social security law provides for tax rates to be gradually increased in future years. The law in effect during 1963, for example, provided for a 7.25 percent tax on payrolls for that year, and the rate was scheduled to rise gradually to 9.25 percent by 1968. In a series of amendments to the Social Security Act during the past ten years, the rate schedule has been raised substantially to pay for benefit increases, including the introduction of Medicare. H.R. 1, now pending in the Congress, would raise the payroll tax rate from 10.4 percent in 1971 to 10.8 percent in 1973, with increases scheduled for future years until the rate reaches 14.8 percent in 1977. In 1963 the maximum wage taxable under social security was $4,800; it is now $9,000 and would be increased to $10,200 under H.R. 1.

If the 1963 schedule of tax rates had remained in effect, and if the wage ceiling had been increased only in line with increased wage rates generally, payroll taxes would have risen from 2.5 percent of GNP in 1963 to 3.3 percent in 1973. Because of legislation increasing the rate schedule and raising the wage ceiling, payroll tax collections have expanded much more rapidly than that, and will reach 4.8 percent of GNP in 1973, almost double the 1963 ratio.

Total federal revenues would have grown from 19.3 percent to 21.6 percent of GNP, had 1963 tax laws remained in effect for the past ten years. The increase in the ratio would have come about principally because of the progressivity of the personal income tax, although payroll taxes would have risen slightly relative to GNP. The net result of all the tax changes during the period, however, was to reduce the ratio of federal taxes to GNP almost back to the level of 1963, and to reduce federal revenues in 1973 by $26 billion below the level that would have been yielded by the tax laws in effect in 1963.

How the Dividend Has Been Distributed

A decade ago, economic expansion clearly promised to generate a growth in federal revenues substantially in excess of the likely growth in expenditures. Defense outlays, with the buildup in strategic arms having already peaked, were likely to decline. Civilian outlays were only 8.7 percent of GNP. Their growth at rates characteristic of the preceding ten years, or even at moderately higher rates, would fall far short of absorbing the annual increase in revenues. This presented both a problem and an opportunity. Failure to take any action would pose a problem of fiscal drag: the potential excess of revenue growth relative to expenditures would tend to depress economic activity and lead to rising unemployment. Indeed, the relatively slow economic growth and high unemployment rates of the late 1950s and early 1960s were attributed by many economists to precisely this cause. On the other hand, the situation could also be viewed as an opportunity: economic growth would yield a fiscal dividend, which could be distributed either in the form of tax cuts or through the introduction of major new federal programs.

In the ten years since 1963, both avenues to distribution of the fiscal dividend have been followed. In order to examine what use the nation has made of this fiscal dividend, revenues and expenditures have been projected to 1973 on the basis of the 1963 outlook:

1. Federal revenues were projected to 1973 on the assumption of a full employment economy and on the basis of federal tax laws in effect in 1963. (This allowed for the scheduled rise in payroll tax rates incorporated in the 1963 social security law.)

2. Federal expenditures were projected on the following assumptions: (a) that after the peak level of outlays on the strategic missile buildup, outlays for the defense–space–foreign affairs complex would decline from $91 billion to $85 billion (in 1973 dollars) and remain constant; (b) that consistent with past experience, social security benefits would be expanded to keep pace with payroll tax revenues; (c) that highway expenditures would grow to about $5 billion a year, as has actually happened; and (d) that other federal expenditures, adjusted for inflation, would expand by 4.5 percent a year, compared to the 3.4 percent annual rate from 1955 to 1960 and the 4.1 percent annual rate from 1960 to 1963.

The results of this projection are shown in the first bank of figures in Table 12-6. Under the assumptions described above, federal revenues at full employment would have been more than $68 billion in excess of expenditures by 1973. Assuming, for the moment, a balanced full employment budget, a $68 billion fiscal dividend would have been available by 1973 for use either in tax reductions, expenditure increases over and above the projection, or some combination of both.

The remaining part of Table 12-6 spells out how the fiscal dividend was used. Since social security taxes were raised while other taxes were being cut, the table separately identifies changes in social security taxes and benefits.

Because of the tax cuts of the past ten years, federal revenues in 1973 (excluding social security taxes) will be $45 billion less than they would have been under 1963 tax laws. Expenditures will be $36 billion above what might have been expected on the basis of trends in effect before 1963. An additional $3.5 billion will be used in 1973 to carry on what is left of the war in Vietnam. Altogether, some $84 billion was distributed in the form of tax cuts and expenditure increases, $16 billion more than the available fiscal dividend. The federal government financed $9 billion of this excess through the sale of various assets,

Table 12-6. Disposition of the 1973 Fiscal Dividend as Projected from the 1963 Outlook
Billions of dollars

	1973		
Description	Budget, excluding social security	Social security	Total budget
Revenues at 1963 tax rates	230.0	41.0	271.0
Expenditures projected from 1963	161.5	41.0	202.6
Potential fiscal dividend	68.5	0.0	68.5
Uses of the potential fiscal dividend			
Tax reductions (−)	−44.5	+18.5	−26.0
Expenditure increases (−)	−36.2	−14.1	−50.3
Vietnam war costs (−)	−3.5	...	−3.5
Total uses	−84.2	+4.4	−79.8
Excess of uses over the potential fiscal dividend (−)			
Portion financed by sales of government assets and so forth (−)	−9.0	...	−9.0
Portion financed by deficit (−)	−6.7	+4.4	−2.3
Total excess of uses	−15.7	+4.4	−11.3

Source: Derived by authors, based on full employment GNP.

principally mortgages in its portfolio and proceeds from oil royalties and leases on the continental shelf. This left a $7 billion full employment deficit in the budget, apart from the social security trust fund.

Increases in payroll taxes, over and above those scheduled in the 1963 law, will add $18.5 billion to social security revenues. Benefits will be $14 billion above those that might have been projected in 1963. The resulting surplus in the social security trust funds in 1973 will offset a large part of the full employment deficit in the remainder of the budget.

Outlook

The prospective growth in federal expenditures in the coming years will be substantially larger than it was ten years ago for three main reasons: (1) Since the overall size of the budget is so much greater, simple growth in "workload" has a larger impact. Even if the conditions of eligibility for federal assistance are not liberalized, keeping up with a growing workload and with sharply rising costs in areas such as construction and medical services will add substantial amounts to the budget each year. (2) As was discussed above, the backlog of unmet demands for federal assistance in each of the new programs is large, the case for expanding these programs is persuasively argued by the groups concerned, and the political benefits of expansion are significant. (3) The forces that led the federal government to assume major new responsibilities in the past decade have not run their course. The people of the United States have increasingly come to believe that the federal government can and should play an important role in dealing with a host of social problems that a short time ago would have been ignored or left to state and local governments. New federal programs have been proposed for a number of these problems—to name only two, the financial plight of central cities and the wide inequalities of educational opportunity that result from reliance on local property taxes to finance elementary and secondary schools. For all of these reasons, the recent 10 to 11 percent annual rate of growth in federal civilian expenditures is not likely to be a temporary phenomenon. It reflects a relatively new but strongly growing demand.

Chapter 13 projects to 1977 the rise in federal revenues that can be expected to accompany economic growth under tax laws currently in effect. It also projects the built-in growth in expenditures likely to occur under existing and currently proposed federal programs—that is, the growth stemming from the first factor listed in the preceding paragraph. The chapter concludes that the fiscal dividend—the gap between the growth in potential revenues and built-in expenditure increases—is likely to be very small, even five years from now.

The demands for additional federal expenditures will, of course, grow more rapidly than the increase in outlays built into present programs and policies. There seems to be no reason why they will grow at a rate slower than in recent years; but from the point of view of financing these demands, the situation will be less favorable. During the past several years, reductions in the real level of defense spending associated with the withdrawals from Vietnam offset part of the rise in civilian outlays. Between 1970 and 1973, the costs of Vietnam, in constant 1973 prices, fell from $20.4 billion to $3.5 billion, while other defense and defense-related spending, after adjustment for inflation, rose only slightly. (See Table 12-3.) Most of the budgetary savings from Vietnam have already been realized, and even a complete withdrawal, accompanied by modest levels of economic and military aid to Vietnam, would yield little further in the way of released budgetary resources. At the same time, as Chapter 3 points out, current defense budget policy will result in sizable increases in the real level of defense spending over the next several years. The impact on the total budget of continued increases in civilian spending of the magnitude of recent years will no longer be moderated by reductions in the real level of defense outlays. And, given the fact that the civilian expenditures of the federal government are now 13.5 percent of GNP, growth in these expenditures at the rates experienced in recent years could be expected to more than absorb the tax revenues generated by economic growth.

In summary, given the tax cuts of recent years and the large built-in growth of federal expenditures, the fiscal dividend in the near future is likely to be much smaller in relation to the size of the economy than historically has been the case in years of peacetime prosperity. At the same time, the growth in the demand for the public services furnished by the federal government is likely to be much greater. In the past, the problem in peacetime was how to deal with the resources channeled into the government by economic growth. For the immediate future at least, the problem appears to be one of trying to find enough resources to finance the growing demand for public services. Paradoxically, the growing absolute affluence of society is now accompanied by a relative squeeze on the resources of the federal government. The problem is compounded by the fact that state and local governments have been steadily raising their tax rates and are meeting growing resistance from taxpayers to further increases. For both of these reasons the problem of setting priorities in the public sector is becoming more, rather than less, acute despite the continuing rise in national income.

13. Revenue and Expenditure Projections: 1973-77

THE PRECEDING CHAPTER EXPLAINED how the United States, during the past ten years, decided to allocate between tax cuts and additional public spending the resources made available to the federal sector by economic growth. It also pointed out some of the future consequences of those decisions. This chapter spells out in more detail the revenue and expenditure framework within which federal budgetary policies will have to be made during the next five years.

National decisions about allocating resources through the federal budget do not have their major consequences immediately. Deciding to procure a large new weapon system, to undertake a new health insurance program, or to increase federal assistance for municipal waste treatment plants normally has little impact on the next year's budget. But such decisions represent important commitments for years beyond that. Similarly, tax cuts reduce the government's revenues not only in the year when they are enacted, but for all subsequent years as well. Explicit decisions about national priorities—about how the nation's resources should be allocated to public purposes—must therefore take into account a longer perspective than a one-year budget. Failure to do so leads to *implicit* priority setting, in which the actual use of resources in a given year reflects not so much the planned results of deliberate decisions, but the unforeseen consequences of past decisions that concentrated only on the near future.

410

In the next five years, economic growth will substantially increase the full employment tax revenues of the federal government. But the expenditures necessary to carry out the existing and proposed policies and programs in the 1973 budget will also rise. A comparison of these two magnitudes—the full employment revenues projected to be available and the future expenditures implied in the current budget—provides a starting point for debate and decision about priority setting.

In summary, the projection shows that over the next two years, from fiscal 1973 to fiscal 1975, expenditures under existing and currently proposed programs are likely to run substantially ahead of full employment revenues. Barring some change either in current policies or in tax laws, a sizable full employment deficit will be forthcoming. Over the subsequent two years the growth of expenditures under existing programs will be somewhat less and the rise in revenues somewhat larger. By fiscal 1977, full employment revenues may be higher than expenditures projected under current and proposed programs, but by a very modest amount, well within the range of error inherent in such projections. And even that modest surplus of revenues is threatened by likely developments in the social security program. In short, given existing and officially proposed expenditure programs, the increase in revenues generated by economic growth over the next five years is already fully committed. Indeed, during the early part of the period, it is overcommitted.

The fact that the projection compares full employment revenues with expenditures does not imply that it is always appropriate national policy for the two magnitudes to be exactly in balance. When demand for goods and services on the part of consumers and private investors is weak, a full employment deficit may be called for, as is the case with the fiscal 1972 budget. Under conditions of very buoyant private demand, a full employment budget surplus will be desirable. And so it may be that in fiscal 1975 or 1977, economic conditions will call for a full employment deficit, or alternatively for a sizable surplus. But it is impossible to forecast the state of private demand so far ahead. As a consequence, longer-run planning for resource allocation purposes cannot prudently rely on future budget deficits as a means of financing long-term program commitments or, conversely, avoid commitments because a large budget surplus may possibly be required at some future date. Marginal adjustments in taxes or expenditures can and should be made when the economic situation becomes clear. For these reasons, the projections in this chapter will use full employment revenues as a measure of the resources available for expenditure programs in future years without implying that a balanced full employment budget is the appropriate policy year in and year out.

Revenues

Projecting the full employment revenues that would be forthcoming under existing tax laws involves two sets of estimates: (1) the level of gross national product (GNP) and the major components of the national income that would be generated under conditions of full employment, and (2) the federal revenues that those incomes would yield if the current tax laws were applied.

Table 13-1 shows the major economic assumptions on which the projections are based. Full employment conditions, with the unemployment rate at 4 percent, are assumed. The increase in GNP between 1971 and 1975 therefore reflects both the growth in economic capacity, at about 4.25 percent a year, and the greater use of capacity as unemployment declines. It is assumed that prices continue to rise, but at a slower rate than in recent years; price increases taper off from the 4.6 percent of 1970–71 to 2.7 percent by 1974 and continue at that rate throughout the remaining years of the projection. In recent years, corporate profits as a percentage of GNP have fallen sharply and by somewhat more than would be expected during periods of recession. The projections assume that profits recover most, but not all, of this loss in their share of GNP. To the extent that this assumption overstates the rise in profits, projected revenues are also overstated, since

Table 13-1. Level of Economic Indicators Used in Budget Projections, Calendar
Years 1971, 1975, and 1977

Dollar amounts in billions

Economic indicator	1971 actual	1975 projected	1977 projected
GNP, current dollars	1,047	1,480	1,690
GNP, 1971 dollars	1,047	1,315	1,420
Personal income less transfers, current dollars	762	1,077	1,229
Corporate profits before taxes, current dollars	85	150	171
Unemployment rate, percent	5.9	4.0	4.0
Private GNP deflator, index	100.0	112.0	117.6

Sources: 1971, *Economic Indicators* (March 1972); 1975, 1977 projections, Brookings Budget Projection Model.

Table 13-2. Projected Federal Revenues, by Source, Fiscal Years 1973, 1975, and 1977

Billions of dollars

Source	1973	1975	1977
Revenues under tax laws in effect before the tax reductions of 1969 and 1971[a]	236	301	363
Individual income taxes	106	140	168
Corporate income taxes	37	49	57
Social insurance taxes and contributions	64	80	102
Excise taxes	18	20	22
All other taxes	11	12	14
Revenue loss from 1969 and 1971 tax reductions[b]	−15	−18	−23
Individual income taxes	−12	−14	−16
Corporate income taxes	−1	−2	−4
Excise taxes	−2	−2½	−3
Actual revenues	221	}283	}340
Full employment revenues	245		

Sources: *The Budget of the United States Government, Fiscal Year 1973*, and the Brookings Budget Projection Model.

a. Excludes individual income tax surcharge. Social insurance taxes are based on the assumptions explained in the text.

b. Includes the effect of liberalized depreciation provisions, promulgated by administration rules in 1971 and, after modification, confirmed in the Revenue Act of 1971.

the rate of tax on corporate profits is higher than the average rate applied to other forms of income.

Using these economic assumptions, the federal revenues that would be forthcoming under existing tax laws are estimated next. Except for social security payroll taxes, revenues were first calculated according to the tax laws in effect in 1969. An estimate was then made of the revenue losses stemming from changes that have occurred in the tax laws since then—the Tax Reform Act of 1969 and the Revenue Act of 1971, both of which reduced taxes substantially. Payroll taxes were estimated on the basis of the tax rates called for in the social security bill (H.R. 1) passed by the House last year and now pending in the Senate.[1] Table 13-2 shows the results of these estimates. Since the economy will be operating during the coming year at less than full employment levels, the actual revenues collected in fiscal 1973 will be less than full employment revenues. But in 1975 and 1977 the projection assumes that full employment conditions will prevail. Hence projected revenues for those years are the same as full employment revenues.

1. The payroll tax estimates also assume that the maximum wage subject to payroll tax is periodically raised to keep up with the projected increase in average wage rates.

The combination of economic growth and sizable increases in payroll tax rates scheduled in the pending social security bill will increase full employment revenues from $245 billion in fiscal 1973 to $283 billion in 1975 and $340 billion in 1977. These revenue projections incorporate tax losses of $18 billion in 1975 and $23 billion in 1977, resulting from the tax cuts of the past three years. Even after taking account of the tax cuts, however, the increase in full employment revenues over the next four budget years is very substantial—$95 billion, or almost 40 percent.

Expenditures

If continuation of the programs and policies incorporated in the 1973 budget also implied a continuation of the 1973 level of expenditures ($244 billion) over the subsequent four years, then the entire $95 billion growth in full employment revenues by 1977 would be available as a fiscal dividend for discretionary use—for expanding the scope of existing programs, inaugurating new ones, cutting taxes, or some combination of all of these policies. But for a number of reasons, expenditures under existing programs and policies will rise sharply, so that much less than the $95 billion will actually be available for discretionary use.

Table 13-3 summarizes the basic factors underlying the projected expansion of budget outlays, given the policies and programs in the 1973 budget. The first of these is inflation.

While price increases are projected to become more moderate, they are not projected to cease. Moreover, since the impact of price increases on many parts of the budget is a delayed one, the projected moderation in the rate of inflation will be reflected in a slower rate of expenditure increases only after a time lag. There is, of course, no immutable necessity for the administration and the Congress to raise expenditures on various federal programs in order to keep pace with inflation. But failure to do so would represent an implicit policy decision to reduce the real level of government services, grants, and income support. The projection assumes that expenditures will be raised to cover higher prices and higher wages for federal military and civilian employees. About $9 billion a year in added federal expenditures will be required for these purposes, given the projected rate of inflation— adding up to about $35 billion over the four-year period.

Beyond the increases required to meet inflation, budget outlays will

Table 13-3. Projected Changes in Federal Outlays, Fiscal Years 1973–75 and
1975–77, and Selected Total Outlays, Fiscal Years 1973, 1975, and 1977
Billions of dollars

	Change in outlays	
Cause of change	1973–75	1975–77
Existing programs		
Pay increases	4.5	4.5
Price increases	12.9	13.0
Increases in workloads, beneficiaries, and so forth[a]	12.2	12.2
Defense programs (excluding effects of pay and price increases)	7.0	4.0
Excess of appropriations over spending[b]	2.0	0
Financial adjustments	6.6	0
New programs		
Revenue sharing	4.0	1.0
Family assistance	5.0	−1.0
Family health insurance	1.7	1.0
Total change	**56.0**	**35.0**

	Total outlays		
Category of outlay	1973	1975	1977
Total federal outlays	**244.3**	**300**	**335**
Military outlays[c]	76.5	90	100
Civilian outlays	167.8	210	235
Outlays under selected programs			
Public assistance	7.6	9.0	10.6
Medicaid	3.4	4.2	5.2
Social security[d]	43.8	49.6	55.7
Medicare[e]	8.9	13.0	15.7
Federal employees retirement (military and civilian)	8.5	10.7	13.2

Sources: *The Budget of the United States Government, Fiscal Year 1973*, and the Brookings Budget Projection Model.
a. Unemployment compensation expenditures in 1973, as well as in subsequent years, assume full employment conditions.
b. Appropriations excess in major civilian programs only. The excess of appropriations over spending in the 1973 military budget is included as an item in the projection of defense spending.
c. Department of Defense, military functions plus military assistance programs.
d. Old age, survivors, and disability insurance (OASDI) payments.
e. Includes proposed Medicare for the disabled.

have to increase to cover growing workloads, rising numbers of beneficiaries, and in some cases legislated improvement in benefit levels under existing programs. The number of aged beneficiaries under the social security and Medicare programs continues to rise, and pending legislation provides an increase in benefit levels. While the recent rate of increase in the number of public assistance beneficiaries is not likely to continue, some further rise is likely. A continuation of the current levels of construction of federally subsidized housing implies a continuing increase in the annual subsidy cost. Each year's construction adds to the stock of housing on which subsidies are paid. An examination of the components of the federal budget suggests that increases of about $5 billion to $6 billion a year will be required to take account of the growth in workload, numbers of beneficiaries, and the like.

Chapter 3 examined the future budgetary implications of the defense policies and programs underlying the 1973 budget. This chapter incorporates those projections. It also assumes that $1 billion a year in budgetary savings is realized from a successful conclusion to the first round of the strategic arms limitation talks (SALT) and, for the sake of conservatism, that only half of the possible cost overruns of weapon systems estimated in Chapter 3 actually occur. On this basis, defense outlays would rise by $10 billion between 1973 and 1977. This is quite apart from the effect of wage and price increases on the military budget, which is included, along with the effect of inflation on the civilian budget, in the first two lines of Table 13-3. Taking into account both real increases and inflation, the projection shows military spending rising from $76.5 billion in fiscal 1973, to $90 billion in 1975, and $100 billion in 1977.

Several other factors will add substantially to budget expenditures during the next several years. In some relatively new or rapidly growing programs, the level of federal commitments or contracts contemplated in 1973 is significantly higher than the level of spending in that year, due to the time lag between making commitments and actually spending the money. Federal agreements to furnish grants for municipal waste treatment plants, for example, will total $2 billion in 1973, and appropriations of that amount are required to make these agreements possible. But since it takes time to get construction under way, actual grant expenditures will total only $1 billion. If the program continues to make commitments at the rate of $2 billion each year, spending will gradually rise to that level. The defense projection already allowed for the 1973 excess of appropriations over expenditures. In civilian agencies, a conservative estimate has been made that a further $2 billion rise in spending will be needed on this account.

As Chapter 1 pointed out, numerous financial transactions contemplated in the 1973 budget are treated in budget accounting as "negative expenditures" and thereby have the effect of holding down the budget totals—estimated sales of $4.6 billion in government mortgages, some $3.1 billion in proceeds from oil royalties and rents through lease of offshore oil rights, $700 million in strategic stockpile sales, a $1 billion switch of public assistance payments from 1973 to the last months of 1972, and several similar items. Such transactions cannot be maintained at this level. Future budget outlays will have to rise by a substantial amount as fewer of these negative expenditure adjustments become available.

The 1973 budget proposes a series of new programs whose expenditures will increase in later years. If President Nixon's general and special revenue sharing proposals are enacted, they will cost $5.6 billion in 1973, $9.8 billion in 1975, and $10.4 billion in 1977, according to estimates presented in the 1973 budget. The family assistance program will require only $350 million in 1973 (for "make ready" costs), but will rise to $5.9 billion in 1975. By 1977, these outlays are expected to decline slightly. Similarly the President's family health insurance program is not proposed to become effective until 1974, but it will add several billion to budget expenditures once it is fully under way. All together, the major new programs proposed in the budget would increase outlays by about $10 billion between 1973 and 1975 and by another $1 billion in 1977.

In total, the military and civilian programs and policies incorporated in the 1973 budget, combined with rising prices, wages, and workloads, imply an increase of $56 billion in full employment budget expenditures between 1973 and 1975, raising total outlays to about $300 billion in that year. Another $35 billion would be added in the next two years, bringing the budget total to $335 billion in 1977.

Revenues and Expenditures Combined

Table 13-4 combines the revenue and expenditure projections. Between 1973 and 1975 the $56 billion rise in expenditures will substantially exceed the $38 billion growth in full employment revenues. With no new programs or discretionary expansion of existing programs beyond what is already implied in the 1973 budget, expenditures will exceed full employment revenues by $17 billion. In the following two years, a faster growth in revenues, coupled with a slower rise in expenditures, will produce a modest fiscal dividend of $5 billion.

Table 13-4. Projected Full Employment Revenues and Expenditures, Fiscal Years 1973, 1975, and 1977

Billions of dollars

Revenue or expenditure item	*1973*	*1975*	*1977*
Full employment revenues before tax cuts of 1969 and 1971	260	301	363
Revenue loss from tax cuts	−15	−18	−23
Full employment revenues after tax cuts of 1969 and 1971	245	283	340
Full employment expenditures	244	300	335
Excess of revenues (+) or expenditures (−)	+1	−17	+5

Sources: *The Budget of the United States Government, Fiscal Year 1973*, and Brookings Budget Projection Model.

Full employment revenues rise more rapidly in the last two years of the projection period than in the first two for several reasons. A roughly constant percentage rate of expansion in the economy is applied each year to a higher base. The absolute increase therefore is larger each year, leading to larger absolute increases in incomes subject to tax. More important, however, are the sharp increases in social security taxes scheduled in pending legislation for the later years of the projection period. (See Table 13-5.) Only part of the large increase in calendar 1975 will be reflected in fiscal year 1975 revenues. But in 1977 this full increase will be in effect as well as half of the next large jump scheduled for January 1, 1977.

Because of these large increases in social security tax rates, there will be a growing excess of social security tax revenues over benefit payments. In the rest of the federal budget, taken as a whole, expenditures will be substantially higher than revenues. (See Table 13-6.) The 1971 report by the Advisory Council on Social Security concluded that the social security system was "overfinanced"—that is, projected

Table 13-5. Social Security Tax Rates Scheduled in H.R. 1, Calendar Years 1972–77 and After

Percent

Year	*Tax rate*[a]
1972–74	10.8
1975–76	12.4
1977 and after	14.8

Source: *Social Security Amendments of 1971*, Report of the Committee on Ways and Means on H.R.1, H. Rept. 92-231, 92 Cong. 1 sess. (1971), p. 24.
a. Combined employer-employee rate.

Table 13-6. Relationship of Federal Revenues to Expenditures under Full Employment for the Total Budget, for the Social Security Program, and for All Other Programs, Fiscal Years 1973, 1975, and 1977
Billions of dollars

	Excess of revenues (+) *or expenditures* (−)		
Program	*1973*	*1975*	*1977*
Total federal budget	+1	−17	+5
Social security (including Medicare)[a]	+4	+6	+20
All other	−3	−23	−15

Source: Brookings Budget Projection Model.
a. Revenues from tax receipts only—excludes interest on federal securities and federal payments to trust funds.

tax rates were more than sufficient to cover projected expenditures.[2] The chairman of the House Ways and Means Committee has expressed his agreement with this finding and has suggested that benefits could be increased by 20 percent, rather than the 5 percent called for in pending legislation and assumed in the projection.[3] Whether the overfinancing is handled by a reduction of scheduled tax rates or an increase in benefits—and history suggests that one of the two results will occur—the small 1977 fiscal dividend projected above for the budget as a whole will thereby be reduced or eliminated.

In summary, full employment revenues under existing tax laws are not likely to be sufficient in 1975 to cover the expenditures forthcoming in that year from a continuation of the policies and programs contained in the 1973 budget, and may fail to do so by a wide margin. While it is not inconceivable that a modest full employment deficit would be necessary in 1975 to promote economic prosperity, it would not be prudent to count on that possibility, and certainly not a deficit of the size projected here ($17 billion).

By 1977 a small margin of revenues over expenditures could open up. But even a small margin would depend on a substantial excess of receipts over expenditures in the social security system—and past experience, the recent report of the Advisory Council on Social Security, and statements of the chairman of the House Ways and Means Committee all suggest that a large surplus will not be allowed to accumu-

2. *Reports of the 1971 Advisory Council on Social Security*, H. Doc. 92-80, 92 Cong. 1 sess. (1971), pp. 64–70.
3. "Increase in Social Security Benefits," *Congressional Record*, daily ed., February 23, 1972, pp. H1413–15.

late. In that case, even by 1977, full employment revenues under existing tax laws may not be large enough to match projected expenditures under current programs and policies.

While the assumptions about the rate of inflation contained in the projections influence both the revenue and expenditure estimates, the use of other assumptions within a reasonable range would not alter the conclusions substantially. A faster than assumed rate of price increase over the next five years would tend to raise revenues by somewhat more than expenditures. Under the personal income tax, the higher monetary incomes that accompany inflation are subjected to higher rates of taxation, and to this extent federal revenues grow more than proportionately with inflation if tax laws are unchanged. In addition, many federal expenditures adjust to price increases only after a time lag, so that the effect of inflation on expenditures is somewhat delayed. These factors, of course, would work in the opposite direction if inflation slowed by more than is assumed in the projection. But the magnitude of these influences would be moderate.

New Program Proposals

Although revenue growth under existing tax laws may be insufficient to cover expenditure growth under existing programs, several new or sharply expanded federal programs are now under serious political discussion, each involving substantial additions to the budget. Many of these were discussed in earlier chapters.

• The replacement of local property taxes devoted to schools by federal financing would cost approximately $12 billion.

• Equalization of expenditures per pupil within states would require an additional $9 billion, part of which would probably have to come from the federal government.

• The pending House and Senate water pollution control bills would add about $3 billion to $4 billion a year to federal grants for waste treatment and related facilities.

• A major congressional initiative for federal support of day care programs was vetoed by President Nixon in 1971. But interest remains high, and as Chapter 8 points out, the provision of day care services for children of the poor and near-poor would involve perhaps from $5 billion to $12 billion a year in federal subsidies.

• National health insurance proposals of widely varying scope are now before the Congress. The administration's proposals are the smallest from a budgetary standpoint, and their cost of $2.6 billion by 1977 has been included in the projections; other and more far-reaching proposals would cost very large amounts—up to $60 billion in the case of the most expensive program.

The specific estimates of revenues and expenditures are, of course, subject to error and may overstate the degree to which current expenditure programs will absorb, or more than absorb, the growth in full employment revenues. In addition some fiscal stimulus in the form of a full employment deficit might be needed in the next few years. But, at a minimum, it is clear that economic growth and current tax laws will not yield sufficient resources to finance any major new federal programs over the next four years. Only two sources of financing are available for new programs: changes in current policies and programs leading to expenditure reductions, and tax increases.

Chapter 5 presented alternative sets of military policies that would reduce budget expenditures below those implied in current policies While the lowest of these options does not represent a radical revision of the U.S. defense posture, it would require a very substantial cutback and cancellation of new weapon procurement and a further reduction in force levels. It would reduce 1977 military outlays, in real terms, by $12 billion below the level assumed in the projection; after inflation is taken into account, the reduction might be $13 billion or $14 billion. Some of this reduction would simply help keep total outlays in line with full employment revenues, particularly in the next two years. Thereafter, some of the reduction might be available for new federal civilian programs.

The two prior volumes of *Setting National Priorities* discussed areas of the civilian budget in which federal expenditures seemed to be yielding only marginal national benefits: farm subsidies, particularly those going to large farms; merchant marine subsidies; aid to "impacted" school districts; public works for navigation and irrigation; and subsidies to owners of private aircraft. But the total sums involved are small compared to the cost of the new program proposals listed above. Moreover, the unsuccessful experience of several administrations in trying to reduce some of these subsidies does not warrant optimism about the possibility of realizing substantial budgetary savings.

For all of these reasons, a major expansion of federal activities

along any one or several of the lines discussed in this book would almost surely require a tax increase. Over the past ten years the nation
has chosen to reduce the major sources of federal revenue, except for
social security payroll taxes. As Chapter 12 pointed out, these reductions will aggregate $45 billion by fiscal 1973. At the same time, the
federal government has been able to undertake large new programs,
sharply raising the proportion of national income devoted to civilian
public objectives. In the decade ahead the choices will be much more
difficult. Lasting new federal initiatives can be financed only with a tax
increase. Various forms of tax increases are possible. The next chapter
discusses alternative sources of additional revenue and evaluates them
by several criteria.

14. Alternative Sources of Federal Revenue

ECONOMIC GROWTH WILL PRODUCE no fiscal dividend for the federal government in the near future. Hence, launching any of the major new federal programs discussed in earlier chapters of this book will require either cutting spending on current programs or raising taxes.[1] While some spending reductions are possible—several options in the defense budget were discussed in Chapter 5—it would not be realistic to rely on them as the sole means of financing new federal programs. Therefore, serious consideration of new programs necessarily involves consideration of tax increases to pay for them.

While one might conceive of numerous ways of raising additional federal revenue, in practice the feasible alternatives narrow down to three: (1) reforming the current structure of the personal income and corporate profit taxes by changing provisions that now give preferential treatment to income from certain sources or to particular categories of taxpayers; (2) raising tax rates on the present personal and corporate income tax base; and (3) finding a new source of revenue not now being taxed by the federal government. The only realistic possibility in the third category is a tax on consumer expenditures. In this chapter these three major alternatives are compared and evaluated.

Criteria for Evaluating Alternative Taxes

Taxes inevitably generate political controversy because no one likes to pay them. Taxpayers may recognize intellectually that taxes are the

1. Financing new programs through large and continuous budget deficits is a third alternative, but it would have serious inflationary effects if full employment were restored.

"prices" they pay for public services, but they seem to resent taxes far more than other prices—presumably because they see no immediate connection between the taxes they pay and the services they receive. When someone pays for an automobile or a steak dinner, however much he may complain about high prices, he can see that the payment produced some tangible benefit to himself. When he pays taxes to support federal programs to equalize educational opportunity or increase national security, the benefits seem intangible, diffuse, and unrelated to his individual tax payment. Hence, while private transactions are normally viewed as a two-way street—one pays money and receives a good or service—taxes are more often seen as purely negative. At best they are a necessary evil.

Moreover, tax decisions inevitably pit one group against another. The particular set of taxes chosen will determine how the cost of government is shared among different groups, and almost everyone feels that others could more fairly be called on to bear a larger share of the total burden.

There are no totally objective ways of distinguishing "good" taxes from "bad" taxes or saying who ought to pay the most. However, at least four questions should be raised in evaluating an existing or proposed tax.

1. *Is the tax equitable?* Most people would agree that "equity" implies among other things that people in the same economic circumstances should pay the same amount of tax. Some violations of the equity principle are obvious—for example, when local property tax assessors place different values on houses in the same neighborhood that turn out, when sold, to have the same market value. Other inequities are more controversial—for example, those resulting from differing federal income tax treatment of individuals or business firms whose economic circumstances are basically similar. Is it equitable to tax income earned as wages or salaries differently from income earned as interest on a municipal bond and still differently from income earned as capital gains on the sale of property or securities—as federal income tax laws now do?

2. *Who bears the burden?* Taxes may be distinguished according to the burden they place on different income groups. A "progressive" tax is one that takes a larger proportion of the income of a rich person than of a poor person; a "regressive" tax takes a higher proportion of

the income of the poor. Most people would agree that the tax system as a whole ought to be progressive. Taxes on the poor cause hardship because they reduce the ability of the poor to pay for the basic necessities of life. Taxes on higher-income persons cut into luxuries rather than necessities. Problems arise, of course, in judging precisely how progressive a tax system ought to be and whether new taxes should make it more or less progressive than it already is.

It is also far from obvious how progressive or regressive a particular tax actually is unless one knows whose real income is ultimately reduced by the tax (the "incidence" of the tax). The person who writes the check to the government for the tax may not be the one who really bears the burden. Is the tax on property borne by the landlord, or does he pass it on to the tenant through higher rent? Is a tax on corporate profits borne by stockholders, or is it passed on to consumers in the form of higher prices?

Economists are fairly certain about the final incidence of general sales taxes and income taxes. In general, the burden of personal income taxes is borne directly by the individual taxpayers. The present federal income tax is progressive, despite numerous provisions that benefit mainly high-income persons. General sales taxes fall on consumers because retailers pass along the full tax in higher prices. Since low-income persons spend higher proportions of their income on consumption, sales taxes tend to be regressive.

With respect to corporate income taxes and property taxes, however, there is considerable disagreement among economists as to the ultimate incidence of these levies. Opinion is divided on how the burden of the property tax is shared between landlord and tenant and how the burden of the corporate tax is shared between owners of corporations and consumers of their products. To the extent that the corporate tax falls on owners of capital, it is progressive, since ownership of capital is concentrated among upper-income groups. To the extent that it falls on consumers, it is regressive.

3. *What are the economic effects of the tax?* Progressive taxes are generally thought to accord more fully with ideas of fairness; but to what extent would an increase in progressivity impair incentives for work and for investment? If tax rates applying to those in upper-income brackets are very high, do they penalize thrift, risk-taking, and investment? No one has the answers to these questions, but the argu-

ment that high tax rates reduce work incentives was used to justify reducing the top bracket rate under the federal individual income tax from its peak of 94 percent in 1945 to its present 70 percent level. Another economic aspect of taxation is the extent to which it distorts the allocation of resources in the economy. Excise taxes on particular commodities or services tend to penalize their production and consumption relative to those of untaxed goods and services. These penalties may be thought desirable in the case of such "harmful" products as liquor and tobacco,[2] but in general, it seems preferable not to interfere with consumer choices.

4. *Is the tax hard to collect or administer?* In the United States, which has an amazingly good record of taxpayer compliance, this question is not as important as it is in some other countries where tax evasion is rampant and the mere passage of a tax law in no way guarantees that the taxes imposed will be collected. Sales and income taxes, however, are generally considered to be far easier to administer than are property taxes, which often involve difficult judgments about property values.

The Current Federal Tax System

Compared with taxes in other industrialized countries, U.S. taxes impose a comparatively light burden on the economy. Because different levels of government perform widely differing functions in different countries, it is necessary to combine all receipts—federal, state, and local—in comparing tax burdens among countries. On this basis, aggregate receipts amounted to 32 percent of the gross national product of the United States in 1969. In the same period, receipts in Norway, the Netherlands, and Sweden exceeded 40 percent of GNP, and in six other countries the total ranged between 35 and 40 percent of GNP. Taxes as a percentage of GNP for the United States and fourteen other countries are shown below:[3]

2. The "excise taxes" on pollution (effluent charges), discussed in Chapter 11, are desirable precisely because pollution is something whose production and consumption society wants to discourage.

3. Organisation for Economic Co-operation and Development, *National Accounts Statistics, 1953–1969.* Data are for 1969, except for Sweden, Austria, and Canada, which are for 1968.

Country	Taxes as percent of gross national product	Country	Taxes as percent of gross national product
Sweden	48	Canada	35
Norway	43	Belgium	34
Netherlands	42	Italy	33
United Kingdom	39	**United States**	**32**
France	38	Switzerland	28
Germany	38	Spain	22
Austria	37	Japan	21
Denmark	37		

Roughly 60 percent of total U.S. taxes are collected by the federal government and the rest by state and local governments. Tax receipts of all levels of government have grown over the years, but in different ways. State and local governments rely heavily on sales and property taxes, and the federal government relies mainly on direct income taxes.

As may be seen in Table 14-1, individual and corporate income taxes are expected to account for 59 percent of total federal revenues in fiscal 1973, and social security and other payroll taxes for 29 percent. The remaining 12 percent will come from customs duties, excise,

Table 14-1. Distribution of Federal Budget Receipts, by Source, Selected Fiscal Years, 1954–73[a]

Percent

Fiscal year	Total	Taxes					
		Individual income	Corporation income	Excises	Estate and gift	Employment[b]	Other[c]
1954	100	42	30	14	1	10	1
1959	100	46	22	13	2	15	2
1964	100	43	21	12	2	20	2
1969	100	46	20	8	2	21	3
1973 est.	100	43	16	7	2	29	3

Sources: 1954 and 1959: *Statistical Appendix to Annual Report of the Secretary of the Treasury on the State of the Finances for the Fiscal Year Ended June 30, 1969*, pp. 14, 17 (1954 data for individual and corporation income, excise, and estate and gift taxes were adjusted by authors to exclude refunds); 1964 and 1969: *Treasury Bulletin* (January 1972), pp. 2–3; 1973: *The Budget of the United States Government, Fiscal Year 1973*, p. 496. Percentages may not add to totals because of rounding.

a. Receipts are on the official unified budget basis and are net of refunds.

b. Includes payroll taxes for social security and unemployment insurance, federal employee contributions for retirement, and contributions for supplementary medical insurance.

c. Includes customs duties, deposits of earnings by Federal Reserve banks, and miscellaneous receipts.

estate and gift taxes, and miscellaneous sources. Major shifts have occurred in the last few years in the relative importance of various types of federal taxes. Excise taxes have been steadily reduced and many of them eliminated in the past two decades. Cuts in corporate profits taxes have also drastically reduced the importance of this source of income to the federal government.

Since the individual income tax is progressive, it could have been expected to rise in importance because it tends to grow faster than other taxes as national income rises. In the past several decades, however, this tendency has been offset by periodic individual income tax cuts—in 1954, 1964, 1969, and 1971. As a consequence, in 1973, revenues from the individual income tax will be about the same percentage of total revenue as they were twenty years ago, despite a more than threefold rise in personal income over the period. Employment (or payroll) taxes, on the other hand, have been rising steadily. Increases in tax rates and in the maximum amount of wages subject to tax have increased the yield of these taxes from 10 percent of federal revenues in 1954 to 29 percent in 1973. Over the past two decades, therefore, the reliance of the federal government on individual income taxes has remained roughly unchanged, while the decreased reliance on corporate income and excise taxes has been balanced by a large increase in payroll taxes.

In considering possible sources of additional federal revenue, some types of taxes can be ruled out. Estate and gift taxes, for example, while badly in need of reform, cannot be counted on to provide significant amounts of new federal revenue. Excise taxes tend to be regressive; they distort relative prices, interfere with consumer choice, and generate considerable political opposition from both producers and consumers. For these reasons, most of the excise taxes introduced during the Second World War and the Korean war have been gradually abandoned; except for the taxes on liquor and tobacco, the remaining federal excises are mainly user charges, such as the tax on gasoline. This trend away from excise taxation is unlikely to be reversed.

Another set of taxes that may be ruled out as a source of increased general revenues are payroll taxes, which are traditionally earmarked for social security and unemployment compensation and are not generally regarded as appropriate sources of revenue for other government programs. Indeed, because of its regressiveness, there are strong reasons to believe that reliance on the payroll tax is already too heavy and that future social security benefits should be financed more out of general revenues and less out of the payroll tax, or that a major restructuring of the tax should be undertaken. The social security payroll tax is in most cases divided into two parts. Half is paid by the employee and half by the employer. Most economists believe that the part paid by the employer is ultimately borne by the worker; his wages are lower than they would be if the employer did not have to pay the social security tax for him. Moreover, the payroll tax at present is levied on only the first $9,000 of wages or salaries, and, unlike the individual income tax, it has no exemptions or deductions. Hence, it is a regressive tax whose burden falls most heavily on low- and moderate-income workers. Those with earnings over $9,000 pay a lower proportion of their income in social security tax.[4]

Among existing taxes, the individual income tax and corporate income tax are the most promising sources of sizable amounts of additional federal revenue. The possibilities of raising more revenue from these taxes are discussed in more detail below.

If the federal government were to seek a new tax source, it would probably have to turn to some kind of general consumption tax.[5] General consumption taxes are used extensively in other countries and by forty-five of the states in the United States, but not by the federal government. The present administration has raised the possibility of such a tax in a slightly different context. It has under consideration a value added tax—essentially a tax on consumer expenditures—whose proceeds would be used to replace the local residential property taxes now devoted to the support of schools. The implications of such a shift for the financing of education are discussed in Chapter 10, and the revenue implications are discussed below.

Although it is impossible to predict the precise amounts of revenue needed in the future, it will be useful to review the alternatives on the assumption that full employment revenue will have to be increased by either 5 percent or 10 percent. In fiscal 1973, a 5 percent increase im-

4. For a discussion of the role of the payroll taxes in the revenue system, see Charles L. Schultze and others, *Setting National Priorities: The 1972 Budget* (Brookings Institution, 1971), Chapter 10, pp. 204–13; and Joseph A. Pechman, *Federal Tax Policy* (rev. ed., Brookings Institution, 1971), Chapter 7, pp. 169–84.

5. Taxes on property and wealth could become a source of general revenue for the federal government only if the Constitution were amended, since Article I, Section 9, requires that such taxes be apportioned among the states in accordance with population. The Sixteenth Amendment was necessary to legalize the federal individual income tax.

plies additional revenue of about $12 billion a year, and a 10 percent increase implies $24 billion. Since fiscal 1973 revenues depend in large measure on calendar year 1972 incomes, all the estimates in this chapter are based on 1972 income levels.

Structural Reforms of the Income Taxes

The revenues yielded by individual and corporate income taxes depend not only on the tax rate, but also on the tax base—the income to which that rate is applied. Over the years, the Congress has made frequent changes in the bases of the individual and corporate income taxes—sometimes to enlarge them but far more frequently to reduce them.

The federal tax bases have been reduced—or eroded—in two major ways. First, certain kinds of income have been excluded from taxation or are taxed at preferential rates. The first $100 a taxpayer receives in dividends is excluded from taxable income; income from oil, gas, and other mineral-producing activities is accorded special treatment through generous depletion allowances; capital gains realized from the sale of assets are subject to a lower tax rate than is ordinary income; and interest on state and local government bonds is completely exempt from taxation. Second, taxpayers have been allowed special deductions from their income for certain kinds of personal expenditures. For example, property taxes, gasoline taxes, medical expenses, and charitable contributions are all deductible in computing taxable income.

These base-reducing provisions were designed to benefit particular groups or industries or to encourage certain activities that are deemed desirable from the national viewpoint. The exemption of interest on state and local government bonds, for example, makes state and local security issues more attractive to investors and lowers the cost of borrowing for these governments. The preferential treatment of mineral industries has been defended in part on national security grounds as a means of stimulating development of domestic mineral resources. The deductibility of charitable contributions provides an incentive for private philanthropy.

However worthy the motives, such provisions reduce federal revenues and enable large numbers of persons, primarily in higher-income brackets, to pay less tax than they otherwise would. In their reports on the Tax Reform Act of 1969, the House Committee on Ways and Means and the Senate Finance Committee stated that "in many cases, although the tax preferences may have been justified at the time of their inception, it is not clear that they are needed or desirable in today's economy."[6]

The loss of revenue is large. In recent years, the Treasury Department has made estimates of what have been called "tax expenditures" —that is, subsidies in the form of tax preferences provided in the tax code rather than paid through direct expenditures. The latest estimates, prepared for the Joint Economic Committee, show that tax expenditures amounted to at least $36 billion in fiscal 1971.[7] Joseph A. Pechman and Benjamin A. Okner have estimated that at 1972 income levels, an additional $77 billion could be raised from the individual income tax alone with present tax rates and exemptions if the tax base were broadened to include all economic income and if most deductions and all preferential tax rates and credits were eliminated.[8] Alternatively, the present yield of the individual income tax could be raised from the broadened tax base with rates that are 43 percent lower, on the average, than the present rates, which begin at 14 percent and rise to a maximum of 70 percent.

Besides cutting into revenues, the erosion of the tax base has the effect of making the personal income tax far less progressive than it would otherwise be. Under existing law, the marginal tax rates (the tax paid on additional dollars earned) rise quite steeply from 14 percent in the lowest bracket up to 70 percent. The schedule of marginal rates makes the tax appear highly progressive. When one looks at average effective rates for each income level, however, one sees that the tax is not really so progressive: the average effective rate now rises from less than 1 percent on incomes under $3,000 to 10.5 percent on

6. The same statement appears in both reports. See *Tax Reform Act of 1969*, Report of the House Committee on Ways and Means, H. Rpt. 91-413 (Pt. 1), 91 Cong. 1 sess. (1969), p. 9; and *Tax Reform Act of 1969*, Report of the Senate Committee on Finance, S. Rpt. 91-552, 91 Cong. 1 sess. (1969), p. 13.

7. *The Economics of Federal Subsidy Programs*, A Staff Study Prepared for the Use of the Joint Economic Committee, 92 Cong. 1 sess. (1972), p. 31.

8. See their study paper, "Individual Income Tax Erosion by Income Classes," in *The Economics of Federal Subsidy Programs*, A Compendium of Papers Prepared for the Use of the Joint Economic Committee, 92 Cong. 2 sess. (1972). The Pechman-Okner estimates are much higher than those of the Treasury Department because their definition of "erosion" includes a number of items not included by the Treasury (for example, the rate advantages of income splitting for married couples), and their estimates are for a later year—calendar 1972 instead of fiscal 1971.

incomes of $15,000 to $20,000. In the $20,000 to $50,000 range, there is little change in average effective rates as incomes rise, and even for incomes over $1,000,000 the average effective tax rate is not much above one-third.

The major factor reducing the progressivity of the income tax is that rich people benefit from preferential tax treatment far more than do those with low incomes. Indeed, in 1970, more than 100 individuals with adjusted gross incomes of more than $200,000 were nontaxable.

Reducing tax preferences therefore would have the double result of increasing federal revenues and making the tax structure more progressive. The Congress, however, is hardly likely to sweep away all the special provisions in the tax laws at one time. The pressures for retaining most of them are strong, and progress typically is made only haltingly. Moreover, some of the tax preferences that constitute major elements in the $36 billion and $77 billion estimates presented above benefit a wide range of average taxpayers, not just the rich. An important example is the ability of homeowners to deduct interest and property taxes from their income as "business expenses" while not being required to pay taxes on the "imputed" income derived from ownership of a home.

Those who support tax reform as a means of raising additional revenue usually do not include *all* the elements of economic income that go untaxed, but confine their attention mainly to those of particular benefit to relatively small groups of taxpayers, principally those in upper-income categories. But even here, the actual accomplishments of tax reform legislation in recent years are modest. The revenue raised as a result of changes in the Tax Reform Act of 1969 amounted to only $3.3 billion a year,[9] and this occurred in a year when tax reform was a popular issue. The Revenue Act of 1971 introduced new tax preferences of $370 million, not including the revenue lost from the adoption of more liberal depreciation allowances and the reinstatement of the investment tax credit.[10]

Three different packages of possible revenue-raising reforms are shown in Table 14-2. They include (1) increasing from 50 to 60 percent the portion of realized capital gains subject to tax; (2) reducing or eliminating some of the allowable deductions from income, such as

9. *General Explanation of the Tax Reform Act of 1969*, prepared by the Staff of the Joint Committee on Internal Revenue Taxation (1970), Table 1, p. 13.
10. *Congressional Record*, daily ed., Dec. 9, 1971, p. H12119.

Table 14-2. Revenue Effect of Various Structural Reforms of the Individual Income Tax under Alternative Packages, 1972 Income Levels
Billions of dollars

Reform provision	Package 1	Package 2	Package 3
Remove maximum tax on earned income	0.1	0.1	0.1
Include 60 percent of realized capital gains in adjusted gross income and remove alternative capital gains tax provision	1.5	1.5	1.5
Eliminate deduction of gasoline taxes	0.5	0.5	0.5
Eliminate deduction of real estate property taxes	...	...	2.3
Remove dividend exclusion	0.4	0.4	0.4
Eliminate 50 percent of excess depletion advantages	0.2	0.2	0.2
Place 3 percent floor on charitable contribution deductions	...	1.9	1.9
Tax unrealized capital gains in excess of $5,000 transferred by gift or bequest at capital gains rates	...	...	0.6
Remove $25,000 exemption allowed for excess investment interest deduction	...	...	1.2
Revise preference income base[a]	0.5	...	...
Revise preference income base[a] and raise tax rate on revised base from 10 to 20 percent	...	1.1	...
Revise preference income base[a] and tax at one-half the regular income tax rates[b]	...	...	2.4
Total revenue effect[c]	**3.1**	**5.6**	**10.2**

Source: Based on the Brookings MERGE File of 30,000 family units for the year 1966 with incomes projected to 1972 level.

a. Revision of preference income base involves inclusion of state-local bond interest as a preference item and removal of deduction for current-year taxes paid.

b. That is, tax the revised base at 7 percent to 35 percent—one-half the regular rates, which range from 14 percent to 70 percent.

c. The total revenue effect of each package is not equal to the sum of the components because various provisions interact with one another.

state gasoline taxes, real estate taxes, and charitable contributions; (3) eliminating the current exclusion from taxable income of the first $100 of dividends; (4) reducing the preferential tax treatment of income from oil, gas, and other mineral-producing activities; and (5) increasing the special tax on all forms of preference income.[11] These

11. The 10 percent tax on preference income is one of the reforms introduced in the Tax Reform Act of 1969. The intent of the provision is to levy a minimum amount of tax on income from certain sources that are recognized as being given preferential treatment under the tax law. For example, one of the items designated as a tax preference is the exclusion of 50 percent of net long-term capital gains. Under the tax on preference income, such excluded gains, minus a $30,000 exclusion and minus any current-year taxes paid, are subject to a minimum tax of 10 percent. However, because of the exclusion and deduction for taxes paid, the provision is not very effective in taxing preferential income. In the case of capital gains, for example, the *maximum* effective rate is increased from 35 to 36.5 percent under this provision.

Table 14-3. Current Effective Individual Income Tax Rates and Rate Increases with a
$13.4 Billion Tax Reform Package,ᵃ by Income Classes, 1972 Income Levels

Income classes in thousands of dollars; other numbers in percent

Income class	Effective rate, current law	Increase in effective rate from reform package
0–3	0.5	0.3
3–5	1.7	0.1
5–10	5.1	0.2
10–15	8.6	0.4
15–20	10.5	0.6
20–25	11.8	0.7
25–50	13.9	1.2
50–100	22.2	3.0
100–500	31.0	8.4
500–1,000	32.8	16.3
1,000 and over	34.2	19.0
All classesᵇ	11.0	1.1

Source: Based on the Brookings MERGE File of 30,000 family units for 1966 with incomes projected to the 1972 level.

a. $3.2 billion of the revenue raised by this reform package would come from the corporation income tax; the tax burden shown in this table arises from the $10.2 billion of revenues derived from the individual income tax as outlined in Table 14-2, package 3.

b. Includes negative income class not shown separately.

would be regarded by most experts as rather substantial revisions and doubtless would be strongly opposed by those taxpayers who would be affected. Most of the changes would not significantly affect the average low- and middle-income taxpayer. The one exception is the group of reforms that limit personal deductions for gasoline and property taxes; these would impinge on a very large number of persons at all income levels. Nevertheless, package 3, which contains the largest number of reforms, would raise only $10.2 billion a year. Most of these reforms would not affect corporations, but those that did would probably increase 1972 revenues by $3.2 billion.[12] Together, these reforms would raise $13.4 billion, or $1.4 billion more than the $12 billion needed to increase full employment revenue by 5 percent.

As may be seen in Table 14-3, package 3 would make the income tax considerably more progressive than it is now. Effective tax rates

12. These include $800 million from eliminating the alternative tax on long-term capital gains, $400 million from removal of half the excess depletion advantages, and $2.0 billion from the revision of the tax on preference income.

would rise only slightly for low- and middle-income persons, but the rise would be steep for those with incomes over $500,000.

Increases in Income Tax Rates

The bases of the two income taxes are very large, even if they are not increased by tax reform. In calendar year 1972, the individual income tax base—the income subject to tax—will amount to about $475 billion, and the corporate income tax base will approach $90 billion. Tax liabilities will be close to $100 billion for individuals and about $35 billion for corporations.

Since the income taxes are the two basic taxes in the federal revenue system, it would be natural to turn to them to raise additional revenue needed for government programs. The individual income tax applies to all income recipients except those with incomes below the officially defined poverty lines;[13] and, as noted earlier, the tax on the whole is progressive. All businesses are subject to tax under either the corporate or the individual tax. Thus, a general increase in the tax rates of both the individual and the corporate income taxes could raise revenue on a progressive basis from the large mass of individuals and business enterprises.

Basically, there are two methods for increasing income tax rates in a systematic way. The first is to increase each bracket rate by the same number of percentage points; the second is to apply a percentage surcharge to all tax liabilities.[14] Under the "percentage point" method every tax rate would be raised equally. If a 2 percentage point increase were enacted, the lowest bracket tax rate, which is now 14 percent, would become 16 percent; the 28 percent rate would become 30 percent; and so on. Under the "surcharge" method, everyone's tax bill, calculated as it is now, would be subject to a proportional increase. If the increase were 8 percent, taxes for those with a $300 annual bill under current law would rise to $324, while taxpayers with a liability of $10,000 would pay $10,800.

13. The minimum taxable level under the individual income tax for a family of four is now $4,300; the poverty line for a four-person family was $4,140 for 1971, and (assuming a 3.5 percent increase in consumer prices) it will be about $4,285 in 1972.

14. A surcharge was used during both the Korean and the Vietnam wars. During the Korean war, the surcharge was moderated at higher income levels to avoid excessively high marginal rates. During the Vietnam war, single persons with taxable incomes of less than $1,000 and married couples with taxable incomes of less than $2,000 were exempted from the surcharge.

The approximate rate increases needed to expand individual and corporate income tax revenues by $12 billion would be 1.8 percentage points in all individual income tax brackets under the first method and 8.5 percent under the surcharge method. To expand revenues by $24 billion would call for increases of 3.6 percentage points and 16.9 percent, respectively. Table 14-4 shows the impact on effective tax rates of raising $12 billion and $24 billion by the two methods. The big difference between the two is that the surcharge is far more progressive than the percentage point method. Current effective rates (tax as a percentage of total income) are shown in column 1. As may be seen in columns 2 and 4 of the table, the surcharge method raises effective rates by increasing amounts as income rises. This is because the surcharge raises taxes proportionately at every income level, and taxes

Table 14-4. Current Effective Individual and Corporation Income Tax Rates and Rate Increases under Surcharge and Percentage Point Methods of Raising Additional Revenue,[a] by Income Classes, 1972 Income Levels

Income classes in thousands of dollars; other numbers in percent

Source of revenue, and income class for individuals	Effective rate, current law (1)	Increase in effective rate			
		$12 billion tax increase		$24 billion tax increase	
		Surcharge method (2)	Percentage point method (3)	Surcharge method (4)	Percentage point method (5)
Individuals, total[b]	**11.0**	**0.9**	**0.9**	**1.8**	**1.8**
Income class					
0–3	0.5	c	c	0.1	0.1
3–5	1.7	0.1	0.2	0.3	0.4
5–10	5.1	0.4	0.6	0.9	1.1
10–15	8.6	0.7	0.8	1.4	1.7
15–20	10.5	0.9	1.1	1.8	2.1
20–25	11.8	1.0	1.1	2.0	2.2
25–50	13.9	1.2	1.2	2.4	2.3
50–100	22.2	1.9	1.3	3.8	2.5
100–500	31.0	2.6	1.2	5.2	2.3
500–1,000	32.8	2.8	0.9	5.6	1.9
1,000 and over	34.2	2.9	0.9	5.8	1.8
Corporations	**40.0**	**3.9**	**3.9**	**7.8**	**7.8**

Sources: Individual income tax, based on the Brookings MERGE File of 30,000 family units for the year 1966 with incomes projected to 1972 level; corporation income tax for 1972, authors' estimate.

a. Under the surcharge method, a percentage surcharge is applied on all tax liabilities; under the percentage point method, each bracket rate is increased by the same number of percentage points.

b. Income for individuals is equal to the sum of adjusted gross income, transfer payments, state and local government bond interest, and excluded realized long-term capital gains. The total includes negative income class not shown separately.

c. Less than 0.05 percent.

already increase more than proportionately as income rises. One would expect the percentage point method to raise effective rates by equal percentage point amounts as income rises, but, as may be seen in columns 3 and 5 of the table, this is not what happens. Effective rates are raised by an increasing number of percentage points as income rises up to $20,000, then by roughly constant percentage point amounts in the $20,000 to $100,000 range, and then by a slightly smaller number of percentage points on incomes above $100,000. Because of exemptions, deductions, and tax preferences, taxable income tends to become a larger fraction of income as incomes rise to about $20,000, remains a roughly constant fraction of income until the $100,000 level is reached, and then declines as a fraction of income.

The increases in effective rates shown in the table indicate the average impacts in each income class. Within the classes, considerable variation would continue to exist. Those who receive a large part of their income in the form of wages and salaries would, particularly under the surcharge method, have their effective tax rates increased by more than would those who receive a large part of their income in the form of capital gains.

A New Revenue Source: Taxing Consumption

If neither tax reform nor increases in income tax rates were chosen as a means of raising additional revenue, the federal government would have to resort to taxing consumption as the only practical alternative. In the United States, the federal government has confined its taxation of consumption to excise taxes, which apply only to selected commodities. But taxation of consumption through the general sales tax is widespread among state and local governments. General consumption taxes are also used in other countries, where income taxation is less well developed. A general sales tax was seriously considered by the U.S. Congress in 1932 and during the Second World War, but the legislation was decisively defeated in 1932 and was never brought to a vote during the war.

There are two major kinds of general consumption taxes: (1) a *sales tax* levied on the sales of final goods and services, and (2) a *value added tax* (VAT) levied on the difference in value between a firm's sales and its purchases. The latter tax is now used extensively in Western Europe.

A truly general sales tax would apply uniformly to all goods and services purchased by consumers. In practice, however, food, rent, and medicine are often excluded from the sales tax base to moderate its impact on low-income families. If the same exclusions and rates are used, a VAT will generally have the same economic effect as a sales tax. For example, the $400 retail price of a color television set is made up of increments added by a large number of firms at various stages in the production process. Mining companies, the manufacturer, the wholesaler, the trucking firm, and the retailer each add some value to the set as it passes along the production and distribution chain. The government could either collect a 3 percent sales tax on the $400 set from the retailer or assess the 3 percent against the value added by each firm along the way. The end result, for all practical purposes, is the same. In both cases the ultimate consumer pays the same amount of tax.[15]

Sales and value added taxes can produce large amounts of revenue because the base to which these taxes apply is large. For example, in 1972 the base of a national sales or value added tax would be about $560 billion if rents and the rental value of owner-occupied homes were exempted from the tax and about $400 billion if food consumed at home and medicine were also exempted. Thus, each percentage point of tax would raise $5.6 billion if levied on the broader base and $4.0 billion on the narrower base. To raise the illustrative $12 billion and $24 billion of revenue at 1972 levels, it would be necessary to levy sales or value added taxes at about 2.2 or 4.3 percent rates on the broader base and at 3.0 and 6.0 percent on the narrower base.

There is little reason to prefer the VAT over the sales tax, particularly in a country like the United States, where tax compliance is generally good. For countries with compliance problems, the VAT may be preferable because it is collected in smaller amounts than the sales tax as products flow through the production and distribution process, even though the final consumer pays the same amount of tax in the form of higher prices. This advantage might be extremely im-

15. Although it is possible that businesses would not raise prices enough to recoup the value added tax for which they are liable (that is, they would accept lower profits), this is unlikely to happen. If the tax is fairly broad and has only a limited number of exemptions, it would in all probability be passed on in full to consumers.

portant in countries where there are large numbers of small retailers who are not good record keepers. In the United States, most retail business is done through firms that may be expected to keep adequate records and to comply with the tax laws. Moreover, with general sales taxes already in existence in forty-five states, retailers should have little trouble in accommodating themselves to a national sales tax. On the other hand, state and local government officials might well resent intrusion by the federal government into the retail sales tax area, which is one of their major revenue sources.

To adopt either a general sales tax or a VAT would require difficult decisions about the kinds of transactions to be included or excluded. Should services—dry cleaning, entertainment, automobile repairs—be taxed? What about legal and medical services or private and parochial schools? What about the sales of (or value added by) publicly owned utilities, such as municipal water systems and electric power companies? Major political pressures and controversies would be generated by questions of this kind.

General sales and broad-based value added taxes are regressive because the poor spend a higher percentage of their income on consumer goods than do the rich. The choice between sales taxes and income taxes for raising additional revenues depends primarily on the relative weight to be placed on protecting work and investment incentives as against the need to avoid placing higher taxes on low-income families. Some believe that income tax rates are already too high and that any increase would discourage extra work effort and incentives to invest. Others point out that the top federal income tax rates have been brought down sharply since the end of the Second World War and that it is unwise social policy to place additional burdens on the poor and the near poor.

As was pointed out above, one way to lessen the regressiveness of retail sales taxes is to exempt food, medicine, and other necessities. Another way of moderating the burden of a consumption tax on the poor and the near poor would be to provide a credit against income taxes for the amount of value added taxes paid by families below a certain income level. The credit would be an estimate of the average amount of value added tax that families of different sizes and income levels would be likely to pay. A table showing the credits for families of various sizes at each income level could then become part of the income tax form. Poor families that pay no income tax would receive a

refund each year equal to their VAT credit. For example, a 100 percent credit for value added taxes paid could be given to families of four
with incomes up to $5,000, with the cutoff appropriately scaled up or
down for families of other sizes. As incomes rose to $20,000, the credit
could be gradually phased out. A family of four with an income of
$12,500 would receive a credit equal to 50 percent of its estimated
VAT. Families with incomes of $20,000 or more would receive no
credit. The rate of the VAT would, of course, have to be increased to
make up for the revenue lost by the low-income credit. And the further up the income scale the credit applied, the higher the value added
tax rate needed to obtain a given amount of revenue.

The value added tax rates needed to raise $12 billion are as follows:
(1) A 2.2 percent rate would be required if the tax were levied on a
broad base, including all consumer expenditures except rent; (2) a 3
percent rate would be needed if the tax were levied on a *narrow base*,
excluding not only rent but food and medical outlays; and (3) a 3.25
percent rate would be needed if a broad base were combined with the
low-income credit described above.

Comparing the Alternatives

In this chapter five possible ways of raising additional federal revenue have been identified that seem worthy of serious consideration:

1. Structural reform of the individual and corporate income taxes
—increasing the tax base by reducing preferential treatment of particular sources of income;

2. Raising income tax rates by imposing a surcharge;

3. Raising income tax rates by a certain number of percentage
points;

4. Enacting a value added tax with exemptions for rent, food, and
medical care; and

5. Enacting a value added tax with a low-income credit but no
exemptions.

Each of the five methods would have different effects on the distribution of income, even if they were to raise approximately the same
amount of revenue. Table 14-5 shows how effective tax rates would be
increased for families at various income levels if approximately $12 bil-

Table 14-5. Current Effective Individual Income Tax Rates and Rate Increases under Various Methods of Raising Additional Revenue, by Income Classes, 1972 Income Levels

Income classes in thousands of dollars; other numbers in percent

Income classb	Effective rate, current law	$10 billion tax increase Income tax reformc	*Increase in effective rate*a $12 billion tax increase			
			Income tax surcharged	Percentage point income tax increasee	Broad-base value added tax with creditf	Narrow-base value added taxg
0–3	0.5	0.3	0.1	0.1	0.1	1.8
3–5	1.7	0.1	0.2	0.3	0.6	1.5
5–10	5.1	0.2	0.6	0.8	0.8	1.5
10–15	8.6	0.4	1.0	1.2	1.1	1.4
15–20	10.5	0.6	1.3	1.5	1.7	1.4
20–25	11.8	0.7	1.4	1.6	1.9	1.3
25–50	13.9	1.2	1.7	1.6	1.7	1.2
50–100	22.2	3.0	2.6	1.8	1.1	0.7
100–500	31.0	8.4	3.5	1.6	0.8	0.5
500–1,000	32.8	16.3	3.9	1.3	0.4	0.2
1,000 and over	34.2	19.0	4.1	1.3	0.2	0.2
All classesh	11.0	1.1	1.3	1.3	1.3	1.3

Source: Based on the Brookings MERGE File of 30,000 family units for the year 1966 with incomes projected to 1972 level.

a. Tax as percent of income.

b. Income is equal to the sum of adjusted gross income, transfer payments, state and local government bond interest, and excluded realized long-term capital gains.

c. Tax reform package 3 outlined in Table 14-2.

d. Surcharge of 11.8 percent on 1972 income tax liabilities.

e. 2.5 percentage point increase applied to each bracket rate.

f. Broad-base value added tax at 3.25 percent with full credit up to $5,000 for a four-person family; credit is phased out completely at $20,000.

g. Narrow-base value added tax at 3.0 percent.

h. Includes negative income class not shown separately.

lion were raised by increases in *individual* taxes under each method.[16] The changes in effective rates are also shown in Figure 14-1 (except for the tax reform alternative).

When the alternatives are compared, it is clear that the tax reform package is by far the most progressive at the high end of the income scale. The reform package would increase average effective rates by less than one percentage point for families with incomes below

16. The increases in individual income tax rates and the value added taxes shown in Table 14-5 and Figure 14-1 would each yield $12 billion; the tax reform package would yield $10.2 billion from individuals, and another $3.2 billion from corporations.

Figure 14-1. Effective Rates of Individual Income Tax Increases and Value Added Taxes Each Yielding $12 Billion, by Income Classes, 1972 Income Levels

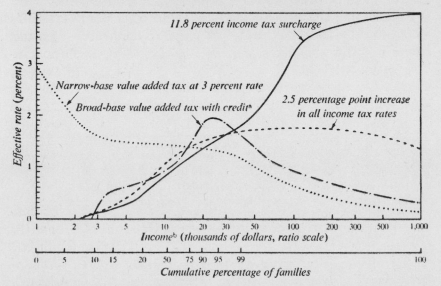

Source: Based on the Brookings MERGE File of 30,000 family units for 1966 with incomes projected to the 1972 level.
a. Rate of 3.25 percent with full credit up to $5,000 for a four-person family; credit is phased out completely at $20,000.
b. Income is equal to the sum of adjusted gross income, transfer payments, state and local government bond interest, and excluded realized long-term capital gains.

$25,000; it would raise effective rates for those in the $50,000 to $100,000 range by 3.0 percentage points; and it would raise effective rates by 19.0 percentage points for families with incomes of $1,000,000 or more. The income tax surcharge would be the next in order of progressivity, with the increase in effective rates ranging from less than 1 percent in the lowest income group to 4.1 percent for those with incomes of more than $1,000,000.

Despite the exemption of rent, food, and medical care, the narrow-base value added tax would be regressive along the entire income scale, increasing taxes for the poor much more heavily than for the rich. The broad-base value added tax, with the low-income credit described above, would have a progressive incidence not very different from that achieved by a constant percentage point increase in all income tax rates on incomes up to about $17,000. For families with incomes between $17,000 and $40,000, the VAT with a credit would increase tax liabilities by somewhat more than the percentage point income tax increase, but for those with incomes above that level the reverse would be true.

The bottom scale in Figure 14-1 shows the proportion of families with incomes at or below the levels shown in the figure. From this scale it is possible to note that for the 75 percent of families whose incomes are below $17,000, the surcharge, the percentage point increase, and the VAT with low-income credit would impose approximately the same additional burden. It is the 25 percent of families with incomes above $17,000 for whom these three alternatives would have quite different impacts.

Substitution of a Value Added Tax for the Property Tax

The value added tax has also been suggested as a partial substitute for the local property tax, which is now the major source of revenue for financing elementary and secondary education in the United States. Since property is unequally distributed among communities, the financial resources available for education are also unequally distributed. The courts in several states have recently ruled that this method of financing leads to unequal educational opportunities for individuals and is unconstitutional. The U.S. Supreme Court has not yet ruled on these cases, but there is substantial public agreement that the present system of financing public education should be drastically modified. Federal assistance to elementary and secondary education, both as a means of equalizing disparities in educational expenditures among school districts and as a substitute for local property tax financing, was discussed in Chapter 10. In addition to the issues brought out in that chapter, full or partial replacement of local residential property taxes for schools by a federal VAT would have significant implications for the distribution of the tax burdens among families at different income levels.

Replacement of the residential property tax by a VAT for financing education would substitute a nationwide tax on consumption for a host of locally established taxes on property. Such a shift would help to reduce the differential burdens of taxation on property in different communities that now prevail because neighboring communities often have quite different property tax rates and assessment practices. Even within a single community, assessment practices are often so variable that levies on properties with the same market value are widely divergent. Such differentials tend to distort land use and planning and have sometimes placed excessive tax burdens on properties in urban areas.

Unfortunately, the distributional effect among those in different income classes of replacing part of the property tax with a consumption tax is particularly difficult to measure. As was pointed out above, economists are not agreed as to whether the owner of the property or the person who pays for the services the property renders ultimately bears the burden of the property tax. The tax on real estate may be thought of in two parts—a tax on the value of the land itself and a tax on the value of buildings and other improvements on the land. With respect to the tax on land, it is generally agreed that the landowner bears the tax and cannot pass it on. But land constitutes, on the average, only about 25 percent of the value of residential property subject to tax. Improvements form the major part of property values, and there are at least two distinct views as to who pays the tax on improvements.

The traditional view of the incidence of the property tax has been that renters pay the tax on residential buildings through higher rent payments and consumers in general pay the property tax on commercial and industrial property in the form of higher prices for the goods they buy. This view assumes that property taxes initially reduce the rate of return to investors in property improvements and that the lower rate of return slows the flow of new investment over time, thereby driving up the prices of business services provided by such assets until the old rate of return to the owners has been restored. Renters and consumers thus end up paying the taxes.

An alternative view is that the initially lower rate of return on property improvements diverts investment into untaxed (or more lightly taxed) areas of the economy, but does not affect the *total level* of investment. This lowers returns on other kinds of investment generally, until a point is reached at which all owners of capital receive a lower rate of return because of the property tax. Under this view, a property tax is ultimately borne in a general way by all owners of capital.[17]

Since there is no consensus on the incidence of the property tax,

17. For a discussion of the traditional and the more recent alternative incidence theories, see Dick Netzer, *Economics of the Property Tax* (Brookings Institution, 1966), Chapter 3, pp. 32–66, and Peter Mieszkowski, "Tax Incidence Theory: The Effects of Taxes on the Distribution of Income," *Journal of Economic Literature*, Vol. 7 (December 1969), pp. 1103–24.

estimates of its distributional effect have been prepared on the basis both of the traditional assumptions and alternative ones. The two sets of assumptions yield very different conclusions about the burden of the property tax at various income levels. (See Table 14-6.) If the property tax is borne by all owners of capital, it takes a high percentage of income at both the bottom and the top of the income scale. At the low end of the income scale is a large concentration of retired people who own their homes. Hence the property tax takes a relatively high proportion of the income of these low-income persons who own capital in the form of residential property. Those at the high end of the income distribution tend to own large amounts of capital of all types, and consequently the tax burden is also a sizable proportion of their income. In the middle of the income distribution, where most income is derived from wages and salaries, the burden of the property tax is much lighter.

Based on the traditional view—that property taxes on improve-

Table 14-6. Effective General Property Tax Rates[a] under Alternative Incidence Assumptions, by Income Classes, 1972 Income Levels

Income classes in thousands of dollars; other numbers in percent

	Effective property tax rate[b] assuming that the tax on improvements is borne by	
Income class[c]	*Capital*[d]	*Renters and consumers*[d]
0–3	7.2	13.0
3–5	5.4	8.0
5–10	3.6	5.9
10–15	2.6	4.9
15–20	2.9	4.7
20–25	3.7	4.4
25–50	5.7	4.4
50–100	14.1	3.7
100–500	22.4	3.5
500–1,000	24.5	3.0
1,000 and over	18.2	2.1
All classes[e]	5.0	5.0

Source: Based on the Brookings MERGE File of 30,000 family units for the year 1966 with incomes projected to 1972 level.

a. Includes all property taxed by state and local governments, such as automobiles; livestock; commercial, industrial, and residential real property; and so forth.

b. Tax as percent of income.

c. Income is equal to the sum of adjusted gross income, transfer payments, state and local government bond interest, and excluded realized long-term capital gains.

d. The tax on land is assumed to be borne by landowners. See text for explanation of the distribution of the taxes on improvements.

e. Includes negative income class not shown separately.

ments are passed on in the form of higher rents and prices—the property tax is similar to a consumption tax, with a particularly heavy emphasis on the consumption of housing services. As a percentage of income it is highest for the very poor, and declines steadily as income rises.[18]

In 1972, total state and local property taxes will amount to almost $46 billion. Even those who favor reducing property tax burdens do not argue for replacing all property tax revenues by a tax on consumption; rather, the suggestion has been made that only the residential property taxes devoted to education be replaced. This view has been supported by various court cases in which there has been a ruling against financing education from property taxes and by recent efforts to provide tax relief to aged homeowners.

As Chapter 10 pointed out, the simple replacement of residential property taxes by a nationwide federal tax would create massive problems concerning the distribution of federal assistance among states and among school districts within a state. But there is also a question as to what such a substitution would imply for the distribution of tax burdens among families in different income classes. Residential property taxes devoted to education currently total about $12 billion. In Table 14-7 combined estimates are shown of the distribution by income classes of the tax burden imposed by $12 billion of revenues raised in three different ways: a federal broad-based value added tax (with low-income credit), an individual income tax surcharge, and a general property tax on residential real estate. The estimates reflect an *average* tax burden in each income class; they do not take into account the tremendous variation in property taxes paid by people in different states and in different communities within states. (See Chapter 10 for a discussion of such variations.) In effect, the calculations assume a property tax levied at the same rate on all residential property in the

18. In Table 14-6, property taxes were distributed as follows. On the assumption that the tax on improvements is borne by capital, all property taxes other than levies on nonfarm motor vehicles and agricultural property were distributed among families on the basis of total property income; the tax on cars was distributed using the value of cars owned by the family; and agricultural taxes were distributed on the basis of gross farm value. In calculating the burdens on the assumption that the tax on improvements is borne by renters and consumers generally, it was assumed that the tax on owner-occupied homes falls on the owner-occupier (since he pays the tax either as a consumer of housing services or as an owner of property) and that the tax on apartments rests on tenants in proportion to rents paid. The tax on commercial and industrial improvements was allocated on the basis of general consumption (on the assumption that higher rentals paid by business would be shifted forward in the form of higher prices), and the tax on farm improvements was allocated among farmers and consumers in general. The tax on land was distributed on the basis of income from capital under both sets of assumptions.

Table 14-7. The Burden of $12 Billion of Tax Revenue Raised from Taxes on Residential Property, a Value Added Tax with a Credit for Low-income Families, and an Income Tax Surcharge, by Income Classes, 1972 Income Levels
Income classes in thousands of dollars; other numbers in percent

	Effective rates of tax[a]			
	Residential real property tax assuming tax on improvements is borne by		*Value added tax with credit*[d]	*Income tax surcharge*[e]
Income class[b]	*Capital*[c]	*Renters and consumers*[c]		
0–3	0.9	3.5	0.1	0.1
3–5	1.0	2.0	0.6	0.2
5–10	0.8	1.5	0.8	0.6
10–15	0.6	1.3	1.1	1.0
15–20	0.7	1.3	1.7	1.3
20–25	1.0	1.2	1.9	1.4
25–50	1.5	1.1	1.7	1.7
50–100	4.2	0.6	1.1	2.6
100–500	7.1	0.6	0.8	3.5
500–1,000	7.8	0.5	0.4	3.9
1,000 and over	5.8	0.4	0.2	4.1
All classes[f]	1.3	1.3	1.3	1.3

Source: Based on the Brookings MERGE File of 30,000 family units for the year 1966 with incomes projected to 1972 level.
a. Tax as percent of income.
b. Income is equal to the sum of adjusted gross income, transfer payments, state and local government bond interest, and excluded realized long-term capital gains.
c. The tax on land is assumed to be borne by landowners. See text for explanation of the distribution of the taxes on improvements.
d. Broad-base value added tax at 3.25 percent with full credit up to $5,000 for a four-person family; credit is phased out completely at $20,000.
e. Surcharge of 11.8 percent on 1972 income tax liabilities.
f. Includes negative income class not shown separately.

nation. And, again, because of the lack of consensus regarding the incidence of the property tax, these calculations were made under the two sets of assumptions described above.[19]

On the assumption that the property tax on improvements is borne by owners of capital, substitution of a *value added tax* (with a low-income credit) for residential property taxes would reduce tax liabilities for families with incomes under $5,000 and for those with incomes of $50,000 and above; families in the $5,000 to $50,000 income range

19. The estimates in Table 14-7 do not reflect the impact on tax burdens resulting from the removal of residential property taxes, which would reduce property tax deductions on federal individual income tax returns and thereby raise income tax revenues. But this is a relatively minor consideration and would not substantially affect the estimates shown. It should also be noted that the calculations include only taxes on residential property and in turn only that portion of those taxes that is devoted to education, a total of $12 billion. The earlier estimates in Table 14-6 cover all property taxes—commercial and industrial as well as residential—totaling $46 billion.

would pay the same or higher taxes. On the assumption that the property tax on improvements rests on renters and consumers, the change in tax liabilities for most income classes would be relatively small, but families with incomes below $15,000 and over $500,000 would pay somewhat lower taxes after the substitution, while those between $15,000 and $500,000 would find their tax liabilities somewhat increased.

Assuming that the property tax on improvements is borne by all owners of capital, replacement of residential property taxes by a personal *income tax surcharge* would reduce tax liabilities at income levels below $10,000, increase them between $10,000 and $50,000, and reduce them for families with incomes above $50,000. If the property tax on improvements is paid by renters and consumers, taxes would be reduced for families with incomes below $15,000, remain unchanged for incomes between $15,000 and $20,000, and be increased for those above $20,000.

Thus, replacing residential property taxes with a VAT would alleviate tax burdens somewhat at the very low end of the income scale, because of the full credit for low-income families used in these computations. But it would also reduce tax burdens substantially at the upper end of the income distribution. In contrast, substituting an income tax surcharge for residential property taxes would greatly increase progressivity for incomes up to $50,000, regardless of what assumption is made about the incidence of the property tax; and it would reduce progressivity for families with incomes above $50,000 only if the property tax on improvements rested entirely on all owners of capital.

These conclusions are only a first approximation. As was noted in Chapter 10, it is not feasible simply to substitute a nationwide federal tax for local property taxes in each locality on a dollar-for-dollar basis because of the inequities this would create among different states and communities. Any realistic plan of substitution would also require significant changes in taxation at the state level, leading to some increases in statewide property or other taxes. After this chain of events took place, tax burdens would be changed again. The ultimate consequences for individuals at different income levels would depend on precisely how the tax laws of each of the states were modified. Nevertheless, Table 14-7 does give some indication of the initial impact on the relative distribution of tax burdens by income class.

15. A New Approach to Priorities

THE LARGE EXPANSION in the role of the federal government during the past decade, coupled with reductions in income and excise tax rates, has added a new dimension to the problem of setting national priorities. Economic growth no longer automatically produces a potential annual growth in revenues that is substantially larger than the expected increase in civilian expenditures.

Still other new dimensions of the priorities problem have emerged in recent years. Not only is the federal government being asked to play a larger role in the nation's economy, it is being asked to play a different role—to take on a new range of responsibilities for providing social services and improving the quality of the environment. Moreover, the public is asking harder questions about federal programs, both new and old. It is asking whether they work. It is no longer enough for politicians and federal officials to show that they have spent the taxpayers' money for approved purposes; they are now being asked to give evidence that the programs are producing results. In many cases, these new activities and attitudes call for a new approach to the setting of priorities.

Traditionally, establishing priorities was viewed as a problem of allocating resources among competing purposes and among different groups of people. How should national resources be divided between public and private needs? What public functions should be carried out by the different levels of government, federal, state, and local? How much should be allocated to each purpose? What groups should benefit, and who should pay—farmer or consumer, North or South, the poor, the rich, or the middle class? From the standpoint of the federal government, this priority-setting problem concentrated political debates on two kinds of questions: *What objectives* should the federal government seek, and *how much money* should be assigned to each? *How* the objectives should be achieved was not considered a major problem.

This emphasis on resource allocation was not surprising, considering the scope and nature of the federal government's civilian activities during most of our history. Until the 1930s, the federal government played a relatively small role in the peacetime life of the nation. Its civilian outlays were less than 1 percent of GNP. This ratio increased to about 5 percent in the 1930s and remained at about that level until the late 1950s.

During the New Deal and the two decades after the Second World War, the federal government expanded its role in several ways. It began using fiscal and monetary policy to maintain full employment, sometimes deliberately incurring budget deficits when they would further that objective. It established a framework of law and regulation to ensure stability and fair dealing in financial markets (the Securities and Exchange Commission, the Federal Deposit Insurance Corporation, and so on) and in labor relations (the National Labor Relations Board). And it undertook programs of income support for the retired, the disabled, the experienced unemployed, the children of families with no male breadwinner, and, through price support programs, the farmer.

The civilian budget of the federal government throughout this period was, with a few exceptions, confined to three kinds of activities: First, income support programs—social security, unemployment compensation, public assistance, veterans' pensions, farm price supports; second, investments in physical assets such as roads, dams, and national parks; third, general housekeeping duties such as maintaining federal prisons, safeguarding navigation, printing the currency, and providing national standards for weights and measures. Programs providing direct services to people—agricultural extension, for example—were minuscule. Health, education, and manpower training programs at the federal level were virtually nonexistent.

The public recognized that competent management was needed to keep social security records properly so that millions of beneficiaries would receive their checks promptly; that hydroelectric power projects required first-class engineering know-how; that it was no easy task to devise the laws and regulations supporting farm prices. But, in general, once it was decided that the federal government should undertake an activity and that a particular amount of money should be allocated to it, getting the job done was not considered an over-riding problem of national policy. Competent civil servants, princi-pally in Washington, could draft the necessary procedures and man-age the programs. Moreover, results were easy to observe; veterans received their pension checks, contracts were let, and dams built. It was considered safe to assume that if federal money were allocated to a particular objective, that objective would be achieved.

New Aspirations

In the 1960s, however, people began asking more of the federal government. First, a variety of new programs were enacted, many of them designed to provide direct services to people, especially poor people. Poverty was to be reduced not just by giving people cash in-come but by providing medical care, preschool programs, job train-ing, legal services, compensatory education, and opportunities for community action. Other new programs were aimed at improving the quality of the environment—reducing air and water pollution, invigo-rating urban planning, and reducing urban blight.

Along with the new activities came the gradual development of new and far more ambitious standards for judging federal programs. For the first time, federal officials—indeed all government officials—were being asked to produce "performance measures" as evidence that their efforts were achieving results. Administrators of education pro-grams were asked, not just to show that money was spent for teachers' salaries or books or equipment, but for evidence that children were learning more. Administrators of water pollution programs were asked to show not only that waste treatment plants had been built, but that water was cleaner. Even transfer programs were judged in a new light. It was not enough to distribute food stamps to a specified number of people. Attention was focused on measurements of nutri-tion or malnutrition. It was not enough that Medicare and Medicaid paid medical bills for the poor and the aged. Attention was focused on the quality of care and the effect of the federal programs on the price of care for the rest of the population.

More demanding goals were laid down for older as well as newer programs. Highway building began to be seen not simply as stretching a ribbon of concrete from one place to another, but as a major influence on the shape of urban communities. The original simple goal of urban renewal—to replace urban slums with high income-yielding property—was modified to take into account the impact of the program on the slum dweller being displaced and on the availability of low-cost housing in the central city.

For a while, the new aspirations and the old approach to setting priorities persisted side by side. It was not immediately recognized that the new demands on the federal government required that attention be paid to *how* federal programs were to be carried out. The problem of setting national priorities in the 1960s was still seen primarily as determining *what* should be done and *how much* should be spent. The idea persisted that if one could identify a problem and allocate some federal money to it, the problem would get solved.

The Initial Discouragement

Perhaps the most noticeable impact of the new aspirations was the widespread discouragement they generated. In many programs, especially social service programs, it proved extremely difficult to measure results. It is not immediately obvious, for example, whether a particular manpower program is "working." The number of trainees who find jobs can be determined, but how many would have found jobs on their own in the absence of the program? Have they found better jobs at higher wages than they would have found without training? To what extent is their success or failure in securing jobs due to the manpower training program rather than to the cyclical ups and downs of the national economy? One manpower training program may appear to be much more successful than another until it is revealed that the one has concentrated on middle-income high school graduates with prior work experience while the other has been aimed at low-income high school dropouts. Moreover, it has become clear that in many of the new areas of federal concern, no one really knew what would work. It was possible to hire an engineer and say "Build a bridge," but it was not possible to hire an educator and say "Improve reading achievement in poverty schools," because educators did not know how.

Many of the newer programs sought to change fundamental behavior patterns of individuals and institutions. They were aimed at improving the quality of education provided to the inner-city poor, not merely at increasing federal financial support for elementary and secondary education; at changing the way in which urban and industrial growth affect the environment, not merely at underwriting municipal waste treatment plants; at ensuring that the poor receive more effective medical care, not simply at giving them money to pay for whatever care is available. It quickly became clear that changing institutional behavior not only is difficult but takes more than federal money. Putting a neighborhood health center into a ghetto or rural area may provide medical service to individual patients, but it does not alter the rest of the health system; nor does it give private doctors incentives to practice in the ghetto or in rural areas; and it does not alter the basic causes of ill health among the poor. Similarly, putting children in preschool programs for a few weeks may improve their performance, at least temporarily, but it does not alter either the homes they come from or the schools they are attending. Earmarking money for the education of disadvantaged children in those public schools may result in additional services, but it does not change the basic attitudes or methods of the school systems. Building municipal waste treatment plants and attempting to guide and supervise state regulation of pollution does not stop thousands of industrial polluters from pouring waste into the air and water or give them an incentive to stop doing it.

It was also clear that the success of many programs depended on how well they were adapted to local conditions and how well they were carried out in particular localities. Cleaning up pollution along the Ohio River depends on the special characteristics of that river and on the responses of cities, towns, and business firms in the river basin. The success of a manpower training program for welfare mothers in Tulsa, Oklahoma, depends on success in matching the particular skills of these women to employment opportunities that actually exist or can be created in Tulsa. Hence, the payoff to the program depends more on the insights and competence of managers on the scene than on the wisdom of those directing the program in Washington.

It is hardly surprising that the major new programs of the 1960s did not achieve instant success. Measurable results were often lacking or discouraging. Increasing criticism was aimed at red tape, inadequate or conflicting regulations, too many federal programs, or the wrong ones in the wrong places. In some places, for example, manpower training programs broke down because the participants needed basic education before they could benefit from training. In other places, basic education programs were effective, but there was no training available for those who had learned the basic skills; in still others there were no jobs for those who had successfully completed training.

Initial discouragement brought several responses, one of which was tighter federal regulation. The failure of early attempts to guide and supervise state regulation of industrial pollution led to proposals for much more direct and centralized regulation by federal officials. Similarly, when the provision of medical benefits to the poor and the elderly under Medicaid and Medicare was accompanied by a sharp escalation of medical prices, federal regulation of the quality and price of medical care began to grow in volume and complexity. When it was revealed that federal funds earmarked for disadvantaged children were being spent by some school districts on services these children would have received out of regular school budgets—or worse, on air conditioners for superintendents' offices—the federal regulations were tightened up. But stricter regulations in all of these areas brought their own problems. They were not always applicable to local conditions, and they were hard to enforce. No one in Washington really knew, for example, how to write regulations that would ensure the effective use of funds for disadvantaged children—regulations that could be both understood and enforced in some 18,000 school districts.

A second call was for "coordination." It seemed reasonable that federal officials handling different programs should communicate with each other and that projects funded under one program should not duplicate or conflict with projects funded under another. Coordinating devices were worked out that required each federal agency to clear a new project with all the other agencies before it could move ahead; joint programs were undertaken in which different federal agencies were supposed to put money into the same comprehensive project. Sometimes coordination worked, but more often it just slowed things down.

A third proposed solution was decentralization of decision making. Since it was clear that the federal government was not managing or regulating these programs particularly well, some people concluded that their management should be turned over to state and local governments with few or no strings attached. At congressional insistence, for example, Title III of the Elementary and Secondary Education Act (ESEA), which provided funds for innovative projects in education, was turned over to the states to administer. The Nixon administration, distressed by the welter of conflicting federal manpower programs, proposed in 1969 that these programs be consolidated and more decision-making authority turned over to state and local "prime sponsors." The same idea turned up in the administration's proposals for special revenue sharing and in more extreme form in the proposal for general revenue sharing with state and local governments.

To some, the lack of quick results in the social programs indicated that not enough money was being spent. Little had been accomplished because appropriations had been too niggardly. If more funds were provided, significant results could be expected. The more usual reaction, however, was just the opposite. The administration and many members of the Congress began arguing that since social programs were not producing obvious results, it was important to be cautious about expanding them and to go slow until it was clear what should be done. Some programs, such as Medicaid, were so structured that they grew almost of their own accord, but many others, such as Title I of ESEA, Head Start, and Model Cities, have simply not been increased appreciably over the last three years.

Giving up the search for solutions to urgent social problems would be both irresponsible and dangerous, but taking refuge in pat, simple answers—decentralize, regulate, coordinate, spend more, spend less—seems unlikely to lead to a workable new strategy. It is time for a new and more realistic look at the federal government and the ways in which it can hope to carry out its activities effectively.

How the Federal Government Does Its Job

Despite the fact that the United States is a large and diverse country in which local conditions, resources, and talents vary tremendously, its population looks increasingly to the federal government for solutions to national problems. The federal government has traditionally undertaken certain kinds of activities and has devised ways to perform them with reasonable efficiency and effectiveness. There are other new activities—especially those aimed at changing the behavior of individuals and institutions in order to improve social services or the quality of the environment—for which the federal government has yet to work out satisfactory techniques.

There are at least three traditional types of activities that the federal government apparently can perform efficiently and effectively and that cannot, in general, be handled satisfactorily at lower levels of government:

1. *Research, demonstration, experimentation, and dissemination of information.* The resources and know-how necessary for a moon shot or a massive medical research program can be mobilized only at the federal level. If the federal government were not channeling resources into research and development, much less of it would be done, since states and local communities have no incentives to undertake major research and development programs whose benefit would go largely to other jurisdictions. Research scholars are in limited supply, and the federal government is much more likely to be able to recruit and build a strong research organization like the National Institutes of Health than are states or localities. Even where the research itself has been largely decentralized, as in the federal agricultural program, federal impetus and money were undoubtedly necessary to achieve results. If the nation were to mount the program of social experimentation discussed later in this chapter, it would have to be financed and managed primarily at the federal level.

2. *Regulation and inspection of national industries.* The regulation of financial institutions clearly is best done at the federal level. The Federal Reserve System, the Federal Deposit Insurance Corporation, and the Securities and Exchange Commission, with all their faults, undoubtedly work far better than do comparable institutions at the state level. Indeed, historical experience has shown that it is not feasible to leave financial regulation to the states. The result would be fifty different sets of regulations, tremendous diversity both in regulations and enforcement, and in efforts to compete with each other by offering financial institutions relatively easy rules or lax enforcement.

The inspection and regulation of products that move across state lines also must be a federal function. When it comes to meat inspection, food and drug regulations, and protection of consumer safety, federal activities are far from perfect, but it would be a step in the wrong direction to turn over these activities to the fifty states.

3. *Redistribution of resources through taxation and subsidy.* The federal government is efficient and effective in collecting money through its tax system and paying it out as transfers to individuals. The tax system, with all the faults discussed in Chapter 14, is relatively progressive and efficient and less resented by taxpayers than are local taxes. The federal tax system could be greatly improved, but for most purposes it works.

Federal programs to support the income of veterans and retired persons also seem to work, in the sense that there are few delays in determining eligibility or mailing out the checks. A social security system run at the state level would be far more costly and would probably be less effective. The arguments for federalizing the welfare system are strong on efficiency grounds alone, quite apart from equity.

But the equity arguments for federal income support programs are also strong. In a society that bases economic rewards on productivity, equal opportunity for good health and a good education are essential if everyone is to be given a fair chance to earn those rewards. It seems unfair for people to have unequal access to such services as day care, health, and higher education because they have low incomes or live in a particular part of the country. Equity argues for federally financed health insurance and student aid programs to equalize access to services that are privately provided at least in part. It also argues for federal efforts to equalize access to publicly provided resources through federal payments to state and local governments, such as aid to education and revenue sharing. There is no doubt that these measures would "work" in the sense that resources would in fact be equalized, though not necessarily in the sense that the service at the local level would be better because federal funds were partially financing it.

The simple transfer of resources is not, however, a sufficient response to the new concerns that were thrust on the federal government in the 1960s: the provision of more effective social services and the improvement of the environment in which people live. Satisfying these new concerns requires finding ways of changing the behavior of individuals and of institutions—making schools and health providers more responsive to the needs of people and changing the way in which thousands of industrial firms make their products and dispose of waste. The federal government has not yet evolved satisfactory ways of bringing about these fundamental behavioral changes. Indeed, the history of the 1960s makes clear that current federal approaches are not particularly effective.

Regulation versus Incentives

There are two principal means by which the federal government could try to influence the behavior of individuals and institutions: by regulation, and by changing the incentives that individuals and institutions face. Explicit federal attempts to influence behavior through incentives are relatively new. The more traditional approach has been to change behavior by regulation. Projects or individuals receiving federal aid are required to have specified characteristics or to meet certain detailed standards. In some instances certain kinds of behavior are simply declared illegal. The regulatory approach, however, has often proved inefficient and ineffective, necessitating constant tightening of the rules or frequent administrative decisions about exceptions necessary to meet local conditions. Hence, in many areas it would be preferable to deemphasize the regulatory approach in favor of creating incentives for desirable behavior. Three examples summarized from earlier chapters will suffice to contrast the regulatory and the incentive approaches to changing behavior: pollution control, ensuring that welfare recipients who can work do so, and controlling medical costs and quality.

Pollution Control

In Chapter 11, the regulatory and incentive approaches to controlling industrial pollution were compared. To date, regulation has proved ineffective. Industrial pollution of air and water has continued to rise in spite of periodic increases in the regulatory authority of the federal government. But instead of turning to a different approach, or supplementing regulation with economic incentives, the pending water pollution control legislation seeks to increase even further the scope and complexity of regulatory power.

The thousands of firms that are sources of industrial pollution operate in many different industries and with widely varying technologies —some with up-to-date and some with obsolete plant and equipment. Setting individual pollution limits plant by plant that take into account the great range of conditions faced by these firms is a task beyond the capability of any administrator. The regulatory approach also generates legal battles on a case-by-case basis, with the attendant delays and the inherent difficulty of securing conviction. Moreover, once a firm has reduced pollution to the limit stipulated by the regulatory authority, it has no reason to seek further reductions. In contrast, the introduction of a heavy tax on each unit of pollution emitted would give firms a self-interest in reducing pollution and would automatically take into account variations in the conditions affecting each. Firms could reduce their taxes by reducing pollution. Not only would existing technology be used to this end, but so long as any pollution remained, firms would have a reason to seek new technology that would provide inexpensive ways of eliminating the remainder.

Work and Welfare

One of the dilemmas of the welfare system grows out of the general consensus both that needy people should receive public help and that people ought to work if they are able to do so. In the past, welfare programs have sought through regulation to avoid freeloading by defining as ineligible for aid those who could be presumed able to work. Welfare programs were limited strictly to the aged, the blind, the disabled, and mothers of dependent children; and the definitions were made stringent to bar the employable. "Disability" had to be permanent and total. Mothers were subjected to strict means tests and even a search of their homes to make sure that no employable male was living there. Regulations kept employable people off the welfare rolls, but they also denied aid to needy persons who did not fall in the eligible categories and created at least potentially perverse incentives. If a man could not earn enough to support his family, he could increase its well-being by deserting and making it eligible for welfare. For these reasons, there has recently been a trend toward extending income maintenance programs beyond the old categories. Adding unemployed fathers was a step in this direction, and the administration's proposed welfare reform, which would add aid to the working poor, will be a further step if it passes the Congress.

Attempts to use regulation to ensure that employable people work, however, have persisted in the context of broader income maintenance programs for the needy. The regulatory device currently favored by the administration and the Congress is a work requirement under which everyone classified as "employable" would be required to register for job placement or enter a training program. Those who refused would have their aid reduced or cut off.

The alternative incentive approach would make it worthwhile for welfare recipients to work by allowing them to keep substantial fractions of their earnings without reducing their welfare benefit. The incentive approach seems likely to be more effective and less resented by the poor and to have far less potential for abuse by public officials. Moreover, unlike the work requirement, it would motivate individuals not just to get any job that will meet the requirement but to increase their earnings as much as possible. The current welfare system, the welfare bill passed by the House, and the different measure recently reported by the Senate Finance Committee all rely heavily on the work requirement approach, but fail to provide appreciable monetary rewards for those welfare recipients who do find employment or increase their earnings.

Controlling Medical Costs

Reimbursement of doctors, hospitals, nursing homes, and other suppliers of services provided under private or national health insurance encourages overuse of expensive kinds of care and even unnecessary surgery, since both doctor and patient know that a third party is paying the bill. This problem could be attacked through regulation—committees of doctors could determine whether procedures were necessary and bureaucratic agencies could regulate the prices charged. This approach would be cumbersome, however, and seems likely to prevent only outrageous abuses. An alternative approach is to try to change the behavior of consumers and health providers by changing their incentives. Consumers can be encouraged to exercise restraint by making sure that they bear part of the cost themselves through coinsurance and deductibles. The ignorance of consumers about medical care, however, and their desire for full insurance coverage make it doubtful that such incentives alone are enough.

In addition to providing consumer incentives, it is important to encourage efficient use of medical resources by changing the incentives facing doctors and hospitals. One way to do this would be to change the way in which suppliers of medical services are reimbursed. Each supplier could receive a single fee set in advance for a complete service to individuals for a period of time rather than reimbursement for each service delivered. Health maintenance organizations, which charge members annual fees, represent one form of this approach. Reimbursement of hospitals on an annual per capita basis is another form. The theory is that such reimbursement schemes would give health providers an incentive to be as efficient as possible, to use preventive techniques to avoid more costly treatment later, and to avoid unnecessary surgery or other procedures.

Conflicting Objectives

If money alone is not enough and if central regulation cannot cope with the complexities of the social problems the federal government faces, then it becomes critically necessary to develop programs with appropriate incentives. But designing the right kind of incentives is extremely difficult, for two reasons: First, programs often have conflicting objectives, so that several sets of desirable incentives have to be balanced; second, little is known about how human behavior actually responds to changes in incentives in particular circumstances.

A particular obstacle to the design of social programs is often the conflict between redistributional or equity objectives on the one hand and productivity or efficiency objectives on the other. The current debate over welfare reform is a prime example of this problem. There is general agreement that a satisfactory income maintenance system ought to (1) ensure adequate incomes for all families, (2) encourage people to work, and (3) treat people in the same economic circumstances in the same way. The present welfare system accomplishes none of these objectives. Large groups of the poor are not covered at all, and those on welfare have little monetary incentive to work. Hence, strong sentiment has risen for shifting toward a new income maintenance system that would provide everyone with a minimum guaranteed income based on family size, and that would reduce the benefit payment by substantially less than one dollar for every dollar earned.

Designing such a system, however, would be difficult in the face of budget constraints. If one could set the guarantee level low (say, $2,000 for a family of four) and reduce payments by a low fraction (say, one-third) of each dollar earned, this would give families ample incentive to work, but it would not provide an adequate income for families that could not work. Alternatively, one could set the guarantee at a higher level (say, $3,600 for a family of four) and reduce payments by a large fraction (say, two-thirds) of each dollar earned. This would provide a more adequate income for those with no other means of support, but it would discourage people from working.

One might suppose that this dilemma could be resolved simply by spending more money, combining a relatively high guarantee level with a low rate of reduction in benefits as earnings rise. But such a solution, besides being extremely expensive, would have other problems. If welfare benefits were related to family size and payment levels reached well into the middle-income ranges (as they must in a generous plan with low rates of reduction), small families would end up paying taxes to support large families with the same earnings—a result that might be regarded as both inequitable and contrary to a policy of moderating population growth. (For a further discussion of these dilemmas, see Chapter 6 and *Setting National Priorities: The 1972 Budget*, Chapter 8.)

As was explained in Chapter 7, similar dilemmas arise in designing a health insurance system. Incentives for consumers and suppliers of medical care are needed to prevent excessive use and escalating prices. But the same features that provide incentives may also become a barrier to needed care or a temptation to reduce the quality of care.

Conflicts also arise in developing federal programs to transfer funds to state and local governments. In the case of federal aid to elementary and secondary education, the objectives are both to equalize expenditures for education within and among states and to encourage state and local governments to make an effort to support education on their own. It is possible to design a formula that does both, but doing so is a complex matter, and present state and federal aid programs accomplish neither objective effectively.

The Need for Experimentation

A second problem that makes the incentive approach difficult and challenging is ignorance of how people and institutions actually respond to changes in incentives. How is the use of medical care affected by changes in health insurance provisions? What effects do changes in tax rates or welfare programs actually have on how hard people look for jobs or strive for increased earnings? Would schools or school districts provide better education if they were rewarded for performance? How would effluent charges actually affect the volume of pollutants discharged into air and water?

Unfortunately there is no way to answer most of these questions by statistical analysis of existing social systems. One cannot find out how the working poor would respond to a particular income maintenance system when no such system exists. One cannot know how health providers would respond to reimbursement on a capitation basis when almost all of them are currently reimbursed on a fee-for-service basis, and those that are not serve atypical populations. Similar difficulties lie in the way of predicting other changes in incentives— voucher systems for education or day care, loans rather than grants for higher education, rewards to educators or other public servants based on performance rather than seniority.

For these reasons, the best way—perhaps the only way—of finding out how individuals and institutions respond to changes in incentives would seem to be to try out the incentives by embarking on a program of social experimentation.

Apart from learning more about how various incentives affect the responses of individuals or groups, there is yet another reason why the federal government needs to conduct social experiments. In many areas of social policy, no one really knows which techniques or approaches are successful and which are not. Even if school officials, hospital administrators, or manpower training specialists have the right incentives to seek efficient and effective courses of action, they often have no way of finding out what works and what does not work. What specific kinds of preschool education or day care are best for disadvantaged children? What are the most effective techniques for monitoring the quality of medical care in a health maintenance organization? While there will never be neatly packaged solutions to these kinds of problems, the federal government can conduct the kind of systematic experiments that might shed some light on them. The purpose of such experiments would be not so much to aid in the design of federal programs as to provide guidance and information for those who must make decisions at the state and local level. It would be simply an extension of the traditional federal role of providing knowledge in areas where private investigations cannot cope with the cost and complexities of the research required.

Not all experiments need be conducted on so large a scale that only the federal government could afford them. The major private foundations could also play a role in sponsoring social experiments. Foundations sometimes have greater freedom of action and are less likely to be wedded to existing programs than are federal bureaucracies.

The Budget Process Itself

Two major themes of this book call attention to the fact that the annual budget process is increasingly ill suited to the intelligent setting of national priorities:

1. Setting priorities no longer involves simply a determination of *how much* of the nation's resources should be devoted to a particular purpose; it also requires difficult decisions about *how* each purpose can best be accomplished.

2. Most important decisions do not have their major budgetary consequences immediately, but only after several years. Effective allocation of resources among alternative goals can be done only with a budgetary outlook extending over time, perhaps many years.

To pretend that a $250 billion federal budget is freshly put together each year is an exercise in self-delusion, for both the Congress and the executive branch. From one year to the next, most of the changes that occur in budget expenditures are "built in"; that is, they result from decisions made in previous years. Thus, in a single year little can be done to restructure priorities. But, as Chapters 1 and 12 emphasized, over a longer period substantial changes in the allocation of budgetary resources can and do occur. Undue concentration on a single year's budget obscures the long-run changes that current decisions will actually bring about. When attempts are made to cut spending, the current annual budget process places most emphasis on actions that affect the coming year's budget, often at the expense of cuts that are more desirable but that may not affect expenditures for several years. Conversely, new programs or military weapon systems are inaugurated with major attention to their cost in the current budget, which may be only a small fraction of their total cost. Tax cuts are enacted with attention to their immediate budget impact and little consideration to their effect on the long-run balance of revenues and expenditures.

While an annual budget is essential for purposes of economic policy, the single-year framework for conducting all of the budgetary procedures has outlived its usefulness. Both the Congress and the executive branch need to view the budget totals and major program decisions in a longer perspective. The following suggestions are one approach to achieving this purpose.

1. Each year the administration should present to the Congress a five-year budgetary outlook. Revenues should be projected forward on the basis of full employment conditions, existing tax laws, and any changes proposed by the administration. The expenditure outlook should reflect the future consequences of existing and currently proposed programs. The outlook should be presented in enough detail to show the factors responsible for major changes in revenues and expenditures: assumptions regarding the movement of prices, wages, and productivity should be stated; major components of the budget should be shown separately; and the causes of projected major changes —for example, military weapon procurement or increasing caseloads in welfare programs—should be spelled out.

2. Shortly after the budget is presented, the Joint Economic Committee of the Congress should hold hearings on the five-year budgetary outlook and issue a report evaluating its implications.

3. Each revenue bill that would change federal revenues by more than some minimum amount (for example, $25 million) should show its projected impact on revenues for three to five years ahead. Any major revenue bill should be accompanied by a restatement of the five-year budget showing how the bill would affect the balance of revenues and expenditures.

4. As was suggested in Chapter 5, the administration should submit to the Congress each year a five-year defense plan showing, by major categories and force components, the funds and expenditures needed annually to realize its objectives. After debate and modification, the Congress should authorize the five-year defense program and appropriate the necessary funds for its first year. In each subsequent year the administration would submit a revised five-year plan, adding on the new fifth year and proposing such changes in the existing five-year program as it deemed appropriate.

5. The civilian programs differ among themselves with respect to their budgetary and financial characteristics. Hence, not one but a number of procedural changes are called for, each tailored to the specific circumstances of the program: (a) *Appropriations for all programs that provide grants-in-aid to state and local governments should*

be made one year in advance. At present, federal grants for a given year are often appropriated after state and local governments have enacted their budgets, making it almost impossible for them to plan their federally aided programs. (b) *Programs should be shifted to a three-year authorization basis.* Some are now authorized annually, some for two years, and some for three years or longer. The programs in the civilian budget should then be divided into roughly three equal groups, with one group authorized each year. A complete review of each program every year is impractical, and facing up to this fact by shifting to three-year authorizations might produce more realistic and effective program reviews by both the Congress and the executive branch. (c) *Annual appropriations should be converted into three-year appropriations where this is consistent with the nature of the program involved.* In some programs, multiyear appropriations would serve little purpose. For example, in programs that pay benefits based on statutory entitlements—such as public assistance, veterans' pensions, and Medicaid—the size of the appropriation does not determine how much is spent; the appropriation simply provides the funds that must be paid to beneficiaries under the law. Similarly, where discrete projects are being funded—a dam or a federal building —appropriations should cover the cost of the entire project regardless of how long it takes to build. But in many other programs of a continuing nature, in which the level of the program can be controlled by the appropriation, conversion from annual to three-year appropriations might be a desirable accompaniment to the three-year authorization process. (d) *Every appropriation bill, as reported to the House and Senate by the Appropriations Committees, should include a five-year projection of expenditures on the programs financed by the appropriation, assuming the continuation of present policies and practices.*

6. Periodically throughout the congressional session, estimates should be prepared and published showing how prior congressional actions on authorizations and appropriations during the session up to that time had affected the five-year budgetary outlook submitted by the administration. At present, a little-known group—the Joint Committee on Reduction of Federal Expenditures, composed of the ranking members of the Senate Finance Committee, the House Ways and Means Committee, and the Senate and House Appropriations Committees, the secretary of the treasury, and the director of the Office of Management and Budget—issues a periodic "scorecard" showing the effects of congressional action on the President's budget requests,

mainly in terms of the current budget year. Perhaps this committee, with appropriate staff resources, could modify its procedures to perform the task described above.

Converting annual into three-year authorizations and appropriations would raise several questions. Would the major substantive and appropriations committees (or subcommittees) of the Congress have nothing to do for two years and then face a major legislative agenda in the third year? Since each committee deals with several programs, the three-year authorizations and appropriations could be so scheduled that each committee would have a work agenda every year. Would the conversion reduce flexibility to adjust expenditures in the light of economic circumstances in accordance with fiscal policy? Even now, with annual appropriations, most expenditures cannot quickly be varied. Through the use of budget amendments to raise or lower previously enacted three-year appropriations, the administration or the Congress could provide the same degree of counter-cyclical flexibility as now exists.

Would a three-year authorization and appropriation cycle hamper an incoming administration in carrying out the objectives for which it was elected? Again, the new procedures would not be an obstacle. A new administration would not have to wait two or three years to make modifications; it could submit budget amendments. More important, however, the new procedures would encourage incoming administrations to realize that effective changes in priorities can be made only in a long-term context, and would help concentrate their attention on making such changes. It is possible, of course, that annual amendments would become so commonplace that annual authorizations and appropriations would, in effect, be restored. Self-restraint in the use of annual amendments by the Congress and the executive branch would be necessary to prevent subversion of the new system. But any procedural reform encounters this difficulty. There is no magic formula to ensure that improved budget procedures will withstand a joint effort by both the Congress and the executive branch to thwart them.

These proposed changes have two basic objectives:

• To provide the Congress and the public with a framework of information about total revenues and expenditures over a five-year period, within which to judge the consequences of particular decisions on taxes or expenditures.

• To shift attention from the very immediate, and often less important, consequences of specific budgetary decisions to their longer-term impact on national priorities.

The information provided by these procedural changes would not bear directly on the merits of any particular tax or expenditure proposal. But it would help the Congress to make explicit decisions about priorities, so that long-run changes in the patterns of expenditures and taxes might become more nearly the result of deliberate choices rather than the unintended consequences of short-run decisions.

3 1543 50083 6004

353.00722
S495n2

715873

DATE DUE

MR 19 74			
DE 17 74			
OC 27 80			

Cressman Library
Cedar Crest College
Allentown, Pa. 18104

WITHDRAWN

DEMCO

TYPESETTING *Monotype Composition Company, Inc., Baltimore*
PRINTING & BINDING *R. R. Donnelley & Sons Company, Chicago*